STRATEGIC MANAGEMENT

Strategic Management
Total Quality and Global Competition

MICHAEL J. STAHL AND DAVID W. GRIGSBY

BLACKWELL
Business

Copyright © Michael J. Stahl and David W. Grigsby, 1997

The right of Michael J. Stahl and David W. Grigsby to be identified as author of this work has been asserted in accordance with the Copyright, Designs and Patents Act 1988.

First published 1997

2 4 6 8 10 9 7 5 3 1

Blackwell Publishers Ltd
108 Cowley Road
Oxford OX4 1JF
UK

Blackwell Publishers Inc
238 Main Street
Cambridge, Massachusetts 02142,
USA

Library of Congress Cataloging-in-Publication Data

Stahl, Michael J.
      Strategic management : total quality and global competition /
Michael J. Stahl and David W. Grigsby.
            p.   cm.
      Includes bibliographical references and index.
      ISBN 1–5578–665–03
      1. Total quality management.   2. Strategic planning.   I. Grigsby,
David W.   II. Title.
HD62.15.S735   1997
658.5′62—dc20   *96–16042*
                                                                                                       CIP

ISBN   1–55578–665–0

British Library Cataloguing in Publication Data

A CIP catalogue record for this book is available from the British Library.

Commissioning Editor: Rolf Janke
Development Editor: Catriona King
Desk Editor: John Taylor
Production Manager/Controller: Lisa Parker

Typeset in 10 on 12 pt Photina
by Graphicraft Typesetters Ltd., Hong Kong
Printed in the USA

This book is printed on acid-free paper

Summary Contents

Detailed Contents

Preface

In writing *Strategic Management: Total Quality and Global Competition*, our objectives were threefold. The first was to offer a comprehensive text that incorporates the latest theory and practice in the field. The second was to make it understandable and appealing to a wide audience by incorporating ample illustrations from real organizations and offering interesting and challenging cases. With cases, exhibits, data, research material and real examples from throughout the world, the book is designed to be used internationally. The third was to approach the subject in a unique way – by coupling global competition and total quality to strategic management.

The result is a text that can be used in a variety of ways on a number of levels. Its emphasis on practical application, with an international exhibit, international case and quality case in each of the 11 chapters, makes it ideal for use as a basic text. Our explanations focus on the results of decisions, and numerous examples of real-world strategic decisions are packed into every chapter. Many of these 33 cases and exhibits are drawn from the popular international business press.

With its full treatment of theoretical concepts, and references to all of the major work in the field, *Strategic Management: Total Quality and Global Competition* can also support a more intensive investigation of the field by serving as a resource for further study. You will find complete explanations of all of the major theories and recent contributions in strategy, and references to many others. Recent research findings are incorporated into the text of each chapter.

Specific chapters on international strategy and business ethics and corporate social responsibility are included. These chapters offer students an appreciation of internationalization, corporate social responsibility and ethics in strategy.

A hierarchical coverage of strategy is included: corporate-level, business-level (two chapters), and functional-level strategies are covered in sequence in four separate chapters. This hierarchical treatment helps students to understand relationships in strategy and to integrate concepts.

Total quality (TQ) concepts are integrated throughout several chapters. This helps the student to understand some linkages between TQ and strategic decisions, since TQ has become a good current example of many strategic management issues.

Because strategy implementation is so important, we devote two chapters to the subject. One covers structure and teams, and the other culture and behavior.

To help students learn the case study process, a detailed case analysis guide, one of the most comprehensive in the industry, is included in the text. A set of 25 detailed cases may be found in the companion book: *Cases in Strategic Management: Total Quality and Global Competition*.

A comprehensive *Instructor's Manual*, with a testbank (discussion, multiple-choice, and true – false questions), answers to cases, answers to discussion questions, and transparency masters, is also available. A separate *Electronic Student Study Guide* is included with the text. This completes a total teaching package.

We appreciate any ideas you have for improvement.

As far as permissions go, every attempt has been made to trace copyright holders. The authors and publishers would like to apologize in advance for any inadvertent use of copyright material.

Acknowledgments

As with any book of this type, this one represents far more than the efforts of its two authors. Consequently, we have many others to thank for this final product.

Much of the success of this project is due to the support and excellent working environments provided to us by The University of Tennessee and Clemson University and to our colleagues who unselfishly offered their suggestions, comments, and encouragement. Special thanks are also due to our students, who cheerfully endured classroom testing of early drafts of the text and cases.

A number of reviewers deserve a special mention here. They worked long and hard on the manuscript and their comments and suggestions proved to be of immeasurable help in improving our work. They are:

Dr Andrew D. M. Anderson, Department of Business and Management, City University of Hong Kong.

Mike Argent, School of Management, Huddersfield University, UK.

Dr Robert P. Bood, Faculty of Economics, University of Groningen, The Netherlands.

Lynne Butel, Plymouth Business School, Plymouth University, UK.

Dr Manton Gibbs, Professor of Strategic Studies, Department of Management and Marketing, Indiana University of Pennsylvania, USA.

Dr Jose Gieskes, Twente Quality Centre, Enschede, The Netherlands.

Dr Steven H. Hanks, Management and Human Resources Department, Utah State University, USA.

Kobus Jonker, Port Elizabeth Technikon, South Africa.

Professor Roland E. Kidwell, College of Business Administration, Louisiana State University in Shreveport, USA.

Professor Peter McKiernan, Department of Management, St Andrews University, UK.

Nigel Munro-Smith, Royal Melbourne Institute of Technology, Australia.

Alex Murdock, South Bank University, London, UK.

Dr M. Oktemgil, Department of Commerce, Birmingham Business School, University of Birmingham, UK.

Dr Stig Ree, Copenhagen Business School, Denmark.

Professor Pieter Smit, Business Economics Department, UNISA, South Africa.

At The University of Tennessee (UT), very special thanks go to Tami Touchstone, who word processed many of the cases, prepared the figures, and provided invaluable administrative assistance throughout the project. Ian Harris, graduate research assistant at UT, researched much of the material for the book and drafted several of the international cases. His thoroughness and innovation contributed to the text.

We also thank our families for understanding us during this time consuming and lengthy process.

Michael J. Stahl and David W. Grigsby

STRATEGIC MANAGEMENT DECISIONS FOR TOTAL QUALITY AND GLOBAL COMPETITION

LEARNING OBJECTIVES

After reading this chapter, you should be able to accomplish the following.

1 *Define the terms total quality management and strategic management, and discuss the relationship between them.*

2 *Discuss the need for business managers and strategic managers in organizations today.*

3 *Describe the various groups of strategic decision makers in an organization.*

4 *Describe the importance of strategy to the manager.*

5 *Elaborate on the idea that strategy is a pattern in a series of decisions.*

6 *Explain the significance of Deming's 14 points of management.*

7 *Explain the global significance of the US Baldrige Quality Award Criteria, the European Quality Award, ISO 9000, the Japanese Deming Prize, and other national quality awards.*

Organizations and the Need for Business Managers

Managers of organizations need to anticipate and adapt to change by keeping in touch with the environment external to the organization. A critical dimension of the external environment is the organization's customers in an era of intensifying global competition. Harley-Davidson almost went bankrupt when its managers lost sight of its customers and the external environment (see quality case at the end of this chapter). As leaders of their organizations and its human resources, managers are expected to articulate a vision, goals and objectives for the future, and manage the business to yield greater value to customers. Thus, we use the following definition in this book.

> Strategic management *refers to the managerial decisions that relate the organization to its environment, guide internal activities, and determine organizational long-term performance.*

Changing external environments

A principal function of managers is to keep the organization in touch with the external environment. With such close contact, the manager is prepared to capitalize on opportunities and avoid threats in the external environment. Effective managers relate the organization to its environment, and then guide internal activities to maximize the external opportunities and minimize the external threats.[1] Managers need to be externally focused despite the temptation to act only in terms of internal organizational activities that assume a life of their own.

Change seems to be a part of organizational life since external organizational environments and customers change. It takes exceptional management to anticipate and profit from change. In the internationally competitive environment of the 1990s, change is virtually assured.

An analysis of *Fortune* magazine's listing of the "most admired corporations" from its debut in 1983 reveals some interesting changes relative to 1995. Only one firm that was on the "most admired" list in 1983 was still among the "most admired" in 1995 (Hewlett-Packard).[2] Three of the 1983 firms (Eastman Kodak, IBM, and Digital) were experiencing financial difficulty in the early 1990s. Eastman Kodak was slow to adapt to customer demands for electronic imaging in cameras. IBM had grown very large and inwardly focused. Digital pursued technology and lost sight of its customers' requirements. All three replaced their chief executive officers in the early 1990s for failure to adapt their organizations to change.

Global competition

Global economic competition has exploded in the past two decades. Many US and European firms have lost market share in several industries to Japanese firms producing higher quality goods at lower ~~...~~ nternational competition is likely to further intensify ~~...~~ first century. The international exhibit shows the strength of ~~...~~ ompetitors.

THE WORLD'S TOP COMPANIES

There are a few different ways to measure the size and strength of international companies. One way is in terms of their stock market value (table 1.1). Another is in terms of their annual revenues (table 1.2). It is useful to examine both measures because currency and stock market fluctuations may present different pictures at different times.

Both tables indicate that international commerce has several strong players from different countries. No one country dominates the listing of the strongest international firms.

Table 1.1 The world's ten largest public companies in 1995

Rank	Company	Country	Market value
1	NTT	Japan	133
2	Royal Dutch/Shell	Netherlands/UK	109
3	General Electric	USA	100
4	Exxon	USA	90
5	AT&T	USA	83
6	Coca-Cola	USA	83
7	Toyota Motor	Japan	78
8	Fuji Bank	Japan	71
9	Industrial Bank of Japan	Japan	70
10	Mitsubishi Bank	Japan	68

Note: Rank is based on stock market value as of July 31, 1995. Market value is in billions of US dollars. Source of data: "World Business", *Wall Street Journal* (October 2, 1995), p. R32.

Table 1.2 The Global 500's top ten in 1995

Rank	Company	Country	Revenue
1	Mitsubishi	Japan	176
2	Mitsui	Japan	172
3	Itochu	Japan	168
4	Sumitomo	Japan	163
5	General Motors	USA	155
6	Marubeni	Japan	150
7	Ford Motor	USA	128
8	Exxon	USA	102
9	Nissho Iwai	Japan	101
10	Royal Dutch/Shell	Netherlands/UK	95

Note: Revenue is in billions of US dollars for 1994. Source of data: "Global 500", *Fortune* (August 7, 1995), p. 136.

After being leveled in the Second World War, Japanese and Western European (especially German) industries rebuilt with new technologies and new capital. The Japanese also devised new management systems based upon ideas of total quality management that increased the quality and lowered the costs of products and services.

> Total quality management (TQM) *is a systems approach to management that aims to continuously improve value to customers by designing and continuously improving organizational processes and systems.*

This definition and the relationship of TQM (or TQ, as the terms are used interchangeably) to strategic management are explored later in this chapter.

In the second half of the twentieth century, international trade barriers declined on a large scale.[3] As those international trade barriers declined, worldwide customers were able to choose among several companies for their purchases. Thus, the customers started to demand high quality and low prices.

Occasionally, patriotic, nationalistic, and protectionist fevers run high. Such sentiments may give domestic firms a temporary respite from international competition as customers buy for reasons other than quality and price. However, domestic firms that rely on such sentiments in the long term, and that fail to offer their customers affordable quality, do so at their own peril. In the long term, most customers will demand affordable quality.

The rebuilding of Japanese and European industry after the Second World War, the spread of TQ as a system of management, the lowering of trade barriers, and the increasing demands of worldwide customers have opened up a globally competitive era. Firms producing consistently high quality products and services at low prices have a strong advantage and should prosper in this new internationally competitive marketplace. The strategic impact of this global competition is a major theme in this book.

To survive and even grow their firms in this internationally competitive marketplace, managers must account for dramatic international cultural and behavioral differences. Using the same assumptions about all customers, other managers, and employees, independent of their national culture, can backfire.

Fons Trompenaars of the Netherlands helped managers to understand international cultural diversity in business and the implications of that cultural diversity for dealing with different customers, managers, and employees.[4] Figure 1.1 contains data showing dramatic differences among people from many different countries on a basic assumption concerning life. These differences, as well as many other cultural differences documented by Trompenaars, indicate that managers need to be sensitive to cultural differences as a major issue in conducting business at the dawn of the twenty-first century. Such differences, and their implications for managers, are explored throughout this book.

Primacy of customers

Today, an increasing number of authors are defining the essence of management in terms of service to the external customer.[5] One of the most popular management books of the 1980s has been Peters and Waterman's book, *In Search of Excellence.*

Percentage of respondents who believe what happens to them is their own doing

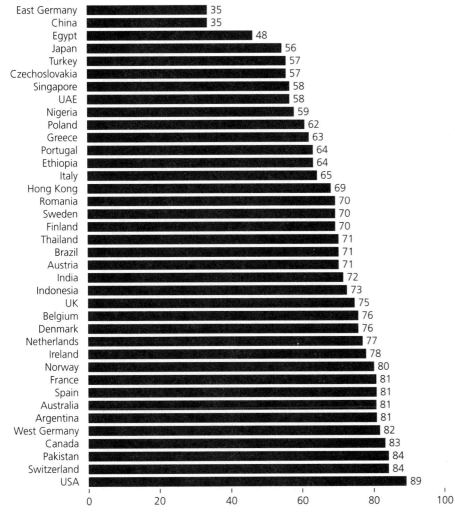

East Germany	35
China	35
Egypt	48
Japan	56
Turkey	57
Czechoslovakia	57
Singapore	58
UAE	58
Nigeria	59
Poland	62
Greece	63
Portugal	64
Ethiopia	64
Italy	65
Hong Kong	69
Romania	70
Sweden	70
Finland	70
Thailand	71
Brazil	71
Austria	71
India	72
Indonesia	73
UK	75
Belgium	76
Denmark	76
Netherlands	77
Ireland	78
Norway	80
France	81
Spain	81
Australia	81
Argentina	81
West Germany	82
Canada	83
Pakistan	84
Switzerland	84
USA	89

Figure 1.1   The captains of their fate.

Source: Trompenaars, F., *Riding the Waves of Culture: Understanding Cultural Diversity in Business.* London: Economist Books (1993), p. 128.

They defined great companies in terms of several characteristics, including "*Close to the customer.* Excellent companies learn from the people they serve. They provide unparalleled quality, service, and reliability – things that work and last. They succeed in differentiating – *à la* Frito-Lay [potato chips], Maytag [washers], or Tupperware – the most commodity-like products."[6]

A pioneer in the quality movement since the 1950s, Armand Feigenbaum understood the primacy of the customer and the implications of quality for managerial behavior. He noted:

As the American consumer continues to place increasing demands on American products and services, business needs to be ready to respond. After all, quality is what the customer says it is. Before American business can effectively address these needs, the following must first take place: Consumers' needs are addressed as quality becomes a fundamental way of managing a company.[7]

This book holds that the customer is the reason for the existence of the entire organization. The primacy of customer value under a TQ umbrella is dealt with further in this chapter and in the entirety of Chapter 7.

Vision, goals, and objectives

Nearly all management scholars agree upon the need for managers to envision and describe the future for the organization. This applies to managers at all levels, where the primary difference may be in the length of the time horizon. As entire managerial levels disappear in many organizations, and as the organizations become flatter and flatter, the remaining managers have become more involved with visions. Once the vision has been articulated, managers translate the vision into more specific goals and objectives for the future.

An increasing number of firms understand that a dramatic commitment to their customers through quality is a necessary part of survival in internationally competitive times. This commitment to quality starts with managerial leaders.

One characteristic common to a number of successful companies is strong leadership – a chief executive who leads the charge with a strong belief in delivering greater value to customers. Leadership is the most important ingredient for launching and sustaining a quality improvement process. Leaders of quality companies establish clear, results-oriented goals for continuous improvement, and communicate their expectations.[8]

Peter Drucker, one of the most noted of all management theorists, summed it up rather succinctly. "The foundation of effective leadership is thinking through the organization's mission, defining it and establishing it, clearly and visibly. The leader sets the goals, sets the priorities, and sets and maintains the standards."[9]

Performance and vision

Once the vision has been established, managers take the lead to insure that the vision is achieved. They do this by steering performance to make it consistent with the vision. Many refer to this managerial behavior as controlling.

Harold Geneen, the well-known tough boss who built ITT into one of the world's largest organizations in the 1970s and 1980s, described the responsibility of managers for performance in the following way. "I think it is an immutable law in business that words are words, explanations are explanations, promises are promises – but only performance is reality. Performance alone is the best measure of your confidence, competence, and courage. Only performance gives you the freedom to grow as yourself. Just remember that: *Performance is your reality.*"[10]

Fortune magazine ran a cover story on managing entitled "America's toughest bosses." In that article, the editors described the role of the boss in insuring performance under the label of toughness. Toughness was defined broadly as demanding and hard to please, for whatever reason. A good toughness pushes people to the limits of their abilities, a   ther, for constructive and legitimate purposes.[11]

Strategic Decision M   s

As with any other important p   he strategic management process requires competent individuals to insu   ccess. Responsibility for strategy normally rests with a small number of ke   ttegic managers within the organization. It is their job to anticipate changes   the environment, customers, and competitors, and to develop responses. *Strategic managers* are the executives responsible for the overall performance of the organization. They are often referred to as general managers for that reason and are noted for their breadth of experience.[12] Alternatively, *functional managers* are responsible for specific functions within the organization. Their expertise is in one narrow domain, such as finance or personnel.

Chief executive officers, presidents, and chairmen

The highest level strategic manager in an organization can go by a variety of titles, but the one most commonly used at the corporate level is chief executive officer (CEO). As the title implies, the *CEO* is the executive with ultimate responsibility for the formulation and implementation of the organization's overall strategy.

The *chairman of the board* is the senior executive on the board of directors. The board of directors is described in a following section. Frequently, the titles of CEO and chairman of the board are held by the same person.

The *president*, sometimes known as the *chief operating officer (COO)*, is the executive charged with implementing the strategy decided upon by the CEO and the board. Daily operations and routine decisions are the province of the president/COO.

All four titles may be vested in one individual. In other organizations, the jobs are held by two, three, or four people, and an executive office is formed with the multiple executives.

Because the insights of these executives play such a critical role, some writers have stressed the importance of matching the characteristics of these executives with the firm's strategies.[13] Drucker, one of management's most noted authors, described effective leadership not in terms of charisma or personality qualities but in terms of strategic behavior.[14]

In pursuing this role as visionary for the organization, the CEO becomes spokesperson for the organization. Examples include Lee Iacocca (CEO, chief salesman, and savior of Chrysler) and Bill Gates (CEO and founder of Microsoft).

Other managers and staff members

At the business level, division vice presidents and group vice presidents manage divisions or groups that are usually organized around a group of products/services, or a group of customers. These decision makers are usually charged with formulating customer and competitive business-level strategies for their businesses. These business level strategies should be consistent with and flow from the corporate-level strategies.

At the functional level, vice presidents for operations, finance, marketing, human resources, research and development, and information systems are involved with strategic decision making. Indeed, Mintzberg argued that strategic decisions are made at multiple levels in many organizations.[15] These functional level strategies need to be consistent with the corporate and business level strategies.

Board of directors

The *board of directors* is the governing body that represents the interests of the stockholders in the affairs of the corporation. In that capacity, it plays an important role in the strategic management process.[16] Recently, the role of the board of directors has been growing in importance because of increasingly vocal stockholders. In 1992 and 1993, the CEOs of both IBM and General Motors were fired by their respective board of directors in part because stockholders were increasingly impatient with poor financial results.

It is common practice for organizations with stock traded on public stock exchanges to have boards of directors containing both outsiders and insiders. The inside directors are corporate executives employed by the organization or retired executives of the organization. They are assumed to be intimately familiar with the firm and are champions of stability, as preserving the status quo that got them to their positions is usually to their benefit. As the inside executives all report to the CEO, it is often difficult to depend on them to provide independent direction to the organization.

Outside directors, on the other hand, are usually experienced executives from other corporations and other public figures who bring a breadth of perspective and independence to the organization. The outsiders are assumed to be in a better position than the insiders to provide independent counsel to management. The outside directors are a check to see that management's ideas do not become too self-serving. The articles of incorporation of most corporations place a legal responsibility on the board of directors to represent the interests of the stockholders whose capital made possible the formation and functioning of the organization.[17]

In order to attract good talent, organizations usually compensate these outside directors liberally. For example, the *Wall Street Journal* reported that the average compensation anticipated for outside directors for Fortune 500 firms in 1995 was US$60,000 for two or three weeks' work a year.[18]

Some have argued that a board dominated by insiders is akin to having the fox guard the chicken coop. There has been a number of charges of irresponsible management of large corporations. Managers have been accused of representing only their own narrow self-interests. Corporate raiders have used this situation to argue that they are a force for more responsible management.[19]

The need for more responsiveness among boards is also reflected in the increasing number of outside members on corporate boards.[20] On many boards, two of every three members are outsiders. The percentage of outside directors on important committees, such as audit, compensation and executive, was even higher, at 75 percent in a recent survey of 250 Fortune 500 companies.[21] As organizations attempt to be responsive to a number of different stakeholders, including customers, suppliers, employees, and stockholders, we forecast that the percentage of outside directors will continue to grow.

The Nature of Strategic Management

Strategic decisions are important in an organization because they are the precursors of many other managerial activities.

Strategic decisions

Strategic decision making is not the exclusive domain of large organizations. It is an important activity in all types of organizations – large and small, for profit and not for profit, private and public. Firms of all sizes and all purposes must learn to direct the strategic management process by engaging in strategic decision making. When your local grocery, bank, or insurance agency decides to offer a new product line or service, it is making a strategic decision. When a hospital or public service agency decides to serve a new clientele, it is making a strategic decision. In short, whenever organizations significantly alter their activities, the strategic management process is at work.

The following three factors distinguish strategic decisions from other business considerations.

1 Strategic decisions deal with concerns that are central to the livelihood and survival of the entire organization and usually involve a large portion of the organizations' resources, at least across two different functions.
2 Strategic decisions represent new activities or areas of concern and typically address issues that are unusual for the organization rather than issues that lend themselves to routine decision making.
3 Strategic decisions have repercussions for the way other, lower-level decisions in the organization are made.

Strategy as a series of decisions

Henry Mintzberg described *strategy* as "a pattern in a stream of decisions."[22] He portrayed this idea by describing the patterns in the many decisions made at Volkswagenwerk over a 54-year period. From those decisions and the patterns in the decisions, the company's strategy of low-priced transportation may be spotted throughout the years that the Volkswagen was marketed throughout the world.

Mintzberg's decision-based concept of strategy has two important implications. First, strategy is not necessarily apparent from the analysis of just one decision. For strategy to be understood fully, it must be viewed in the context of several decisions and the consistency among the decisions.[23] Second, the organization must be aware of decision alternatives in all of its decisions. Strategy may be viewed as the logic that governs the firm's choices among all its decision options.

For example, a tobacco company, faced with long-term declining sales of tobacco products, might diversify into the consumer foods industry. In its diversification decisions, it may opt for branded consumer foods where the tobacco company can continue to use its advertising and marketing expertise. This can be seen in the example of R. J. Reynolds Industries' acquisition of Nabisco in 1987 to become the giant consumer goods company RJR–Nabisco.[24] A product strategy of branded consumer products emerges as a pattern from these decisions. Thus, strategy defines the firm's business as a response to its environment.

Deliberate and emergent strategy

Is strategy always a purposeful process? Is strategy always the outcome of a planned effort toward goals that results in a pattern in a series of decisions? The cumulative effect of making small decisions regularly can result in a pattern in the stream of decisions.

Mintzberg contrasted *deliberate strategy* with *emergent strategy*.[25] Deliberate strategy had been viewed as a result of the strategic planning process. *Deliberate strategy* consists of a firm deciding on its goals and implementing intended strategy to realize the goals. This view of strategy as a deliberate process neglects several possibilities.[26] Sometimes, a firm may not intentionally set strategy. The firm's strategy may emerge from the lower levels of the organization because of its daily activities. Such emergent strategies might also be the result of the implementation process. Alterations in goals based on feedback during implementation may produce strategies that vary from their original design.

Emergent strategies are those strategies actually in place in the organization that were never intended. Uncontrollable changes in the external environment or poor implementation can result in emergent strategies different from deliberate strategy.

These two views of strategy also help us to recognize that the strategic formulation process is not always a top-down process. Sometimes the process is bottom-up as lower-level managers contribute to strategy by their daily actions. Sometimes executives start the strategic management process with input from lower levels in the organization.

Why understand strategy?

Why do managers throughout the organization need to understand strategy? Is not strategy the province of the most senior executives in the firm?

In an earlier, more stable, era, with very few international competitors, executives were solely responsible for strategy. Today, managers throughout the organization should be involved in strategy formulation and implementation for several reasons.[27]

Most importantly, due to the rebuilding of other nations' industries after the Second World War and the elimination of many trade barriers, international competition has become feverish. Chapter 3 is devoted to describing this international competition. Before the 1970s, the USA had few significant international industrial competitors. Then, American firms could stay in markets for a long time with benign domestic competition. Today, rapid change is the name of the game. Such change mandates that managers understand the forces requiring strategic change. With that understanding, they can help to formulate a new strategic plan and implement the new strategy.

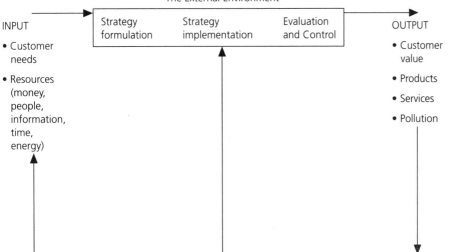

Figure 1.2 The strategic management process.

As the pace of technological change accelerates, the strategy, products, customers, and markets of many firms change at a quickening rate. Managers need to understand the customer, and technological and economic forces, so that they can help to shape and implement the new strategies and managerial processes. As leaders, managers must understand the corporation's strategy so that they can explain the strategy and elicit support from others.

Strategy formulation, implementation, evaluation, and control

The strategic management process involves the range of strategic decisions, from planning the strategy through control of operations. There are three major steps in the strategic management process, known as strategy formulation, implementation, evaluation and control. *Strategy formulation* involves the decisions that determine the organization's mission and establish its objectives and strategies. Some refer to strategy formulation as planning. *Strategy implementation* involves the activities and decisions that are made to install new strategies or support existing strategies. Some refer to strategy implementation as operational management. *Evaluation and control* involve the activities and decisions that keep the process on track. Evaluation and control include following up on goal accomplishment and feeding back the results to decision makers.

Figure 1.2 depicts these three major steps of strategy formulation, implementation, and evaluation and control in the strategic management process. The centrality of the customer to the strategic management process and to TQ is noted in figure 1.2 and throughout this book. A key feature of the external environment is international competition. Other features of the external environment, and a way to conduct an analysis of the external environment, are reviewed in the next chapter.

Total Quality and Management

Are managers' roles changing due to intense global competition? Are managers' jobs changing due to more demanding customers?

Total quality management

To understand the importance of customers to the organization, we develop the concept of TQM, sometimes referred to simply as TQ. TQ involves all employees and extends backwards and forwards to i︎ ︎le the supply chain and the customer chain.[28] As the first word "total" i︎ ︎M is concerned with managing the entire system as opposed to sub-s︎ ︎unctional departments. *Processes* are groups of activities that take a︎ ︎ value to it, and provide an output to an internal or external custome︎ ︎re collections of processes and resources.

Xerox almost went ban︎ ︎o inferior quality products in the face of high-quality, lower-priced pr︎ ︎om Japanese competitors. Faced with organizational death, Xerox s︎ ︎ntly launched TQ efforts which earned it renewal, a Baldrige National Quality Award, and a European Quality Award (see next section). Xerox's efforts include continuously improving quality by working horizontally across departments, by working with suppliers to provide consistent quality, and by working closely with customers to deliver superior value.

From this definition of TQ, we see the reason for management as the provision of customer value. We also see the theme of integration of processes across functions and departments.

In discussing the importance of TQ to all of management, an examiner for a national quality award remarked: "Quality management has coalesced into a major management movement which has influenced nearly every industry. 'Quality management' in this context, means the recognition by senior management that quality is a key strategic issue and therefore an important focus for *all* levels of the organization."[29] Some refer to strategic quality management as aligning the organization and relating it to its environment and its customers.[30]

Herein lies a major theme of this book. Through the mechanism of aligning the entire organization to exceed customer requirements, TQ and strategy have become intertwined. By relating the organization to its external customers and by managing horizontally across the entire organization, *TQ has become a good current example of many strategic management issues*. In many companies throughout the world, TQ is an umbrella description of strategic thinking and action within the companies' chosen businesses. Although it is not a substitute for strategic management, it is easier to find programs, practices, and policies with the TQ label than the strategic management label in many organizations. This book attempts to show how TQ has been incorporated into the practice of strategic management at many firms after the firm has decided the business(es) in which it wishes to operate. Several recent publications in both the USA and Europe have further explored how TQ, as a current example of strategic behavior, relates the organization to its customers and works across large parts of the organization.[31]

Continuous improvement is the continual refinement and improvement of products, services and organizational systems to yield improved value to customers. The term continuous improvement derives from the Japanese term *kaizen*, meaning small, but continuous, improvement.

To see how pervasive globalization and TQ have been as two themes driving many organizations, it is useful to examine some characteristics of current admired corporations per the international exhibit.

GLOBALIZATION AND TOTAL QUALITY AT AMERICA'S MOST ADMIRED CORPORATIONS

Over the past 13 years, Fortune *magazine has ranked "America's most admired corporations." The rankings result from* Fortune's *Corporate Reputations Survey.*

For the 1995 data, 10,000 senior executives, outside directors, and financial analysts were asked to rate firms on eight attributes: quality of management; quality of products or services; innovativeness; long-term investment value; financial soundness; ability to attract, develop, and keep talented people; responsibility to the community and the environment; and wise use of corporate assets.[a]

In defining overall corporate reputation, the polled executives, analysts and directors cited quality of management as the primary attribute. Quality of products or services was rated as the second most important attribute.[b]

Table 1.3 contains the list of the most admired from 1995. Two important characteristics of the firms in the most admired list are worth discussing. The first notable characteristic indicated by the raters is the quality of products and services. Indeed, the firms' commitments to quality go beyond today's products and services. Three of the top ten firms (Motorola, 3M, and Procter & Gamble) have been actively disseminating TQ material to academia. All of the top ten firms are close to their customers – a key characteristic of TQ as discussed throughout this book.

The second notable characteristic is the international presence of the most admired firms in table 1.3. Several of the firms (Coca-Cola in soft drinks, 3M in scientific, photo and control equipment, Motorola in electronics, and Procter & Gamble in consumer products) receive the majority of their sales internationally. The average international sales as a percentage of total sales was about one-third.[c] The data demonstrate that the most admired firms had adapted to the international business environment of the 1990s.

Table 1.3 America's most admired corporations (1995)

Rank	Company	Area
1	Rubbermaid	Rubber and plastic products
2	Microsoft	Computer software
3	Coca-Cola	Beverages
4	Motorola	Electronics
5	Home Depot	Specialist retailers
6	Intel	Electronics
7	Procter & Gamble	Soaps, cosmetics
8	3M	Scientific, photo and control equipment
9	United Parcel Service	Trucking
10	Hewlett-Packard	Computers, office equipment

Source: [a] "America's Most Admired Corporations", *Fortune* (March 6, 1995), p. 54; [b] "America's Most Admired Corporations", *Fortune* (February 10, 1992), p. 43; [c] *Value Line Investment Survey.* New York: Value Line Publishing, Inc. (May 1995).

By reviewing the prescriptions of W. Edwards Deming, we may understand the breadth of managerial changes required to compete in this new era. He and a few others are credited with remaking Japanese industry after the Second World War.

Deming's 14 points of management

Deming's 14 points are widely viewed as prescriptions for a new way to manage. Deming described his 14 points as no less than a complete agenda for managerial action. "The 14 points are the basis for transformation of American industry. It will not suffice merely to solve problems, big or little. Adoption and action on the 14 points are a signal that the management intends to stay in business and aim to protect investors and jobs."[32] The points are:

1   Management must demonstrate constantly their commitment to a widely published statement of the purposes of the company.
2   Learn the new philosophy, top management and everybody.
3   Understand the purpose of inspection, for improvement of processes and reduction of costs.
4   End the practice of awarding business on the basis of price tag alone.
5   Improve constantly and forever the system of production and service.
6   Institute training.
7   Teach and institute leadership.
8   Drive out fear. Create trust. Create a climate for innovation.
9   Optimize toward the purposes of the company the efforts of teams, groups, staff areas.
10   Eliminate exhortations for the workforce.
11a   Eliminate numerical quotas for production and institute methods for improvement.
11b   Eliminate management by objective and improve the capabilities of processes.
12   Remove barriers that rob people of pride of workmanship.
13   Encourage education and self-improvement for everyone.
14   Take action to accomplish the transformation.

Deming's prescriptions are anything but business as usual. He stresses themes of quality, leadership, horizontal management, continuous improvement, employee involvement, and training. His model is substantially different from the old bureaucratic model of inwardly looking administrators whose primary interest is in directing and controlling the behavior of others. Deming's themes are used throughout this book and influence managerial action throughout the world.

Deming was not the only quality pioneer. In some areas, others made even greater contributions to the advancement of quality in organizations. They helped managers to realize that the practice of management had evolved in the twilight of the twentieth century.

Other quality pioneers

Joseph Juran viewed quality as a cross-functional integration issue. He was concerned with processes that spanned at least two functions of design, production, marketing, or finance. Juran recently described the critical role that quality management plays in executive leadership of the entire enterprise and the overall strategy of the firm to deliver greater value to customers.[33] His ideas are treated in detail in this book, especially in the subjects of cross-functional processes and organizational design. His ideas have influenced the way managers structure organizations and teams today.

Kaoru Ishikawa was concerned with the prevention of defects before they occurred. Some of his work in systems and process improvement is reviewed in chapter 11. His work has much to do with the managerial emphasis on process improvement today, and the Japanese emphasis on *kaizen* or continuous improvement.

Philip Crosby is noted for his work concerning the cost of quality and motivational aspects of quality improvement, including the concept of zero defects as a performance criterion for managers.[34] The *cost of quality* refers to the costs incurred due to producing poor quality products and services. Crosby helped US managers to understand that *increased quality could lead to lower costs* if the product/service and the process which yielded it were designed correctly. This understanding helped many managers to see the importance of improving many parts of the organization, like engineering design and the manufacturing/service operations process, not just inspection. The same holds true for service operations where design of the service and the process of delivery are important ingredients to acceptance by customers in the market.

Another way to examine trends in management and organizations in the 1990s concerning quality and international competitiveness is to review a number of prominent organizational awards and managerial criteria in several different countries. Some of the more popular awards and criteria include the Malcolm Baldrige National Quality Award in the USA, the European Quality Award, ISO 9000 in Europe, the Deming Prize in Japan, and other national quality awards from Canada, Europe and Russia.

Malcolm Baldrige Quality Award process

The *Malcolm Baldrige National Quality Award* is a US national award given annually to recognize US companies for business excellence and quality achievement. The Baldrige was started on August 20, 1987, with the enactment of US Public Law 100–17, to recognize firms who were leaders in providing increased quality and value to their customers in an internationally competitive era.[35]

Although there have been some complaints about the amount of work needed to satisfy all the Baldrige criteria, the criteria have been used by many managers as a guide for managerial and organizational improvements. For example, some companies require their suppliers to apply the Baldrige criteria to their firms to improve their operations. The summary Baldrige criteria are repeated in table 1.4. Figure 1.3 shows the relationships among the award criteria.

There has been some criticism of the Baldrige Award.[36] However, the Baldrige criteria help to show how management has changed in the internationally competitive era of the 1990s, with rapidly changing technology and demanding customers who have alternatives. Many firms winning the Baldrige are leaders in

Table 1.4   Malcolm Baldrige National Quality Award Criteria

Examination category/item	Maximum points
1.0 Leadership	90
2.0 Information and analysis	75
3.0 Strategic planning	55
4.0 Human resource development and management	140
5.0 Process management	140
6.0 Business results	250
7.0 Customer focus and satisfaction	250
Total points	1,000

Source: Malcolm Baldrige National Quality Award: 1995 Award Criteria. Washington, DC: United States Department of Commerce (1995), p. 20.

this new era, and are providing new models of management for the twenty-first century. Note the emphases in the Baldrige criteria on customer satisfaction and quality. These areas are at the very core of managerial attention and action at the dawn of the twenty-first century.

There are other quality criteria and other quality awards in Europe, Japan, Canada, and the Pacific Rim, to name a few, that are also influencing managerial action throughout the world.

European Quality Award
Just as there is a national award for exemplary quality in the USA, there is an award for exemplary quality in Europe, known as the European Quality Award. The *European Quality Award (EQA)* is a European award given annually to recognize European companies for business excellence and quality achievement. The EQA is administered by the European Foundation for Quality Management (EFQM). The EFQM consisted of about 300 European organizations (corporations and universities) in 1995. The EQA criteria shown in figure 1.4 are similar to the Baldrige criteria. The EFQM and the EQA help to underscore the importance given to TQ as a competitive weapon in Europe.

In 1994, three firms were publicly recognized by the EFQM for their exemplary quality improvement efforts in Europe with a first place EQA or one of two European Quality Prizes (EQP). Design to Distribution Ltd (D2D), based in the United Kingdom and active in electronics manufacturing, won the first place EQA. Ericcson SA, based in Spain and active in telecommunications systems, and, IBM Italy, South Europe, Middle East, and Africa (SEMEA), both tied for the EQP.[37]

ISO 9000
In some industries, it is difficult for non-European firms to compete in the European Union because of International Standards Organization (ISO) 9000. *ISO 9000* is a comprehensive standard specifying the management systems and processes a

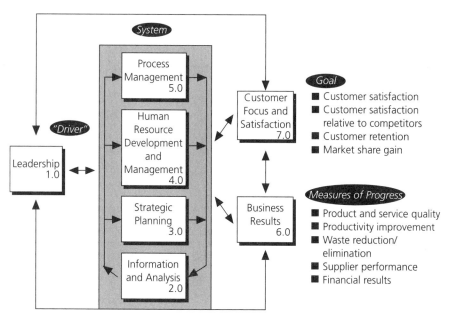

Figure 1.3 Malcolm Baldrige National Quality Award criteria framework: dynamic relationships.

Source: Malcolm Baldrige National Quality Award: 1995 Award Criteria. Washington, DC: US Department of Commerce (1995), p. 5.

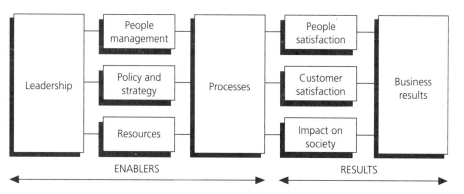

Figure 1.4 Framework of the European Quality Award.

Source: Total Quality Management: the European Model for Self-appraisal. Eindhoven: European Foundation for Quality Management (1993).

firm must possess to market certain products in the EU. ISO 9000 is an entire series of quality management system standards, including 9000, 9001, 9002, and 9003.[38] Without ISO 9000 certification, a firm with regulated products in the health, safety, or environmental sectors may be prohibited from marketing its products in Europe. Very many products have a health, safety, or environmental impact.

Because of their quality themes, there are multiple comparisons between the Baldrige Quality Award, the European Quality Award, and ISO 9000. Many US and European firms have qualified themselves under all three criteria as a statement of their commitment to the quality of their products and services.[39]

Deming Prize

Prior to the implementation of the Baldrige Award, the European Quality Award, and ISO 9000, the Japanese had implemented the Deming Prize. The *Deming Prize* is a Japanese award given annually to recognize companies for business excellence and quality achievement. Partly in recognition of Dr Deming's many contributions to quality improvement in Japanese industry, the award was given to a firm with exemplary and sustained quality improvement systems and processes. For the first time ever, the Deming Prize was given to a US firm when it was awarded to Florida Power and Light in the late 1980s.[40]

Other quality awards

As a system of management and as a strategy, TQ has spread to many parts of the world. That spread has been marked by national competitions and quality awards.

About 30 individual states in the United States have started their own state-wide quality awards. Canada has Canada's Award for Excellence. The United Kingdom started the UK Quality Award in 1994.[41] Annual quality awards are also given in Belgium, Bulgaria, Denmark, Finland, France, Germany, Greece, Iceland, Ireland, The Netherlands, Norway, Poland, Portugal, Russia, Slovakia, Slovenia, Spain, and Sweden.[42]

We forecast that more countries will start their own quality awards as they recognize that TQ is an engine for national competitiveness. Crosby tried to communicate the role of TQ in competitiveness with the title of an award: The Philip B. Crosby Medal for Outstanding Competitiveness through Quality.

Total quality and global competitiveness

A number of countries have discovered that in the era of demanding customers with alternatives due to international competition, TQ and global competitiveness go together. The European Commission recently published an international comparison on the role of quality in various countries. A summary is presented in table 1.5. At the time of the study in 1995, the European Commission was also promoting a European Quality Promotion Policy, including European Quality Week.[43]

▮ Summary ▮

International competition and demanding customers yield potent forces operating on managers today. These themes are reviewed throughout the book as they shape the concepts and practices of strategic management.

Managers are the primary force for keeping an organization in touch with the environment surrounding it and with the customers served by the organization. As such, managers develop and communicate a vision for the future of the organization

Table 1.5 The role of quality and the various countries

Country or region	Role of quality in management	Level of awareness of quality
Japan	Quality is the key element of overall management.	Excellent
United States	Quality is gaining in importance.	Good
Europe	Quality is seen as a special professional problem of management In certain countries, authorities are taking measures to promote quality.	Not sufficient
Central and Eastern European countries and certain other countries	Quality is seen as a specific problem generally linked to the workers.	Limited

Source: The European Way towards Excellence. Brussels: European Commission (1995), p. 21.

and set goals and objectives. Managers are also charged with guiding performance to ensure that the vision and the goals are reached.

Strategic decision makers are categorized in terms of the outsiders on the board of directors and the inside executives employed by the organization. Today, a higher percentage of board members are outsiders than in the past. This trend is part of an attempt to require the inside executives to be more accountable to the board and the stockholders.

Corporate level strategic decision makers include the chief executive officer, the president, the chief operating officer and the chairman of the board. In some organizations, these jobs are held by one or two powerful individuals, whereas in other organizations the jobs are held by three or four individuals in an executive office. Corporate level vice presidents are also included in the list of corporate level strategic decision makers. Division and group vice presidents are among the strategic decision makers at the business level. At the functional level, manufacturing vice presidents, marketing vice presidents, and other functional vice presidents are typically involved with strategic decision making.

Following the lead of Mintzberg, we view strategy as a pattern in a series of decisions. The unit of analysis in the study of strategy is the strategic decision rather than a long-range plan, annual report, or news release.

Deming's 14 points of management are viewed as a new prescription for managing and doing business in a world where intense international competition gives customers choices. The Baldrige Quality Award, the Deming Prize, the European Quality Award, ISO 9000, and other national quality awards provide standards throughout the world for organizations focusing on customers. Deming, Juran, Ishikawa, Crosby, and these standards combine with the practice of TQ to yield a concept of management focusing on continuous improvement, organizational systems, and customer value. Thus, TQ has become an application of many strategic management concepts throughout the world.

DISCUSSION QUESTIONS

1 Describe the need for business managers and strategic managers in organizations today.

2 Do you expect the need for managers to stay in touch with the environment and customers to strengthen or weaken in the next decade? Why?

3 Describe the advantages and disadvantages of increasing outside representation on the board of directors.

4 Why is strategy important for managers? How have changes in quality and technology impacted on the importance of strategy for managers?

5 Compare and contrast the view that strategy is a pattern in a series of decisions with the view that strategy can be found in the firm's latest annual report.

6 How does TQ relate to strategic management?

7 Describe the significance of Deming's 14 points of management for managers today. Apply your answer to a manager in an airline, a restaurant, and a computer manufacturer.

8 How will the Malcolm Baldrige National Quality Award, the Deming Prize, the European Quality Award, ISO 9000, and other national quality awards lead to greater customer value globally?

KEY TERMS

The board of directors	is the governing body that represents the interests of the stockholders in the affairs of the corporation.
The chief executive officer	is the executive with ultimate responsibility for the formulation and implementation of the organization's overall strategy.
The chairman of the board	is the senior executive on the board.
Continuous improvement	is the continual refinement and improvement of products, services, and organizational systems to yield improved value to customers.
The cost of quality	refers to the costs incurred due to producing poor quality products and services.
Cross-functional processes	are activities linked to providing value to customers that span at least two functions of design, production, marketing or finance.
Deliberate strategy	consists of a firm deciding on its goals and implementing intended strategy to realize the goals.
The Deming Prize	is a Japanese award given annually to recognize companies for business excellence and quality achievement.
Emergent strategies	are those strategies actually in place in the organization.
The European Quality Award	is a European award given annually to recognize European companies for business excellence and quality achievement.

Evaluation and control	involve the activities and decisions that keep the process on track.
Functional managers	are responsible for specific functions within the organization.
ISO 9000	is a comprehensive standard specifying the management systems and processes a firm must possess to market certain products in the EU.
The Malcolm Baldrige National Quality Award	is a US national award given annually to recognize US companies for business excellence and quality achievement.
The president,	sometimes known as the chief operating officer, is the executive charged with implementing the strategy decided upon by the CEO and the board.
Processes	are groups of activities that take an input, add value to it, and provide an output to an internal or external customer.
Strategic managers	are the executives responsible for the overall performance of the organization.
Strategic management	refers to the managerial decisions that relate the organization to its environment, guide internal activities, and determine organizational long-term performance.
Strategy	is a pattern in a stream of decisions.
Strategy formulation	involves the decisions that determine the organization's mission and establish its objectives and strategies.
Strategy implementation	involves the activities and decisions that are made to install new strategies or support existing strategies.
Systems	are collections of processes and resources.
Total quality management (TQM)	is a systems approach to management that aims to continuously improve value to customers by designing and continuously improving organizational processes and systems.

Harley-Davidson Beats Back a Japanese Motorcycle Invasion with Quality and Exports

QUALITY CASE

Harley-Davidson (H-D) is a remarkable story of a 90 year old US company that nearly went bankrupt because its managers lost sight of its customers. The near bankruptcy is all the more remarkable when you consider that big, loud, Harley "hogs," as the bikes were known, are icons of Americana. The bankruptcy was avoided and many of the customers returned after H-D's managers refocused on customers by making a massive investment in quality.

In 1903, three brothers, William, Walter, and Arthur Davidson, invented the first Harley-Davidson motorcycle. In the ensuing years, H-D survived two world wars and the Great Depression. Partly because Harley focused on super heavyweight bikes (engine sizes greater than 850 c.c.), hogs personified "the American desire for power, speed, and personal freedom."[a] Due to the popularity of H-D hogs, by 1953 H-D was the sole domestic maker of motorcycles in the USA.[b] H-D made its initial public stock offering in 1965.

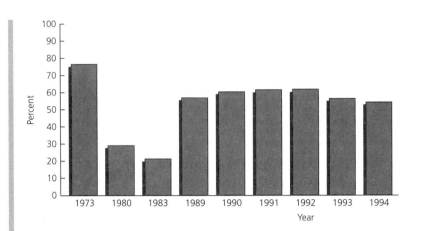

Figure 1.5   Harley-Davidson: share of US super-heavyweight motorcycle market.

The AMF Corporation acquired H-D three years later, partly on the basis of plans to invest in H-D and grow it.[c] Ironically, AMF increased production dramatically and drove down quality. Hogs were failing final quality inspection more than 50 percent of the time and many defects were showing up in the hands of customers.[d]

This was about the time that Japanese motorcycle companies in the form of Honda, Suzuki, Yamaha, Kawasaki, and others were invading the US motorcycle market with high-quality bikes. Soichiro Honda, the founder of the Honda Company, described his strategy. "If you turn out a superior product, it will be patronized by the public. Our policy is not simply to turn out a product because there is demand, but to turn out a superior product and create a demand."[e]

Honda entered the USA by creating demand at the low end of the market with lightweight bikes. Harley Davidson's managers initially ignored the international competitors. The attitude of Harley's managers concerning lightweight bikes was typified by a comment of William H. Davidson, the firm's president and son of the founder. "Basically, we don't believe in the lightweight market."[f] While H-D was disbelieving and ignoring the threat, international competitors first built substantial market share in the lightweight segment and then attacked H-D by selling super heavyweight bikes.

Because of the attack with high-quality bikes by Japanese firms and H-D's quality problems, H-D's market share plummeted. Its domestic market share fell by more than two-thirds from more than three out of every four bikes in 1973 to fewer than one out of every four bikes in 1983 (see figure 1.5).

Associated with the market share loss, H-D lost money in 1981, and lost about US$25 million in 1982 (see figure 1.6). Based upon those market and financial losses, bankruptcy seemed imminent. How could Harley's managers rescue the company and save an American institution from international attack?

Forecasting that the future contained bankruptcy, given its dismal results under AMF, Harley's executives bought the company back from AMF.[g] With the weakened market and financial conditions, the executives lobbied for and achieved substantial tariff protection from the US Congress for five years against foreign motorcycles.[h] This gave the executives five years to rescue the company as the tariffs raised the price of foreign bikes and thereby limited their market growth.

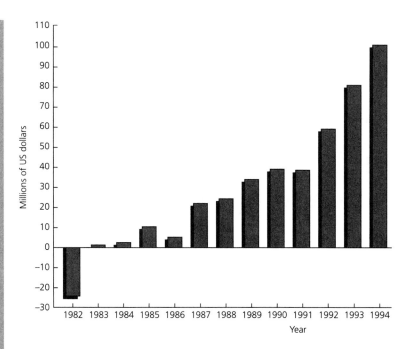

Figure 1.6   Harley-Davidson: annual net income.

The executives tried a number of programs, including wage cuts and automation. Nothing they tried seemed to work until they implemented quality improvement, including employee involvement.

Harley's executives dared to rebuild the company and win back customers by making a massive commitment to improving the quality of H-D hogs. As part of their commitment to the customer, Harley executives traveled to HOG (Harley Owner Group) rallies on their bikes on weekends to assess customer needs and customer satisfaction with current products.[i] Partly as a result of those executive trips to assess customer needs, Harley's managers purposely designed their bikes with the motor and parts not covered with sheet metal, as is the case with the more aerodynamic looking Japanese bikes.

Harley's quality improvement efforts also included supplier training and supplier partnerships. Harley cut the number of its suppliers from 320 to 120 and taught the remaining firms TQ concepts. Gary E. Kirkham, H-D's manufacturing manager, says: "We buy 50 percent of the dollar value of our motorcycles from suppliers. So improvements we made [internally] only got us halfway."[j]

Changes were made on several other fronts to improve quality. Massive worker training in TQ ideas and methods, and the active buy-in from the union, were part of the quality improvement change. The organization started using cross-functional quality teams with representatives from different functions, such as manufacturing, purchasing, and marketing. A flatter organization structure was implemented, with fewer layers of managers, as the employees were now better trained and working together across departmental boundaries. Statistical process control was implemented to control the manufacturing process before defects were produced. Just-in-time (materials as needed) manufacturing is also part of H-D's commitment to quality improvement.[k]

As they do in H-D, executives must "walk the talk" and lead the commitment for such a system of management to succeed. The near bankruptcy, quality rebirth, and dramatic turnaround at Harley-Davidson prove the importance of managers focusing on the customer in an era of intense international competition.

As a result of its commitment to its customers and their quality requirements, H-D's market share reached 63 percent in 1992.[l] Market share declined slightly in 1993 and 1994 because H-D would not quickly increase output and jepordize quality in the face of rising demand. Indeed, the wait to buy a new hog approximated a year at the time. H-D's profitability had increased dramatically and its stock price increased 30-fold from 1986 to 1994.[m] Increasing international sales of hogs were helping to fuel the profit and sales growth. In 1995, there were rumors that H-D would start to manufacture its bikes in Europe.

In the quality transformation, owning a hog had become respectable. Jay Leno talked about his hog on his *Tonight Show*, and actors like Arnold Schwarzenegger were helping to make the bikes popular by driving around Hollywood on them.[n] As a measure of the bike's respectability, one in three Harley-Davidson buyers in the early 1990s was a professional or a manager.[o]

The Harley-Davidson trademark alone has a new impact. H-D has recently licensed its name to a shoe manufacturer that plans to invade the "industrial chic" boot market.[p] It has also licensed the theme-restaurant chain which operates the Harley-Davidson Cafe in New York City to use the company name.[q] Both the shoe company and the restaurant chain expect to cash in on the legendary status of Harley-Davidson as a symbol of US culture and quality rebirth in the late twentieth century.

Discussion Questions

1 How important is quality to the rebirth of H-D?

2 What were H-D's chances of surviving under the corporate structure of AMF?

3 Discuss the advantages and disadvantages of H-D targeting other segments of the motorcycle market.

4 Discuss the advantages and disadvantages of H-D making its bikes in Europe to help meet rising demand from Europeans.

Note: the case book that accompanies this text contains a full-length case on H-D.
Sources: a. Marvel, Mark, "The gentrified hog," *Esquire* (July, 1989), pp. 25–26;   b. Rose, R. "Vrooming back," *Wall Street Journal* (August 31, 1990), p. 1;   c. Reid, P., *Well Made in America*: Lessons from Harley-Davidson on Being the Best, New York: McGraw-Hill (1990), p. 9;   d. Ibid, p. 25;   e. *Journal of Commerce*, (November 6, 1965), p. 23;   f. Rowan, T. "Harley sets new drive to boost market share," *Advertising Age* (January 29, 1973), p. 34;   g. Willis, R., "Harley-Davidson comes roaring back," *Management Review* (March, 1986), pp. 20–27;   h. Rose, R., "Vrooming back", p. 1;   i. "The payoff from a good reputation," *Fortune* (February 10, 1992), p. 77;   j. "Learning from Japan," *Business Week* (January 27, 1992), p. 59;   k. Draper, S., Dundon, A., North, A., Smith, R., Adams, S. and Griffin, A. "Harley Davidson, Inc.," in Grigsby, D. and Stahl, M., *Strategic Management Cases*. Boston: PWS-Kent (1993), pp. 352–77;   l. "Learning from Japan," p. 59; "The enduring Harley mystique," *The Charlotte Observer* (July 27, 1993), pp. D1–2;   m. Gold, H. R., "Harley splits stocks, revs up dividend," *Barrons* (August, 1994);   n. "Harley-Davidson," *Value Line Investment Survey* (September 3, 1993), p. 1763;   o. Rose, R., "Vrooming back," *Wall Street Journal* (August 31, 1990), p. 1;   p. Schroer, J., "Selling clodhopper chic , Harley, Caterpiller try boots for size," *USA Today* (December 9, 1993), p. 6B;   q. Gold, H. R., "Harley splits stocks, revs up dividend," p. 39.

WOMEN AND GENDER DIVERSITY IN THE WORLDWIDE WORKFORCE

There are few human resource issues as widely debated throughout the world as the role of women in the workforce. The Fourth United Nations World Conference on Women, held in Beijing during the summer of 1995, focused international media attention on the plight and progress of women in the world of work, as well as in other human dimensions.[a]

One of the underlying themes to the debate is that of unequal economic power between the genders. Women's economic power is associated with the percentage of the workforce that is female, which averages 29 percent in developing countries and 44 percent in developed countries.[b]

Another measure of unequal economic power between the genders is women's salaries relative to men's salaries (see table 1.6). These data indicate that there is much variance throughout the world concerning the utilization of women in the workforce. In addition to the data in table 1.6 indicating that Japanese women earn 51 percent of Japanese men's salaries, there are other data suggesting that Japan underutilizes the women in its workforce.[c] As the world becomes an increasingly competitive global marketplace, those firms that learn how to equitably use both genders in their workforces will reap a competitive advantage as their customers are increasingly of both genders.

Women fulfill a positive role in working with a gender diverse workforce and gender diverse customers. The percentage of managers who are women is a recognition of that role. That percentage varies considerably across US industries (table 1.7). The data indicate that some non-manufacturing industries recognize the role that women managers can fulfill in working with a gender diverse workforce and gender diverse customers. As the percentage of customers who are women increases, and as the percentage of the non-managerial workforce that is women increases, there should be an increased percentage of women managers in a variety of industries.

Another measure of the increased gender diversity of women in the workforce is the percentage of women in executive positions. An increasing number of women are breaking the glass ceiling, which is a perceived invisible barrier keeping women and minorities out of executive ranks. The United States Department of Labor published a report with some encouraging data on the upward mobility of women. The report showed that among 90,000 contractors who reported to the department, women accounted for 25 percent of the total officers and managers in 1991. This was up from 18 percent in 1981.[d]

This progress is especially noteworthy at the very top of corporate America – in the board room. The presence of women is being increasingly noted on corporate boards of directors. The *Wall Street Journal* reported that the proportion of corporate boards appointing women in 1992 reached a record of 60 percent.[e] Since such boards are the pinnacle of power in most firms, women's presence on these boards may lead the way to shattering the glass ceiling for other women. Especially since women are increasingly functioning on powerful committees of those boards, their ability to influence corporate practices is growing. "Token women on boards are dead. Today's women board members, armed with more business knowledge and experience, can be found heading powerful executive and audit committees. Others are influencing policy in finance, acquisitions and executive pay."[f]

However, progress is not uniform, as stumbling blocks remain to be conquered. Many womens' managerial experience is relatively short, narrow, and in areas that have not been associated with executive career paths, e.g. communications.[g] Women are also finding that they are not accepted as equals by managers in many other countries when conducting international business. In many foreign countries, business is still more of a man's world than in the USA. Thus, women face problems being accepted as professionals.[h]

Table 1.6   A worldwide gender wage gap

Country	Women's earnings (percent)
Turkey	93
Kenya	85
France	81
United States	76
United Kingdom	71
Switzerland	66
Hong Kong	63
Japan	51

Note: Women's earnings are expressed as percentage of men's for non-agricultural employment.
Source of data: International Labor Organization (1993–4) "The roads to Beijing," *The Washington Post* (August 27, 1995), p. C3.

Table 1.7   Percentage of women managers

Industry	Percentage
Finance, insurance, real estate	41
Services	39
Retail trade	39
Wholesale trade	21
Manufacturing	16
Mining	10

Source of data: Federal Glass Ceiling Commission, (1995) "How workplaces may look without affirmative action" *Wall Street Journal* (March 20, 1995), B1.

To counter these roadblocks, women are increasingly seeking line managerial experience in marketing and operations. As international experience is increasingly demanded for executive careers, some women are placing more emphases on international experiences and assignments. Such international experience, combined with breadth in line managerial positions, should lead to further disintegration of the glass ceiling for women.

Discussion Questions

1   How should the salaries of women relate to the salaries of men? Relate your answer to the concept of discrimination which refers to human resource actions based on criteria that are not job relevant.

2   Describe the appropriate percentage of managers in an industry who should be women. Relate your answer to the concept of discrimination.

3 Why has the responsibility of managers for the gender diversity of their workforce received so much attention in the past ten years? What is your forecast for the next ten years?

Sources: **a.** "Women debate 'Platform for Action'," *International Herald Tribune* (September 5, 1995), p. 1; **b.** "The roads to Beijing," *The Washington Post* (August 27, 1995), p. C3; **c.** "The great Japanese secret," in Schonberger, R. J., *Building a Chain of Customers*. New York: The Free Press (1990), p. 130; **d.** "Progress seen in breaking 'glass ceilings'," *Wall Street Journal* (August 12, 1992), p. B1; **e.** "Once male enclaves, corporate boards now comb executive suites for women," *Wall Street Journal* (January, 22, 1993), p. B1; **f.** Ibid.; **g.** "Doors still closed to women, CEO survey says," *USA Today* (September 3, 1992), p. 7B; **h.** "Gender gap: businesswomen face formidable barriers when they venture overseas," *Wall Street Journal* (October 16, 1992), p. R20.

NOTES

1 Stahl, M. J. and Grigsby, D. W., *Strategic Management for Decision Making*. Boston: PWS-Kent (1991), p. 4.

2 "Ranking corporate reputations," *Fortune* (January 1983), p. 35.

3 "Australia presses APEC to take concrete free-trade action," *International Herald Tribune* (September 1, 1995), p. 7; "Europe builds ties in East Asia: after many chilly decades, a new climate for trade," *International Herald Tribune* (September 22, 1995), p. 17; "NAFTA: so far, so good," *Wall Street Journal* (October 28, 1994), pp. R1–R14; "Pretoria invigorates 12-nation African development group," *International Herald Tribune* (August 30, 1995), p. 13.

4 Trompenaars, F., *Riding the Waves of Culture: Understanding Cultural Diversity in Business*. London: Economist Books (1993).

5 Carothers, G. H., Bounds, G. M. and Stahl, M. J., "Managerial leadership," in Stahl, M. J. and Bounds, G. M. (eds), *Competing Globally through Customer Value: the Management of Strategic Suprasystems*. Westport, CT: Quorum Books (1991), p. 80; Band, W. A., *Creating Value for Customers*. New York: Wiley (1991).

6 Peters, T. and Waterman, R., *In Search of Excellence*. New York: Warner Books (1982), p. 14.

7 Feigenbaum, A. V., "How to implement total quality control," *Executive Excellence* (November, 1989), p. 15.

8 Bowles, J. and Hammond, J., *Beyond Quality: How 50 Winning Companies Use Continuous Improvement*. New York: G. P. Putnam's Sons (1991), pp. 119–21.

9 Drucker, P., "Leadership: more doing than dash," *Wall Street Journal* (January 6, 1988), p. 14.

10 Geneen, H. and Moscow, A., *Managing*, Garden City, NY: Doubleday (1984), p. 285.

11 "America's toughest bosses," *Fortune* (February 27, 1989), p. 40.

12 Norburn, D., "The chief executive: a breed apart," *Strategic Management Journal*, 10 (1989), pp. 1–15.

13 Quick, J., Nelson, D. and Quick, J., "Successful executives: how independent?" *Academy of Management Executive*, 1 (May 1987).

14 Drucker, P., "Leadership: more doing than dash," *Wall Street Journal* (January 6, 1988), p. 14.

15 Mintzberg, H., "The design school: reconsidering the basic premises of strategic management," *Strategic Management Journal*, 11 (March–April 1990), pp. 171–96.

16 Goodstein, J., Gautam, K. and W. Boeker, "The effects of board size and diversity on strategic change," *Strategic Management Journal* (March 1994), pp. 241–250.

17 "The battle for corporate control," *Business Week* (May 18, 1987), pp. 102–109.

18 "Directors earn much more in benefits than shareholders think," *Wall Street Journal* (January 5, 1995), p. A1.

19 "Power investors," *Business Week* (June 20, 1988), pp. 116–23.

20 Kesner, I. and Johnson, R., "An investigation of the relationship between board composition and stockholder suits," *Strategic Management Journal*, 11 (May–June 1990), pp. 327–36.

21 Kesner, I., "Director's characteristics and committee membership," *Academy of Management Journal*, 31 (March 1988), pp. 66–84.

22 Mintzberg, H., "Patterns in strategy formation," *Management Science*, 24 (1978), pp. 934–48.

23 Mintzberg, H. and J. A. Waters, "Of strategies, deliberate and emergent," *Strategic Management Journal*, 6 (1985), pp. 257–71.

24 Wilson, J. T., "Strategic planning at R. J. Reynolds industries," *Journal of Business Strategy*, 6 (1985), pp. 22–8.

NOTES CONT.

25 Mintzberg, H. and A. McHugh, "Strategy formation in an adhocracy," *Administrative Science Quarterly*, 30, (June 1985), pp. 160–97.

26 Mintzberg, H., "The design school," pp. 171–96.

27 Ireland, R. D. et al., "Strategy formulation process," *Strategic Management Journal*, 8, (1987), pp. 469–86.

28 Rampey, J. and Roberts, H., "Core body of knowledge working council: perspectives on total quality," in Report of the Total Quality Leadership Steering Committee and Working Councils, Cincinnati, OH: Procter & Gamble (November 1992), pp. 2–2.

29 Easton, G., "The 1993 state of US total quality management: a Baldrige examiner's perspective," *California Management Review*, 35 (Spring 1993), pp. 32–54.

30 Godfrey, A. B., "Ten areas for future research in TQM," *Quality Management Journal* (October 1993), pp. 47–70.

31 Cole, W. and Mogab, J., *The Economics of Total Quality Management: Clashing Paradigms in the Global Market*. Oxford: Blackwell (1995); Hackman, J. R. and Wageman, R., "Total quality management: empirical, conceptual, and practical issues," *Administrative Science Quarterly*, 40 (1995), pp. 309–42; Powell, T., "Total quality management as competitive advantage: a review and empirical study," *Strategic Management Journal*, 16 (January 1995), pp. 15–38; "Special issue: Total quality management," *California Management Review*, 35 (Spring, 1993); "Special issue: Total quality management," *Canadian Journal of Administrative Sciences*, 12 (June, 1995); "Total quality special issue," *Academy of Management Review*, 19 (July 1994).

32 Deming, W. E., *Out of the Crisis*. Cambridge, MA: MIT Press (1986), p. 23.

33 Juran, J. (ed.) *A History of Managing for Quality*. Milwaukee, WI: ASQC Quality Press (1995), pp. 650–1.

34 Crosby, P., "Quality leadership," *Executive Excellence* (May 1993), pp. 3–4; Crosby, P., *Quality without Tears: the Art of Hassle-free Management*. New York: McGraw-Hill (1984).

35 *Malcolm Baldrige National Quality Award: 1991 Application Guidelines*. Washington, DC: United States Department of Commerce (1991), p. 43.

36 "Does the Baldrige Award really work?" *Harvard Business Review* (January–February, 1992), pp. 126–47; "The Baldrige boondoggle," *Machine Design* (August 6, 1992), pp. 25–9.

37 "1994 European Quality Award Prize winner profiles," *European Quality*, 1 (November/December 1994), pp. 18–45.

38 Brumm, E., "Managing records for ISO 9000 compliance," *Quality Progress* (January 1995), pp. 73–7.

39 Askey, J. M. and Dale, B. G., "From ISO series registration to TQM,' *Quality Management Journal* (July 1994), pp. 67–76.

40 Evelyn, J. J. and DeCarlo, N., "Customer focus helps utility see the light," *Journal of Business Strategy* (January–February 1992), pp. 8–12.

41 Shergold, K., "UK Quality Award," *UK Quality* (February 1994), p. 8; *The 1995 UK Quality Award*. London: British Quality Foundation (1994).

42 "Annual Report of European Organization for Quality," *European Quality*, 1, 3 (1994), pp. 56–94.

43 *The European Way towards Excellence*. Brussels: European Commission (1995), p. 21.

THE ENVIRONMENT AND THE STRATEGIC PLAN

LEARNING OBJECTIVES

After reading this chapter, you should be able to accomplish the following.

1 Define the ideas of strengths, weaknesses, opportunities, and threats from a SWOT analysis and relate the four ideas.

2 Define the ideas of mission, objectives, and strategies from a strategic plan and explain the three ideas.

3 Describe the uses and limitations of the product/market/industry life cycles.

4 Explain the use of the BCG matrix as a portfolio planning tool.

5 Describe the use of learning curves in market entry and pricing decisions.

Table 2.1   Primary SWOT issues

Internal strengths and weaknesses	External opportunities and threats
Horizontal processes	Customer value trends
Organizational structure	Social trends
Corporate culture	Demographic trends
Management	Economic trends
Financial position	Technological trends
Operations	Regulatory trends
Marketing	Physical trends
Human resources	Competitive trends
Research and development	
Information systems	

Source: Adapted from Stahl, M. J., *Management: Total Quality in a Global Environment*. Oxford, UK: Blackwell (1995), p. 150.

Throughout recorded history, there have been various managerial and organizational practices in vogue to fit the demands of the times.[1] Just as the managers at AT&T showed (see quality case), managers must change strategies and managerial practices to fit the environment.

Analyzing the Environment: SWOT Analysis

As discussed in chapter 1, there are three major steps in the strategic management process, known as strategy formulation, implementation, evaluation and control. To effectively formulate strategy, strategic decision makers need to understand and forecast environmental trends. The case analysis guide in the appendix to this chapter is meant to help one understand "how to do" such an environmental analysis.

SWOT analysis

To understand environmental trends, managers must analyze conditions in the internal environment of the organization *and* conditions in the external environment.[2] This analysis of the internal environment and the external environment is so pervasive in strategic planning that it has its own acronym. This analysis of internal Strengths and Weaknesses and external Opportunities and Threats is called a *SWOT analysis*.

Table 2.1 shows the primary internal and external issues/conditions examined in a SWOT analysis.

Internal strengths and weaknesses

Conditions internal to the organization are called internal strengths and weaknesses. A *strength* is a condition or issue internal to the organization that may lead to a customer benefit or a competitive advantage. Alternatively, a *weakness* is a condition or issue internal to the organization that may lead to negative customer value or a competitive disadvantage. Most of these internal strengths and weaknesses are the result of prior management decisions.[3]

Horizontal processes, a flat organizational structure with few layers of management, and a customer-oriented corporate culture are obvious internal strengths. *Horizontal processes* are flows of work and activities that span vertical functions like purchasing, design, production, and marketing. These strengths are common to many firms who are serious about providing superior value to customers as a way to compete globally.

These strengths can be contrasted to bureaucratically oriented organizations with tall, vertical organization structures, many levels of non-value-added management, and strict job descriptions. These features discourage people from solving problems or improving systems outside their immediate jobs. How often is the cry of "That's not my job!" an excuse for not satisfying the customer?

Competent, experienced, flexible managers are a definite asset. Managers who understand customers and competitors, who are dedicated to continuous improvement, information sharing, and involvement in planning and implementing change are an indispensable asset.[4]

Strong finances can facilitate most decisions that management wishes to implement. Alternatively, a weak financial position with disastrous debt levels weakens and constrains any organization. A weak financial position can prohibit a firm from responding to external opportunities and makes the firm more susceptible to external threats.

In the early 1990s, Trans World Airlines (TWA) was struggling for its very survival, with high debt levels and mounting losses. Because of the weak financial position, it had sold some of its more lucrative international routes to raise cash. Selling the crown jewels left TWA in a weakened position to compete in the future.[5] In contrast, financially stronger Delta Airlines, American Airlines, and United Airlines were buying aircraft and lucrative, growing international routes from ailing airlines. Such purchases made those three airlines even stronger to serve customers and to compete in the future.

Strengths in production/operations and in marketing are usually the internal strengths that brought an organization to its current strong position. Some examples of strengths in productions/operations are systems capable of producing quality products and services, modern plant and equipment, flexible manufacturing systems, and state-of-the-art technology. Examples of strengths in marketing are a strong distribution system, products or services demanded by customers, systems to understand customer requirements, competitive prices, and effective advertising.

Some examples of strengths in human resources are the energy and training of the firm's human resources. The potential of trained human resources is not realized if work rules are restrictive, as General Motors learned. GM spent much effort in the 1980s and 1990s pursuing looser work rules to improve the productivity and the quality of its operations. In deciding on which plants to close as part of a restructuring in 1992, one GM plant was kept open and another

GM plant was closed, partly because of the looser work rules and higher quality at the plant kept open.[6]

Today, many firms that truly understand the role of employees in delivering value to customers are investing 5–8 percent of their payroll in employee training. These are numbers unheard of a few years ago, when spending 1 percent on training was viewed as an expense to be minimized.

Training in horizontal systems and processes is usually part of the training to produce higher quality and productivity, as the Capsugel Division of the pharmaceutical firm Warner-Lambert discovered.[7] Capsugel used such training so that its personnel would think horizontally in accord with the way value was created for its customers.

Computerized information systems can be a strength in providing products and services to the firm's customers. For some firms, strong information systems can provide value directly to customers. American Airlines' Sabre reservation system allows travel agents to quickly book reservations for their customers.[8]

A research and development program that continually turns out new and valuable products is an internal strength that can pay dividends for years into the future. As new product development cycle times shorten and as customers demand new technologies and new products *now*, R&D will receive increasing attention.[9] Merck has a very productive R&D program, with many new pharmaceutical products in the R&D pipeline. This R&D strength helped Merck top the list of *Fortune*'s most-admired companies for every year from 1987 through 1993.[10] After completing the merger with Medco, Merck was using the Medco distribution system in 1995 to help distribute its own pharmaceutical products.

Internal strengths and weaknesses are inside the organization and under the influence of managers. Therefore, it is assumed that the weaknesses can be changed. External threats can be more trying than the internal conditions since external threats are not under the control of the firm's managers.

External opportunities and threats

An *opportunity* is an issue or condition in the environment external to the firm that may help it reach its goals. A *threat* is an issue or condition in the external environment that may prevent the firm from reaching its goals. Very strong external opportunities or threats may even cause the firm to evolve its goals and strategies.

Opportunities and threats in the external environment are not under the direct control of the firm's managers. However, external opportunities and threats must be responded to if the firm wishes to remain healthy and grow. Analyzing the external environment is labeled as *environmental scanning*.[11] High organizational performance is associated with frequent and broad environmental scanning.[12]

The trends listed in table 2.1 under "external opportunities and threats" may be opportunities or may be threats, depending on the nature of the trend. Unlike the issues listed under "internal strengths and weaknesses", external trends are not under the control of management. However, management can anticipate and respond to the external trends with adequate environmental scanning and strategic planning.

Managers must understand and even anticipate customer value trends as those trends can affect the products/services demanded and the way the firm operates. A good example of customer value trends affecting the way the firm operates is the switch to firm, non-negotiable pricing ("no-dicker stickers") at many General Motors dealers in the 1990s. Saturn dealers had such success with the concept of no haggling on price that other parts of GM copied the practice. Sales usually double about the first month or so, then stabilize into a pace 20–50 percent ahead of sales before the switch. No-dicker dealers slash expenses, mainly by cutting employees. Advertising expenses can also be cut because satisfied customers advertise widely by word of mouth.[13] Understanding and delivering value to customers is so central to strategic management that chapter 7 of this volume is devoted to the subject.

Social and demographic trends usually have slowly developing, yet long-lasting, effects on the organization. For example, the shift to dual-career couples in the United States took many years to develop. Now that the trend is in place, it will be a long time before the USA and much of the developed world returns to only one family member working. (See international case in chapter 1.) The dual-career couple has been associated with the popularity of disposable diapers and other labor saving products. Now that the demand is established, the demand for such products should stay strong for some time.

A powerful demographic trend occurring in several developed countries is the aging of the population. Figure 2.1 shows the aging population for Germany,

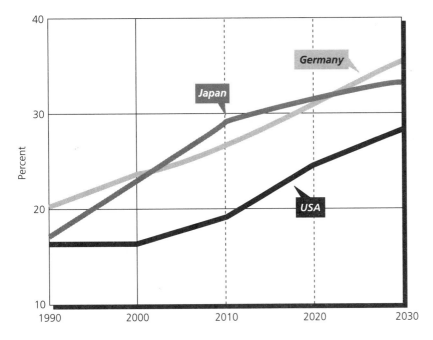

Figure 2.1   Older and older: percentage of population over age 60.
Source: The Wall Street Journal (September 11, 1995), p. A1. Copyright © 1995 Dow Jones & Co., Inc. All rights reserved worldwide.

Japan and the USA projected to the year 2030. Demographers forecast that such powerful, long-lasting trends will have widespread impacts on business. These changes include the design of products to accommodate older customers, increased demand for health care, an older workforce, increased savings rates, and increased retiree pension costs. The increased percentage of retired workers in Japan and Germany could even impact their international competitiveness beyond the year 2000.

To recognize the changes in the economic environment, organizations spend considerable time and money on economic forecasts. Economic forecasts concerning recessions, expansions, inflation, international exchange rates, and other economic changes aid managers as they plan strategic moves.[14]

Firms also spend considerable amounts of time, money and personnel on technological forecasting. The effects of technology and technological change on the firm, its customers, and its competitors are so important that they are analyzed in detail in chapter 8 of this volume.

Changes in government regulation can have an extreme, sudden impact because the rules of conducting business are sometimes changed abruptly with the power of law. Effective strategic managers pay close attention to potential regulatory changes. Frequently, managers join industry associations to monitor potential changes and to influence the nature of the regulation.

A good example of government regulation that could impact millions of people and the way firms conduct business concerns legislation about smoking tobacco. In an attempt to show how onerous that legislation could be due to its detailed specifications, Philip Morris Europe SA ran an ad in European newspapers addressed to Europe's 97 million smokers. The ad stated: "The Ten Commandments contain 179 words; The American Declaration of Independence contains 300 words; and, Recent legislation in Europe concerning when and where you can smoke contains 24,942 words".[15]

Changes in the physical environment, like acid rain or global warming, usually occur at a slow rate. Therefore, the trends are easier to counter with a strategic plan. For example, as the amount of garbage grows and landfills overflow, pressure for recycling and conservation will grow. Since those trends take years to develop, firms have time to mount effective responses.

Changes in competition, such as the entrance of a new competitor, can be a dramatic threat. Such extensive changes due to competitive threats underscore the importance of competitive strategy and competitor analysis. Chapter 6 is devoted to understanding those competitive issues.

The Strategic Plan

After the SWOT analysis has been performed with the analysis of internal strengths and weaknesses, as well as external opportunities and threats, then managers are able to formulate the strategic plan. The *strategic plan* includes a mission, objectives, and strategies.

The strategic plan should be formulated to capitalize on external opportunities and internal strengths, and to work around external threats and internal weaknesses. *Grow-and-invest situations* are those in which firms can capitalize on external opportunities with internal strengths. *Shrinkage or withdrawal situations* are those in which firms have significant internal weaknesses or external threats that they cannot overcome.

Mission

A *mission statement* describes what business(es) the firm is in. The mission indicates why the organization exists.[16] As the mission refers to the whole enterprise, there is usually only one mission statement per enterprise. However, a highly diversified firm may operate in substantially different businesses and require each different business unit to design its own mission statement.

The mission should be written from the perspective of the customers rather than the stockholders, or any other group. The customer focus is a primary characteristic of TQ and an area in which TQ and strategic management intersect.[17]

Mission statements usually describe the firm's chief products or services, the customers or market served, the customer value provided, and the firm's activities. An example of a mission statement printed in Lilly's Annual Report follows. "Eli Lilly and Company is a global research-based corporation that develops, manufactures, and markets pharmaceuticals, medical instruments and diagnostic products, and animal health products. The company markets its products in 110 countries around the world".[18] Understanding what its customers require in 110 countries is a primary function of Lilly's management.

Objectives

After the *why* of the business has been defined, it is appropriate to describe the *what*. *Objectives or goals* refer to the kinds of results the firm seeks to achieve. Corporate objectives/goals refer to results targeted for the entire corporation. Goals can also exist at the business level, the functional-area level like marketing, and lower levels in the organization.

Objectives should be specific, measurable, time phased, and realistic. The realistic characteristic explains why objectives are considered *after* the mission. The mission statement broadly determines what is achievable and desirable, as well as the context. For example, a 30 percent rate of growth in sales may be realistic in a rapidly growing biotechnology company like Amgen. However, such an objective is not realistic in Caterpillar, Inc. for worldwide sales of earth moving equipment or Royal Dutch/Shell for worldwide sales of petroleum products.

Increasing attention is being paid to market share and sales growth objectives as these goals show relative changes in value realized by customers. Many firms are concentrating on providing customer value in the 1990s as a competitive mandate.[19]

One year or less refers to a short-term objective, and five years or more refer to a long-term objective. The time between refers to a medium-term objective. Table 2.2 contains several examples of short and long term objectives.

There are three themes that may be found in objectives. One is growth. In a growth theme, the firm attempts to grow and expand through significantly increased sales. Many firms in the biotechnology and computer software industry

Table 2.2 Examples of objectives

Objective	Measure	Short term (6 months)	Long term (5 years)
Customer satisfaction	Percent satisfied	60	95
Market share	Percent	10	15
Growth	$ sales	8 million	12 million
Profitability	ROA (percent)	12	16
Stockholder value	EPS ($)	1.40	1.90
Employee stability	Turnover (percent)	40	15

Note: ROA is return on assets. EPS is earnings per share. (See the appendix for explanations of key financial ratios.)

Table 2.3 Frequency of use of quality information to evaluate business performance (percentages)

	Less than annually or not at all	Annually	Quarterly	Monthly or more frequently
Canada	14	7	28	54
Germany	9	24	12	55
Japan	2	10	18	70
USA	18	11	16	55

Source: American Quality Foundation and Ernst & Young, *International Quality Study: the Definitive Study of the Best International Quality Management Practices*. Cleveland, OH: Ernst & Young (1991), p. 16. Copyright © 1991. All rights reserved. International Quality Study is a service mark of Ernst & Young LLP.

pursue growth. Another theme is stability. Firms in mature industries that do not expect significant growth, like the aluminum industry, pursue stability. The third theme is restructuring. *Restructuring* is a series of actions aimed at downsizing or cutting back the scope of the firm. Firms in shrinking industries like the steel industry have restructured.

An increasing number of firms have established quality goals, in addition to marketing and financial goals, to evaluate business performance. Table 2.3 shows how frequently companies in Canada, Germany, Japan, and the USA use quality goals to evaluate business performance. These data are consistent with the data in Table 1.6 from the European Commission, showing that in Japan, "Quality is the key element of overall management."[20]

Managers in different countries attach different priorities to various organizational goals. The data in Table 2.4 show the variance on organizational goals for samples of managers from the USA, Japan, Korea, Australia, and India. The differences in the data suggest that managers from different countries are not

Table 2.4 Priority of organizational goals in five countries

Goal	Australia	India	Japan	Korea	USA
High productivity	62	62	<u>79</u>	67	63
Organizational efficiency	64	69	62	<u>49</u>	65
Organizational growth	<u>29</u>	47	<u>72</u>	<u>61</u>	50
Profit maximization	<u>38</u>	<u>36</u>	<u>61</u>	45	58
Organizational stability	41	<u>58</u>	<u>58</u>	55	41
Industry leadership	44	38	<u>50</u>	<u>30</u>	43
Employee welfare	<u>45</u>	<u>44</u>	<u>21</u>	<u>20</u>	34

Note: Goals are underlined for any country when they vary from the average by 10 percent or more. A 10 percent difference is both statistically and practically significant. The numbers refer to the percentage of managers in that country's sample who viewed the goal as highly important.
Source: England, G., *The Manager and His Values: an International Perspective from the United States, Japan, Korea, India, and Australia.* Cambridge, MA: Ballinger (1975), p. 30.

equally committed to the same goals and those managers formulating or implementing a strategic plan need to act accordingly.

Strategies

After the objectives have been decided, the managers can decide how to achieve them. *Strategy* refers to *how* the organization will achieve its objectives and may be observed as a pattern in a stream of decisions. The choice of strategies at the corporate, business, and functional levels is central to the understanding of strategic management, and is examined in chapters 5 to 8.

International cultures and strategic plans

Understanding local issues well enough to implement a strategic plan is a formidable challenge. Failure to understand them in another culture is potentially embarrassing and can produce losses as noted in the following international exhibit.

INTERNATIONAL EXHIBIT

INTERNATIONAL BUSINESS BLUNDERS

1 Timing The Tandy Corporation scheduled its first Christmas promotion of Radio Shack stores in Holland around December 25. After realizing sales below their expectations, Tandy discovered that the Dutch trade gifts on December 6, St Nicholas Day.[a]

2 Language An insurance company doing business in Brazil named its branch there "SAI do Brasil". The locals pronounced it "Saee do Brasil", which when translated meant "Get out of Brasil."[b] McDonald's used the term "Gran Mac" when introducing the Big Mac in France. Only after the promotional literature had been printed did someone point out that "Gran Mac" in French translated into "master pimp."[c]

> Chevrolet's "Nova" was spoken as "no va" in Spanish, which means "it doesn't go."[d] Coca-Cola in Chinese characters became "bite the wax tadpole" or "a wax-flattened mare."[e] Ford's "Fiera" meant "ugly old woman" in Spanish.[f]
>
> 3 Symbols   The hand sign for perfection in the USA, making a circle of the index finger and the thumb while pointing the three other fingers skyward, is a hand sign meaning an obscenity in Australia. It is analogous to holding up the middle finger in the USA.
>
> 4 Color   Black is associated with death in the USA and Europe. In Japan, white is associated with death. In Latin America, purple is associated with death. The choice of color can be exasperating in packaging.[g]
>
> **Sources:** **a.** "Radio Shack's rough trip," Business Week (May 30, 1977), p. 55; **b.** Lowen, I., "Eyes on Europe", Direct Marketing (October, 1990), p. 45; **c.** Ibid.; **d.** Ricks, D., Blunders in International Business. Oxford, UK: Blackwell Publishers (1993), p. 34–6; **e.** Ibid.; **f.** Ibid.; **g.** Ibid., p. 30.

There are numerous examples in which well intended managers from one country were just not aware of local customs or language nuances in another country. For example, the Japanese have learned how to use silence as a weapon in negotiations. "Japanese people understand that in face-to-face negotiating sessions, Americans often become nervous when there is a lull in the conversation, so they will use that as a weapon."[21]

Careful planning and study of the potential international market, including hiring citizens of the host country, are essential. Who can help the international firm to understand customer requirements in the host country better than locals? Errors in language translations and ignorance of local customs can destroy the best positioned international product, just as ignorance of domestic customers can destroy a domestic product. This subject is dealt with in much greater detail in the next chapter.

Consistency and fit

In relating the strategic decisions to the environment, there are at least two important considerations. First is the necessary condition of internal consistency. The strategic decisions on mission, objectives and strategies must be consistent with each other. For example, failure of the strategic plan is nearly guaranteed if the mission proposes to design, develop, produce and market the world's most advanced wireless communications system, yet the R&D budget is being starved due to a corporate cash squeeze.

If internal consistency is a necessary condition for the success of the plan, then external fit of the plan with the environment is a sufficient condition. External fit refers to how well the internal elements of the plan relate to the external environment.[22] How well do the internal strengths and weaknesses of the strategic plan relate the organization to the opportunities and threats in the external environment?

A good example of consistency and fit in a strategic plan is that of the Swatch watch, manufactured and distributed by SMH of Switzerland. The success of the Swatch is all the more remarkable in light of the devastation of the Swiss watch industry by the Japanese watch industry. In 1982, the Swiss watch industry, which had dominated worldwide demand for watches in an earlier era, saw its worldwide market share plunge to 25 percent with many bankruptcies. In a competitive world, with customers demanding high-quality and low-priced watches, the East Asians adapted quality and electronic technology to meet those demands. Meanwhile, many Swiss watch manufacturers stayed with high-priced, less accurate mechanical movements that limited quality. SMH resisted Swiss watch making tradition and designed a quality quartz movement in an all plastic case with multiple colors for a low price. Based on customer demands for low price, SMH has kept the price of the Swatch constant in Swiss francs since 1982, at 50 Swiss francs or US$36 in 1994. Since 1982, SMH has sold many millions of the Swatch, including 28 million in 1993 alone.[23]

Strategic Decision Making Aids

As the strategic decision makers evaluate several alternatives in their decision making process, they use some commonly accepted tools or strategic decision making aids. Although the data for the tools may be gathered by other managers, or strategic planners, or industry associations, the executives use the data in the tools to help formulate strategic decisions.

We review three commonly accepted strategic decision making aids that are sometimes used to decide what business/industry to enter. Sometimes executives use these aids to decide on strategies within a chosen business. In chapter 6, we review Porter's five forces model and competitive group analysis for analysis within a chosen business.

Product/market/industry life cycles

One of the most widely used strategic decision making aids is the life cycle concept. The *life cycle concept* holds that products, markets, and industries develop, grow rapidly, mature, saturate, and decline in a somewhat predictable fashion.[24] If sales are plotted as a function of time, this predictable pattern is a lazy-S shaped curve as in figure 2.2.

In the introduction phase, the product/service is initially offered to customers, and sales are slowly built up as more customers become aware of the product/service. After demand has been established, sales take off at an exponential growth rate as increasingly large numbers of new customers demand the product for the first time. Such sales attract entrant firms into the industry. This results in competitive turbulence and shakeout of the weaker competitors. As initial demand is satisfied and sales become replacement sales, the industry reaches maturity. At this stage, further sales gains for one firm come at the expense of other firms rather than from first time customers. As technology makes the product/service obsolete, or as substitute products arrive, sales decline. Some firms leave the industry, and the remaining firms "milk" the product/service for profits with little new investment.

There are problems with using the life cycle concept as a precise, predictive decision making tool. *A priori*, it is impossible to predict how long a certain phase

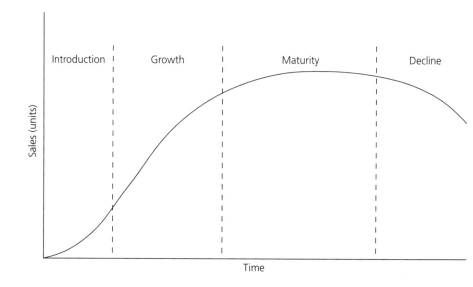

Figure 2.2 Product/market/industry life cycle.

will last. It is also impossible to know *a priori* how many units will be sold. Thus, the concept's use as a forecasting tool is very limited.

However, if a firm can determine what stage it is in at the time, it can pursue certain strategic actions to lengthen the phase (like product modification), or increase its profitability (like process improvement). Helping executives to decide what strategic and competitive moves are appropriate in a given phase may be the most important advantage of the life cycle concept. One may grow, invest, and market aggressively in the early stages. But it appears that harvesting profits and decreasing financial commitments are more appropriate in the later stages.

Most large companies are somewhat diversified. Typically, they have products/ services at different stages of the life cycle. An implication of the life cycle concept for a diversified firm is that a firm should have new products/services at various early stages to provide for the future growth of the firm as older products/services mature and decline.

Business/product portfolio matrices

Recognizing that some firms have products of varying strength, the Boston Consulting Group is credited with developing a matrix that portrays the strength of various products or businesses.[25] The tool has been used in corporate strategic decisions, as one of the original purposes was to help executives decide which businesses to grow and which to exit.[26] The matrix is sometimes used at the business level to help executives decide if they need different products within the given business.

The *BCG matrix* is a business/product portfolio matrix with two dimensions of relative market share and market (or industry) growth rate. The matrix is sometimes referred to as the "market share growth matrix". The matrix has only four

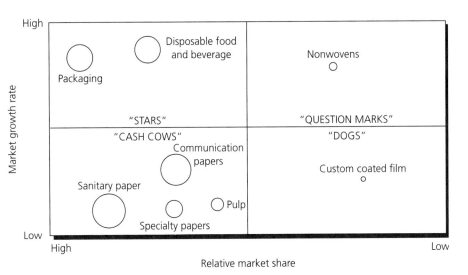

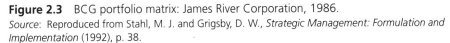

Figure 2.3 BCG portfolio matrix: James River Corporation, 1986.
Source: Reproduced from Stahl, M. J. and Grigsby, D. W., *Strategic Management: Formulation and Implementation* (1992), p. 38.

cells arising from high and low levels of the two variables representing the two dimensions. The horizontal dimension is relative market share, the ratio of the firm's market share to the market share of the largest rival firm. The vertical dimension is market (or industry) growth rate, preferably in constant dollars. Each product is represented by a circle whose area is in accord with the relative importance of that product to the firm as a fraction of the firm's total sales. Figure 2.3 contains an example of a BCG matrix.

The cells and the conditions behind them have obvious strategic implications. The "cash cows" can be used to generate cash flow to grow other products. The "stars" are well positioned, with relatively high market share, and are in markets with high growth rates. "Question marks" need careful scrutiny to see if they should be divested or aggressively invested in for growth. Typically, "dogs" are divested or liquidated. As a lesson in continuous improvement for the future, firms try to determine how a product became a "dog".

An example of a "cash cow" was the Lotus *1–2–3* spreadsheet of the Lotus Development Corporation in the late 1980s. That product generated the majority of Lotus's revenue at that time. Recognizing the huge and growing cash flow from spreadsheets, other competitors were stepping up their development of spreadsheets. Lotus was having trouble introducing new products. It is difficult to grow when a firm has one very strong "cash cow" and no other apparent developing "star" products.[27]

There are more complicated portfolio matrices, like the GE business screen.[28] It has different dimensions dealing with industry attractiveness and competitive position, and complicated weights and rankings to derive the two-dimensional scores in nine cells. The GE business screen is not often used partly because its complicated ordinal rankings and weights can be manipulated to show almost any desired answer. However, the BCG matrix is enjoying renewed popularity partly because its two objective dimensions are consistent with an external customer focus.

Learning/experience curves

Another powerful strategic decision making tool is the learning or experience curve. The curve is often used to justify aggressive pricing decisions of new products and to discourage potential new entrant firms from entering into the business.[29]

The *learning curve* shows the constant percentage decline in the deflated marginal cost of production each time the cumulative volume of production doubles. Simply put, "practice makes perfect." Increased labor and material productivity, as well as process improvement, are associated with learning curve effects. Marginal costs, not fixed costs, decline at a fixed rate. Deflated costs are used so that the effects of inflation in multi-year production runs do not mask the learning.

The learning curve slope refers to the percentage of learning. This is the percentage level to which marginal costs fall each time cumulative output *doubles*. An 80 percent learning curve means that marginal costs fall to 80 percent of their previous level each time cumulative output doubles.

Figure 2.4 is a graph of an 80 percent learning curve. Progressively higher and higher cumulative output levels are required to realize the same percentage marginal cost reduction because the volume must double.

Typical learning curve slopes are 80 and 90 percent. Table 2.5 shows the costs for cumulative volume and the two learning percentages. The table contains at least two messages. First, the marginal cost declines dramatically with higher cumulative volume. Second, there is a substantial difference in marginal cost as a function of the percentage of learning, especially at higher cumulative volumes. Different slopes are realized in different firms due to the willingness to incorporate continuous improvement and process improvement as ways of life.

Two potential pitfalls are apparent. Overestimating the volume can lead to dramatic cost underestimates. Similarly, overestimating the amount of learning can also lead to dramatic cost underestimates.

Pricing decisions, profit projections, volume plans, and capital expenditure plans associated with new products or businesses and competitor signaling are primary uses of learning curves.[30] There are at least two different pricing strategies based on the learning curve. A firm can follow a short-run pricing strategy in which the firm reaps large profits early by keeping its prices high while its marginal cost of production declines (see period A in the left part of figure 2.5). If held too long, this strategy encourages competitors to enter the market, which may result in steep price declines or shakeout (see period B). As a result of the competition, profit margins remain thin in period C.

Alternatively, the firm may follow a barrier pricing strategy in which it aggressively lowers prices as its costs decline. Such lowered prices act as a deterrent to new market entrants and keep the firm's market share high. The firm's profit margins

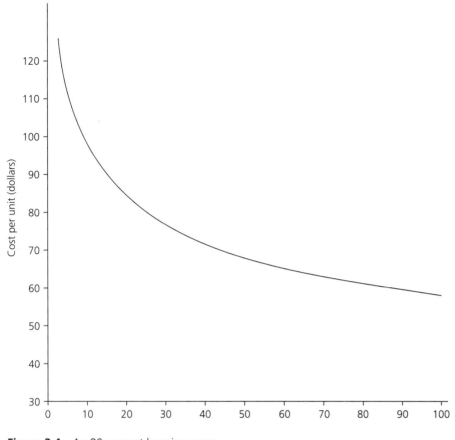

Figure 2.4 An 80 percent learning curve.

Table 2.5 Marginal costs for two different learning curves

Cumulative no. of units	90 percent L-C ($)	80 percent L-C ($)
1	10.00	10.00
2	9.00	8.00
4	8.10	6.40
8	7.29	5.12
1,000	3.50	1.08
10,000	2.47	0.52
1,000,000	1.22	0.12

Note: The marginal costs are for a specific unit with all units having a first-unit deflated cost of $10.00.
Source of data: Yelle, L., "Industrial life cycles and learning curves", *Industrial Marketing Management*, 9 (1980), p. 314.

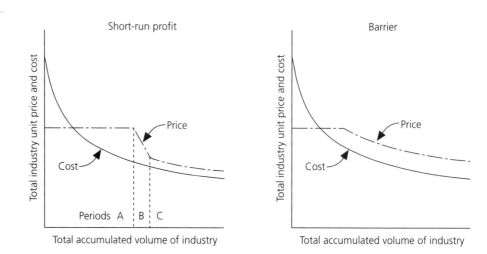

Figure 2.5 Two pricing strategies and learning.
Source: Reproduced from Stahl, M. J. and Grigsby, D. W., *Strategic Management: Formulation and Implementation* (1992), p. 45.

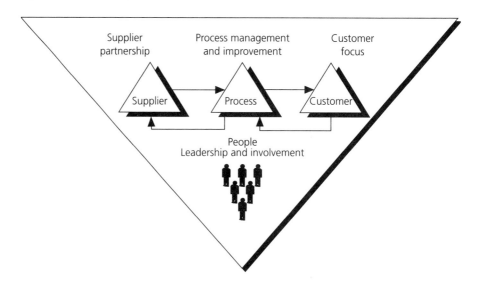

Figure 2.6 AT&T's total quality approach.
Source: AT&T, New York (1992).

may be modest, but long-term profits and market share tend to be stable (see the right half of figure 2.5). Whichever pricing strategy is followed, there are strong reasons for the firm to enter the market early and build cumulative volume, so that its costs decline. It can then offer more sustainable value to customers. One way that the Swiss watch maker SMH has kept the price of the Swatch watch constant since its 1982 introduction is by realizing learning effects with cumulative production of tens of millions of watches.[31]

▌ Summary ▌

All organizations interact with and are affected by the external environment in which they function. An analysis of internal environmental issues (strengths and weaknesses) and the external environment (opportunities and threats) is preparatory to deciding on the strategic plan, Such a SWOT analysis is an integral part of strategy formulation.

There are external opportunities to be capitalized on and external threats to be avoided. These external environmental issues include customer value, social, demographic, economic, technological, regulatory, physical, and competitive trends.

Similarly, there are internal environmental issues that must be considered in formulating a strategic plan. These issues include horizontal processes, organizational structure, corporate culture, management, financial position, operations, marketing, human resources, research and development, and information systems. The internal strengths must be capitalized on, and the internal weaknesses overcome when formulating and implementing the strategic plan.

The corporate strategic plan contains at least three elements: the mission (why), objectives (what), and strategy (how). The main element is the mission statement. It describes the business(es) the firm is in. Objectives are the specific kinds of results the organization hopes to achieve. Objectives should be specific, measurable, time phased, and achievable. Strategies refer to the how of the plan.

To be successful, the strategic decisions must meet the two important considerations of consistency and fit. The strategic decisions on mission, objectives, and strategies must be consistent with each other. If internal consistency is a necessary condition for the success of the plan, then fit of the plan with the external environment is a sufficient condition.

This chapter reviews three commonly used strategic decision making tools. The product/market/industry life cycle concept indicates that products, markets, and industries develop, rapidly grow, mature, saturate, and decline in a somewhat predictable fashion. The position of the firm's products/services on this lazy-S shaped curve has implications for the formulation of the strategic plan.

The BCG matrix is one of the simplest of the business and product portfolio matrix approaches to strategic planning. The BCG matrix is a four-cell matrix with high – low scores on the two dimensions of relative market share and market growth rate. These two customer-relevant dimensions are associated with renewed interest in this matrix.

The learning/experience curve is used to justify aggressive pricing decisions of new products, and to discourage potential new entrants from entering into the business. These curves are based on the constant dollar decline in the marginal cost of production each time cumulative output doubles.

DISCUSSION QUESTIONS

1 As the pace of change quickens at the dawn of the twenty-first century due to international competition and technology, discuss the importance of a frequent SWOT analysis.

2 How do mission, objectives, and strategies relate to each other in a strategic plan?

3 Is the deliberate formulation of mission, objectives, and strategies more or less important in a rapidly changing internationally competitive marketplace with demanding customers than in a stable non-competitive environment? Explain.

4 How can the product/market/industry life cycle concept be used as a forecasting tool?

5 How is the BCG matrix related to customer focus?

6 How are learning curves used in market entry and pricing decisions?

KEY TERMS

The BCG matrix	is a business/product portfolio matrix with two dimensions of relative market share and market (or industry) growth rate.
Environmental scanning	is analyzing the external environment.
Grow-and-invest situations	are those in which firms can capitalize on external opportunities with internal strengths.
Horizontal processes	are flows of work and activities that span vertical functions like purchasing, design, production, and marketing.
The learning curve	shows the constant percentage decline in the deflated marginal cost of production each time the cumulative volume of production doubles.
The life cycle concept	holds that products, markets, and industries develop, grow rapidly, mature, saturate, and decline in a somewhat predictable fashion.
A mission statement	describes what business(es) the firm is in.
Objectives or goals	refer to the kinds of results the firm seeks to achieve.
An opportunity	is an issue or condition in the environment external to the firm that may help it reach its goals.
Restructuring	is a series of actions aimed at downsizing or cutting back the scope of the firm.
Shrinkage or withdrawal situations	are those in which firms have significant internal weaknesses or external threats that they cannot overcome.
Strategy	refers to how the organization will achieve its goals.
The strategic plan	includes a mission, objectives, and strategies.
A strength	is a condition or issue internal to the organization that may lead to a customer benefit or a competitive advantage.
A SWOT analysis	is an analysis of internal strengths and weaknesses and external opportunities and threats.
A threat	is an issue or condition in the external environment that may prevent the firm from reaching its goals.
A weakness	is a condition or issue internal to the organization that may lead to negative customer value or a competitive disadvantage.

AT&T Awakens to Compete Globally through Quality

American Telephone and Telegraph (AT&T) had been a very large, inwardly focused, tradition bound, slow to respond symbol of corporate America prior to divestiture and deregulation in the 1980s. As a secure, lifetime employer of hundreds of thousands of managers and employees in the USA, AT&T had the somewhat affectionate title of "Ma Bell." For most of this century, managers joined the firm and expected to work for "The Phone Company" until they retired. Additionally, AT&T had the protection of the US government, which treated AT&T as a monopoly in communications.

As a large, stable firm in a non-competitive market with fat profits, the firm received the approval of corporate America. Many financial advisers referred to AT&T as a "widow and orphans stock," since AT&T stock could be counted on to produce healthy dividends, while maintaining price stability. AT&T was one of the ten most admired corporations in America in 1983.[a]

Much of that stability changed on January 1, 1984. The federal government ordered AT&T to divest itself of its local operating companies effective on that date. AT&T was allowed to retain 23 percent of the former firm's assets, including its long-distance lines, Bell Laboratories, and Western Electric, the manufacturer of telecommunications equipment.[b] The divestiture also removed the monopoly from the long-distance market. Other long distance carriers were allowed to form and compete with AT&T for long-distance services. Within a short period of time, MCI and Sprint were formed to compete with AT&T in the long distance market. AT&T's long-distance market share shrank from over 90 percent in 1984 to 62 percent in 1992, and the company shed 140,000 employees in less than ten years.[c]

For the first time in its corporate existence, AT&T managers were forced to compete in a deregulated marketplace. How would they compete in such a strange competitive marketplace without the monopolistic protection of the government?

For a few years, the new, deregulated AT&T floundered. It is hard to compete in a deregulated internationally competitive market when the corporate history was written around a monopoly. Between 1984 and 1988, AT&T lost dramatic market share and many employees.

In 1988, Bob Allen became Chief Executive Officer with a vision of telecommunications "anytime, anywhere." He hired a number of outside executives to help breathe new life into the hidebound, internally focused culture at AT&T. The two new watchwords became global and quality.

In the telecommunications industry, consumer electronics, cable TV, computing, communications including wireless cellular communications, and multimedia were all converging. To help make AT&T the master of the convergence of those industries, Allen engineered a number of acquisitions to position AT&T in areas where it had no historical strength and to help change its corporate culture. In 1991, AT&T acquired National Cash Register (NCR) for US$7.5 billion to rescue AT&T's fledgling computer business. In 1993, AT&T acquired the number one cellular phone company, McGaw Cellular, for US$12.6 billion. These acquisitions and several lesser ones not only built strengths in areas where AT&T needed them, but also helped turn the old AT&T's inward focus outward to the customer. The CEO of McGaw Cellular, Craig O. McGaw, remarked: "We've been invited to cause a little trouble within AT&T."[d]

A number of the acquisitions helped to improve AT&T's global reach. Allen was asked about his goal of 50 percent of the business being global. "Fifty-fifty is not magic. What is magic is that we be a global company. The growth opportunities in our industry are much higher outside the USA than they are here. More and more of our business customers are global. Many of our customers travel abroad as business people and want AT&T connections and service. Our competitors are global."[e]

Examples of AT&T's global presence are found in Europe, as it has established a presence in all the major European countries. AT&T is represented in Europe by AT&T Network Systems International, headquartered in the Netherlands. At the firm's first European Forum on Quality Leadership, two examples of its customer focus in a competitive world were presented. In Poland, AT&T Network Systems International won a contract to design and install an entire network of up to 100,000 lines. In Germany, the firm won a contract to design and install a fiber optic, broad band communication system into Eastern German homes, which will leapfrog existing technology.[f]

To deliver more value to its customers and to turn the focus of AT&T managers outward to the customer, AT&T pursued total quality with a vengeance. As of 1995, it was the only company to have won three Baldrige National Quality Awards for three different parts of the company. AT&T described its total quality approach with the following (see also figure 2.6). "For more than a century, AT&T has stood for quality. Much has changed for AT&T – and the world – since our company was founded in 1885. But our commitment to quality has not. Our fundamental principles continue to guide us:

- The customer comes first.
- Quality happens through people.
- All work is part of a process.
- Suppliers are an integral part of our business.
- Prevention is achieved through planning.
- Quality improvement never ends."[g]

In the mid-1990s, AT&T was on a roll. Its stock had quadrupled since the divestiture of 1984. In 1995, the value of its stock made it one of the largest companies in the world. With revenues of about US$80 billion in 1995, and a goal to more than double revenues in about ten years, AT&T was clearly positioned for growth.[h] In September 1995, AT&T announced that it would divest its manufacturing and computer operations to further focus on its core area of telecommunications in a global market.

In less than the ten years since the government mandated divestiture that removed the protection of monopoly, AT&T had come a long way. With acquisitions, divestitures and outside executives changing its old, internally focused culture, a major TQ effort to focus on the customer, and a globalization program, AT&T managers were a new breed. They had awakened from an environment of a government protected monopoly to compete globally through quality.

Discussion Questions

1 How important was the globalization program at AT&T to changing its management and culture?

2 Why was the TQ effort and its focus on the customer important to achieving change at AT&T?

3 In what way did bringing in several key outside executives contribute to the transformation at AT&T?

Sources: a. "Ranking corporate reputations," *Fortune* (January 10, 1983), p. 35; b. "AT&T," *Value Line Investment Survey* (July 16, 1993), p. 749; c. "Could AT&T rule the world?" *Fortune* (May 17, 1993), p. 62; d. "AT&T's bold bet," *Business Week* (August 30, 1993), p. 29; e. "Could AT&T rule the world?" p. 57; f. "The global connection," *European Quality*, 1 (1) (1994), pp. 44–9. g. "AT&T's total quality approach", AT&T, New York (1992), p. 2; h. "Could AT&T rule the world?" p. 55, "AT&T," *Value Line Investment Survey* (April 14, 1995), p. 745.

ROLLING OUT THE ROLLS-ROYCE

Since 1906, Rolls-Royce has built its name into one of the most famous, recognizable brand names on earth. Rolls-Royce Motor Cars Ltd manufactures what many people believe are the finest, most luxurious automobiles available. The flying lady hood ornament and the double R logo are symbols of the highest degree of luxury and quality.

Growing at a 12 to 14 percent annual rate in the 1980s, Rolls-Royce was the jewel in the crown of its parent company, Vickers PLC. As the biggest and most profitable division, Rolls-Royce's progress appeared set on cruise control as it passed corporate milestones with ease. In 1990, it broke divisional records by selling a total of 3333 Rolls-Royce and Bentley cars worldwide. Turnover was more than £278 million (US$536.5 million), and annual profits reached a high of £24.4 million (US$47.1 million).[a] The company was enjoying such good times that the Rolls-Royce management did not pay much attention to strategic planning. In addition, it was widely believed that luxury items were relatively recession proof.[b]

In just the first few months of 1991, the economy proved that luxury goods were not immune to recession. Sales dropped by 48 percent as the North American market for luxury autos collapsed under the weight of new luxury taxes and the world's deepest recession since the Second World War. Layoffs began immediately, but the depths of the widening abyss only became clear as the year progressed. The company eliminated almost 700 jobs at the main factory in Crewe, England. The Mulliner plant in London was closed, resulting in the loss of 500 additional jobs. By the end of the year, Rolls-Royce had lost 46 percent of its work force, falling from 5900 to 3200 employees.[c]

As drastic as the workforce reduction was, it still did not keep pace with the simultaneous slowing of sales. In 1991, Rolls-Royce only sold 1723 new cars, about half of the previous year's volume. This dramatic reversal of fortunes resulted in losses of £60 million (US$112 million).

The same cars that received such favorable press just a year earlier were now criticized for archaic manufacturing processes. What management had thought was impossible had become a brutal reality – Rolls-Royce cars were being unfavorably compared to the technologically more advanced Japanese autos. *The Financial Times* wrote, "Manufacturers need more than the smell of leather and the glint of burled walnut to retain a reputation for luxury. They need to master modern manufacturing technologies as well."[e] Attempts to sell the auto maker proved fruitless. The most likely purchasers, BMW and Toyota, were not interested in the floundering company.[f]

In response to the crisis, Michael J. Donovan was named managing director of Rolls-Royce. Mr Donovan had previously been responsible for strategic changes at Land Rover. Under his guidance, management began to completely redesign the company. It adopted a combination of Japanese production techniques, modern technology, traditional crafted automobile concepts, and teamwork from marketing to manufacturing. Mr Donovan said, "I'm not talking about multifunctional teams to implement a new product. Lots of people do that. I'm talking about going all the way back to the pre-concept stage before you even have a notion of the conceptual idea. You research the marketplace needs, not just with marketing specialists, but with marketing, sales, manufacturing, purchasing, and financial people."[g]

Donovan and management implemented a transformational strategy that included the following three key components:

1   To maximize profitability by increasing productivity and reducing the sales break-even point from 2700 units in 1990 to 1300 units and matching production to the level of demand.

2 To anticipate and exceed customer expectations in terms of quality, craftsmanship, reliability, safety, and comfort.

3 To concentrate exclusively on the core activity of designing, developing, and building the best cars in the world.

Rolls-Royce used a conceptualization of the ideal manufacturing site that produced cars to the highest international standards as a mental model and guide. It then applied this measuring rod to every aspect of the company and made drastic changes from management to the shop floor.[h]

In order to attain these goals, Rolls-Royce further reduced its workforce to 2400 employees, delayered the management hierarchy, changed the manufacturing environment, reduced inventory from approximately 140 days to 65 days, and implemented information technology to get real-time input from customers around the globe.[i]

The factory was divided into 16 zones that act like small business units in a customer–supplier relationship with other zones. Each zone is fully responsible for the cost, quality, and the delivery of product to the next zone, and has instant access to productivity and cost data. All workers can continuously monitor performance against key indicators of improvement.[j]

Rolls-Royce also began to use outside sources for services and supplies that were not considered essential to the Rolls-Royce name or image. For example, computer services are now supplied by an independent vendor, and exhaust systems are manufactured by a copper manufacturer with excess capacity. At the end of 1994, Rolls-Royce announced a partnership with BMW in which the German manufacturer would supply engines for Rolls-Royce's newest model line.[k] However, the burled walnut and leather seating, elements considered essential to the image of Rolls-Royce, are kept under direct management control.

Although Rolls-Royce knew that it would have to survive as a smaller company, it was determined to exit the recession as a greatly improved company. At the risk of throwing good money after bad, Rolls-Royce and its parent company increased investment in R&D. Based on customer research, the company believed that its customer base was still intact, and that 80 percent of them intended to eventually replace their Rolls-Royce with a new one. Despite their optimism, it was an extremely difficult investment in light of the large reductions in other areas, but the R&D investment was essential.[l]

In only two years, the pain of restructure and risky investment began to make a difference. Vickers PLC losses in 1991 and 1992 turned into pre-tax profits of £32.2 million (US$47.3 million) in 1993 and £44.8 million (US$69.8 million) in 1994. This trend continued into 1995, when pre-tax profits reached £68 million (US$107 million). This turnaround in profitability was fueled by the improvements made at Rolls-Royce.[m]

The changes at Rolls-Royce have created a more responsive, customer-driven organization. Finding outside sources for many of its non-core functions has allowed Rolls-Royce to concentrate heavily on product design. Rolls-Royce has introduced four new models since 1992 and made extensive changes across all its models to better meet the needs of its market. In addition, increased flexibility has enabled Rolls-Royce to increase revenues in the production of limited edition models and one-of-a-kind variations, which increase the scarcity value and exclusivity of the latest models. In particular, the use of BMW engines in the new model range will free up funds, enabling Rolls-Royce to enhance exterior and interior features for which the Rolls-Royce and Bentley cars are renowned.[n]

The market outlook for luxury cars is good, despite uncertainty about future market conditions. This, together with the new strategic focus of Rolls-Royce management, means that the road ahead looks more promising. Even if the market does not grow, Rolls-Royce is now able to make a profit on a much lower sales volume than ever before.

Discussion Questions

1 How important was is it in 1991 for top management to realize that half of the market for Rolls-Royce and Bentley cars had evaporated for the foreseeable future?

2 Describe the significance of focusing on marketplace needs during the restructure of Rolls-Royce.

3 Why did Rolls-Royce concentrate more on the interior and exterior design of its automobiles than the engine or exhaust systems?

Sources: **a.** "Rough ride at Rolls-Royce," *Management Today* (UK), (February, 1993), p. 38; **b.** "Rolls-Royce, in for service," *The Economist* (July 10, 1993), p. 63; **c.** "Rough ride at Rolls-Royce," p. 38; **d.** Ibid.; **e.** "Perilous niches," *The Financial Times* (February 26, 1992), p. 16; **f.** "Rough ride at Rolls-Royce," p. 39; **g.** "The rescue of the gilded lady," *Industry Week* (January 17, 1994), p. 15; **h.** Ibid., p. 16; **i.** Ibid.; **j.** "Rough ride at Rolls-Royce," p. 40; **k.** "Rolls-Royce fuels profits at Vickers", *International Herald Tribune* (September 8, 1995), p. 13; **l.** "The rescue of the gilded lady," p. 17; **m.** "Vickers PLC," *Compact Disclosure Database* (1995); **n.** "Vickers – Company Report", Charles Stanley & Co. Ltd, *InvesText Database* (March 22, 1995).

NOTES

1 Wren, D., *The Evolution of Management Thought*, 4th edn. New York: Wiley (1994).

2 Ireland, R. D. et al., "Strategy formulation process," *Strategic Management Journal*, 8 (1987), pp. 469–86.

3 Mintzberg, H., "The design school: reconsidering the basic premises of strategic management," *Strategic Management Journal*, 11 (March–April 1990), pp. 171–96.

4 Schonberger, R. J., "Is strategy strategic? Impact of total quality management on strategy," *Academy of Management Executive*, 6 (3) (August 1992), pp. 80–7.

5 "TWA may go to creditors, employees: rescue plan needs union, investor approval," *USA Today* (August 4, 1992), p. B1.

6 "GM posts record loss of $4.45 billion, sends tough message to UAW on closings", *Wall Street Journal* (February 25, 1992), p. A3.

7 Judge, W., Stahl, M., Scott, R. and Millender, R., "Long-term quality improvement and cost reduction at Capsugel," in Stahl, M. J. and Bounds, G. M. (eds), *Competing Globally Through Customer Value*. Bridgeport, CT: Quorum Books (1991), pp. 703–9.

8 Harris, C., "Information power," *Business Week* (October 14, 1985), pp. 53–5.

9 Wilson, C., Kennedy, M. and Trammell, C., *Superior Product Development*. Oxford, UK: Blackwell (1996).

10 "America's most admired corporations," *Fortune* (February 8, 1993), pp. 40–72.

11 Hambrick, D. C., "Environmental scanning and organizational strategy," *Strategic Management Journal*, 3 (1982), pp. 159–74.

12 Daft, R. L., Sormunen, J. and Parks, D., "Chief executive scanning, environmental characteristics, and company performance," *Strategic Management Journal*, 9 (March–April 1988), pp. 123–39.

13 "'No-dicker sticker' car deals ignite: buyers tired of getting beaten up", *USA Today* (August 4, 1992), p. A1.

14 Armstrong, J. S., "The value of formal planning for strategic decisions," *Strategic Management Journal* (1982), p. 197–211.

15 "Ad from Philip Morris Europe SA," *The European* (July 13, 1995), p. 7.

16 Cochran, D. S., David, F. R. and Gibson, C. K., "A framework for developing an effective mission statement," *Journal of Business Strategies*, 2 (1985), pp. 4–17.

17 Carothers, H., Bounds, G. and Stahl, M., "Managerial-leadership," in *Competing Globally Through Customer Value*, chapter 3.

18 Eli Lilly and Company: Report to Shareholders, 1991, p. 1.

19 "King customer," *Business Week* (March 12, 1990), pp. 88–94; Kearns, D. A., "Leadership through quality," *Academy of Management Executive* (May 1990), pp. 86–9.

20 "The European way towards excellence," European Commission, Brussels, Belgium (1995), p. 21.

21 "Avoiding business faux pas abroad," *International Herald Tribune* (September 21, 1995), p. 13.

22 Mintzberg, H., "The design school," pp. 171–96.

NOTES CONT.

23 "The secrets of Swatch," *European Quality*, 1 (4) (1994), pp. 18–24.

24 Levitt, T., "Exploit the product life cycle," *Harvard Business Review* (November–December 1965), pp. 81–94; Thorelli, H. B. and Burnett, S. C., "The nature of product life cycles for industrial goods businesses," *Journal of Marketing*, 45 (4) (1981), pp. 97–108.

25 Hedley, B., "Strategy and the business portfolio," *Long Range Planning* (February 1977), pp. 2–12.

26 MacMillan, I. C., Hambrick, D. C. and Day, D. L., "Strategic attributes and performance in the BCG matrix," *Academy of Management Journal*, 25 (December 1982), pp. 510–31.

27 "After years of glory, Lotus is stumbling in software market," *Wall Street Journal* (August 30, 1988), p. 1.

28 Hall, W. K., "SBU's: hot new topic in the management of diversification," *Business Horizons* (February 1978), p. 20; Hofer, C. W. and Schendel, D., *Strategy Formulation: Analytical Concepts*. St Paul: West Publishing Co. (1978), pp. 31–2.

29 Leiberman, M. B., "The learning curve, diffusion, and competitive strategy," *Strategic Management Journal*, 8 (5) (September–October 1987), pp. 441–52.

30 Clarke, R. H., Darrough, M. W. and Heineke, J. M., "Optional pricing policy in the presence of experience effects," *Journal of Business*, 55 (1982), pp. 517–30.

31 "The secrets of Swatch", pp. 18–24.

Appendix: Case Analysis Guide

Introduction

If your strategic management course is like most, the instructor will make extensive use of case analysis. You will study business strategy cases, which are accounts of actual business situations, and be placed in the role of a top-level decision maker. By introducing a variety of situations, the case method provides a wide range of opportunities for you to apply the skills learned in this course and other business courses and to begin building confidence in your decision-making ability.

Although case study may be a new experience for you and therefore confusing at first, you will quickly see that it can increase your understanding of the complex world of strategic decision making and sharpen your analytical skills. Case study will also enhance your knowledge of the strategic conditions in different industries. Although there is no substitute for real-world management experience, case study is "the next best thing to being there."

The cases you will be assigned to analyze will represent a broad range of strategic decisions, usually taken from real life. They may include: large and small businesses; for-profit and not-for-profit organizations; and companies engaged in manufacturing, service industries, and distribution activities. The cases will often feature successful organizations, but you may also encounter organizations that are struggling. Occasionally, the company and the names of managers will have been disguised, but many cases feature organizations that you will readily recognize.

This case study guide is offered to familiarize you with the expectations of you as a student. It will help to guide you through your first case and will show you how to prepare the analyses that will be required.

Reading and studying the case

Because you are expected not only to read cases as they are assigned, but to analyze them and develop sound, reasoned judgments that will lead to recommendations, the case method requires a level of preparation that often goes well beyond that required in a traditional lecture course. It is important, therefore, that you devote considerable time to studying and analyzing each case.

To get the most out of a case, read it at least two times and, if possible, separate the two readings in time. On the first reading, go through the case rather quickly, without trying to take notes or underline. Read it as you would a magazine article or short story. Get a general idea of the situation the company is in – its industry, its position within the industry, and its competition. Note the date of the latest case information. Treat the tables and financial statements merely as illustrations rather than trying to analyze them at this time. Before your second reading, stop and think about the case. Ask yourself, "What are the central issues?" and "What do I need to try and uncover in my analysis?" All business strategy cases revolve around one or, at most, two or three major problems or decision points. The earlier you can identify these the better, as they will guide your analysis. During your second reading of the case, take notes on the case facts that are important for analysis.

There will undoubtedly be instances when you feel that you do not have all the information you need to make the best decision. The information provided in case reports is often incomplete by design. Just as real-world managers are often called on to make decisions without extensive information, this aspect of the case method is not unlike real experience. One of the most important steps towards becoming an effective strategic decision maker is knowing how to make the most of the limited amounts of information the environment provides.

The time frame for decisions is an important element in any case. That is, you should make decisions based only on information that was available to the managers at the time of the case date, although it may seem a bit artificial at times. You may even be required to ignore some information you may have about the company or its situation. For instance, if you are analyzing a 1986 case, your knowledge of the stock market crash of October 1987 should not affect your handling of the case. Although you are encouraged to do outside research, you should resist the temptation to second-guess the decision makers on the basis of information they could not have had.

Your professor may assign you or other class members the responsibility of updating the case by researching recent information on the company. Later information about the strategies that were actually adopted and their subsequent outcomes often proves to be an interesting way to complete the study of the case. A company's actual strategy should not be taken as the "right" answer, however, even if it proved to be a very profitable one for the company, as any number of other recommended strategies might also have been successful.

Doing the analysis

Organizing the case facts
Cases sometimes present a bewildering number of names, titles, dates, and other facts that are hard to keep straight. Before proceeding with an in-depth analysis of the case, make sure you have a sufficient grasp of the facts. Sometimes it may be necessary to construct a chronology to help you keep in mind the sequence of significant case events and their relationships. To keep names, organizational titles, and relationships in focus, you may need to sketch a rough organization chart if one is not provided in the case. Once you have an adequate grasp of the case facts and the central issues, you are ready to begin an in-depth analysis.

Start with financial analysis
"Number crunching" is nearly always the best way to begin a case analysis, as it gives you an objective assessment of the company's performance and can help to identify problem areas for further analysis. Key financial ratios must be calculated so that you can get a reading on the company's financial performance and

condition. Exhibit 2.1 provides a review of the most often used financial ratios (in case your ratio analysis skills are a bit rusty). Keep in mind that ratios should be interpreted only in light of the organization's situation, and remember that trends are always important. For that reason, two or more years of financial statements are usually included in the cases so that any trends in the ratios can be discerned. Industry averages with which to compare the key ratios are also helpful; if not contained in the case, these averages are available from a number of reporting services.

Converting the financial statements to "common-size" ones is also helpful. The balance sheet is common-sized by setting total assets equal to 100 percent and then calculating each balance sheet account as a percentage of total assets. Income statements are common-sized by setting net sales equal to 100 percent and then calculating each item as a percentage of net sales. With common-size statements, relative relationships among the various accounts can readily be seen and trends noted over time. These relationships and trends can indicate other problems to be investigated. Common-size statement information is best used in combination with other information. For example, a steadily increasing cost of goods sold as a percentage of net sales may indicate waste, loss of efficiencies in production, increased raw materials prices that have not been passed on to buyers, or some combination of these factors.

Financial analysis can be one of the most time-consuming parts of your preparation. You can save yourself a lot of time if you do only those analyses that you need rather than using the same standard analyses for every case. Thus, you need to use your head at least as much as your calculator or computer spread sheet. The focus should be on developing information to help you understand the company and to provide the basis for recommendations to solve its problems.

Exhibit A2.1   Key Financial Ratios

Ratio	Formula	Expressed as
Profitability ratios		
Return on investment	$\dfrac{\text{Net income after taxes}}{\text{Total assets}}$	percentage
Return on stockholders equity	$\dfrac{\text{Net income after taxes}}{\text{Total stockholder's equity}}$	percentage
Earnings per share	$\dfrac{\text{NIAT-preferred dividends}}{\text{No. common shares outstanding}}$	dollars
Gross profit margin	$\dfrac{\text{Sales} - \text{CGS}}{\text{Sales}}$	percentage
Operating profit margin	$\dfrac{\text{Net income before taxes and interest}}{\text{Sales}}$	percentage
Net profit margin	$\dfrac{\text{Net income after taxes}}{\text{Sales}}$	percentage

Exhibit A2.1 Cont.

Ratio	Formula	Expressed as
Liquidity ratios		
Current ratio	$\dfrac{\text{Current assets}}{\text{Current liabilities}}$	decimal
Quick (acid-test) ratio	$\dfrac{\text{Current asset-inventories}}{\text{Current liabilities}}$	decimal
Inventories to net working capital	$\dfrac{\text{Inventories}}{\text{Current assets} - \text{current liabilities}}$	decimal
Leverage ratios		
Debt to assets	$\dfrac{\text{Total debt}}{\text{Total assets}}$	percentage
Debt to equity	$\dfrac{\text{Total debt}}{\text{Total stockholders equity}}$	percentage
Long-term debt to equity	$\dfrac{\text{Long-term debt}}{\text{Total stockholders equity}}$	percentage
Times-interest earned	$\dfrac{\text{NI before taxes and interest}}{\text{Interest expenses}}$	decimal
Fixed-charge coverage	$\dfrac{\text{NI before taxes and interest} + \text{lease obligations}}{\text{Interest expenses} + \text{lease expenses}}$	decimal
Activity ratios		
Total asset turnover	$\dfrac{\text{Sales}}{\text{Total assets}}$	decimal
Fixed asset turnover	$\dfrac{\text{Sales}}{\text{Fixed assets}}$	decimal
Net working capital turnover	$\dfrac{\text{Sales}}{\text{Current assets} - \text{current liabilities}}$	decimal
Inventory turnover	$\dfrac{\text{Sales}}{\text{Average inventory of finished goods}}$	decimal
Collection period for receivables	$\dfrac{\text{Average accounts receivable}}{\text{Annual credit sales/365}}$	days
Investment ratios		
Price-earnings ratio	$\dfrac{\text{Market price per share}}{\text{EPS}}$	decimal
Dividend payout	$\dfrac{\text{Annual dividends per share}}{\text{EPS}}$	percentage
Common stock dividend yield	$\dfrac{\text{Annual dividends per share}}{\text{Market price per share}}$	percentage

Focus your analysis

Effective case analysis must include both an internal analysis of the firm and an external analysis of the firm's operating environment. Internal analysis is usually handled by taking a functional approach, first making sure you understand the organization's top management and its corporate- and business-level objectives and strategies, and then moving on to analyze each of the company's functional-level objectives and strategies. Part II of exhibit 2.4 contains a step-by step internal analysis plan.

External analysis can best be accomplished by breaking the environment down into sectors and analyzing the influence of each sector separately. Consider the possible effects of the economy, demographics, and social change. Analyze the regulatory environment, resource availability, and technological change. Above all, do a thorough analysis of the competitive environment. Part III of exhibit 2.4 lists some questions to consider in external analysis.

The analysis process can be very time consuming if one tries to analyze every aspect in detail. For that reason, you should let the key issues in each case indicate which aspects of the case you will treat in detail. Exhibit 2.4 can help you through the analytical process. Keep in mind that it is intended as a comprehensive resource rather than a structured checklist. You will probably want to emphasize different aspects of analysis for each individual case, as the focal points in each case are different.

Make recommendations

The end result of your analyses will be your recommendations. These should be based solely on the findings of your analysis and should include supporting evidence for any judgmental elements included. Although real-world business decisions are often subject to intuitive processes, more analytical processes are always preferred unless the decision makers have a great deal of first-hand experience with the type of strategic problems encountered in the case. Therefore, a statement such as "My analysis shows the following . . ." is always better than "I believe the company should . . ."

Most professors prefer that you prepare a list of several feasible alternatives to the case problems. This process allows you to compare competing solutions from which you select your recommendations. In drafting the solution, implementation issues should not be ignored, especially financial ones. A recommendation is always strengthened considerably if you can show that the company has the resources to accomplish it and if you present a well laid-out implementation scheme including as much detail as facts allow. If you recommend a strategic change, include a timetable and budget for accomplishing the new strategy, assign specific managers the responsibility for carrying it out, and tell how the company should follow up to make sure the new strategy is successful.

Perhaps one of the hardest adjustments to make to the case method is the realization that there is no such thing as the "right" answer or even the "right" approach. After all the work you put in, there is a natural tendency to wonder, "Did I get it right?" Remember that strategic decision making is not an exact science. Just as two businesses that adopt completely different courses of action while competing in the same markets are often both successful, different approaches and solutions to the same case also are often both "right." (It is exactly that quality that makes strategic management a challenging and interesting field.) Although no single solution or approach is the only "right" one, there are always some decisions that are better than others and some ways to approach a decision situation that are superior to other approaches. As you develop and refine your case analysis skills, you will also increase your ability to identify the conditions under which different approaches and solutions may be successful. The important thing to remember in case analysis is to justify and support your recommendations with thorough analysis.

Class discussions

Instructors have a number of ways of handling case discussions in class. These range from structured discussion, in which specific questions about the case are asked and sometimes distributed in advance, to unstructured discussions in which the students are given some latitude in identifying the important issues in the case and in presenting their analyses and recommendations. As most business strategy courses utilize the unstructured approach, and few students have encountered it before, we discuss it here.

A good case discussion can be a very rewarding class experience for everyone, but its success depends on good preparation by you and the right set of expectations. Keep the following in mind:

1 Before class, reduce your analysis to two or three pages of notes. Your notes should include your list of the key issues in the case, a SWOT summary (identifying strengths, weaknesses, opportunities, and threats), key financial ratios, a list of two or three feasible alternatives, and your recommendations. Refer to these notes often during the discussion, and add any new ideas that arise.

2 One of the most important things to bring to class with you is an open mind. Once the discussion starts, you will undoubtedly find that there are nearly as many approaches to the case as there are class members. Although there is merit in standing by your convictions, keep in mind that most complicated management problems can best be approached by the refinement process, which requires decision makers to be open to a variety of views.

3 Make the classroom time count by not rehashing case facts. Assume that everyone is familiar with the facts and get right into identifying key issues and problems and analyzing them. Strive to reach the decision-making level of participation (see exhibit 2.2).

4 Remember that you cannot test your ideas if you remain silent. In an active class, that may mean that you have to assert yourself to get the floor. Be careful not to equate "air time" with participation, however. Do not dominate the conversation, especially if you have little to add.

5 If a class discussion is going well, you will discover that the professor has done very little of the talking. His or her role in the discussion is to keep the flow of ideas coming, challenge opinions that are offered, insist on reasons behind your statements, and occasionally summarize the analysis.

Exhibit A2.2   Four Levels of Case Discussion

Fact sharing
The lowest level of discussion. The class simply goes over case facts without really analyzing them. Symptoms of underlying problems are discussed without uncovering the problems themselves.

Problem finding
A step above fact sharing. The class goes through a structured analysis of the company. Strengths, weaknesses, opportunities, and threats are uncovered, and the problems underlying the symptoms are identified.

Problem solving
The third level of class discussion. Attention is directed to the problem areas, problems are prioritized, and recommended solutions are developed for each problem area.

Decision making
The highest level of class discussion. Organizational problems are seen as a whole. Solutions are merged into an overall strategic plan, and implementation considerations are included.

Oral presentations

Students are sometimes assigned cases to present orally, usually in teams of three or four students. The degree of formality in the presentation is up to the professor, but regardless of the formality, preparation for the presentation and the actual conduct of the case in class will differ markedly from the informal class discussion. Thorough preparation will naturally be important, as the entire presentation of issues, analysis, and decision may be up to you and the other members of your team. Here are some points to keep in mind if you are assigned an oral case presentation:

1   Make sure the audience knows the case facts. If the case has not been assigned to the rest of the class to read, the first part of the presentation will have to be devoted to factual material. Although this step is important, keep it brief to allow time for your analysis. Handing out fact sheets is a good way to move this step along quickly.
2   It often helps to identify a role for yourself. The role of the outside analyst or consultant is usually preferable to the role of corporate official, as it allows you to speak more objectively.
3   Organization is important, and communicating the organization of your talk early in the presentation is a good idea. Identify the issues early in the presentation so that you can focus on them throughout the analysis. Summarize at several points to remind the audience of where you are.
4   Visual aids can significantly improve a presentation, but they also can be overdone. Prepare a few good charts and graphs to help tell the story, but don't bury the audience in needless detail.
5   Make your recommendations as thorough as you can. Always include financial and staffing plans for the implementation of your recommendations and provide for evaluation and follow-up.

6 Take questions from the floor if allowed. They are a good way to demonstrate your knowledge of the case and depth of thinking. You should set up ground rules for questions at the beginning, however, so you won't be interrupted at unwanted times.

Written case assignments

A written case analysis may be assigned, either as a structured paper in which you are asked to address specific issues or topics in the case, or as a comprehensive analysis. To prepare a written analysis, you should go through much the same preparation for class discussions, but here your analysis would probably need to be more thorough.

The written format of your paper will vary according to the particular case and the wishes of your professor. If the assignment is a structured one, you may want to address the questions one by one and present your recommendations. If the unstructured approach is taken, you may need some suggestions as to how you should organize the contents of the paper. The outline in exhibit 2.3 is offered as an example that applies to most business strategy cases in your casebook.

Doing additional research

Case analysis sometimes requires research to find additional information about the firm or its industry in order to recommend a course of action. You may, for example, want to update the information in a case that is several years old or to investigate more thoroughly the firm's environment or competition. You may also use the library to develop your own business strategy case from secondary sources.

Fortunately, most college and university libraries and public libraries are well equipped to provide the necessary resources. The companies themselves can also be important sources of current information, and many of them will willingly provide you with copies of their quarterly and annual reports as well as other information. Company sources should not be relied on exclusively, however, as information that is unfavorable to one company is unlikely to be obtained that way.

Exhibit A2.3   Suggested Outline for Written Cases

I   *Introduction*
Give a brief statement of the purpose of the report and how the report is organized. You might also include some basic facts about the company as a way of introduction.

II   *Internal Analysis*
A   Present situation. Discuss the firm's present strategy. Describe its markets, products or services; its competitive orientation; and the scope of its activities. What is being attempted, and how? How well is it working?
B   Financial resources. Describe the financial condition of the company and assess its ability to meet the demands of its environment and to provide for future growth.
C   Strengths and weaknesses. Discuss the company's strong and weak points as uncovered in your analysis of the various functional areas.

Exhibit A2.3 Cont.

III *External Analysis*

A General environment. Describe any feature of the economic, technological, regulatory, physical, and social environments that are relative to the organization's future.

B Operating environment. Describe the competitive environment. Who are the competitors? What are their strengths and weaknesses? Describe the customer environment. Who are the customers? What are their requirements? How does the firm provide value to them?

C Opportunities and threats. Summarize all of the relevant issues uncovered by your external analysis.

IV *Key Decisions*

Identify the main points at issue in the case. What are the problems and decisions the company faces? What should be the focus of the recommendations?

V *Alternatives*

Describe each of the possible strategies the firm could adopt. Discuss each one and include its strong and weak points.

VI *Recommended Decisions*

Tell what you think the company should do. What should be its strategy? Justify your choice on the basis of analysis. Discuss implementation, evaluation, and follow-up. Include time estimates for implementation and financial staffing plans where appropriate.

VII *Appendices, Tables, and Graphs*

Keep in mind that sometimes the cases use disguised company names that are impossible to research directly. Also, most privately held companies do not make it a practice to share financial information with the public, as publicly held companies are required to do. This limitation can make it difficult to obtain the latest information on some companies, although you can usually obtain information about their industries. The major financial reporting services often report estimates of the sales, profits, and key ratios for private companies, and their estimates are considered quite accurate.

It is generally true that the larger the company is, the more information you will find. Most of the Global 1000 size companies discussed in the cases are the subjects of many news articles, industry analyses, and trade reports, and therefore make excellent subjects for secondary case research.

Working in teams

Just as strategic decisions in real businesses are often the products of teams of managers working together, professors frequently assign class members to teams for the preparation of case reports in order to provide a more realistic experience in the decision-making process. Teamwork may be a new experience for you and other members of your team. The following points may make your team experience a more successful and satisfying one:

1 Determine the relative strengths and skills of team members and divide the work to take advantage of them. Breaking the analysis down into distinctive parts will avoid duplication of effort.

2 Meet often and work as a team. Remember that your performance on the assignment depends on each other. Make sure that meetings are scheduled when all members can attend and that meetings are planned ahead of time.

3 Use consensus processes and make decisions jointly. Make sure the final product is consistent throughout. Teams often make the mistake of presenting the final paper or presentation that is simply an accumulation of parts instead of a single analysis with a unified set of recommendations.

Summary

The chapter presents a general framework for analyzing strategic management cases and developing case reports. These guidelines may seem long to you now, but as you become more familiar with the process, much of it will become automatic. The purpose is to get you started on the road to formulating effective strategic decisions and communicating the results of your analyses.

Case analysis, like any other valuable skill, takes time to develop and requires concentration and hard work. The rewards are plentiful, however. In addition, case analysis is very personal. Every successful decision maker eventually adopts a style that is his or her own. For that reason, you will probably find it necessary to modify the framework presented in this chapter to fit your own work habits and decision style. We suggest that you follow this guide closely until you feel comfortable with the process, and then use if only occasionally to review your own procedure and analysis.

Exhibit A2.4   Case Analysis Outline

I The Present Situation

A *Mission, Objectives, Strategies, Policies*
   1 Mission. What business(es) is the company in? Is the mission relatively stable or undergoing change.
   2 Objectives. What is the company trying to accomplish? Are corporate-level, business-level, and functional objectives consistent with the corporate mission and with each other? Are objectives written down, or must they be inferred from performances?
   3 Strategies. How is the company attempting to achieve its objectives? Are the strategies consistent with the mission and objectives? Are strategies coordinated, or do they appear to be developed piece-meal?
   4 Policies. Does the corporation have well-developed guidelines for carrying out its strategies? Do they seem to enhance or hinder goal accomplishments?

B *Corporate Performance*
   1 Financial performance. Is the company's financial performance adequate? What is its net profit margin, its return on investment, and earnings per share? What are the trends in these overall measures of performance?

Exhibit A2.4   Cont.

2   Goals. How well is the organization meeting its objectives? Does present performance match expectations?

3   Competitive stance. Is the company remaining competitive in its industry? Is it maintaining or enhancing its market share?

II Internal Analysis – Strengths and Weaknesses

A   *Organizational Structure and Corporate Culture*

1   Type. What type of organizational structure does the firm have: simple, functional, divisional, horizontal, or matrix?

2   Centralization. Is decision making centralized at top management levels, or decentralized throughout the organization?

3   Culture. Is there a well-defined culture? Is the culture market-oriented, product-oriented, or technology-oriented?

4   Consistency. Are the company's structure and culture consistent with the firm's objectives and strategies?

B   *Top Management and Board of Directors*

1   The CEO. How would you rate the CEO in terms of knowledge, skills, and abilities? Is his or her overall management style autocratic or participative?

2   The board. Is the board of directors directly involved in the strategic management process, or is it a "rubber-stamp" board?

3   Top managers. How would you rate the overall capability of the top management team? Is there an adequate plan for executive succession and training for top management positions?

C   *Financial Management*

1   Functional objectives and strategies. Does the company have clearly stated financial objectives and strategies? Are they consistent with the company's overall objectives?

2   Profitability. How is the company performing in terms of profitability ratios? How does this performance compare with past performance and industry averages? Does a common-sized income statement reveal any discrepancies in the components of net income?

3   Liquidity and cash management. How is the firm performing in terms of its liquidity ratios? Are cash-flow problems indicated? How do the ratios compare with past performance and industry averages?

4   Leverage and capital management. Is the firm's leverage appropriate, as evidenced by its leverage ratios? Is the amount of leverage in keeping with the industry and the company's strategies for expansion?

5   Asset management. Are inventories, fixed assets, and other resources being effectively managed as indicated by the activity ratios? How do these ratios compare with the firm's past performance and other firms in the industry?

6   Financial planning and control. What individuals are involved in the firm's financial planning? How often are budgets prepared? How closely are spending decisions monitored, and who has the authority to control financial resources? How sophisticated are the financial and asset management systems of the firm?

D   *Operations Management*

1   Technical core. Does the technical core of the organization center on production, service, or merchandising?

2   Capacity. Is the productive capacity of the firm adequate for present needs and for future growth in operations?

Exhibit A2.4 Cont.

3 Quality. Is the quality of the product or service in keeping with customers' expectations and the company's goals? Are quality assurance systems in place and functioning properly?

4 Efficiency. Is operating efficiency adequate? Can it be improved?

E *Marketing Management*

1 Product. What is the company's present mix of products and/or services? At what stages in their product life cycles are they? Who are the firm's target customers? Is there a readily identifiable product-mission philosophy?

2 Price. Are prices competitive and in keeping with product quality and the target market? Is price determination demand-based, competitive, or on a cost-plus basis?

3 Place. Is the distribution system adequate? Does the company maintain its own sales team or depend on outside firms? Is it an integrated part of the company or separately controlled? Are relations with the sales force and distributors good? Do compensation systems provide the right amount of incentives?

4 Promotion. How does the company advertise and promote its products or services? Is the promotion effective? Is promotion designed in-house or by outside firms?

5 Marketing information systems. How does the company identify new markets or target groups? Is the marketing department involved in the development of new products? How does the company exchange information with the distribution system?

F *Human Resources Management*

1 Human resources planning. Is there an effective human resources planning effort? Are personnel requirements included in strategy formulation and facilities planning?

2 Obtaining personnel. Are adequate processes in place for obtaining qualified personnel? How are personnel recruited and selected?

3 Retaining and improving human resources. Are training programs effective? Are performance evaluation and improvement managed effectively? Are grievances handled well?

4 Compensation. Is the compensation system effective and fair? Is pay generally competitive or above competitive levels? Are fringe benefits high or low for the industry? Does the firm have a profit-sharing plan?

5 Labor relations. If the company is unionized, are relations with labor organizations congenial or combative?

G *Research and Development*

1 Organization. Is there one centralized R&D department, or is R&D decentralized?

2 Level of R&D effort. What percentage of the firm's resources are devoted to the R&D effort? How does this compare with competitors?

3 Control. How is the R&D effort controlled? Where in the organization is policy established for R&D?

4 Product development. How effective is R&D in bringing new products to market?

H *Management Information Systems*

1 Is a management information system in use at all levels – operational, middle management, and top management?

2 Is the system adequate to meet information needs at each level?

3 Does the organization use a centralized MIS or independent decentralized systems for various departments and functions?

4 Is the MIS cost-effective?

Exhibit A2.4 Cont.

5 Does the strategic management process make use of a decision support system (DSS) to aid in strategic analysis?

III External Analysis – Opportunities and Threats

A *Economic Environment*
What is forecast for the industry, and how are economic events likely to affect this firm? How would an inflationary period or a recession affect product demand?

B *Technological Environment*
What innovations are likely to occur that will affect either products and services or production processes? Is the rate of change in technology increasing or slowing?

C *Regulatory Environment*
Are there any present or expected government and/or industry regulations that present either threats or opportunities? Are there ongoing efforts to monitor or actively participate in the regulatory process?

D *Physical Environment*
Can we expect any significant depletion of needed resources? Will there be any changes in the physical surroundings of the organization that might affect the accomplishment of its goals or present opportunities?

E *Social/Demographic Environment*
Are any important demographic changes in customers, suppliers, or the labor pool expected? Are tastes and preferences changing in a way that might affect this firm?

F *Competitive Environment*
Who are the firm's competitors? What are their market shares? How effective are they? How likely is the entrance of new competition? Are there close substitutes for the company's products or services?

G *Customer Environment*
Who are the current and future customers? What are their requirements? How does the firm provide value to current customers? How will the firm provide value to future customers?

CHAPTER
3
THREE

INTERNATIONAL STRATEGIC DECISIONS

LEARNING OBJECTIVES

After reading this chapter, you should be able to accomplish the following:

1 Describe recent developments that have contributed to the increasing importance of international strategic decisions.

2 Discuss the range of contextual factors affecting international strategy.

3 Compare and contrast four strategic dispositions found in multinational corporations.

4 Describe the range of international strategic alternatives

available to the firm, including import–export strategies, foreign direct investment, and international strategic alliances.

5 Discuss Bartlett and Ghoshal's "goals and means" model of international strategy formulation.

6 Compare and contrast multidomestic, global, and transnational strategic configurations.

7 Describe Porter's four-factor model of national industry competitiveness.

The Importance of International Strategic Decisions

Through the 1980s and early 1990s, the most rapidly expanding area of strategic management has been that of international, or global, strategy. Businesses and industries that were once purely domestic, such as the one featured in the quality case at the end of this chapter, have been transformed rapidly into global ones. Moreover, the challenges facing the multinational corporation (MNC) have expanded rapidly. In this chapter, we shall investigate the increasing importance of strategic decisions in this new environment and discuss the consequences of this transformation for the tasks of strategic decision makers.

Two forces have combined to create this new environment, and with it, the rapid internationalization of strategic management: (a) the convergence of markets throughout the world and the advent of global products to serve them; and (b) the search for increased operating efficiencies. These forces are dynamic in nature and interrelated in the ways that they affect international business decisions.

Market convergence

The product preferences of consumers around the world are converging. Whereas in the past consumers in different parts of the world purchased very different sets of goods and services, the world now wants Sony CD players, Armani suits, and MTV. Behind this globalization of product markets are a number of causal factors.

Technological improvements in mass communications have played a role in disseminating up-to-date product information and enhancing brand awareness. Instantaneous communication via satellite television transmission makes consumers around the world aware of products soon after they are introduced. This more rapid diffusion of product information also has the effect of shortening product life cycles, as new products replace older ones more frequently than ever before.

Rising affluence in some parts of the world has also contributed to the opening of new markets for sophisticated products and services. The newly industrialized economies of the Far East, such as Taiwan, Singapore and Korea, have produced millions of middle-class consumers, as have the middle-income economies of Latin America. According to *Fortune*, there are over 30 million new middle-class consumers in India, a country that was once considered to be an unattractive market.[1] This new army of customers around the world demands more "upscale" goods, better entertainment, financial services, and a host of other products that have not been available in their countries until very recently.

The demand for quality has also been an important factor in the market convergence process. As consumers become more sophisticated, have more money to spend, and learn more about products, they become increasingly dissatisfied with anything less than high-quality products. Product quality has therefore become a "given" for any firm wanting to compete in global markets as well as domestic ones.

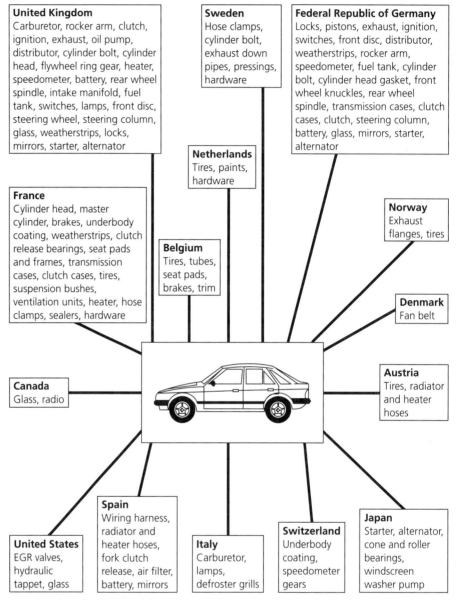

United Kingdom
Carburetor, rocker arm, clutch, ignition, exhaust, oil pump, distributor, cylinder bolt, cylinder head, flywheel ring gear, heater, speedometer, battery, rear wheel spindle, intake manifold, fuel tank, switches, lamps, front disc, steering wheel, steering column, glass, weatherstrips, locks, mirrors, starter, alternator

Sweden
Hose clamps, cylinder bolt, exhaust down pipes, pressings, hardware

Federal Republic of Germany
Locks, pistons, exhaust, ignition, switches, front disc, distributor, weatherstrips, rocker arm, speedometer, fuel tank, cylinder bolt, cylinder head gasket, front wheel knuckles, rear wheel spindle, transmission cases, clutch cases, clutch, steering column, battery, glass, mirrors, starter, alternator

Netherlands
Tires, paints, hardware

France
Cylinder head, master cylinder, brakes, underbody coating, weatherstrips, clutch release bearings, seat pads and frames, transmission cases, clutch cases, tires, suspension bushes, ventilation units, heater, hose clamps, sealers, hardware

Norway
Exhaust flanges, tires

Belgium
Tires, tubes, seat pads, brakes, trim

Denmark
Fan belt

Canada
Glass, radio

Austria
Tires, radiator and heater hoses

Spain
Wiring harness, radiator and heater hoses, fork clutch release, air filter, battery, mirrors

United States
EGR valves, hydraulic tappet, glass

Italy
Carburetor, lamps, defroster grills

Switzerland
Underbody coating, speedometer gears

Japan
Starter, alternator, cone and roller bearings, windscreen washer pump

Final assembly takes place in Halewood (United Kingdom) and Saarlouis (Federal Republic of Germany).

Figure 3.1 Global manufacturing: the component network for the Ford Escort in Europe.
Source: World Development Report 1987. New York: Oxford University Press (1987), p. 39.

The search for efficiency

The second force that is driving the rapid internationalization of strategic management is the quest for more efficient operation. Intensified competition has caused strategic decision makers to seek out new ways of reducing costs and optimizing their companies' investments. This search for the competitive advantages afforded through international sources of increased efficiency has taken on two basic forms.

Global sourcing of raw materials and component parts has increased in recent years. A growing number of companies have realized that tremendous cost savings can accrue to their businesses by utilizing those suppliers who can more efficiently provide needed inputs, regardless of where they are geographically located. The global component network employed by Ford Motor Company in the production of its Escort model in Europe is an example of the extent to which this strategy may be employed. Ford uses components from 15 countries, including 12 European sites, the USA, Japan, and Canada, to build the Escort in its assembly plants in Halewood, UK and Saarlouis, Germany.[2] Figure 3.1 is a graphic depiction of this global sourcing network.

The *relocation* of production plants to countries where labor costs are lower is also a strategy that is rapidly growing in popularity. The most often cited reason for locating production in foreign countries is to take advantage of lower labor costs. BMW's management decided, in 1993, to locate its first plant outside Germany. A site near Greenville, South Carolina, in the southern United States, was chosen. Among the reasons cited for the location choice were lower labor costs. Average annual wages at BMW's new South Carolina facility are approximately US$25,000, as compared to $40,000 at the company's main plant in Munich.[3] Relocating production facilities can also provide other savings to a multinational company. Locating closer to the market often reduces transportation costs, and becoming a direct participant in local economies can lead to a reduction in a firm's regulation by the host government.

The Context of International Strategic Decisions

Operating a multinational corporation, rather than a purely domestic one, implies that there are important contextual differences in the environment. The geographic spread of markets and the necessity of dealing with foreign cultures and governments are but two of the complicating factors in an international firm. Whether these differences significantly affect the way that decisions are made has been the subject of debate, however. Herbert argued that global expansion is no different from domestic geographic diversification, and that globalizing a business simply requires the extension of the same principles.[4] Kogut, on the other hand, pointed out that strategic formulation in a international context requires management decisions based on more complex factors, such as differences in host-country laws and cultures.[5] Miller observed that the number of risk factors to which a firm is exposed is greater in a MNC.[6]

Sources of authority and denominations of value

Sundaram and Black noted that in the environment of the MNC there are a number of factors present that the purely domestic firm does not experience. The two distinguishing aspects of these are (a) multiple sources of external authority, and (b) multiple denominations of value. The fact that MNCs operate across borders and under different legal systems means that they are subject to conflicts among the laws, political institutions, official languages, norms of behavior, and cultures, i.e. multiple sources of authority. The second distinguishing aspect, multiple denominations of value, arises from the fact that the firm's operations are housed in different countries, and its cash flows are subject to the vicissitudes of exchange rate fluctuations. The firm's revenues, its profits, and the value of its assets are therefore subject to a great deal of exchange exposure. That is not the case in a purely domestic firm.[7]

Strategic dispositions in the multinational corporation

According to Chakravarthy and Perlmutter, three important contextual factors define the challenges for strategic planning in the MNC:

1 The *economic imperative* that determines where the MNC should locate various elements of the production and distribution chain for a given business.
2 The *political imperative* as shaped by the demands of host countries in which the MNC operates.
3 The MNC's own *strategic disposition*.[8]

The last of these, strategic disposition (or *orientation*) is especially important for understanding how strategic choices are made in multinational firms. Among MNCs, there are significant differences in the way that international operations are viewed. In an earlier work, Perlmutter identified three basic orientations adopted by headquarters toward their international subsidiaries. They are (a) ethnocentrism, (b) polycentrism, and (c) geocentrism.[9]

In the *ethnocentric* firm, the values and interests of the parent company dominate the strategic decision making process. Foreign subsidiary operations are viewed simply as extensions of the parent firm's strategy, and the culture of the firm's home country becomes the dominant culture of all its operations. A single global strategy, based on the experiences of the company in its home markets, is enacted worldwide. For example, a USA-based MNC adopting an ethnocentric orientation might attempt to promote successful US products as global ones, and to operate its subsidiaries abroad in the same manner that it conducts its US operations. The dominant logic is that good business practices are universal, and "if it works at home, it will work abroad." Although this orientation often provides an efficient way to disseminate knowledge and "best practices" gained from experiences, it runs the risk of failing to recognize important differences in market preferences and cultures in the host countries of its operations.

The *polycentric* firm, on the other hand, tailors its strategic plan to meet the needs of each country in which it operates. Subsidiaries abroad are given latitude in deciding upon the objectives they will pursue, and in the methods for accomplishing them. Product characteristics may be altered to conform to local tastes and preferences, and operating procedures adjusted to conform to cultural differences in the workforce. National responsiveness, rather than global integration, is the key feature of the firm's international strategy. For example, a European firm adopting a polycentric orientation in Asia would research local product preferences and design strategies to capture those markets, rather than assuming that a product that was successful in Europe might automatically appeal to Asian consumers. Sonoco Products Company, a large USA-based packaging firm, conducts separate strategies in each of the 25 countries where it conducts food packaging operations. Sonoco management stresses the flexibility and autonomy that this arrangement affords its local managers, who must be responsive to local needs in food packaging that vary widely from country to country.[10] Although more responsive to local needs, the polycentric orientation runs the risk of become inefficient as the company's products and operations diverge to meet the needs of its various markets.

A more all-inclusive approach characterizes *geocentric* firms. These companies view their operations on a global basis, and seek to integrate their subsidiaries through a worldwide systems approach. A global strategy is enacted, whereby the best ideas and practices from around the world are brought into an overall plan. For example, in a Japanese firm adopting a geocentric orientation, marketing information from North America might be used to alter the design of the company's products sold throughout the world, or a manufacturing innovation arising from a Korean factory might be applied in manufacturing plants in Europe and North America. The attempt is to be simultaneously responsive *and* efficient. The most difficult aspect in enacting a global strategy in the geocentrically oriented firm is knowing when and where to trade off efficiency for responsiveness. To the extent possible, global products are designed to meet the needs of consumers everywhere, with local adaptations made where necessary to serve the market, i.e. global products with local variations. Likewise, the firm's operations are designed to take advantage of the experience gained throughout the network of subsidiaries, with local variations made only where necessary to adapt to customs and practices. An example of a geocentric firm is Ford Motor Company. In 1993, Ford introduced a new automobile model, the CDW27 sedan, that would be sold as a "global" product in all of Ford's markets around the world.[11]

More recently, a fourth orientation, regiocentrism, has been identified.[12] The *regiocentric* firm eschews both a local and a global strategy in favor of a regional one. Instead of attempting to integrate its strategy throughout the world, the firm enacts regional ones. A single European strategy, for example, recognizes the similarities in European markets and operations, and seeks to gain efficiency by treating the company's European subsidiaries as single strategic unit. At the same time, a different strategy may be enacted by the same MNC in Asia. By grouping similar markets under regional strategies, the firm seeks to gain some of the efficiency afforded by global integration while retaining important aspects of regional responsiveness. The regiocentric orientation may be seen as a compromise of sorts, and like all compromises runs the risk of achieving only partial satisfaction of important objectives. An example of a regiocentric firm is the USA-based appliance company, Whirlpool Corporation. Following the acquisition of

Table 3.1   Strategic orientations of multinational enterprises

Orientation of the firm	Ethnocentric	Polycentric	Regiocentric	Geocentric
Mission	Profitability (viability)	Public acceptance (legitimacy)	Both profitability and public acceptance (viability and legitimacy)	Both profitability and public acceptance (viability and legitimacy)
Governance	Top-down	Bottom-up (Each subsidiary decides upon local objectives)	Mutually negotiated between region and subsidiaries	Mutually negotiated at all levels of the firm
Strategy	Global integrative	National responsiveness	Regional integrative and national responsiveness	Global integrative and national responsiveness
Structure	Hierarchical product divisions	Hierarchical area divisions with autonomous national units	Products and regional organizations tied through a matrix	A network of organizations
Culture	Home country	Host country	Regional	Global
Product planning	Determined by needs of home country customers	Local product development based on local needs	Standardize within region, but not across	Global product with local variations
Finance objective	Repatriation of profit to home country	Retention of profits in host country	Redistribution within region	Redistribution globally
Personnel practices	Home country citizens developed for key positions worldwide	Local citizens developed for key positions in the country	Regional managers developed for key positions anywhere within the region	Best people everywhere in the world developed for key positions throughout the firm
Evaluation and control	Home standards applied everywhere	Determined locally	Determined regionally	Standards which are universal, weighted to suit local conditions

Source: Adapted from Balaji. S. C. and Perlmutter, H. V.. "Strategic planning for a global business." Columbia Journal of World Business (Summer 1985), pp. 5–6.

several foreign subsidiaries and the establishment of a European joint venture with Philips, Whirlpool established separate strategic areas for North America, Europe, and Asia, rather than trying to standardize its markets and products globally.[13]

Whatever the particular orientation of the firm in question, understanding the MNC's strategic orientation toward its subsidiaries is important to analyzing the basis for its international strategy, as we have seen. There are also important implications for understanding the MNC's structure and governance. According to Chakravarthy and Perlmutter, ethnocentric firms tend to be hierarchically structured, and use top-down decision making. Polycentric, regiocentric, and geocentric firms, on the other hand, are more autonomously structured and adopt more participative styles in strategic decision making. A MNC's strategic orientation also carries important implications for functional level strategies. Marketing, finance, personnel, and evaluation and control systems all vary markedly among firms with different orientations.[14] Table 3.1 presents a comparison of the four strategic orientations of MNCs on several important dimensions.

International Strategic Alternatives

The strategic alternatives available to firms wishing to enter the international arena range from minimal involvement to substantial investments of the firm's strategic attention and its resource base. Beginning with the simplest of these, import and export strategies, we shall discuss the range of alternative strategies in the international environment.

Merchandise imports and exports

The importing or exporting of goods, whether it is raw materials, component parts, or finished products, is typically the first type of international activity undertaken by a firm. The main reason for this is that importing or exporting requires the least commitment of company resources, and usually involves the least risk. These strategies are also the easiest to implement. Trade intermediaries, such as import and export brokers, are prevalent in practically every part of the world. For a fee, these intermediaries will handle all of a company's import and/or export functions, thereby eliminating the need for a company to acquire its own in-house expertise.

The rising popularity of import–export strategies is also due, in part, to the development of a much more favorable climate for world trade over the past two decades. Trade restrictions have been eased in virtually all of the world's markets through the successful implementation of the General Agreement on Tariffs and Trade (GATT), and by economic cooperation pacts such as the European Union and the North American Free Trade Agreement. In 1992, world trade in the form of imports and exports of goods totaled well over US$3.6 trillion , representing a ten-fold increase since 1972.[15]

Accounting for much of that increase has been the propensity of manufacturing firms to use more foreign sources for raw materials and component parts, a practice generally referred to as *global sourcing*. Among US firms, foreign purchases – measured as a percentage of all purchases by the firm – rose from 8 percent in 1980 to over 15 percent in 1985, and to nearly 20 percent in 1992.

Some of the early part of this growth was fueled by the strength of the dollar on world money markets. More of it can be explained, however, by the increased availability of cheap, dependable sources abroad. Many US and European manufacturers have found that global sourcing, particularly from the newly industrialized countries of the Far East, is cheaper, and the quality is better than that available from domestic suppliers.[16]

Although a merchandise import and/or export strategy is usually the first international strategy adopted, companies typically do not abandon it as they expand their international activities to other realms, but rather use importing and exporting to supplement their more involved strategies. For example, a company establishing a production facility in a country to which it formerly exported will continue to use exporting and importing to equip and supply the new facility, and to supply markets abroad from the new facility's products.

Service imports and exports

Just as domestic markets for services are expanding rapidly, so are international markets for all types of service products. Although often referred to as *invisibles*, because of their intangible nature, the services are anything but invisible on world markets. Service exports and imports take on many forms, including entertainment, travel and tourism, and business services. Among the fastest growing global businesses in recent years have been entertainment, business consulting, and financial services.

In some ways, service sector strategies represent a more involved level of international participation on the part of the firm than do import–export strategies. In services, value is created at the point of sale, as opposed to being embodied in the product itself. Therefore, company representatives must often be physically present in the markets that are being served. Take international consulting, for example. The consultant must often interact directly with the client firm to achieve results. Market intermediaries are neither desirable nor feasible when customer satisfaction is dependent on the delivery of services.

Of growing importance among service export strategies are management contracts and turnkey operations. A *management contract* is an arrangement whereby a company provides personnel to perform either general or specialized management functions for another, often in conjunction with a construction project. General Electric (GE) often agrees to provide management services for a period of time following the construction of electric generating plants. Electric power utilities in the host country pay fees to GE for this service for a period of one to two years. This arrangement provides an opportunity for host country personnel to become familiar with the new technology before assuming full responsibility for its operation. The term *turnkey operation* generally refers to a project performed under contract by a multinational construction firm. The facilities are transferred to the host country owners when they are ready to begin operation.

Licensing and franchising

In some ways similar to service products, in the sense that intangibles are involved, licensing and franchising arrangements offer another alternative for international business strategy. These sectors are growing rapidly, and are expected to continue to expand at a faster level than import–export markets well into the twentieth-first century.

Licensing involves the sale of the rights to intangible assets, such as trademarks, patents, copyrights, or other intellectual property. The number and value of international licensing transactions rose sharply during the 1980s and early 1990s, especially in the entertainment and computer software industries. Protection for intellectual property rights was an important feature of the Uruguay round of the GATT concluded in 1994,[17] and has been the subject of much controversy between the government of the People's Republic of China and the entertainment industry.[18]

Franchising, another of the most rapidly growing international businesses, may be thought of as a specialized form of licensing whereby the franchisor not only conveys rights to use the company's trademarks and images, but also assists in the operation of the business. American fast-food franchising operations such as McDonald's, Pizza Hut and KFC, have reached global proportions within the past two decades, and their growth is projected to continue well into the twenty-first century.[19]

Investment strategies

The most involved international business strategies are those in which a firm invests in assets abroad. For purposes of discussion, we shall make a distinction between portfolio investment and foreign direct investment.

Portfolio investment is a strategy which gives the investing business either a minority ownership position in a foreign company or some ownership of its outstanding obligations. It is used primarily for short-term financial gain. Corporate treasurers routinely move investment funds among countries to take advantage of the higher yields that result from differences in reported earnings, or differences in exchange rates or interest rates abroad. These portfolio investments may take a number of forms: shares of either voting or non-voting stock in the foreign company; or loans in the form of bonds, bills, or negotiable notes.[20]

Foreign direct investment (FDI) is a strategy that gives the investing firm a controlling interest in a foreign company. FDIs represent the highest level of commitment a company can make to international business. The decision to engage in a FDI typically involves not only financial resources, but the transfer of other valuable resources to the foreign subsidiary, such as technology and personnel. Unlike portfolio investments, FDI usually represents a long term obligation on the part of the investing business.

As of 1992, over 37,000 companies worldwide had foreign direct investments, the total value of which was approximately US$2 trillion.[21] The sales from all FDIs totaled US$5.5 trillion in 1992. Although many small companies engage in FDI, large MNCs control a disproportionate share of this type of investment. Approximately 1 percent of all companies holding controlling interests in foreign subsidiaries own half of the total. These are mostly members of the elite "Global 500," the world's largest industrial firms.[22]

Strategic alliances

Some of the most rapidly growing forms of international strategies are those involving strategic alliances between companies. Practically all Global 500 firms engage in one or more types of strategic alliances. According to *Fortune*, one type, the international joint venture, grew at an average annual rate of 27 percent between 1985 and 1991.[23] International strategic alliances can take a variety of forms, including collaborations without equity, cash-neutral exchange of assets, equity ownership agreements, and, of course, the establishment of joint ventures.

In a *collaboration without equity*, MNCs simply form loose associations, usually for a special purpose. Technology sharing arrangements are common examples of this. Mitsubishi, the Japanese trading company, and Daimler-Benz, the giant German manufacturing company, have successfully shared technologies over the years on a range of products, including automobiles, aerospace, and integrated circuits.[24] Sony often shares its research staff and production facilities with small companies in collaborative efforts to develop promising new technologies.

Cash-neutral exchanges of assets is another form of strategic alliance that is rapidly gaining in popularity. One of the most prevalent types is the cross-licensing agreement. In a cross-licensing of product rights, for example, a domestic company grants the foreign rights to use its property to a company abroad in exchange for acquiring rights to distribute that company's products in its own market. Each firm can therefore extend its product lines without engaging in expensive and often redundant product development. It can also speed product introductions abroad with the help of its partner, and can avoid expensive start-up time in learning new markets.

Equity ownership arrangements involve either one-way or mutual purchases of equity stakes in foreign companies. By trading ownership shares through the exchange of stock, companies often formalize working agreements across global markets. Equity arrangements open the door to wholesale exchanges of assets. Often, products are marketed jointly in both home countries and technology sharing improves the offerings of both partners. Perhaps the most widely publicized equity ownership alliance has been that of Ford and Toyo Kogyo Co. (Mazda). Ford owns a 25 percent stake in Mazda, and the two companies assist each other's marketing efforts in both the USA and Japan. Mazda and Ford products also share common designs, such as that of Mazda's MX6 and Ford's Probe sports sedans.[25]

The international *joint venture* (JV) is an alliance in which a new firm is created, jointly owned by two or more partners. The joint venture has become a very important market entry strategy, since host governments often require foreign corporations to have a local partner before doing business there. Technology-sharing JVs are also common. AUTECS, a supplier of computerized automotive parts, is just such a JV. The company is jointly owned by Robert Bosch, the German auto parts supplier, and Nissan Motor Manufacturing. Located on the campus of one of Bosch's larger US manufacturing facilities, the venture combines Bosch's automotive computer technology and Nissan's manufacturing expertise to provide an important component assembly for Nissan products manufactured worldwide.

The *reasons for creating international strategic alliances* are about as varied as the alliances themselves. Five common ones are as follows.

- Penetrating new markets – strategic partners abroad can ease market-entry problems by introducing mangers to important customers, aiding in the use of distribution channels, and interpreting the culture.
- Sharing costs of research and development – the investment required to launch a new global product is often prohibitive for one company working alone, even a for giant MNC. For example, the development costs of a new 16-megabit DRAM chip for applications in the computer industry were shared by Texas Instruments and Hitachi.[26]
- Sharing risks (particularly the risks of large-scale projects) – often the scale of operations required to compete in any meaningful way in world markets requires resources that are not available from a single company, and even if they were, would put the entire firm's survival at risk. In order to compete with Boeing and McDonnell-Douglas in the global passenger aircraft industry, European firms joined forces to create Airbus Industries, a joint venture composed of British, French, German and Spanish companies.[27]
- Counterattacking the moves of a common competitor – although not as common a motivation as some of the others, sometimes global competitors find it necessary to form a coalition to beat back the competitive threat of a powerful predator. In order to combat the Japanese presence in the European personal computer market, IBM formed alliances with several of its European rivals, including an agreement with Siemens to share in the development of the 64-megabit processor.[28]
- Learning from partners – although sharing critical knowledge and skills with foreign partners runs the risk of creating future competitors, the learning motive is a powerful reason to engage in alliances. A classic example of this is the establishment of New United Motors Manufacturing (NUMMI), a joint venture established in 1984 by General Motors and Toyota in Fremont, California to manufacture automobiles for the American market.[29] While GM learned Toyota's manufacturing techniques, Toyota gained the knowledge and experience of dealing with American workers and supplier companies, which it was able to put to use some years later when it built its own manufacturing facility in Kentucky.

Strategic alliances are not without their downside, however. Many international alliances have suffered from unresolvable clashes between cultures, and the disappointment of unrealized expectations. A firm contemplating an international alliance should also be aware of the potential for losing sovereignty over its decision making processes. Larger partners, especially, often dominate smaller ones. Local firms, by virtue of their familiarity with the operating environment and their contacts and political influence, frequently overpower their foreign partners, regardless of the actual equity stakes in the business. Above all, there is the risk that the transference of knowledge can result in losing one's core competence to the partner, who may then become a powerful competitor. After teaching its local

Table 3.2 Worldwide advantage: goals and means

Strategic objectives	Sources of competitive advantage		
	National differences	Scale economies	Scope economies
Achieving efficiency in current operations	Benefiting from differences in factor costs, wages and cost of capital	Expanding and exploiting potential scale economies in each activity	Sharing of investments and costs across markets and businesses
Managing risks through multinational flexibility	Managing different kinds of risks arising from market- or policy-induced changes in comparative advantages of different countries	Balancing scale with strategic and operational flexibility	Portfolio diversification of risks and creation of options and side bets
Innovation, learning, and adaptation	Learning from societal differences in organizational and managerial processes and systems	Benefiting from experience, cost reduction and innovation	Shared learning across organizational components in different products, markets, or businesses

Source: Bartlett, C. A. and Ghoshal, S.. *Transnational Management: Text, Cases, and Readings in Cross-Border Management.* 2ed. Homewood, IL: Richard D. Irwin (1995), p. 247.

partner in India the soft drink business, Coca-Cola subsequently found itself out of the country and the former partner selling Coca-Cola look-alike products.[30]

Despite their possible shortcomings and risks, strategic alliances are an essential feature of the global economy. The noted strategist Kenichi Ohmae, writing in *Harvard Business Review*, stated: "Globalization mandates alliances, makes them absolutely essential to strategy."[31] Chapter 5 of this book contains a more detailed discussion of strategic alliances as a competitive strategy, including strategies for making an alliance work to the firm's advantage.

Strategy and Structure in the Multinational Corporation

Achieving global competitive advantage: goals and means

Given the range of strategic choices available to the decision makers of global companies, it is important to examine the motivations underlying various alternatives. Christopher A. Bartlett and Sumantra Ghoshal have developed an interesting model of strategic choice featuring the strategic objectives (goals) of the firm and the sources of competitive advantage (means) available for achieving them.[32] Building upon earlier work by Ghoshal,[33] they assert that a company must achieve three strategic goals in order to develop a worldwide advantage:

1 It must build global-scale efficiency in its existing activities.
2 It must develop multinational flexibility so as to manage diverse country-specific risks and opportunities.
3 It must create the ability to learn from its international exposure and opportunities and to exploit that learning on a world-wide basis.[34]

In a global business, the means for achieving these goals, and consequently building worldwide competitive advantages, according Bartlett and Ghoshal, lie in three fundamental tools:

1 Exploiting differences in sourcing and market potential across countries.
2 Exploiting economies of scale.
3 Exploiting economies of scope.[35]

Table 3.2 illustrates how Bartlett and Ghoshal's three basic strategic objectives interact with the their three sources of competitive advantage to produce viable strategies in the global firm.

Balancing global vision and local demand

Although Bartlett and Ghoshal provide a comprehensive model of global strategic decisions, it is important to point out that the three goals of efficiency, flexibility, and learning may not always be of equal importance in a given decision context. In their groundbreaking book, *The Multinational Mission*, C. K. Prahalad and Yves Doz provide a contingency-based model of strategic response to the

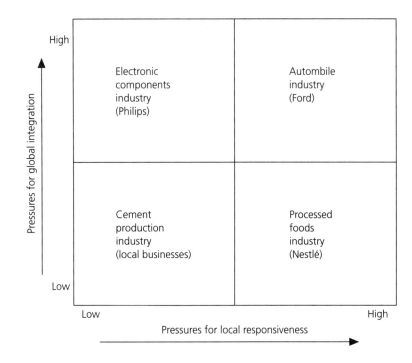

Figure 3.2 Pressures for local responsiveness and global integration.
Source: Adapted with permission of The Free Press, a division of Simon and Schuster, from Prahalad, C. K. and Doz, Y. L., *The Multinational Mission: Balancing Local Demands and Global Vision*. New York: Free Press (1987), p. 24. Copyright © 1986 by The Free Press.

environment.[36] According to Prahalad and Doz, different global industries present varying degrees of efficiency to be gained from global integration and local (or national) responsiveness. If we view the MNC as an input–output system, and its overall efficiency as the relative value of its outputs as compared to its inputs, then it is clear that global efficiency may be served either by reducing input costs (for example, by accessing least-cost sources of labor and component materials) or by increasing outputs (for example, by serving new markets with appropriate product offerings).

The degree to which either of these opportunities is available distinguishes global industries from each other along the two dimensions depicted in figure 3.2. Along the horizontal axis, industries differ by the extent to which there exist benefits from differentiating a firm's products and services among the various national markets served. In the packaged food industry, for example, firms such as Nestlé gain competitive advantage by catering specifically to the different tastes and preferences of customers around the world. Nestlé's product offerings in Europe are quite different from those offered in North America, and different still from those the company markets in Asia.[37] By contrast, in an industry such as consumer electronics, product preferences are much the same the world over.

Along the vertical dimension of Prahalad and Doz's matrix, certain industries can gain efficiency benefits through the global integration of their activities, while others cannot. In the consumer electronics business, for example, companies such as Philips can benefit significantly from scale economies, and use a few very efficient sourcing points to serve world markets. Philips's decision to source all of its European automobile radio products from a new single plant located in Portugal is an example. In the packaged foods business, however, minimum efficient plant size is quite small – so there are few, if any, advantages available along this dimension, even to very large companies such as Nestlé.

In certain industries, benefits can accrue to MNCs through global integration and local responsiveness *simultaneously*. In the automobile industry, for example, product differentiation across world markets is still very much the case. Although North American auto drivers have become more value-conscious and more mindful of fuel efficiency in recent years, the average auto purchased there is still larger, and engineered very differently, compared to the the average European or Asian product. Responding to those differences in markets, while also attempting to gain global efficiency through the integration of its production and supply activities, poses a dual challenge for global automakers such as General Motors, Volkswagen, and Ford.[38] On the other hand, some industry environments offer neither possibility. For that reason, industries such as cement production remain largely domestic ones.

Configuring the multinational corporation for maximum strategic advantage

The two-dimensional model proposed by Prahalad and Doz carries with it implications for the design of global firms. If pressures for local responsiveness dominate, as in the packaged foods industry, we may assume that industry competition in each country, or region as the case may be, is essentially independent of competition in other countries or regions. In that case, according Michael E. Porter, the correct response for a MNC would be to configure its business as a multidomestic one. Under the "*pure multidomestic*" strategy, a great deal of autonomy is given to managers at the subsidiary level, so that functional strategies may be tailored to fit the conditions existing in each market. Although the MNC may benefit from transfers of know-how and infusions of capital from headquarters to its foreign locations, the firm's products and operating policies are adapted to the needs of the particular markets in which it operates. The competitive advantages of the multidomestic firm, then, are largely specific to each country, and the industry may be viewed as a collection of essentially domestic industries.[39]

On the other hand, if pressures for global integration dominate, then the appropriate response is to configure the firm as a "global" one. The definition of global as used here simply means that a firm's competitive position in one country or region is significantly affected by its strategy in others. The "*pure global*" strategy views the world as a single market, and its subsidiaries as a linked set of productive resources for serving that market. The firm's goal is to capitalize on highly centralized scale-intensive manufacturing and R&D operations, and to leverage these through worldwide exports of standardized global products.[40]

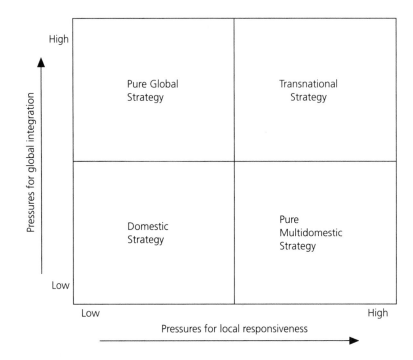

Figure 3.3 Configurations of multinational enterprises in response to pressures for national responsiveness and global integration.
Source: Adapted with permission of The Free Press, a division of Simon and Schuster from Prahalad, C. K. and Doz, Y. L., *The Multinational Mission: Balancing Local Demands and Global Vision*. New York: Free Press (1987), p. 24. Copyright © 1986 by The Free Press.

In their very popular book, *Managing Across Borders: the Transnational Solution*, Christopher Bartlett and Sumantra Ghoshal describe the ideal configuration for industries in which there are significant pressures for global integration and, simultaneously, for local responsiveness. They argue that the emergence of what they term "*transnational*" industries requires concurrent attention to global efficiency, national responsiveness, and worldwide innovation. The tasks for achieving this are, understandably, demanding and complex. Companies must build global efficiency through a worldwide infrastructure of distributed, but specialized, assets and capabilities that are directed toward exploiting comparative advantages, scale economies, and scope economies simultaneously. Unlike the purely global company, in which expertise flows directly from headquarters to the foreign subsidiaries, expertise in the transnational firm exists in the various local operations, where it has been acquired through exposure to local market conditions and operational level experience. This distributed network of expertise and other specialized assets is then coordinated through flexible linkages, to design new products, solve problems that arise, and attack new markets on a worldwide basis.[41] Figure 3.3 illustrates the position of the three MNC strategies – pure global, pure multidomestic, and transnational – as responses to pressures for globalization and pressures for local responsiveness.

"TRANSNATIONAL LINKAGES AT PROCTER & GAMBLE"

At Procter & Gamble (P&G), the story of the development of the company's global liquid laundry detergent illustrates the transnational approach, and demonstrates how flexible linkages allow the efforts of multiple organizational units around the world to be combined effectively. In 1981, P&G had launched the liquid laundry detergent "Vizir," as the company's first "Euro brand." Experience gained on that project provided core marketing and management skills needed to coordinate future cross-market campaigns. Meanwhile, researchers in the United States had discovered a way to improve "builders." Those are the ingredients in liquid laundry detergent which prevent redeposition of dirt in the wash, a problem that was especially important in the USA, where soils contain large amounts of clay. At the same time, P&G's Japanese research labs had produced liquids with superior surfactants, the ingredients which improve a detergent's ability to remove greasy stains – even in the cold water washes common to Japanese households. By 1984, each unit had developed effective responses to its local needs. When these achievements were combined through the efforts of the company's International Technology Coordination Group, the result was a single liquid laundry detergent, incorporating the best developments created in each major subsidiary, which was then offered in all three markets. The product was sold as Liquid Tide in the USA, Liquid Cheer in Japan, and Liquid Ariel in Europe.

Sources: *Bartlett, C. A., Procter and Gamble Europe: the Vizir Launch, Harvard Business School case no. 384–139; Bartlett, C. A. and Ghoshal, S., Transnational Management. Homewood, IL : Richard D. Irwin (1992), p. 649.*

In order to make the transnational approach work effectively, the MNC must be staffed with a highly trained set of specialists who develop the company's product, market, and technical expertise, and leverage them on world markets – no easy task. A *Harvard Business Review* article entitled "What is a global manager?" describes Electrolux Corporation's scheme for staffing the transnational company. Electrolux developed four distinct managerial positions, which are coordinated in the firm's matrix configuration. The interaction of the four managerial roles results in simultaneous attention being paid to the firm's product lines, its functional activities, and its markets.

- Global *business managers* are in charge of Electrolux product groups worldwide. Their overriding responsibility is to further the firm's global-scale efficiency and competitiveness.
- *Country managers* are responsible for the performance of Electrolux's national subsidiaries. Their main concern is to be sensitive and responsive to the local market.
- *Functional managers* are each given responsibility for Electrolux's technical functions across product groups and countries. Their concern is disseminating information and cross-pollinating ideas.
- *Corporate managers* at Electrolux strive to tie the other managerial roles together in the matrix. Coordinating the activities of the other three types of managers is their primary concern.[42]

Location decisions

Whatever the configuration chosen, it is important that the MNC make a proper determination of the best locations in which to locate its various activities. According to Peter Dicken, these decisions involve much more than simply the location decision as it is traditionally handled in economic geography. They include decisions about the number, size, function, and geography of all the firm's activities.[43]

Locational decisions must therefore be understood as an integral part of firms' overall strategy. While some location decisions are simply about the choice of a new location for a particular activity, most involve decisions about the reallocation of the company's resources and activities among its existing facilities as well. Dicken termed these decisions "spatial change," and described two types of spatial change: *in situ change* and *locational shift. In situ* change is the reallocation of activities and resources among existing geographically dispersed operations in a MNC. Capacities of existing operations can be increased to achieve economies, technology can be relocated to serve different activities, and the importance of locations changed within the spatial network. Locational shifts involve investment at a new location, disinvestment at an existing site, or acquisition of a facility from another firm.[44]

Locational shifts are a consideration for any MNC, regardless of whether the strategic configuration of the firm is multidomestic, global, or transnational. *In situ* change, on the other hand, would be a strategic option only for global and transnational MNCs, since that type of spatial change involves shifting resources among geographic locations.

Competitiveness in world markets: Porter's "diamond" model

The strategic location decision in the MNC has also been addressed from the perspective of attempting to identify the best countries in which to locate activities. In his best-selling book, *The Competitive Advantage of Nations*, Michael E. Porter examined the conditions which contribute to the competitiveness of industries in the world's ten leading economies. The fifty leading industries of each nation were studied to determine the conditions that led to their success. In constructing their study, Porter and his team of researchers challenged the accepted logic of international economics, which held that the availability of production factors is the primary determinant of an industry's competitiveness on world markets. Porter cited four factors that, together, determine the success of a nation's products in world competition.

Factor conditions. The availability of production factors, as economics suggests, does play an important role, but its importance has been exaggerated. If factor conditions alone determined competitiveness, then Japan, with its lack of energy resources and an economy that was devastated at the end of the Second World War, might never have been able to develop into the economic superpower of the 1980s. Porter points out that factors are not simply "givens," they can also be developed. The manner in which the Netherlands has created special factors to produce flowers and Italy to produce specialty steel manufacturing are prime examples. Factor substitution is also an important consideration. The USA and Germany have developed factory automation in response to high labor costs in their countries.

Demand conditions. The existence of strong local demand builds and shapes industries on the home front, which in turn prepares them for international competition. Japan, for example, has the world's most demanding consumers of electronics. This makes its home market perfect for testing new ideas. Automobile

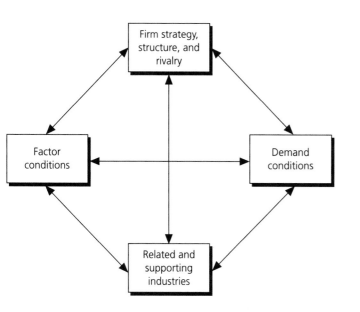

Figure 3.4 The determinants of national advantage.
Source: Reprinted with the permission of The Free Press, a division of Simon and Schuster, from Porter, M. E., *The Competitive Advantage of Nations*. New York: Free Press (1990), p. 72. Copyright © 1990 by Michael E. Porter.

buyers in the USA are very receptive to new ideas, and are especially safety conscious. This makes the USA a good place to produce and test such innovations as anti-lock braking systems.

Related and supporting industries. Porter's research also indicated that when suppliers of essential inputs are based in the home country, the entire industry becomes stronger, and therefore more likely to be successful in world markets. For example, the existence of a strong steel industry in Japan contributes to making the industrial machinery business better. Leather processors in Italy, arguably the world's best, are responsible for much of the success of the Italian shoe industry. In the USA, so-called "knowledge industries," such as the computer software business, are supplied talent by some of the world's leading universities. Suppliers can also be a valuable source of information about innovations, and about competitors. For this reason, Porter argues that the practice of using "captive suppliers" can hurt a company's competitiveness in the long run.

Firm strategy, structure and rivalry. A "fit" between the firm's management and the national characteristics of its home market (i.e. cultural fit) is essential. Industries which require "patient capital" do better in Japan than in the USA, while risk-taking is more likely to be rewarded in the USA. Structure also plays a role. Often the size of a firm is better suited to some countries than to others. Germany, for example, is a country in which small firms tend to do well. Porter also notes that successful firms "cluster" in countries where conditions are favorable. This suggests that industry leaders derive advantages from each other through healthy rivalry. Figure 3.4 depicts the four aspects of Porter's competitiveness model, and the interactions among them.

▌ Summary ▌

Throughout the 1980s and early 1990s, international strategic management has seen a meteoric rise in its importance to the competitive firm. Although many factors have contributed to this, the convergence of world markets and the intensified search for efficiency have been primary contributors. Aided by technological improvements in mass communications, firms have sought out new world markets and the newly affluent consumer. The prevalence of global sourcing and direct investment in production facilities abroad have also increased dramatically.

Distinguishing international strategic decisions from domestic ones are the necessity of dealing with multiple sources of authority, and the necessity of risking the firm's assets through multiple denominations of value. Four prototypical strategic orientations may be observed which affect the choice of strategic alternatives: ethnocentric, polycentric, geocentric, and regiocentric.

Strategic alternatives available to the multinational corporation range from minimal involvement via export – import strategies, which risk little, to very risky, but more profitable, foreign direct investments. Among the fastest growing strategic alternatives are strategic alliances – collaborations without equity, cash-neutral exchanges of assets, equity ownership arrangements, and joint ventures.

The choice among international strategies may be described as seeking to achieve three basic goals (achieving efficiency, managing risk, and exploiting learning) by applying three fundamental tools on a global basis (national differences, scale economies, and scope economies). Configurations of international industries may be seen as responses to varying levels of pressure for local responsiveness and for global integration.

In response to significant pressure for local responsiveness, the MNC may take on the characteristics of the "pure multidomestic" business, in which national subsidiaries conduct their own strategies. In response to heavy pressure for global integration, the international firm takes on a "pure global" strategy, in which its entire set of international subsidiaries act on a single, integrated world strategy. When both pressures are present to a significant degree, the MNC takes on the characteristics of the "transnational" firm, in which global strategies are enacted, but are implemented with local adaptations.

Competitiveness of national industries in world markets may be viewed as the result of the interaction of four sets of forces. Factor conditions in the home market predispose the country and its industries toward certain sets of activities. Demand conditions in the home market strengthen domestic business in preparation for international competition. Related and supporting industries provide strategic partners and critical sources of information. Finally, the strategies, structures, and rivalry among firms provide appropriate fit for competing abroad.

DISCUSSION QUESTIONS

1 Discuss the phenomenal growth of international strategies in recent years. What major factors have contributed to internationalization?

2 Do you agree or disagree with the following statement? "International strategy is no different from domestic strategy, it is simply the same decisions made across a larger geographic area." Explain.

3 Compare and contrast the four prototypical international strategic dispositions – ethnocentric, polycentric, geocentric, and regiocentric.

4 What are the advantages and disadvantages of engaging in foreign direct investments, versus other less involved strategies, such as export – import or licensing?

5 What factors explain the rapid increase in the use of strategic alliances in international strategy, and the international joint venture in particular?

6 Using Bartlett and Ghoshal's "goals and means" model (table 3.2), give an example of an international activity to fit each of the nine cells.

7 Choose a well-known industry associated with its country of origin, such as Japanese consumer electronics, US computer software, or German luxury automobiles. Explain the industry's success using aspects of Porter's "diamond" model of national competitiveness.

KEY TERMS

Foreign direct investment.	A strategy which gives the investing firm a controlling interest in a foreign subsidiary.
Foreign portfolio investment.	A strategy which gives the investing business either a minority ownership position in a foreign company or minority ownership of its outstanding obligations.
Global sourcing.	A production strategy which depends on the importation of raw materials and/or component assemblies.
***In situ* change.**	The reallocation of activities and resources among existing geographically dispersed operations in a MNC.
International franchise agreement.	The conveyance of rights to an international trademark, accompanied by assistance in the operation of the business.
International licensing agreement.	The sale of rights to intangible assets such as patents, copyrights, or trademarks.
International management contract.	An agreement whereby a MNC provides personnel to perform either general or specialized management functions, for a fee, in a foreign country.
International turnkey operation.	A project performed under contract to deliver a finished facility, ready to begin operation, in a foreign country.
International strategic alliance.	Any one of a number of strategies whereby a MNC cooperates with one or more foreign partner firms. The types are: *collaboration without equity*, loose associations of firms, usually for a single purpose; *cash-neutral exchange of assets*, agreement to trade assets, usually technological products or product rights, between companies; *equity ownership arrangement*, mutual exchange of ownership shares between companies; *joint venture*, an agreement whereby a new firm is created, jointly owned by international partners.

Invisibles.

Another term for service imports and exports. So called because of their often intangible nature.

Locational shifts.

Investment at a new location, disinvestment at an existing site, or acquisition of a facility from another firm.

Multinational corporation (MNC).

A corporation which conducts a significant percentage of its business outside its home country.

Multiple denominations of value

refer to the fact that the MNC's revenues, assets, and cash flows are subject to exchange rate exposure.

Multiple sources of authority

refers to fact that the MNC operates in an environment that is subject to conflicts among laws, political institutions, official languages, norms of behavior, and customs.

Pure global strategy.

Prototypical international strategy in which the MNC's subsidiary operations are treated as parts of an integrated system, with each subsidiary contributing to a single global strategy formulated and executed by headquarters.

Pure multidomestic strategy.

Prototypical international strategy in which the MNC's subsidiary operations are treated as independent strategic units.

Strategic disposition (orientation).

The predisposition of strategic decision makers toward international activities. The four prototypes are: *ethnocentric*, in which the values and interests of the parent company and home country dominate decision processes; *polycentric*, in which the values and interests of the subsidiary and host country dominate decision processes; *geocentric*, in which the MNC's operations are viewed as parts of an overall global system; and *regiocentric*, in which the MNC's operations are viewed as consisting of several regional systems.

Transnational strategy.

Prototypical international strategy in which the MNC's subsidiaries are treated as a distributed network composed of centers of expertise, and strategy is executed as flexible responses to conditions arising out of the global web.

QUALITY CASE

IKEA Redefines the Value-creation Process

Customers entering an IKEA store for the first time know immediately that something is different. Instead of the typical displays found in other furniture outlets, IKEA stores feature a carefully laid-out "script" that carries customers from one setting to another, illustrating the role that IKEA furniture can play in improving one's home and life. To its over 96 million devoted customers worldwide, shopping in one of IKEA's giant 20,000 square-meter stores is a form of entertainment. There are in-store coffee shops, playrooms where toddlers may be dropped off, and even restaurants where a family can have lunch while making decisions. Although stores are designed to make furniture buying fun, IKEA's purpose is serious one – to create an organization that reinvents value and a business system that delivers quality through an entire cast of economic actors.

In less than two decades, IKEA has been transformed from a small Swedish mail-order company into the world's first and largest global home furnishing business. In 1992, IKEA's store network contained over 100 outlets, which generated revenues of US$4.3 billion, and an average annual growth rate of 15 percent. The key elements of IKEA's winning formula have been well publicized: simple yet high-quality Scandinavian-designed products, prices anywhere from 25 to 50 percent below its competitors, the "family outing" atmosphere of its stores, global sourcing of components, and knock-down kits that allow customers to transport and assemble their own purchases. Behind these visible elements of a winning global strategy, however, lie a philosophy of value creation that is unique.

IKEA is able to keep costs and prices down because the company has found ways to redefine the roles and relationships of every participant in the value-added chain. The result is a strategy that focuses on quality at every turn. Customers, by assembling and transporting their own furniture, become *participants* in the value-creation process rather than consumers of value. IKEA management sees its role as assisting in this value-creation process, not only by "scripting" the customer's new role, but also by making it easier for the customer to assume the role. Catalogs and in-store assistants carefully detail the assembly process, and free car-top racks are available at every IKEA location. The result? IKEA's customer receives a level of quality that is not available elsewhere, let alone at IKEA's prices.

Quality considerations at IKEA actually begin long before the customer arrives in the store. Management has found unique ways of bringing suppliers into the value-creation process as well. Through its thirty buying offices located around the world, IKEA takes enormous care in finding, evaluating, and developing suppliers. The result is a dedicated network of over 1,800 suppliers located in more than fifty countries. Once suppliers become part of IKEA's system, they receive regular technical assistance, leased equipment, and advice on bringing their products up to IKEA's exacting world-quality standards and keeping them there. Instead of viewing suppliers simply as providers of standardized parts, IKEA sees its relationship to them as one of providing the means for suppliers to create value for themselves. By reinventing the role of suppliers, IKEA is able to systematically reduce the delivered cost of high quality products throughout its global system.

IKEA views its enormous network of warehouses differently, too. Its 14 world distribution centers, the largest of which is over 135,000 square meters, operate as logistical control points employing the latest systems of stock consolidation and transport planning. Taking the burden of stock checking and reordering off local managers, this system allows the store manager to concentrate on facilitating the value-creation process at the store level through improved customer service.

Supporting all of this is also a unique view of the company's structure. IKEA's founder, Ingvar Kamprad, describes the structure as a "reverse pyramid," in which customers stand on the top step, served by local stores, which in turn are served by regional headquarters, and finally by headquarters. That is why the company has no titles and no perks for executives. According to Kamprar, IKEA engages in cooperative adaptation to its markets and customers. The company's purpose, ultimately, is all about learning.

Discussion Questions

1   How does IKEA's approach to shopping for furniture compare with its competitors'? In what way does this account for the company's success?

2   How does "reinventing" the roles of customer and supplier contribute to the creation of value and, ultimately, higher quality at IKEA?

3   Analyze the statement that the company's purpose is "all about learning." What role do you think this played in IKEA's becoming the world's largest furniture retailer?

Sources: Normann, R. and Ramirez, R., "From to value constellation: Designing interactive strategy," *Harvard Business Review* (July–August 1993), pp. 65–77. Bartlett, C. A. and Nanda, A., Ingvar Kamprad and IKEA, Harvard Business School Case no. 390–132. Sasporito, B., "IKEA's got 'em lining up," *Fortune* (March 11, 1991), p. 72. Burton, J., "Rearranging the furniture," *International Management* (September 1991), pp. 58–61.

BMW USA

The announcement, in the summer of 1992, by Bayerische Motoren Werke (BMW) came as a shock to many in the automotive industry. That BMW would locate its newest plant outside its native Germany was unthinkable. Moreover, the location chosen was to be in the southern United States, near Spartanburg, South Carolina. BMW in South Carolina? How could BMW manufacture its line of luxury cars there and preserve the legendary BMW quality?

As BMW revealed more about its plan to build the 1.9 million square-foot (180,000 square-meter) factory, the logic seemed clearer. BMW's products had sold well in the USA for nearly a decade, with unit sales surpassing those of its arch-rival, Mercedes-Benz, for the first time in 1991. Sales of luxury cars in the USA were predicted to increase from 1.25 million units in 1992 to over 1.5 million by 1995. Competition in this market was getting tougher, however. Toyota's Lexus and Nissan's Infinity models were capturing a large share of the market that had previously gone to the two German rivals. Prices for all foreign-made autos were rising rapidly as the US dollar's value fell. To make matters worse, a new luxury tax added US$187 million per year to German car prices.

According to its CEO, Eberhard von Kuenheim, BMW's aim was "to maintain, secure, and build up" its position in the US luxury car market. The United States plant would be a key element in this strategy. The South Carolina site would be the sole plant producing a new model based on BMW's hot-selling 3-Series compact cars. The new car, which would sell for around $22,000, would be designed especially for the North American driver, and cost savings were a key to making the new model competitive. By producing cars in the USA instead of in Germany, the company would save approximately $2,500 in shipping costs per automobile. Its manufacturing costs were expected to be between $2,000 and $3,000 lower in South Carolina. According to Corporate Planning Director Helmut Panke, a major component of the manufacturing cost reduction would be lower labor costs. Average wages for the 2,000 or so young American workers that BMW expected to hire would be one-third lower than at BMW's plants in Germany, where workers were paid $28 per hour, including fringe benefits. Other cost savings would ensue from a generous incentives offered to BMW by the state of South Carolina. The state's offer included income tax credits, assistance in purchasing the 900-acre (365-hectare) tract of land, funding of site preparation costs and road building, plus picking up the tab for training workers – in all, a package estimated at nearly $135 million. The factory would make 30,000 autos per year initially, on an investment of $400 million. BMW's plans included eventual expansion of the plant investment to $640 million to turn out over 70,000 BMWs per year.

Still, the quality question lingered. Could BMW expect to achieve the level of product quality in South Carolina that had become synonymous with the company's name? The last time a German automaker had attempted to produce cars in America, the result had been a disaster. Volkswagen's Westmoreland, Pennsylvania, Rabbit plant closed in 1987, after losing over $1.5 billion. Members of the press doubted that BMW could fare much better. A *Newsday* business columnist compared the move to a US manufacturer fleeing to Mexico, and predicted that the company would never achieve its quality goals in the the USA.

BMW officials admitted that the venture was risky, but they had a well thought-out plan for ensuring that quality goals were met. American workers were sent to Germany to observe BMW production processes first-hand, and to soak up some the company's rich quality-oriented culture. When production finally began in South Carolina in 1994, the first cars were assembled using mainly German parts. As the initial kinks were worked out of the production process, BMW gradually began increasing the US-made content of the cars coming from the plant. Within a year's time, quality goals had been met. BMW announced, in the summer of 1995, that an independent audit of the company's products had pronounced the US BMWs equal in quality to those produced in Germany. The company's confidence in its US subsidiary was confirmed in the fall of 1995, when it was announced that the South Carolina plant would be the sole production site for BMW's newest model, the Z-3 roadster, which was featured in the James Bond movie *Goldeneye*.

Discussion Questions

1 To what extent does BMW's international strategy typify a global, multidomestic, or transnational type? Explain.

2 How would you assess BMW's chances of competing successfully in the US luxury car market? Would your assessment be different if the quality issue had not been resolved?

3 As BMW devised its strategy for competing in the US luxury car market, what other options were available to it, other than the decision to build a US factory? Why was the US plant option the one chosen?

Sources: Walechia K., Could anything be finah than to be in Carolina?" *Business Week* (June 1 1992), pp. 33–4; Templeton, J. and Woodruff, D., "The Beemer spotlight falls on Spartanburg, USA," *Business Week* (July 6 1992), p. 38; Davis, M., "Europe loves Dixie: BMW's move into South Carolina highlights region's Eurosuccess," *Europe* (October 1992), pp. 30–6; Brooke, L., "Carolina motor works," *Automotive Industries* (January 1994), pp. 44–6; "BMW introduces the Z-3 roadster." *The Greenville News* (Greenville, South Carolina) (October 14, 1995), pp. 1A.

NOTES

1 Jacob, R., "The big rise: middle classes explode around the globe, bringing new markets and prosperity," *Fortune* (May 30, 1994), pp. 74–90.

2 Dicken, P., *Global Shift: Industrial Change in a Turbulent World*. London: Harper and Row (1986).

3 Fleet, L. A. "BMW: measuring the cost," *The Greenville News* (May 3, 1992), p. 1A.

4 Herbert, T. T., "Strategy and multinational organization structure: an interorganizational relationships perspective," *Academy of Management Review*, 9 (1984), pp. 259–71.

5 Kogut, Bruce. Normative observations on the international value-added chain and strategic groups," *Journal of International Business Studies*, 15(2) (1984), pp. 151–67.

6 Miller, K. D. "A framework for integrated risk management in international business," *Journal of International Business Studies*, 23 (1992), pp. 311–31.

7 Sundaraman, A. K. and Black, J. S., "The environment and internal organization of multinational enterprises," *Academy of Management Review*, 17 (1992), pp. 729–57.

8 Chakravarthy, B. S. and Perlmutter, H. V., "Strategic planning for a global business," *Columbia Journal of World Business* (Summer, 1985), pp. 3–10.

9 Perlmutter, H. V., "The tortuous evolution of the multinational corporation," *Columbia Journal of World Business*, January–February (1969), pp. 9–18.

10 Sonoco Products Company, Annual Report for 1994, p. 4.

11 "Ford world car won't replace Tempo," *Ward's Auto World*, 29 (February 1993), p. 10.

12 Chakravarthy and Perlmutter, p. 5.

13 "Call it worldpool," *Business Week* (November 28, 1994), p. 98.

14 Chakravarthy and Perlmutter, p. 7.

15 International Monetary Fund, *Direction of Trade Statistics Yearbook* (1993), p. 9.

16 "US MNCs increase global sourcing despite contrary trends," *Business International* (September 21, 1987), p. 302.

17 Boskin, M. J. "Pass GATT now," *Fortune* (December 12, 1994), pp. 137–8.

18 Kraar, L., "The risks are rising in China," *Fortune* (March 6, 1995), pp. 179–80.

19 Welch, L. S., "Developments in international franchising," *Journal of Global Marketing*, 6(1/2) (1992), pp. 81–96.

20 Daniels, J. B. and Radebaugh, L. H., *International Business: Environments and Operations*, 7th edn. Reading, MA: Addison-Wesley (1995), p. 18.

21 United Nations Conference on Trade and Development, Programme on Transnational

NOTES CONT.

Corporations, *World Development Report, 1993: an Executive Summary*. New York: United Nations (1993), pp. 1–4.

22 "The Global 500," *Fortune* (July 25, 1994), pp. 137–96.

23 Sherman, S., "Are strategic alliances working?" *Fortune* (September 21, 1991), pp. 77–8.

24 Phatak, A. V., *International Dimensions of Management*, 3rd edn. Boston, MA: PWS-Kent (1992), p. 105.

25 Muller, J., "Ford – Mazda alliance seen as forerunner for future of industry," *Detroit Free Press* (February 20, 1994), p. 2A.

26 Selwyn, M., "Making marriages of convenience," *Asian Business* (January 1991), p. 26.

27 Greenhouse, S., "There's no stopping Europe's Airbus now," *New York Times* (June 23, 1991), sec. 3, pp. 1, 6.

28 Levine, J. B. and Schares, G. E.,. "IBM Europe starts swinging back," *Business Week* (May 6, 1991), pp. 52–3.

29 Main, J., "Making global alliances work," *Fortune* (December 17, 1990), p. 124.

30 Daniels, J. D. and Radebaugh, L. H., "PepsiCo in India," *International Business: Environments and Operations*, 7th edn. Reading, MA: Addison-Wesley (1994), p. 482.

31 Ohmae, K., "The global logic of strategic alliances," *Harvard Business Review* (March–April 1989), pp. 143–54.

32 Bartlett, C. A. and Ghoshal, S., *Transnational Management*. Homewood, IL: Richard D. Irwin (1992), pp. 272–92.

33 Ghoshal, S., "Global strategy: an organizing framework," *Strategic Management Journal*, 8 (1987), pp. 425–40.

34 Bartlett and Ghoshal, *Transnational Management*, p. 273.

35 Bartlett and Ghoshal, *Transnational Management*, p. 278.

36 Prahalad, C. K. and Doz, Y., *The Multinational Mission*. New York: Free Press (1988).

37 Quelch, J. A. and Hoff, E. J., "Customizing global marketing, *Harvard Business Review* (May–June 1986), pp. 59–68.

38 Taylor, A. III, "New ideas from Europe's automakers," *Fortune* (December 22, 1994), pp. 159–72.

39 Porter, M. E., "Changing patterns of international competition," *California Management Review*, 28(2) (1986), pp. 9–40.

40 Barlett and Ghoshal, *Transnational Management*, p. 116.

41 Bartlett, C. A. and Ghoshal, S., *Managing Across Borders: the Transnational Solution*. Boston, MA: Harvard Business School Press (1991).

42 Bartlett, C. A. and Ghoshal, S., "What is a global manager?" *Harvard Business Review* (September–October 1992), pp. 124–32.

43 Dicken, P., *Global Shift*, p. 318.

44 Dicken, P., *Global Shift*, p. 318.

4

FOUR

BUSINESS ETHICS AND CORPORATE SOCIAL RESPONSIBILITY

ETHICS, ORGANIZATIONAL PROCESSES, AND MANAGEMENT
Concept of ethics
Ethics and organizational processes
Ethics bases for managers
Which ethics base?
International ethics

THE CORPORATE SOCIAL RESPONSIBILITY DEBATE
International corporate social responsibility
International Exhibit: The Body Shop: Trade – Not Aid
Liberal corporate social responsibility
Conservative corporate social responsibility
Corporate social responsibility positions

MULTIPLE STAKEHOLDER VIEW
Equity stake
Economic stake

Influencer stake
A stakeholder grid
Stakeholder conflict and total quality

INFLUENCES ON CORPORATE SOCIAL RESPONSIBILITY
Government and regulatory influences
Ethical influences
Societal influences
Competitive influences

SUMMARY

DISCUSSION QUESTIONS

KEY TERMS

QUALITY CASE: JOHNSON & JOHNSON RECALLS TYLENOL

INTERNATIONAL CASE: ROUSSEL-UCLAF AND RU-486

NOTES

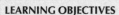

LEARNING OBJECTIVES

After reading this chapter, you should be able to accomplish the following.

1 *Discuss the implications of the definition of ethics, i.e. doing the right thing right the first time, for managerial decisions and behavior.*

2 *Compare and contrast the five different managerial ethics bases.*

3 *Discuss the arguments for a liberal corporate social responsibility on the part of managers.*

4 *Discuss the arguments for a conservative corporate social responsibility on the part of managers.*

5 *Describe the various positions a firm's managers might take on corporate social responsibility issues.*

6 *Compare and contrast the three different kinds of stakeholder interest in corporations.*

7 *Describe the relative importance of the government, ethical, societal, and competitive influences operating to shape corporate social responsibility decisions.*

The subjects of business ethics and managerial ethical decision making have received much attention in organizations lately. A recent survey of ethics practices in business revealed that 45 percent of firms have enacted ethics codes since 1987. More than 80 percent of US firms had ethics codes in the early 1990s.[1]

Ethics, Organizational Processes, and Management

There has been an increasing number of cases of managers and the organizations they represent acting in highly publicized, unethical, yet legal ways. There are also other cases in which managers have acted in highly visible, ethical, and admirable ways, as did the managers at Johnson & Johnson in the Tylenol recall (see quality case at the end of this chapter). This chapter explores the different approaches to dealing with ethical decisions for managers and then broadens the discussion to the larger issue of corporate social responsibility.

Concept of ethics

Ethics is defined as doing the right thing right the first time. This concise definition underscores the importance of describing what is the "right thing." If there were not disagreements on what is the "right thing," then the issue of ethical behavior by managers would be far less controversial.

It is difficult to describe what is the right thing because there are so many different bases of ethics. A different base of ethics may give a different answer in a given situation. Later in this chapter we review five primary ethics bases for managers.

Some equate an individual's sense of ethics to conscience. Since individual conscience is associated with one's religion and upbringing, it is easy to see why ethics means different things to different people.

Decisions involving ethics usually occur in the context that someone will be hurt or harmed in some way by the decision. Is it ethical to shut down a plant that is the lifeblood of a company town? Is it ethical to fire someone who has worked for a company for many years and is near retirement? These are but two of the ethical questions posed in business involving harm to someone.

Those few situations in which all bases of ethics produce the same answer are usually the easy questions that all agree upon. Is it ethical to continue to market a product that is known only by its producers to kill or mutilate its users? Prior to reviewing the ethics bases, it is important to understand the rest of the definition of ethics concerning doing the right thing right the first time.

Ethics and organizational processes

There is a close link between total quality management and managerial ethics.[2] TQM is concerned with the continuous improvement of organizational processes and systems to prevent defects. Nearly all organizations claim that they wish their managers to act ethically in deciding business issues. Therefore, unethical managerial behavior can be described as a result of a defect in an organizational system or process.[3]

The defect may be in terms of inadequate training for the manager, in which the organization glossed over the importance of ethical decisions. This indicates that the training system needs to be improved. There may be conflicting signals from the reward system, in which short-term profits are stressed over all else. Thus, the reward system needs to be clarified. Once the organizational processes are aligned, then managers may be predisposed to do the right thing right the first time.

Managers assume responsibility for the ethical conduct of their employees and their organization. This issue is receiving increased attention due in part to some highly publicized ethics cases. To communicate the importance of ethical decisions to managers, many organizations have published codes of ethics. McDonnell Douglas offers a code of ethics and an ethical decision-making checklist.[4]

Ethics bases for managers

Ethics questions would be easy to decide if all questions could be decided with the same ethics base. The five different bases reviewed show how different answers are possible to an ethical dilemma depending on which ethics base the manager is using.[5]

Eternal Law (rule-based ethics)

The *Eternal Law* approach to ethics holds that there is a common set of moral standards apparent in Nature or revealed in the Holy Scripture. This set of moral standards should be obvious to anyone who takes the time to study either Nature or the Scripture. Everyone should act in accordance with the common set of standards (Eternal Law). Some refer to the Eternal Law as "rule-based ethics" because it holds that one should adopt a set of general rules, or principles, that guide one's actions.[6]

Apparently, Thomas Jefferson was influenced by the Eternal Law in the framing of the Declaration of Independence in the United States in 1776. He wrote that certain truths were "self-evident," and that certain rights were "inalienable," including the rights to "life, liberty, and the pursuit of happiness." Another good example of the Eternal Law is the Golden Rule: "Do unto others as you would have others do unto you."

Religion is associated with the Eternal Law. Frequently, religious leaders interpret the eternal truths in Scripture. However, not all subscribe to the same religious leaders. A disadvantage of the Eternal Law is that few individuals or religious leaders interpret Nature or Scripture in the same way. Today, many do not accept Scripture. There is no commonly accepted way to choose among the different interpretations. Therefore, one interpretation of the Eternal Law that guides one's actions may be different from another interpretation of the Eternal Law that guides another's actions.

Utilitarianism

Utilitarianism, or the utilitarian principle, means that a manager should act in ways to create the greatest benefits for the largest number of people. Utilitarianism arises from *teleological theory*, which stresses the outcome, not the intent, of managerial actions. Teleology comes from the Greek word which means outcome or result. Thus, a managerial decision is "right" if it results in benefits for others, and the decision is "wrong" if results in damage or harm to others.

If following the utilitarian principle, a manager should be aware of the benefits and damages of a managerial action, like closing a plant. If literally followed, the utilitarian principle would suggest seizing the assets of the few wealthy people who own Rolls-Royce autos and distributing those assets to large numbers of impoverished individuals. Herein lies the biggest drawback with utilitarianism – the possibility of exploitation. The possibility exists of justifying benefits for the great majority of the population by extracting sacrifices from a small minority. This is the ethical fallacy in the "soak the rich" tax schemes that sometimes spring up in politics.

Universalism

Universalism holds that the ethics of a decision depends on the motives or intentions of the decision maker. Universalism arises from deontological theory, which is the opposite of teleological theory. Deontology is derived from another Greek word that means the duties or obligations of the individual. Thus, personal intentions or personal motives can be translated into personal duties or obligations because all would behave in the same universal fashion given the same situation.

A manager who scrupulously adhered to terms of a contract may have done so because the manager believed in the sanctity of contracts. Such a belief in the sanctity of contracts is consistent with universalism.

A disadvantage of universalism is the problem with objective interpretation. Persons subject to self-deception, or beliefs of self-grandeur, can justify unethical decisions by referring to their "lofty" motives. When distributing products with many defects in the market, a manager might argue that the company was trying to keep the price of the products low. In truth, the manager may have been covering up a shoddy management system.

Utilitarianism and universalism are the two most popular ethical bases for managers. However, those two theories cannot be used to judge all ethical issues in all circumstances. Thus, the next two ethical bases have been developed more on the bases of values, than on the bases of principles.

Distributive justice

Distributive justice is based upon the primacy of the single value of justice. According to the idea of distributive justice, managers should act to ensure a more equitable distribution of benefits. This is assumed to be essential for social cooperation. The manager who attempted to hire the largest number of people to distribute salaries widely would be acting in accord with the idea of distributive justice.

An obvious problem with distributive justice is the basis of the distribution of benefits. Should benefits be distributed in accordance with needs, or in accordance with accomplishments? Since social cooperation, needs, and equity are highlighted, a problem is that individual effort, risk taking, incentives, and achievement are downplayed.

Personal liberty

Personal liberty is based upon the primacy of the single value of liberty. A managerial decision that violates individual liberty, even if it results in greater benefits for others, is not consistent with the idea of personal liberty. It is based upon equal opportunities for individual choice and exchange, not upon equal distributions of benefits. A pay system that pays individuals in accordance with their own choices of how hard to work is consistent with the idea of personal liberty.

A problem with personal liberty is that it does not insure some minimum level of existence if the individual is not capable of working. Personal liberty assumes that others will voluntarily provide for the incapacitated individual through charity.

Which ethics base?

There does not appear to be a single ethics base, with standards for managerial decisions and actions, that can guide managers in all situations. A proposed ethical decision must be analyzed with the multiple ethics bases to see how it holds up under the scrutiny of the multiple approaches. Only after informed thought and analyses relative to the different ethics bases can the manager make rational and

es decisions concerning ethics
different ethics standards in
ational manager's decisions

ght the first time, it is hard for
w what is the right thing, as
ifts or gratuities are expected
t prohibits such actions for US
by the realization that some
ards being forced on them.[8] In
ating in another culture must
it culture.

ent international cultures,
rading on insider information
on. "You have just come from the secret meeting of the board of directors of a company. You have a close friend who will be ruined unless she can get out of the market before the board's decision becomes known. You happen to be having dinner at the friend's home this evening. What right does your friend have to expect you to tip her off? 1a She has a definite right as a friend to expect me to tip her off. 1b She has some right as a friend to expect me to tip her off. 1c She has no right as a friend to expect me to tip her off. Would you tip her off in view of your obligations to the company and your obligation to your friend? 1d Yes. 1e No."[9]

Respondents from nearly forty different countries provided the answers reproduced in figure 4.1. These data underscore the idea that ethics means different things to different people, and ethics means different things to different cultures. Some countries have laws against trading on insider information and some countries do not.

Since we posed the question "which ethics base?", it may be instructive to

Percentage of respondents who would not tip off a friend or gives him or her no right (answers c or b+e)

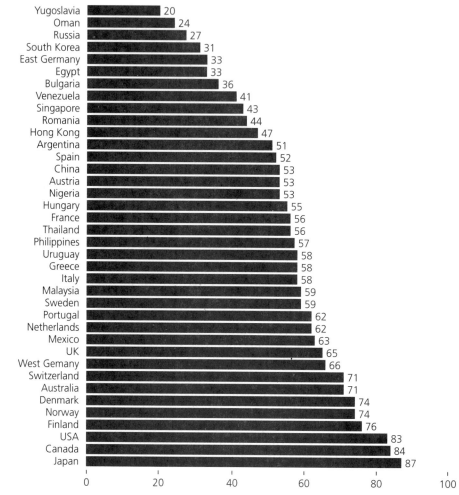

Country	Value
Yugoslavia	20
Oman	24
Russia	27
South Korea	31
East Germany	33
Egypt	33
Bulgaria	36
Venezuela	41
Singapore	43
Romania	44
Hong Kong	47
Argentina	51
Spain	52
China	53
Austria	53
Nigeria	53
Hungary	55
France	56
Thailand	56
Philippines	57
Uruguay	58
Greece	58
Italy	58
Malaysia	59
Sweden	59
Portugal	62
Netherlands	62
Mexico	63
UK	65
West Gemany	66
Switzerland	71
Australia	71
Denmark	74
Norway	74
Finland	76
USA	83
Canada	84
Japan	87

Figure 4.1 Insider information.

Source: Trompenaars, F., *Riding the Waves of Culture: Understanding Cultural Diversity in Business*. London: Economist Books (1993), p. 39.

analyze this situation from the five different ethics bases. In this analysis, we assume a country in which there is a law against divulging insider information. The Eternal Law base suggests relying on the Golden Rule, "Do unto others as you would have others do unto you," and tip off the friend. The utilitarian principle suggests that it is OK to tip off the friend, since you are providing a benefit to her without harming others. If the motive in tipping off the friend is to win favor with her, then universalism suggests that it would be unethical to tip her off. Alternatively, if the only motive was altruistic, based on a genuine desire to protect her from harm, then universalism suggests that it would be OK to tip her off. Distributive justice suggests that it is not ethical to tip off the friend since only one person benefits. Personal liberty suggests that it is ethical to tip off the friend since such behavior allows for her individual choice to escape from a potentially ruinous financial situation. As indicated, different ethical bases provide different answers even within the same country. Involving different cultures and different ethical bases can yield exasperating dilemmas.

The Corporate Social Responsibility Debate

There are different ways for a manager to make a decision. The manager may use economic analysis, legal analysis, or ethics analysis.[10] The preceding section shows the number of different ethics bases for the manager to consider when trying to decide on doing the right thing right the first time. Now the question needs to be addressed of how the manager combines the economic, legal and ethics analyses to make decisions that benefit society.

Corporate social responsibility refers to the obligation of the firm to use its resources in ways to benefit society. This is sometimes known as a social action program, social policy, and community responsiveness. There is considerable debate concerning how managers and firms should fulfill that responsibility. This section reviews the various arguments in the debate.[11]

International corporate social responsibility

There are different assumptions in various parts of the world concerning the corporate social responsibility of companies. As the European Union consists of several different countries, the Commission of the European Communities has been leading the effort to articulate the options and define a European Social Policy.[12] Although some member countries have well developed social policies, others have questioned the relationship with economic growth.

The Body Shop, a British retailer specializing in bath items, sources products from countries all over the world. Partly to improve the existence of the people in those countries, the Body Shop prefers to source directly from the people in those countries as the international exhibit indicates.

INTERNATIONAL EXHIBIT

THE BODY SHOP: TRADE – NOT AID

The Body Shop believes that direct sourcing – purchasing ingredients and products to sell in our stores – in the developing world can help relieve economic pressures on communities in need. Rather than foster their dependence on charity, we prefer to provide sustainable trade which helps these communities support themselves by earning an income.

Trade Not Aid is our umbrella title for sourcing ingredients and products directly from the producers. All Trade Not Aid projects should be commercially viable and encourage a long-term trading relationship. They are built on mutual benefit and trust rather than the demoralizing feeling of dependence which can characterize traditional aid programs. Although direct sourcing is currently a small percentage of our trade, we intend to increase this practice whenever possible.

Source: *The Body Shop, Wake Forest, NC, USA.*

Liberal corporate social responsibility

Many arguments in favor of liberal corporate social responsibility start by reviewing the role of business in society. Some argue that there are three primary reasons why business should voluntarily assume a liberal corporate social responsibility.[13]

First, society expects it. This argument holds that since firms are creatures of society, they have an obligation to return something to their creators. If the firms do not fulfill those obligations to the society that created them, then that society will place restrictions on their power.

Second, businesses' long-term self-interests are best served when those responsibilities are fulfilled. This "enlightened self-interest" stance is a long-term view of profitability. It argues that firms with such a stance have a competitive advantage in the long term through greater appeal to customers, and lower long-term costs by doing things right the first time.[14] This argument also holds that individuals with healthy physical environments, good educations, reasonable incomes, and secure jobs make better employees and customers than those who are poor or ignorant.[15]

Third, the firm will avoid future government regulation. Much of the current regulation of business has arisen from complaints over past business practices. For example, complaints in the 1970s over pollution of the environment led to the establishment of the US Environmental Protection Agency. This argument holds that a proactive stance by business will prevent the establishment of future burdensome regulations and entire regulatory agencies by government. There will be costs to proactively push new forms of corporate social responsibility before it is demanded by the government. However, it is generally less expensive to implement programs unhampered by government restrictions than to react to government restrictions.

Conservative corporate social responsibility

Many managers counter that the most socially responsible action a company can engage in is to maximize its profits legally. This more conservative view is founded on four ideas.

First, profit maximization is the only legitimate purpose of business in capitalism. In capitalism, managers are hired by owners and stockholders solely to maximize profits. Milton Friedman, the Nobel Prize winning economist, forcefully expressed this view and tied it into the role of capitalism in a free society. "There is one and only one social responsibility of business – to use its resources and engage in activities designed to increase its profits so long as it stays within the rules of the game. Few trends could so thoroughly undermine the very foundations of our free society as the acceptance by corporate officials of a social responsibility other than to make as much money for their stockholders as possible."[16]

Second, social responsibility subverts the market system. When firms pursue social action programs, they incur costs that must eventually be passed on to consumers. Friedman argues that the allocative mechanism of price in the marketplace will then be distorted because of the added social costs.[17] Then some goods will be artificially priced out of the market.

Third, the roles of business and government become confused. Many argue that the role of government is to implement social programs through the electoral process. Voters elect individuals who will implement those desired social goals. When business implements social goals, voters do not have an opportunity to participate in the selection of those social goals. This thwarts the purpose of an elected legislative body in a free society.

Fourth, business can become too powerful. If corporations become a primary instrument for social change, then they will have an added dimension of power at their disposal. Combined with their economic power, such firms could be too powerful in a free society that relies on checks and balances.

Corporate social responsibility positions

Given the conflicting arguments, there are at least three different positions that managers might employ. These three positions are described in terms of increasing social activism.

One position might be labeled as *minimum legal compliance* which means that the managers comply with the minimum social requirements of the law. Some firms adopt this position because their slender profit margins and concern for short term survival do not provide the flexibility of much else.

Enlightened self-interest involves the use of social programs to gain an advantage in the marketplace. Such firms use social responsibility programs as a strategic weapon to communicate to the market that they are "better than" competitors. This is consistent with the long-run best interest of the firm argument, expected to lead to long-term profitability. Some firms adopt this position, or the "minimum legal compliance" position, because they believe it to be the proper position.

With *proactive change*, the firm actively uses its assets to improve society independent of a direct benefit to the firm. Managers taking such positions risk disapproval from owners and stockholders for taking positions that are so far beyond the requirements of today's laws.

Managers might take different positions as a function of the nature of the decision and the firm's customers. This would lead to a situation like that depicted in the corporate social responsibility matrix for an aluminum smelter in figure 4.2.

In a total quality sense, the position might be tied into the interests of the firm's customers. Some decisions might be made in terms of "minimum legal compliance" if the firm's customers have little interest in those decisions beyond what is already in the law. Some decisions might be made in terms of "enlightened self-interest" if the firm's customers have a particular interest in that social issue.

For example, the customers of a bank with a regional check processing facility in a lumbering area like the US northwest may have little interest in whether the checks are written on recycled paper. Thus, "minimum legal compliance" may be the appropriate position on recycling. The same customers may not even want the bank to go beyond "minimum legal compliance" on animal rights issues, because it might lead to unemployment, as with the Endangered Species Act. That Act has been used to prohibit logging in vast areas in the US northwest, with a resultant dramatic increase in unemployment. In other decisions, the same bank's customers may want the bank to act in terms of "enlightened self-interest". Because of

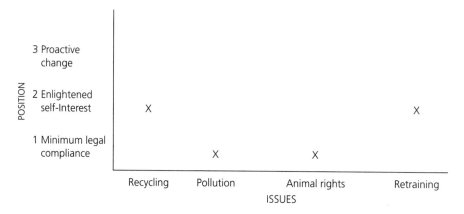

Figure 4.2 Corporate social responsibility matrix for an aluminum smelter.

the unemployment discussed, the bank's customers may want the bank to actively implement worker retraining programs. The bank's customers may prize their clean air and thus expect the bank to take an "enlightened self-interest" position on pollution.

Sometimes the best intended corporate social responsibility policy does not meet expectations. Then, managers must decide if it is in the enlightened self-interest of the organization to continue with the policy.

Multiple Stakeholder View

Stakeholders are the individuals and organizations that have an interest or stake in the activities of a firm. As industrial organizations have grown large after the Second World War, their power to affect the lives of many people has also grown. Thus, there are an increasing number of stakeholders associated with the typical firm. These stakeholders have an equity, economic, and/or influencer stake in the firm.

Equity stake

An *equity stake* in the company is associated with an ownership position. The equity stake varies as a function of the kind of power held by the stakeholder. The following examples refer to the primary orientation of the stakeholder.

The ownership position can range from formal ownership or voting positions of power, as with stockholders, directors, and other minority equity interests, to economic positions of power, as with employees or owners, to political positions of power, as with dissident stockholders.

There has been considerable criticism of many managers in the USA for overly focusing on the stakeholders with an equity stake and formal/voting power by stressing short-term profits. Such a focus has been associated with ignoring customers and losing them to international competitors who provide more value to customers. An increasing number of managers have realized that the best way to serve the interests of equity stockholders is by building a firm which provides more value to customers and increases market share in the long term.

Economic stake

An *economic stake* is due to direct market involvement with the company's marketplace actions. Formal or voting power is exercised by preferred debt holders. Economic power is exercised by a large group of stakeholders, including suppliers, debt holders, customers, employees, and competitors. Political power is exercised by local and foreign governments, consumer lobbies, and unions who have an economic stake in the firm.

Influencer stake

Those with an influencer stake meet the expanded definition of stakeholders because these groups do not have much economic or equity interest. An *influencer stake* is interest associated with the firm's activities not due to marketplace or equity involvement.[18] Influencers include those with formal or voting power, such as outside directors and licensing bodies; those with economic power, such as regulatory agencies that can affect prices; those with political power, such as federal and state governments, trade associations, and environmental groups.

In recent years, there has been an increasing number of laws which provide some of these groups with considerable legal power to back up their interest in the firm. In such situations, managers must comply by force of law and government sanctions. Two examples are the US Environmental Protection Agency and the Occupational Safety and Health Administration, which regulate issues concerning pollution and workplace safety, respectively.

A stakeholder grid

These various stakeholders can be described as a function of the kind of stake and the kind of power. Various stakeholder groups could be placed in more than one cell in figure 4.3. The figure shows the primary orientation of each group.

At least two points need to be made from figure 4.3. First, there are many individuals and groups with a stake in the typical firm. Second, the nature of the stakeholders' interests varies as a function of the kind of power possessed.

Stakeholder conflict and total quality

Given the large number of stakeholders with different interests and different power bases, there will be situations of conflict among the various stakeholders. Managers can deal with the conflict partly by prioritizing the various groups.

Historically, stakeholder conflict was thought to be a zero-sum game in which one group gained advantage only at the expense of another group. By definition, total quality stresses the primacy of the customer, and the importance of employees and suppliers in the system of management of the firm. TQ strives to increase the health of the firm by strengthening the priority of the customer, supplier and employee groups.[19] A healthier firm should be better able to serve the equity and economic interests of the other stakeholder groups, as all ships rise with a rising tide.

Influences on Corporate Social Responsibility

There are a number of influences on any social responsibility decision, which can be categorized as government and regulatory influences, ethical influences,

POWER

	Formal or voting	Economic	Political
Equity	Stockholders Directors Minority interests	Employee/owners	Dissident stockholders
Economic	Preferred debt holders	Suppliers Debt holders Customers Employees Competitors	Local governments Foreign governments Consumer lobbies Unions
Influencers	Outside directors Licensing bodies	Regulatory agencies	Federal and state government Trade associations Environmental groups

STAKE

Grid location denotes the primary but not necessarily the sole orientation of each stakeholder.

Figure 4.3   A real world stakeholder grid.
Source: Freeman, R. E., *Strategic Management: a Stakeholder Approach*. London: Pitman (1984), p. 63.

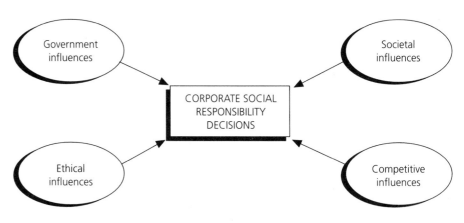

Figure 4.4   Constraining influences on the corporate social responsibility decision.
Source: Reproduced from Stahl, M. J. and Grigsby, D. W., *Strategic Management: Formulation and Implementation* (1992), p. 182.

societal influences, and competitive influences. Figure 4.4 shows the influences acting on corporate social responsibility decisions.

Government and regulatory influences

The powers of governments to regulate business in their countries are wide and deep. The US Congress controls much business activity under the authority to regulate interstate commerce as stated in the United States Constitution.

To implement its regulatory function, the federal government has established a number of regulatory agencies. A few of the more important ones follow. The Environmental Protection Agency (EPA) develops and enforces standards for pollution. The Equal Employment Opportunity Commission (EEOC) prosecutes employment discrimination complaints based on race, gender, religion, creed, or national origin. The Food and Drug Administration (FDA) enforces standards for the purity and labeling of foods, drugs, cosmetics, and hazardous consumer products. The Occupational Safety and Health Administration (OSHA) regulates safety and health conditions in the workplace. These and other federal and state regulatory agencies are significant forces towards liberal corporate social responsibility decisions.

In Europe, each country has its own government with various degrees of regulation. Additionally, the European Union in Brussels disseminates series of regulations for the entire EU. Other countries in other parts of the world have varying degrees of regulation. Managers operating internationally need to be aware of the differing regulations in the host countries.

Ethical influences

As discussed earlier, there are at least five different managerial ethics bases. These bases act as an internal self-regulating force for corporate social responsibility decisions. Interest in managerial ethics is at a high point. Today, a manager's ethical standards are increasingly being evaluated as part of the manager's performance.[20]

For a manager to apply his or her own personal ethical standards to corporate decisions can be a complicated process. Even if the individual manager has been able to analyze the situation in terms of several of the five ethics bases and feels reasonably comfortable with the decision, then there are different stakeholder interests to satisfy. To deal with this situation, more than 80 percent of US firms had ethics codes in the early 1990s to act as guides.[21]

Societal influences

There are at least three different ways that society exercises its influence on a firm's corporate responsibility stance. The first and most powerful way is through market forces. The cumulative buying decisions of individual customers in the marketplace communicate society's preferences. If society prefers to buy "safe" autos and not buy "unsafe" autos, then society has voted its preferences on this corporate social responsibility issue.

The second way is through the electoral process. By voting for candidates with certain views concerning social responsibility issues, society expresses its preferences.

The third way is through the activities of influence groups. Influence groups use a variety of tactics including lobbying public officials, informing the public on certain issues, and organizing boycotts. Some examples of US influence groups include Ralph Nader's Public Citizen (a consumer organization), the Sierra Club (an environmental organization), and Action for Children's Television (a special interest organization).

Competitive influences

Competitors directly affect the social responsibility decisions of managers in the areas of product quality, safety, and economy. The TQ movement grew mostly because Japanese and German firms gave US customers high-quality, reasonable priced products from which to choose. In the mid-1990s, it was very difficult to sell an auto without anti-lock brakes and air bags because most of the competitors offered them and customers demanded them.

Competitors help to establish the norms in an industry concerning employment practices. Those firms that violate the norms on the downside usually suffer the loss of skilled personnel.

▌ Summary ▌

Ethics is defined as doing the right thing right the first time. Unethical managerial behavior can be described as a result of a defect in an organizational system.

It is difficult to describe what is the right thing because there are so many different bases of ethics. There does not appear to be a single ethics base, with standards for managerial decisions and actions, that can guide managers in all situations. A proposed ethical decision must be analyzed with the multiple ethics bases to see how it holds up under the multiple approaches. Five different ethics bases are reviewed.

The Eternal Law approach to ethics holds that there is a common set of moral standards apparent in Nature or revealed in the Holy Scripture. Some refer to the Eternal Law as "rule-based ethics," because it holds that one should adopt a set of general rules, or principles, that guide one's actions.

Utilitarianism, or the utilitarian principle, means that a manager should act in ways to create the greatest benefits for the largest number of people. A managerial decision is "right" if it results in benefits for others, and the decision is "wrong" if it results in damage or harm to others.

Universalism holds that the ethics of a decision depends on the motives or intentions of the decision maker. Personal intentions or personal motives can be translated into personal duties or obligations because all would behave in the same universal fashion given the same situation.

Distributive justice is based upon the primacy of the single value of justice. Thus, managers should act to ensure a more equitable distribution of benefits.

Personal liberty is based upon the primacy of the single value of liberty. A managerial decision that violates individual liberty, even if it results in greater benefits for others, is not consistent with the idea of personal liberty.

Corporate social responsibility refers to the obligation of the firm to use its resources in ways to benefit society. Many arguments in favor of a liberal corporate social responsibility start by reviewing the role of business in society. First, society expects a liberal corporate social responsibility. Second, businesses' long-term self-interests are best served when those responsibilities are fulfilled. Third, the firm will avoid future government regulation.

Many managers counter that the most socially responsible action a company can engage in is to maximize its profits. This more conservative view is founded on four ideas. First, profit maximization is the only legitimate purpose of business in capitalism. Second, corporate social responsibility subverts the market system.

Third, the roles of business and government become confused. Fourth, business can become too powerful.

Given the conflicting arguments, there are at least three different positions that managers might employ. One position might be labeled as "minimum legal compliance," which means that the managers comply with the minimum social requirements of the law. "Enlightened self-interest" involves the use of social programs to gain an advantage in the marketplace. "Proactive change" refers to actively using the firm's assets to improve society independent of a direct benefit to the firm.

Stakeholders are the individuals and organizations that have an interest or stake in the activities of a firm. These stakeholders have an equity, economic, and/or influencer stake in the firm. An equity stake in the company is associated with an ownership position. An economic stake is due to direct market involvement with the company's marketplace actions. An influencer stake is interest associated with the firm's activities not due to marketplace or equity involvement.

In addition to the previously mentioned arguments in favor of a liberal corporate social responsibility, there are a number of influences on any social responsibility decision. These influences can be summarized in the four categories of government and regulatory influences, ethical influences, societal influences, and competitive influences.

DISCUSSION QUESTIONS

1 Compare and contrast each of the five different managerial ethics bases with the requirements of the law in general, and with the requirements of the law concerning product liability in specific.

2 What are the implications of the definition of ethics for managerial training?

3 Six months into a new job as a manager, your manager directs you to implement a decision contrary to your sense of ethics. Discuss your alternatives.

4 Discuss the arguments for a liberal corporate social responsibility and the arguments for a conservative corporate social responsibility.

5 Describe five important social responsibility issues for a chemical manufacturer. Complete a corporate social responsibility matrix for the firm on those issues.

6 Total quality management stresses the primacy of the customer, and the importance of employees and suppliers in the system of management of the firm. How will those TQ themes relate to the interests of the other stakeholders?

7 In the 1970s and 1980s, there were significant reductions in US regulation in a variety of industries, including airlines, railroads, trucking, natural gas distributors, financial institutions, oil pipeline companies, and parts of the telecommunications industry. Forecast the trend of federal regulation of business in the next ten years.

8 How are competitors an influence for liberal corporate social responsibility decisions? How are competitors an influence for conservative corporate social responsibility decisions?

KEY TERMS

Corporate social responsibility	refers to the obligation of the firm to use its resources in ways to benefit society.
Distributive justice	is based upon the primacy of the single value of justice.
An economic stake	is due to direct market involvement with the company's marketplace actions.
Enlightened self-interest	involves the use of social programs to gain an advantage in the marketplace.
An equity stake	in the company is associated with an ownership position.
Eternal Law	holds that there is a common set of moral standards apparent in Nature or revealed in the Holy Scripture.
Ethics	is defined as doing the right thing right the first time.
An influencer stake	is interest associated with the firm's activities not due to marketplace or equity involvement.
Minimum legal compliance	means that the managers comply with the minimum social requirements of the law.
Personal liberty	is based upon the primacy of the single value of liberty.
Proactive change	refers to actively using the firm's assets to improve society independent of a direct benefit to the firm.
Stakeholders	are the individuals and organizations that have an interest or stake in the activities of a firm.
Teleological theory	stresses the outcome, not the intent, of managerial actions.
Universalism	holds that the ethics of a decision depends on the motives or intentions of the decision maker.
Utilitarianism, or the utilitarian principle,	means that a manager should act in ways to create the greatest benefits for the largest number of people.

Johnson & Johnson Recalls Tylenol

On September 30, 1982, Johnson & Johnson (J&J) announced that three people died as a result of consuming Tylenol capsules laced with cyanide. Within the next two days, four more deaths were announced from consumption of cyanide-laced Tylenol capsules.[a] J&J's handling of the situation is regarded as a must read for anyone studying managerial ethics and product liability issues.

At the time of the poisonings, Tylenol was a major brand for J&J in capsule and tablet forms. Through years of concentrated marketing and advertising, J&J had built Tylenol into the number one over-the-counter analgesic brand with 35.3 percent of that market.[b] Sales of Tylenol in 1982 were $350 million (US) accounting for seven percent of all J&J sales and 17 percent of all profits.[c]

What were J&J managers to do? Some of their customers were dying from consuming one of their flagship products! The CEO and Chairman of J&J, James E. Burke, stressed that the following J&J credo, which had been originally written in 1947 and modified in 1979, played a critical role when the company fashioned its response to the crisis.[d]

Johnson & Johnson's Corporate Credo

"We believe our first responsibility is to the doctors, nurses and patients, to mothers and fathers and all others who use our products and services. In meeting their needs everything we do must be of high quality. We must constantly strive to reduce our costs in order to maintain reasonable prices. Customers' orders must be serviced promptly and accurately. Our suppliers and distributors must have an opportunity to make a fair profit.

"We are responsible to our employees, the men and women who work with us throughout the world. Everyone must be considered as an individual. We must respect their dignity and recognize their merit. They must have a sense of security in their jobs. Compensation must be fair and adequate, and working conditions clean, orderly and safe. We must be mindful of ways to help our employees fulfill their family responsibilities. Employees must feel free to make suggestions and complaints. There must be equal opportunity for employment, development and advancement for those qualified. We must provide competent management, and their actions must be just and ethical.

"We are responsible to the communities in which we live and work and to the world community as well. We must be good citizens – support good works and charities and bear our fair share of taxes. We must encourage civic improvements and better health and education. We must maintain in good order the property we are privileged to use, protecting the environment and natural resources.

"Our final responsibility is to our stockholders. Business must make a sound profit. We must experiment with new ideas. Research must be carried on, innovative programs developed and mistakes paid for. New equipment must be purchased, new facilities provided and new products launched. Reserves must be created to provide for adverse times. When we operate according to these principles, the stockholders should realize a fair return." (*Source*: Johnson & Johnson Corp.)

The poisonings became a publicity event without precedent in US business. About 125,000 stories appeared in the print media and it was estimated that the Tylenol brand received over US$1 billion in adverse publicity. Soon after the poisonings, the market share of the entire Tylenol line fell by 80 percent.[e]

J&J quickly issued the largest product recall in the history of the USA – 31 million bottles of capsules with a retail value of over US$100 million. Through ads and $2.50 coupons which offered to exchange tablets for capsules, through 500,000 messages to the medical community and distributors, and through public press releases, J&J forcefully communicated its actions.[f]

These actions were taken by J&J even though it had been established that the poisonings were not due to a malfunction in J&J's manufacturing process. It was established that someone had purchased bottles of Tylenol capsules, injected cyanide into the capsules, and reintroduced the capsules into the distribution chain in the Chicago area. Only capsules were involved in the poisonings since tablets were much harder to tamper with.

In a few months, J&J reintroduced the capsule form of Tylenol with a triple-sealed, tamper-resistant package. The flaps of the box were glued shut, the bottle's cap and neck were covered with a plastic seal, and the mouth of the bottle was covered with a foil seal. The box and the bottle were marked with the warning "Do not use if safety seals are broken".[g]

The out-of-pocket costs associated with J&J's decisive actions approached $200 million.[h] However, it appeared that J&J's forceful and quick actions had reestablished the public's trust in its products. In less than one year from the poisonings, Tylenol had regained nearly all of its former market share, approaching 35 percent.[i]

Calamity struck Tylenol capsules again in February 1986, when a Westchester, NY, woman died from cyanide-laced Tylenol capsules. Since J&J felt that it could no longer guarantee the safety of the product, it decided to stop manufacturing capsules. Instead, J&J would market only tablets and a new product called a caplet, which is an elongated, coated, easy to swallow tablet. That decision cost the firm about $150 million. Apparently it was a wise decision, as Tylenol's market share stood at 32 percent by July 1986.[j] In describing the actions, J&J's president commented: "People think of this company as extraordinarily trustworthy and responsible, and we do not want to do anything to damage that."[k]

That trustworthiness continues to be a major asset for J&J. Today, J&J is one of the world's leading manufacturers and marketers of healthcare products. It offers a broad line of consumer products, prescription and over-the-counter pharmaceuticals, and various other medical and dental items.[l]

Sales in 1995 were about US$19 billion, with about 50 percent of those sales outside of the USA, in Europe, Africa, and Asia.[m] The firm's reputation has been maintained, as J&J was one of only two firms ranked as one of America's ten most admired corporations in both 1992 and 1983.[n]

Discussion Questions

1 Was the money that management spent on a recall and product repackaging justified?

2 Apparently the poison was added by an outsider, not at J&J manufacturing or distribution facilities. Should management have blamed the outsider(s) and kept the product as it was?

3 Compare Johnson & Johnson's response to the response of some other firms involved in product liability cases.

Sources: a. Mitchell, M. L., "The impact of external parties on brand-name capital: the 1982 Tylenol poisonings and subsequent cases," *Economic Inquiry* (October 1989), pp. 601–18;   b. "A death blow for Tylenol?" *Business Week* (October 18, 1982), p. 151;   c. Hartley, R., *Management Mistakes and Successes*, 3rd edn. New York: Wiley (1991), p. 365;   d. Jacobs, R., "Products liability: a technical and ethical challenge," *Quality Progress* (December 1988), p. 28;   e. Mitchell, M. L., "The impact of external parties on brand-name capital," pp. 601–3; f. Hartley, R., *Management Mistakes and Successes*, p. 368;   g. Ibid., p. 369.   h. Mitchell, M. L., "The impact of external parties on brand-name capital," p. 611;   i. Hartley, R., *Management Mistakes and Successes*, p. 371; j. Ibid.;   k. "Johnson & Johnson's recovery," *New York Times* (July 5, 1986), p. 33;   l. "Johnson & Johnson," *Standard & Poors Reports*, Standard & Poors Corporation (May 28, 1993), p. 1268;   m. "Johnson & Johnson," *The Value Line Investment Survey* (March 17, 1995), p. 221;   n. "America's most admired corporations," *Fortune* (February 10, 1992), p. 41; "Ranking corporate reputations," *Fortune* (January 10, 1983), p. 35.

INTERNATIONAL

C   A   S   E

"ROUSSEL-UCLAF AND RU-486"

It has become popular in the past decade for corporations to espouse socially responsible policies. More than ever, corporate annual reports contain discussions of their social credo. Nevertheless, it is not always clear how to translate this into meaningful action.

Among the many different types of dilemmas faced by multinational corporations, few are as difficult as bringing a product to market in a foreign country where ethical standards are different or more stringent than at home. The most debated cases may be those surrounding biomedical, biochemical, and pharmaceutical products, which can challenge the most fundamental beliefs within some societies.

Roussel-Uclaf Pharmaceuticals, a Paris-based company, faced such a dilemma when it introduced a controversial new compound to market in 1988. Roussel-Uclaf is 55 percent owned by Hoechst AG (a German multinational conglomerate of 250 companies), 36 percent owned by the French government, and 9 percent publicly owned.[a]

Roussel-Uclaf scientists developed RU-486, a steroid compound that prevents a fertilized embryo from implanting in the womb or causes a fertilized embryo to "slough off". Named mifepristone, the drug was designed to be used between conception and the end of the first trimester of a pregnancy in order to terminate the pregnancy. The product was successfully tested in France, Britain, Scandinavia, and other countries, where it demonstrated a 95.5 percent success rate for safety and effectiveness.[b]

Roussel and the French Health Ministry brought the product to the French market in 1988 with considerable enthusiasm and fanfare. At the same time, a protest movement developed that called for a worldwide boycott of all Hoechst (the parent company) products. Cardinal Jean-Marie Lustiger of Paris lambasted RU-486 as "savage liberalism" and a "chemical weapon" against the unborn. This prompted Roussel to remove mifepristone from the market. The subsequent backlash was even stronger. Dr Baulieu, the discoverer of the drug, criticized the removal as "morally scandalous." Within two days of the decision, the French government (36 percent owners) intervened and ordered RU-486 back on the market.[c]

This turmoil at home made it apparent to Roussel-Uclaf executives that distribution abroad could be a very complex question. Nevertheless, soon after its introduction in France, manufacturers in Great Britain, Sweden, Holland, and a few other countries applied for and were granted licenses to produce RU-486 in their countries.[d]

Although well aware of the controversy surrounding the product, Roussel-Uclaf probably was not prepared for the strength of the backlash it encountered in the United States. When Roussel-Uclaf tried to license RU-486 in the US market through Hoechst-Roussel Pharmaceuticals (a division of Hoechst AG primarily devoted to bringing prescription drugs to the US market), not one major US manufacturer approached Hoechst-Roussel for a license to produce RU-486. Despite the enormous profit potential, most believed the potential liability to be even greater.[e]

Political and religious opposition began almost from the time of the drug's inception. The National Right to Life Committee played an important role in preventing RU-486 from being introduced in the United States. It dubbed RU-486 the "abortion pill," representing the view that human life begins at conception. Opposition was not targeted just at Roussel-Uclaf, but also at the parent company, Hoechst AG. The committee pressured Hoechst by calling for a boycott of all its products, not just pharmaceuticals. It persuaded Hoechst AG to limit distribution to its current markets. The medical community's view was divided on the matter.[f]

There was also strong support for RU-486 from other political and social organizations. Planned Parenthood, the World Health Organization, the Population Council, and feminist groups defended a woman's decision to end her pregnancy. In addition to the increased level of privacy, they supported RU-486 on the grounds of safety and effectiveness.[g]

The management of Hoechst-Roussel was accountable for the decision to try to license RU-486 in the USA. It was already clear that this decision could have extensive consequences for the company stockholders, potential customers, the medical community, and US society at large. Fearing that anti-abortion activists would pursue a more organized boycott of all Hoechst products, the company decided not to seek permission to sell and market RU-486 directly to the United States market. In 1994, after years of deliberation, Roussel-Uclaf donated the rights of clinical testing, distribution (should the situation arise), and patents to The Population Council, a non-profit population-research organization located in New York and California.[h]

Although Roussel-Uclaf may think that its traumatic experience in the US market may be over, it is hard to predict what the residual effects on the reputation of Roussel-Uclaf and Hoechst AG may be. Multinational corporations need to better anticipate potential conflicts and be prepared to respond in ways that justify company decisions and respond to the legitimate concerns of critics and the interests of the public.

Discussion questions

1 What social and cultural considerations should multinational companies consider when marketing products in a foreign country?

2 It is clear that Roussel-Uclaf severely underestimated the level of resistance to RU-486. If you were a business consultant, how would you suggest that Roussel approach marketing decisions in the future?

3 What say, if any, do you think society should have in the management of a firm conducting research in biochemical products like RU-486?

Sources: **a.** Lader, L., *RU 486*. Reading, MA: Addison-Wesley (1991), p. 41; **b.** Bol, J. W. and Rosenthal, D. W., "Hoechst-Roussel Pharmaceuticals, Inc.: RU 486," *Case Research Journal* (1993), p. 6; **c.** Lader, L., *RU 486*, pp. 50–2; **d.** Boland, R., "RU 486 in France and England: corporate ethics and compulsory licensing," *Law, Medicine, and Health Care*, 20(3) (1992), p. 226; **e.** "Abortion pill maker urged to apply for US trials," *Journal of Commerce* (December 18, 1992), p. 9A; **f.** Bol, J. W. and Rosenthal, D. W., "Hoechst-Roussel Pharmaceuticals, Inc.: RU 486," p. 12; **g.** Ibid., p. 14; **h.** "US-Organisation darf Abtreibungspille erproben," *Suddeutsche Zeitung* (April 22, 1993), p. 2.

NOTES

1 Berenbeim, R. E., "The corporate ethics test," *Business and Society Review* (Spring 1992), pp. 77–80.

2 Buban, M., "Factoring ethics into the TQM equation," *Quality Progress* (October 1995), pp. 97–9.

3 Fisscher, O., "Ethics and social value", *European Quality*, 1(4) (1994), pp. 34–6.

4 "Five keys to self-renewal," MDC Policy Manual – Policy 2, McDonnell Douglas Corporation (1993).

5 These five rules are described in greater detail in Hosmer, L. T., *The Ethics of Management*, 2nd edn. Homewood, IL: R. D. Irwin (1991), pp. 108–20.

6 Stahl, M. J. and Grigsby, D. G., *Strategic Management for Decision Making*. Boston: PWS-Kent (1992), p. 185.

7 Singer, A., "Ethics: are standards lower overseas?," In *Across the Board*. New York: The Conference Board; "How US concerns compete in countries where bribes flourish," *Wall Street Journal* (September 29, 1995), pp. A1.

8 Vogel, D., "Is US business obsessed with ethics?," *California Management Review*, 35(1) (Fall 1992), pp. 31–3.

9 Trompenaars, F., *Riding the Waves of Culture: Understanding Cultural Diversity in Business*. London: Economist Books (1993), p. 38.

10 Hosmer, L. T., *The Ethics of Management*, 2nd edn. Homewood, IL: R. D. Irwin (1991), p. 102.

11 This section was heavily influenced by Stahl, M. J. and Grigsby, D. G., *Strategic Management for Decision Making*. Boston: PWS-Kent (1992), pp. 189–93.

12 European Social Policy: Options for the Union. Brussels: Commission of the European Communities (1994).

13 Steiner, G. A. and Steiner, J. F., *Business, Government, and Society*. New York: Random House (1988), p. 182.

14 Dechant, K. and Altman, B., "Environmental leadership: from compliance to competitive advantage," *Academy of Management Executive*, VIII(3) (August 1994), pp. 7–20.

15 Committee for Economic Development, *Social Responsibilities of Business Corporations*. New York: CED (1981), pp. 25–6.

16 Friedman, M., *Capitalism and Freedom*. Chicago: University of Chicago Press (1962), p. 24.

17 Friedman, M., "The social responsibility of business is to increase its profits," *New York Times Magazine* (September 13, 1970).

18 Freeman, R., *Strategic Management: a Stakeholder Approach*. Boston: Pitman Publishing Company (1984), p. 58.

19 Buban, M., "Factoring ethics into the TQM equation," *Quality Progress* (October 1995), pp. 97–9.

20 Bennett, A., "Ethics codes spread despite skepticism," *Wall Street Journal* (July 15, 1988), p. 17.

21 Berenbeim, R. E. "The corporate ethics test," *Business and Society Review* (Spring 1992), pp. 77–80.

CORPORATE STRATEGY

LEARNING OBJECTIVES

After reading this chapter, you should be able to accomplish the following.

1 *Relate the concepts of strategic fit, core competency, and related diversification.*

2 *Compare and contrast the concepts of horizontal diversification and vertical integration.*

3 *Discuss the advantages and the risks of concentration strategies.*

4 *Describe the advantages and disadvantages of horizontal diversification and vertical integration.*

5 *Describe why so many mergers and acquisitions fail.*

6 *Explain the advantages and the risks of pursuing a joint venture versus a merger.*

7 *Describe the advantages and the risks of restructuring.*

8 *Discuss the role of the customer in strategic planning as international competition intensifies.*

9 *Describe the impact of total quality on concentration and diversification strategies.*

This chapter deals with the broad and long lasting decisions referred to as corporate strategy. *Corporate level strategy* refers to decisions on what business(es) the firm should be in.

By definition, a decision implies that a choice is made among alternatives. However the corporate-level strategic decision is made, all organizations are faced with choices among possible businesses or industries. These decisions may result in an overall mission statement, such as "The mission of Apple Computer is to design, manufacture, and market personal computers to the business, educational, and professional user." Once such a mission has been decided, the organization must decide how to enter, improve, or exit the chosen business(es).

These decisions are grouped into strategies concerning corporate direction (concentration, horizontal diversification, and vertical integration), strategies concerning corporate means (merger and acquisition, joint venture), and strategies concerning restructuring (retrenchment, divestiture, bankruptcy, and liquidation).

Strategies Concerning Corporate Direction

At the corporate level, decisions concerning what business(es) the firm should be in address underlying issues of concentration and diversification. The concepts of strategic fit and core competency describe major issues in the debate concerning concentration versus diversification

Strategic fit and core competency

The concepts of strategic fit and core competency provide the rationale behind concentration. *Strategic fit* refers to the relatedness of activities in an organization. The concept argues that there should be a common thread throughout the firm's activities, so that there is resulting synergy and a common focus. *Synergy* is the hoped for non-linear benefit arising from the combination of two activities yielding results greater than a linear combination predicts. Some refer to synergy as $2 + 2 = 5$.

Thompson and Strickland identified three types of strategic fit.[1] *Product – market fit* is the use of common distribution channels, sales forces, promotion techniques, or customers for more than one product or service. A good example is Anheuser Busch's decision to use its beer distribution channels and marketing techniques to market a line of Eagle Brand snack foods. *Operating fit* is the realization of economies from internal operations, such as purchasing, warehousing, production and operations, research and development, or personnel from more than one product or service. For example, Levi Strauss capitalized on its experience in the manufacture and marketing of denim jeans, and decided to manufacture and market jackets and other apparel. *Management fit* is the benefit from managerial experience in similar areas. Thus, the company can tap years of accumulated exposure from one line of business to another. For example, a successful insurance company might decide to sell common stock mutual funds.

Core competency is that set of activities or functions in which the organization is

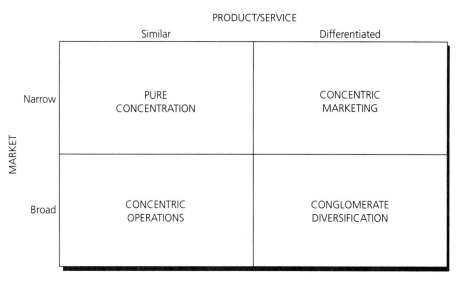

PRODUCT/SERVICE

	Similar	Differentiated
Narrow	PURE CONCENTRATION	CONCENTRIC MARKETING
Broad	CONCENTRIC OPERATIONS	CONGLOMERATE DIVERSIFICATION

MARKET

Figure 5.1 Product-market matrix.

Source: Reproduced from Stahl, M. J. and Grigsby, D. W., *Strategic Management: Formulation and Implementation* (1992), p. 58.

particularly skilled. Prahalad and Hamel argued that core competency should determine the businesses in which the organization operates, i.e. the firm should do what it is good at doing.[2] The concept of core competency goes one step beyond strategic fit by arguing that not only should the activities within a firm be related, but that the firm should be expert at those activities. A company builds on the activities in which it already has competence and operates in a core area. Strategic fit assumes that a corporation should pursue only those activities in which it has some distinctive competence.

A good example of core competency in the late 1980s was observed in some visible acquisitions and divestitures in retailing. Kmart acquired some specialty retail chains in office products, sporting goods and bookstores for its battle against Wal-Mart. After finding that specialty retailing did not fit with its core competency in discount retailing, Kmart decided to divest the specialty retailers in 1995.[3]

Concentration

The combination of product and market considered in concentration strategies can be visualized in the product – market matrix in figure 5.1. The three upper and left cells in figure 5.1 are concentration or related/concentric diversification strategies. As the figure indicates, the two concentric diversification strategies are somewhat broader concentration strategies than pure concentration. The differentiated products – broad markets cell is a conglomerate diversification strategy in that it refers to diversified products. Firms sometimes choose such a position to diversify risk.

Pure concentration refers to offering similar products or services in narrow markets. *Concentric marketing* refers to offering differentiated products or services in a narrow market. Concentric marketing is based on the concept of product – market fit. *Concentric operations* refers to the production of similar products or services for broad markets. Concentric operations are based on the concept of operating fit.

There are several reasons for choosing concentration strategies. The strategic decision makers may feel comfortable with familiar markets and products/ services, and may shun the unfamiliarity of other markets or products/services. Even if they are willing to consider alternatives, there may be little economy of scale due to expansion, primarily because of the technology employed. Reduced costs associated with learning effects may not be possible in other markets or other products/services. Both of these reasons may be relevant in service industries in which the service may be produced at the point of delivery. There may be little marketing fit or operating fit with other products/services or other markets.

There are three forms of pure concentration. *Penetration strategies* seek to increase market share. A good example is the cola wars between Coke and Pepsi. *Product development strategies* slightly modify basic product lines to capture more of the market. Kellogg's introduction of a new cereal is a good example. *Market development* seeks to expand the customer base for present product lines. For example, an airline discount fare targeted at college students might try to draw new customers.

Hair styling salons, banks, car repair shops, and other service organizations can be characterized by the matrix in figure 5.1. Most styling salons are multiple-product yet narrow-market organizations. Their expertise or distinctive competence is in the delivery of their services to a local clientele. Although they may start as single product/service firms offering only services dealing with hair, they may grow into other personal appearance services/products. Some offer retail hair care products, some offer tanning facilities, and some offer manicures. As there is little marketing fit to enter broader markets and few economies of scale to expand geographic coverage, such firms usually stay local.

TNT Express of the UK concentrates on time-sensitive freight in Europe. Through penetration strategies and market development, the firm has grown its sales 50-fold in 15 years.[4]

Historically, banks have been narrow-market firms that specialized in offering personalized services to local customers. Under times of government regulation limiting interstate banking, such concentration was logical. When the banking laws were changed to allow interstate banking in the early 1980s in the USA, several superregional banks were formed to lower their cost structures. An example is NCNB National Bank, headquartered in Charlotte, North Carolina. It had branches in several southeastern states and an asset base approaching US$30 billion in 1988. Although it had grown dramatically through merger and acquisition activity since banking deregulation, few expected NCNB to diversify from financial products/services. With its subsequent acquisitions in Texas, NCNB continued to concentrate on financial products/services while serving a broader market. After the acquisitions in Texas, the assets of NCNB National Bank reached about $60 billion in 1990. It subsequently changed its name to NationsBank when it merged with C&S/Sovran and had assets of $168 billion in 1995. NationsBank had become the third-largest bank holding company in the United States.[5]

A third example of concentration is the retail auto repair industry. Shops that specialize in the services they offer tend to be local firms. They may specialize in similar kinds of autos or certain levels of repair. Other firms have decided due to a distinctive competence in a specific product or a specific service to concentrate on that specific product/service in a national market. Midas (mufflers) and Jiffy Lube (oil change) are two US national examples. Although their market is broader, their products/services are few. Such concentration allows them to "stick to their knitting" and develop a distinctive competence, as suggested in the popular book *In Search of Excellence*.[6] In so doing, they may even lower their cost structure through familiarity with national purchasing trends, economies of scale, standardization, advertising, and the spread of fixed costs over a large business base.

Concentrically or relatedly diversified firms follow the dictates of strategic fit and stick to a distinctive competence principally in terms of operating fit or marketing fit. Good examples include Champion International, which is focused around the concept of producing forest products that include paper products and wood building supply products. Similarly, Procter & Gamble builds on marketing fit and is focused around the concept of marketing many consumer products directly to the end-use consumer. Merrill Lynch, by building on operating and marketing fit, offers a number of related financial services.

There are costs and risks associated with concentration, as variability in earnings may be high. The concentrator may be subject to survival threats due to the formation of competitors, or the development of substitute products/services.

Horizontal diversification

Some decision makers hold the view that big is better. If the strategic decision makers at the executive level are compensated in part on the basis of the size of the firm (for example, annual sales volume or growth), it is easy to imagine a built-in bias for dramatic growth, which frequently implies diversification.

There are few topics in corporate-level strategic decision analysis that have received as much attention from strategy researchers as the issue of diversification.[7] To insulate the firm from risk of downturns in one product or market, should the firm diversify horizontally into products or markets that are related to its core business?[8] To further spread financial risk, should the firm diversify into unrelated products and markets and transform the corporation into a conglomerate?[9] *A conglomerate* is a widely diversified firm with unrelated products and markets.

This question of diversification can be viewed as an expansion of the differentiated products–broad market cell from figure 5.1. Figure 5.2 shows this diversification dimension.

The reader may wish to think of conglomerate diversification as the logical extreme of low relatedness applied to the design of organizations. In order to diversify risk, the strategic decision makers enter many unrelated or even contracyclical markets with different earnings streams. In financial theory, this evens out the

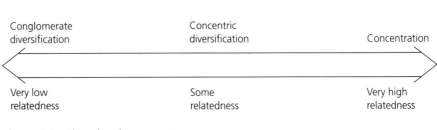

Figure 5.2 The relatedness spectrum.

Figure 5.3 The vertical integration spectrum.

fluctuations in the corporate earnings by reducing the variability of the total return stream.[10] Such a firm also finds itself in totally unrelated industries in which there is little or no strategic fit. Hanson PLC, the British conglomerate, purchased Britain's largest electric company, Eastern Group PLC, in 1995. Hanson's other operations included gold mining, chemicals, coal mining, cigarettes, and golf clubs.[11] ITT, under the direction of Harold Geneen, was in businesses as diverse as telecommunications and insurance during the 1970s. TRW (Thompson-Ramo-Woolridge) was in industries as diverse as aerospace, auto parts, and water meters. Conglomerates frequently have multiple letters or names in their titles, which reflect the history of the merger of several corporate entities.

Conglomerates were in vogue in the 1970s during a merger boom as a growth strategy. Many CEOs liked conglomerates if their compensation was tied to growth or the size of the firm.

As competition heated up internationally in the 1980s and as investors began to see that the profitability of conglomerates was less than the earnings of other forms of organizations, many firms spun off businesses in which they had little distinctive competence and refocused on core areas.[12] If investors wished to diversify the financial risk in their investments in the 1990s, many bought common stock mutual funds. The low price-earnings multiples attached to the stocks of conglomerates in the 1990s indicated that investors were devaluing conglomerates.

Vertical integration

Vertical integration is the operation of the firm near to both the end-use consumer, and to the source of raw material at the same time. *Backward vertical or upstream integration* is operation near to the stage of raw materials production. *Forward vertical or downstream integration* is operation near to retailing the product/service directly to the consumer. Figure 5.3 depicts the concept of vertical integration.

Backward vertical integration is associated with upstream companies. Such firms are frequently characterized by commodity products, standardization, low-cost production, process improvements, capital intensity, and technological skills. Alternatively, forward vertical integration is associated with downstream companies. They are characterized by proprietary products, customization, high-margined marketing, product innovation, people intensity, and marketing expertise.

Some firms seek upstream activities to protect a source of supply or to insulate the parent firm from price fluctuations in the raw material. An example is the ownership and growth of forests by firms in the paper industry. Champion International owned a large part of the trees that were used in its production of paper. In contrast, the James River Corporation owned a small fraction of the trees used in its paper production and sought its distinctive competence in the paper production process itself.[13]

Others seek forward vertical integration so that the customer will identify with the firm and demand its product by name. For example, in the textile and apparel industries, the fabric producers (textile firms) are frequently different from the garment cutters/assemblers (apparel firms). Milliken and Company, one of the USA and Europe's largest textile producers, had an agreement with some of its apparel customers to identify garments made from Milliken's material.[14]

Firms that are integrated across the entire vertical integration dimension depicted in figure 5.3 are known as "fully integrated" companies. Good examples are Shell Oil and British Petroleum (BP). The firms have operations ranging from exploration for crude oil, to oil drilling, to refining, to wholesaling, and to retailing petroleum products under their names in their own retail outlets.

Increasing vertical integration from the position on the vertical integration dimension where the firm currently operates is a form of diversification. Such a move to become more integrated in addition to one's current position spreads risk and leads to areas in which management has limited competence. This is conceptually similar to increased horizontal diversification.

Highly vertically integrated firms have had lower profitability than others.[15] Apparently, the diversification activities required of increased vertical integration detract attention and resources from the firm's core of distinctive competence. This yields lower profitability just as unrelated horizontal diversification does. One step away from current operations on the vertical integration dimension may be analogous to related diversification. Several steps away from current operations is similar to conglomerate diversification.

Strategies Concerning Corporate Means

Once the organization has decided the issues of concentration, diversification, and vertical integration, it must deal with questions of the means it uses to enter those businesses.

Merger and acquisition
The single most controversial and newsworthy corporate strategy in the late 1980s was merger and acquisition, commonly referred to as M&A. As the abbreviation

implies, the terms are usually used together in reference to the joining of two separate corporations or organizational entities. The term may also imply the purchase by firm X of one division that is being divested by firm Y. Separately, the two words, merger and acquisition, have different connotations. A *Merger* is the friendly joining together of two organizations as in a corporate marriage, usually with the sanction of both firms' top strategic decision makers. A merger typically involves firms of about the same size. *Acquisition* usually implies an unfriendly or hostile takeover without the sanction of the acquired firm. Firms of smaller size are typically acquired by firms of larger size.

Whether friendly or not, M&A is controversial and newsworthy for several reasons. First, the sums of money involved are typically huge, reaching into several billions of dollars. Second, the very survival of the firm as currently known to management, workers, and other vested interests is at stake. Third, the control and management of the firm are in question, particularly in a hostile takeover. Top executives often lose their jobs after a hostile takeover.[16] The M&A area is so controversial and newsworthy that it has spawned some of its own language, as indicated in the following list.

- A *raider* is a wealthy individual who attempts to take over corporations for near-term profit. Due to the receipt of either "greenmail" or profits through subsequent piecemeal divestiture, the raider's primary interest is usually short-term profit rather than long-term management of the corporation.
- A *golden parachute* is a severance package for the top-level executives of the purchased company. As an exit incentive, the packages are usually lucrative, reaching into seven figures.
- *Greenmail* is the corporate purchase of stock from a corporate raider at a premium. The raider is paid an above-market price not paid to other stockholders. Greenmail is outlawed in many places as it does not serve the best interests of all stockholders.
- *Junk bonds* are corporate bonds with very low ratings and high interest rates. Such risky financial instruments were often used to finance hostile takeovers.
- *Leveraged buyout (LBO)* refers to using or pledging the assets of the acquired firm to repay or secure the debt from the purchase. Top management often uses an LBO to maintain control of a firm by taking it private.
- A *poison pill* is a measure implemented to deter a hostile takeover. An example is the assumption of onerous debt in the event of a takeover.
- A *white knight* is an organization or individual that rescues a company involved in a hostile takeover by buying the company on more friendly terms. White knights typically offer higher prices than the corporate raider and/or promise not to fire top management.

Other than short-term profit, there are several reasons why firms are involved in M&A activity. Merger and acquisition can be a way to implement other strategies. In pursuit of concentration, a firm might try to buy its competitors, although this type of acquisition is controlled by the federal government. M&A is a way to pursue either concentric or conglomerate diversification. It is

Table 5.1 M&A in the worldwide pharmaceutical industry

Parent Firm	Junior Firm	$ billion (US)
Eli Lilly	PCS Health Systems	4.0
Merck	Medco	6.6
SmithKline Beecham	Diversified Pharmaceutical	2.3
Roche Holding	Syntex	5.3
SmithKline & Bayer	Sterling Winthrop	2.9
Glaxo	Wellcome	14.9
Hoechst	Marion Merrell Dow	tbd

Note: tbd means to be determined.
Source of data: "Drug industry takeovers mean more cost-cutting, less research spending," *Wall Street Journal* (February 1, 1995), p. B1.

used extensively by conglomerate firms, which typically do not develop their own products/services as a way to enter new markets. Merger and acquisition may also be used by a firm to vertically integrate. Instant market share can be achieved with M&A activity, whereas internal product development activity may take several years before substantial market share is realized. If executives are compensated on the basis of market share growth or the firm's size, there may be a built-in bias toward M&A.

Good examples of M&A are contained in the waves of consolidation in the worldwide pharmaceutical industry starting in 1993 and extending into 1995. The activity involved a number of US, British, Swiss and German firms. Table 5.1 summarizes some of the activity. The first three entries (Lilly, Merck, and SmithKline Beecham) are noteworthy as they involve vertical integration activity of getting closer to customers by acquiring pharmacy benefit management firms.

The grandaddy of all mergers in the international banking industry was announced in March 1995 and would create the world's largest bank by far. Mitsubishi Bank and Bank of Tokyo announced that they were merging, creating a colossus with about $820 billion in assets. The merger was so large that some hoped that it would help revitalize the ailing Japanese economy in early 1995. The Bank of Tokyo was already a major global player with major operations in California and more US employees than Japanese.[17]

The corporate world contains many examples of failed acquisitions. One article gave examples of several failed mergers and offered "The seven deadly sins in mergers and acquisitions":

1 Paying too much.
2 Assuming a boom market won't crash.
3 Leaping before looking.
4 Straying too far afield.
5 Swallowing something too big.

6 Marrying disparate corporate cultures.
7 Counting on key managers staying.[18]

In an examination of the relationship between business-level competitive advantage and corporate strategy, Porter reported on the acquisition and subsequent divestiture history of 33 large US companies over a 35-year time period. He found that most of them had divested many more acquisitions than they had kept.[19] Although M&A is a glamorous, high-stakes game, the size of the game and the failure rate should send up warning signs about its dangers. Far too many of today's corporate marriages end up in the divorce courts of tomorrow's divestitures. (Divestiture is discussed later in this chapter.)

Joint venture

Sometimes the dangers of merger and acquisition are recognized, but the firm needs a temporary partner for a variety of reasons. These reasons might include the amount of capital involved, a desire to share the financial risk, a lack of technical expertise, and a need to penetrate a market rapidly. Rather than pursuing M&A as a long-term marriage of two corporations, firms sometimes pool resources and risk by pursuing a temporary legal, business relationship, referred to as a *joint venture*.[20] Joint ventures are typically more involved than supplier – customer contractual business transactions. The size of joint ventures sometimes runs into billions of dollars. There may also be a pooling of personnel, plants, equipment, management expertise, and technical expertise.

Stahl found that there were three important reasons for entering into joint ventures among executives from large corporations.[21] These decision makers decided to pursue joint ventures primarily for technology/knowledge acquisition; secondarily for financial risk minimization; and, thirdly for market penetration.

A recent example of a joint venture for the apparent sake of technology/knowledge acquisition was the General Motors – Toyota joint venture in California to manufacture Chevrolet Nova automobiles. It appeared that GM entered into that joint venture because it wished to know more about Toyota's managerial and quality control programs.[22]

It also appears that technology/knowledge acquisition was instrumental in the joint venture between Hewlett-Packard (H-P) and Canon to produce and market laser printers for microcomputers. During the joint venture, most of the production of the laser printers was done by Canon and the marketing was done by H-P under H-P's label. After the joint venture, H-P did both.

Market penetration seemed to be associated with a joint venture in German telecommunicatins in 1995. Communications Network International, an alliance of Mannesmann AG, Deutsche Bank AG, and RWE AG, entered into a joint venture with AT&T and Unisource, a European telecommunications conglomerate. The joint venture was designed to sell voice and data telephone service and apply for a German telephone license.[23]

In a joint venture, typically one partner pursues the arrangement for one set of reasons while the other partner has other reasons. In 1995, three different joint ventures were announced to start auto, truck, and motorcycle production in

Vietnam. Honda and Toyota announced a joint venture with Vietnam Engine and Agricultural Machinery Corp. for motorcycles and compact autos. Ford announced a joint venture with Song Cong Diesel Co. to produce small cars. Chrysler announced a joint venture with Vinappro to produce trucks.[24] It appears that the Vietnamese firms were interested in the financial capital of the other firms and acquisition of technical knowledge. The Japanese and US firms gained market share.

Strategies Concerning Restructuring

There are four restructuring substrategies: retrenchment, divestiture, bankruptcy, and liquidation. They are listed in the order from least to most severe in terms of impact upon the organization. They all have in common the concept that the organization is being made smaller for a changed market.[25]

Retrenchment

Retrenchment is downsizing and cost cutting to meet a marketplace with reduced demand for the firm's products or services. The retrenchment may include layoffs, cuts in salary, hiring freezes, and plant closings. Because of the hardships associated with some of these approaches, retrenchments are usually controversial, and it is not unusual for firms to delay restructuring past the time when it is needed.[26] By that time, the restructuring is more painful because the corporate fat and waste have become more ingrained.

It is not uncommon to see firms retrench during a business contraction or recession. If a firm retrenches during a healthy business expansion, one wonders if it was suffering from severe competition in its markets.

Good examples of retrenchment were in the American and European automobile industries of the past two decades. Chrysler almost went bankrupt before undergoing a massive restructuring under the leadership of chairman Lee Iacocca. His decisions (combined with federal loan guarantees) to restructure, slim down, cut back, and refocus a bloated company that was out of control and out of touch with customers are credited with the survival of the company. Partly because of his restructuring success, Iacocca became an American folk hero.[27]

The Ford Motor Company restructured shortly after losing nearly US$2 billion in 1980. It emerged in the late 1980s to report the highest profits of the American auto firms, even surpassing GM for the first time in several decades. GM delayed restructuring until after its competitors restructured. It finally took the bitter medicine in the late 1980s and early 1990s. There was some evidence that GM did not restructure in time to prevent serious erosion of its market share to the Japanese. Between imports and transplant production in the United States, Japanese auto market share was about one-third of the US market in the mid 1990s.

European auto manufacturers delayed restructuring until their cost grew so high that they lost market share. To lower costs and regain market share, both BMW and Mercedes were building plants in the United States in the mid-1990s, and reducing manufacturing in Europe.

The French telecommunications maker, Alcatel, announced a major retrenchment involving job losses and asset sales to turn the company around after reporting huge losses. Although no major divestitures of businesses were planned, the retrenchment involved a charge of US$2 billion in 1995.[28]

Divestiture

Divestiture refers to selling a division or business unit of the firm. The recent trend in corporate divestiture represents a remarkable turnaround from the 1960s, when it was thought that acquisitions were the key to the continued success of the firm. Much attention has been given to the strategic option of acquisition, but relatively little light has been shed on the alternate issue of divestiture. This situation stems in part from the perception that a divestment represented a failure on the part of the management team that was involved. Consequently, prior to the early 1970s, few divestments took place, and the executives who were involved were reluctant to discuss their parts in the decision process.[29]

As many firms have reevaluated the divestment process and its impact on the company's overall performance (particularly its impact on stock prices), more divestments have taken place. Thus, it is reasonable to consider divestment a management tool that will be used more frequently in the future.[30]

Hayes suggested that many managers see divestiture as simply the reverse side of acquisition.[31] When considered from a corporate strategy perspective, however, divestiture is quite different from acquisition. Specifically, the manager cannot simply take acquisition decision processes and do the reverse to accommodate divestiture decisions.[32]

A fundamental reason for a divestment is to clarify the divesting firm's image as perceived by the stock market. Potential investors cannot fully value a conglomerate firm's many diverse business units because the overall strategy and resulting direction are unclear to the stock buyer. As a result, the stock price of the conglomerate firm is priced artificially low.[33] Indeed, a number of researchers have noted the tendency for share prices to rise after a divestiture announcements.

Divestiture is not only a way to refocus the firm. It contains an element of power for a new strategic decision maker who attempts to assert independence from past policies. Stahl examined the divestiture decisions of 339 executives and found that nearly all of their decisions were influenced by the absence of the executive who had made the acquisition earlier.[34]

Sometimes, divestitures are required by governments due to concern about the size or monopoly power of some firms. In 1995, a government sponsored panel recommended that the Japanese government split up NTT, the Japanese telecommunications giant. The panel cited the need for competition to lower prices. At the time, telephone calls between different regions of Japan were sometimes so expensive that it was cheaper to use an overseas telephone carrier and route calls through another country.[35]

Bankruptcy

Bankruptcy varies from one country to another because of various bankruptcy laws. Differing national laws provide differing degrees of protection from creditors while the firm attempts to reschedule its debt payments and correct the situation that caused the financial difficulty. This section deals with US bankruptcy laws because some of the highly publicized cases involving firms using bankruptcy as a temporary strategy and reemerging as a viable firm have occurred under those laws.

Some executives use a declaration of bankruptcy under Chapter 11 of the US bankruptcy laws as a temporary way to seek legal protection from their creditors. The time gained is usually used to restructure the firm and its debts. The firm usually emerges in a leaner form from bankruptcy and resumes operations. Examples are Continental Airlines, which used bankruptcy to void a union contract, and Braniff Airlines, which used bankruptcy to restructure. The John Manville Corporation filed for protection of the courts under the bankruptcy laws while deciding how to handle its asbestos-related lawsuits. In 1989, Eastern Airlines used bankruptcy as a way to stop negative cash flow during a labor strike. If a firm is unable to restructure while in bankruptcy, it may liquidate the entire firm or at least divest major parts.

For a retailer, bankruptcy may have particular risks. In early 1990, as part of the largest retailing bankruptcy in history, the Campeau Corporation used Chapter 11 as a way to seek protection from its creditors.[36] As a retailer, B. Altman & Co. found that liquidation may be inevitable due to the unwillingness of suppliers to ship inventory.[37]

Liquidation

Perhaps the most dramatic admission of failure of all the restructuring strategies is liquidation. A visible example is Eastern Airline's liquidation in 1991. Grounded Eastern aircraft awaiting sale in the Atlanta airport in 1991 were a reminder that even large corporations can fail and be dismantled.

Corporate Strategies and SWOT

There are generic corporate strategies that tend to be more appropriate for certain combinations of internal strengths and weaknesses with external opportunities and threats than other combinations. Figure 5.4 relates the generic corporate strategies to various SWOT combinations.

The "grow" quadrant is the most enviable of the four quadrants. With numerous environmental opportunities and substantial internal strengths, the firm can grow and invest. Concentrating on the current products and markets or pursuing M&A as a growth strategy are relevant.

The "shrink" quadrant is just the opposite. With major environmental threats and critical internal weaknesses, downsizing and withdrawal are appropriate.

The "transport strength" quadrant, with substantial internal strengths and major environmental threats, suggests that the firm should use its strengths in slightly different arenas. Therefore, diversifying into related areas and pursuing M&A with others in related areas are appropriate strategies.

The "overcome weaknesses" quadrant, with numerous environmental opportunities and critical internal weaknesses, suggests that the firm take strategic actions

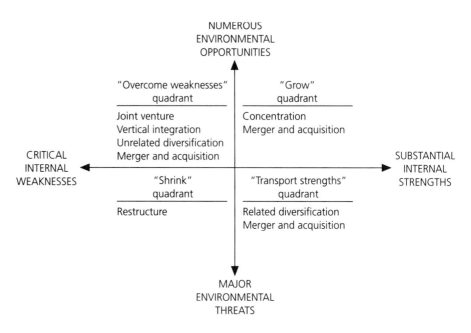

Figure 5.4 SWOT and corporate strategies.
Source: Reproduced from Stahl, M. J. and Grigsby, D. W., *Strategic Management: Formulation and Implementation* (1992), p. 47.

to overcome or avoid the weaknesses. Temporary (joint venture) or long-term partnerships (M&A) with others, integration back to the source of raw material or forward to the retail consumer, or diversification into other areas that avoid the weaknesses may be appropriate strategies. The existence of M&A in three of the four quadrants indicates that the M&A strategy can be used as a complement to different objectives.

HOW THE JAPANESE WON THE BATTLE FOR VCRs

The videocassette recorder was first developed by Ampex in the United States and shortly thereafter by RCA and Philips of Eindhoven in the Netherlands. But as with most breakthrough products, these were seen as high-margin niche products for industrial and professional application in broadcasting studios. The strategy was to reap the rewards of innovation before others caught up, and the product was priced at over US$1500 to maximize profits.

The Japanese strategy was to look for a massively enlarged market of ordinary consumers. Thus, companies like Victor, Sharp, and Sony-Betamax aimed for the consumer electronics market and a price below $500 (now below $250). What was needed was the development and refinement of a low-cost reliable product. The authors of Made in America *comment:*

> *One key factor in Japanese success was superior engineering. Another was the willingness to invest heavily in both product development and process development for more than two decades while cash returns were low and growing only very slowly. American industry proved much less ready to do this. Over the same period, many*

American firms were actually retreating from consumer-electronics markets, progressively ceding products and functions to foreign competitors and diversifying into less risky and more profitable businesses such as car rentals and financial services, unrelated to their original line of work. We think we have detected a systematic unwillingness or inability of US companies to "stick to their knitting" and maintain technological leadership after the first big returns have been captured.

There was a sad sequel. Ampex, which had pioneered the product but had failed to commercialize it for consumers, now finds its niche market for sophisticated studio equipment eroding, as Japanese competitors, using the cost saving from their high-volume business, systematically underprice it. It is more strategically effective to go for broadened markets first and then mop up the high margin niches, than to go for profitable niches initially.

Sources: Hampden-Turner, C. and Trompenaars, A., The Seven Cultures of Capitalism: Value Systems for Creating Wealth in the United States, Japan, Germany, France, Britain, Sweden and the Netherlands. *New York: Doubleday (1993), p. 184; Dertouzas, M., Lester, R. and Solow, R.,* Made in America: Regaining the Productive Edge. *Cambridge, MA: MIT Press (1989).*

Total Quality and Corporate Strategies

What is the implication of TQM for corporate strategy? Does the era of international competition in which customers have many choices have any implications for corporate strategy?

The customer and corporate strategy

Before the advent of intense global competition, many managers chose corporate strategies with little regard for customer value. Many strategy models were based upon complex financial calculations, with shareholder return as a primary criterion.

Lower trade barriers and deregulated global commerce yield a new internationally competitive era. Now, customers can vote with their money among competing international firms for the one providing the best value. This globally competitive environment forces managers to decide strategy with a customer focus. Therefore, there are certain corporate strategies that will flourish in such a competitive, customer-focused environment.

The strength of concentration and weakness of diversification

Understanding customers and their needs in narrowly defined markets is a formidable challenge. Market share battles in autos, telecommunications, beer, consumer electronics, motorcycles, and earth moving equipment show how hard it is to provide and continually improve superior value to customers in one industry.

It is virtually impossible for managers in a widely diversified firm like LTV or Hanson to provide superior value to customers and continually improve that value in each of the different markets. Focused global competitors in one market will not stand still while diversified managers are tending to several other markets and other customers.

Table 5.2   Winners of European Quality Award

Year	Winner	Area of concentration
1992	Rank Xerox Limited	Office machines
1993	Milliken European Division	Textiles
1994	Design to Distribution Ltd (D2D of ICL Computers)	Contract electronics
1995	Texas Instruments Europe	Semiconductors and electronics

Source: 1995 European Quality Award Special Report. Brussels: European Foundation for Quality Management (1995), pp. 34, 54.

Therefore, it is forecast that concentration or related diversification will be the corporate strategies of choice in an era of global competition and TQM. In contrast, it is forecasted that conglomerate diversification will decline in importance in an era of global competition, demanding customers, and continuous improvement.

It is no accident that America's ten most admired corporations that consistently show up in *Fortune* magazine in the 1990s are firms pursuing concentration or related diversification. Firms like Merck, AT&T, Rubbermaid, Wal-Mart, Liz Claiborne, J&J, Levi Strauss, Coca-Cola, 3M, Pepsico, and P&G repeatedly appear in the lists. These firms concentrate on certain products and markets.

Similarly, the firms that won the European Quality Award from 1992 to 1995 concentrate on certain products and markets. Each of these firms in table 5.2 became world class at providing superior value to customers in specific markets.[38]

In 1995, some Chinese corporations were exceptions to the trend toward concentration. Some believed that size and diversification were assets. Zheng Duxun, President of Sinochem, China's largest company, with operations in oil, chemicals, exporting, and importing, described the aim of the $15 billion firm: "We must diversify in all areas and very rapidly to compete".[39] Such firms often contained banks and export-import companies to help gain financing and international distribution.

Sustained competitive advantage

The sustainability of competence in a type of competition must be considered.[40] Sustained competitive advantage is likely if the company is committed to a particular kind of competitive strategy throughout its operations.[41] Gale recently argued that firms should enter and invest only in businesses where they can be quality and value leaders since such leadership provided sustained competitive advantage.[42]

An example of a firm having a sustained competitive advantage is the Wal-Mart Corporation. Its sustained competitive advantage is in terms of the low cost of its operations. Concern for low-cost operations permeates the organization. For example, its locations are low cost; it owns its own transportation and distribution network; and it uses information systems to link point of sale information at the cash register to automatic reordering from strategically located warehouses or directly from major vendors.[43] Partly because of its low costs, which were translated into low prices, Wal-Mart has become the world's largest discount retailer, with estimated 1996 sales of about US$105 billion.[44]

▌ Summary ▌

This chapter explores the corporate-level strategic decisions associated with the question, "What business(es) should we be in?" International competition, concepts of TQM, strategic fit and core competency, and current practice support concentration in corporate-level strategy. Often, conglomerate diversification is an admission of failure to compete.

Six different corporate-level strategies are covered in this chapter. Certain generic corporate strategies seem to be appropriate for certain SWOT conditions.

Concentration strategies include both similar product/service and narrow-market focus firms. Such concentrated firms stay closest to their specialized competence but suffer the risk of variability in earnings more than many other firms.

Partly to address those risks, diversification strategies are formulated. Horizontal diversification strategies include both related/concentric diversification and unrelated/conglomerate diversification. In the related category, there is some form of corporate synergy, fit, or focus related to distinctive competence that ties the business units together. In the conglomerate mode, there is no common theme tying the unrelated businesses together. Ideally, the unrelatedness itself insulates the firm from variability in earnings. Considerable evidence supports concentric fit as a way to diversify and stick to a profitable core competence.

Forward vertical integration, as a corporate strategy, involves integrating the firm forward or downstream to move closer to the end-use customer. Alternatively, backward integration is an upstream move closer to raw material sources. Company operations along many stages of the vertical integration dimension can be viewed as a form of vertical diversification.

The strategic world of mergers and acquisition is a world unto itself with its own language. With high-stakes games ranging into the billions of dollars, M&A is pursued for a variety of reasons. If there is a lack of fit between the two organizations it is not unusual for the merger or acquisition to fail and be dissolved in a subsequent divestiture.

Joint ventures are an increasingly popular form of temporary corporate strategic linkage. Due to the need to acquire the technological expertise of another or the need to gain access to markets, a number of firms, particularly those with international operations, are pursuing such temporary corporate marriages.

Partly due to intense international competition, there was a wave of corporate restructuring in the USA in the mid and late 1980s. A number of European firms restructured in the 1990s. As companies attempted to refocus on what they did best, there was much retrenchment activity, including plant closings, layoffs, salary cuts, and corporate slimming exercises. Divestiture is a strategy to help a firm refocus and increase its profitability by shedding business units unrelated to its core competence.

DISCUSSION QUESTIONS

1 How do the concepts of strategic fit, core competency, and related diversification compare to one another?

2 How do the concepts of unrelatedness and conglomerate diversification relate to one another?

3 Discuss the advantages and the disadvantages of concentration strategies.

4 Compare and contrast the concepts of horizontal diversification and vertical integration. Describe the advantages and disadvantages of each.

5 Why do so many mergers and acquisitions fail?

6 Describe the advantages and the risks of pursuing a joint venture versus a merger.

7 Describe the advantages and the risks of restructuring.

8 How will international competition cause the customer to grow in importance in strategic planning in the 1990s?

9 Describe the impact of total quality on concentration and diversification strategies in the 1990s.

KEY TERMS

Acquisition	usually implies an unfriendly or hostile takeover without the sanction of the acquired firm.
Backward vertical or upstream integration	is operation near to the stage of raw materials production.
Concentric marketing	refers to offering differentiated products or services in a narrow market.
Concentric operations	refers to the production of similar products or services for broad markets.
A conglomerate	is a widely diversified firm with unrelated products and markets.
Core competency	is that set of activities or functions in which the organization is particularly skilled.
Corporate-level strategy	refers to decisions on what business(es) the firm should be in.
Divestiture	refers to selling a division or business unit.
Forward vertical or downstream integration	is operation near to retailing the product/service directly to the consumer.
A golden parachute	is a severance package for the top-level executives of the purchased company.

Greenmail	is the corporate purchase of stock from a corporate raider at a premium.
A joint venture	is a pooling of resources and risk by pursuing a temporary legal, business relationship.
Junk bonds	are corporate bonds with very low ratings and high interest rates.
Leveraged buyout (LBO)	refers to using or pledging the assets of the acquired firm to repay or secure the debt from the purchase.
Liquidation	refers to selling the firm's assets, usually under the supervision of the courts, to satisfy the firm's out-of-control indebtness, and ceasing operations as an entity.
Management fit	is the benefit from managerial experience in similar areas.
Market development	seeks to expand the customer base for present product lines.
A merger	is the friendly joining together of two organizations as in a corporate marriage.
Operating fit	is the realization of economies from internal operations, such as purchasing, warehousing, production and operations, research and development, or personnel from more than one product or service.
Penetration strategies	seek to increase market share.
Poison pills	are measures implemented to deter hostile takeovers.
Product development strategies	slightly modify basic product lines to capture more of the market.
Product–market fit	is the use of common distribution channels, sales forces, promotion techniques, or customers for more than one product or service.
Pure concentration	refers to offering similar products or services in narrow markets.
A raider	is a wealthy individual who attempts to take over corporations for near-term profit.
Retrenchment	is downsizing and cost cutting to meet a marketplace with reduced demand for the firm's products or services.
Strategic fit	refers to the relatedness of activities in an organization.
Synergy	is the hoped for non-linear benefit arising from the combination of two activities yielding results greater than a linear combination predicts.
A white knight	is an organization or individual that rescues a company involved in a hostile takeover by buying the company on more friendly terms.
Vertical integration	is the operation of the firm near to both the end-use consumer and the source of raw material at the same time.

QUALITY CASE

Caterpillar and Komatsu Compete Globally through Quality: Cat Concentrates and Komatsu Diversifies

Caterpillar, Inc. (Cat) is the world's largest producer of earth moving machinery. Its products include tractors, scrapers, graders, compactors, loaders, off-highway trucks, and pipelayers. Cat also makes diesel and turbine engines and lift trucks. Sales in 1995 reached US$16 billion, with nearly 50 percent coming from international sales.[a] The percentage of international sales is expected to approach 75 percent by 2010. Cat's big yellow equipment is found throughout the world.

Cat's fiercest global rival throughout the 1980s and 1990s has been Komatsu Ltd of Tokyo. Komatsu's 1994 global construction equipment sales were forecast at US$7.5 billion. Komatsu's rally cry had been, "Catch up to Caterpillar and surpass it."[b]

It appeared for a while that Cat might lose. Komatsu had lower cost labor in the 1980s. Cat's work force was relatively more expensive in the 1980s.

In the mid-1980s, Komatsu's US market share was near 15 percent. In 1988, Komatsu started a joint venture in the USA with Dresser Industries, for manufacturing and distribution in Cat's backyard. The combined Komatsu – Dresser US market share leaped to 20 percent. With Cat's US market share in 1988 around 35 percent and holding, it appeared that Komatsu – Dresser might overtake Cat. In the face of such growing international competition, what was Cat to do?

Rather than shrinking in the face of fierce Japanese competition, Cat fought back and fought back hard on at least three fronts. First, Cat made a dramatic investment in and commitment to quality. Its Plant With A Future (PWAF) idea includes total quality control (TQC), computer integrated manufacturing (CIM), and just-in-time (JIT) production. Conceptually, "PWAF is a purely customer driven manufacturing philosophy."[c] CIM used computers throughout the manufacturing process for scheduling, machine control, and inventory tracking. JIT scheduled the delivery of parts as they were needed rather than hold them in inventory. This helped to spot quality problems as they occurred. Part of Cat's commitment to quality includes educating its suppliers in quality improvement methods at the Caterpillar Quality Institute.[d]

Second, Cat kept a lid on its costs so that Komatsu did not achieve a substantial competitive cost advantage. This global competition highlighted Cat's higher labor costs. To keep labor costs in line, Cat suffered a bitter, highly visible strike in 1992 by the United Auto Workers, which was resolved only after Cat threatened to hire permanent replacements.[e] Another strike that began in 1994 has had little impact on sales. Despite the strike, Cat has achieved record sales, production, and shipment records, with a high percentage of temporary employees.[f] Cat also kept its supplier costs low by educating its suppliers to use quality techniques as a way to reduce the cost of manufacturing.[g]

Third, Cat kept its dealer network strong to provide service to its customers. In 1992, Cat estimated that its 65 full line US dealers had a net worth of $1.72 billion, versus Komatsu – Dresser's net worth of $300 million for its 60 US and Canadian dealers.[h] Cat recognized the importance of suppliers and dealers as part of Cat's system to provide value to customers. Providing value to its customers was a large part of Cat's business strategy.

Cat's commitment to quality, its cost controls, and its networks of suppliers and dealers paid off in the early 1990s. Cat gained market share at Komatsu's expense in the USA. "In four key products (crawler tractors, crawler loaders, hydraulic excavators and wheel loaders), Komatsu/Dresser's unit market share dropped from 20.3 percent in 1988 to 18 percent in 1991. Caterpillar's US market share rose from 34.5 percent to 36.4 percent in the same period."[i] Komatsu – Dresser's joint venture had problems in terms of realizing the goal of overtaking Cat.[j] After suffering a loss associated with the strike in 1992, Cat's profits grew strongly in 1993 and 1994.[k]

Komatsu decided to diversify away from construction equipment with only half of its sales in the mid-1990s in construction equipment. " 'Komatsu isn't only for a bulldozer anymore,' says Satoru Anzaki, executive managing director of Komatsu's international operations."[l]

Cat concentrated on its construction equipment business with quality, cost control, and networks of suppliers and dealers. Its strategy of providing value to its customers became part of its business strategy. This helped Komatsu to answer the corporate strategy question of what business they were in by diversifying away from construction equipment.

Discussion Questions

1 How important was Cat's strategy of providing value to its customers through quality, price and dealer networks to its corporate objectives?

2 How did Komatsu's decision to diversify affect its competitive strength in construction equipment?

Sources: **a.** "Caterpillar, Inc.," in *Hoover's Masterlist Database*. Austin, TX: The Reference Press (1996); **b.** "Komatsu throttles back on construction equipment," *The Wall Street Journal* (May 13, 1992), p. A5; **c.** Vichas, R. P. and Mroczkowski, T., "Caterpillar, Inc. in Latin America," in Stahl, M. J. and Grigsby, D. W. (eds), *Strategic Management for Decision Making* (1992), pp. 922–42; **d.** Cayer, S. "Welcome to Caterpillar's Quality Institute," *Purchasing* (August 16, 1990), pp. 80–4; **e.** "Caterpillar's Don Fites: why he didn't blink," *Business Week* (August 10, 1992), pp. 56–7; **f.** Rose, R., "Caterpillar had a record profit in fourth quarter," *The Wall Street Journal* (January 25, 1995), p. A2; **g.** Cayer; **h.** "Komatsu throttles back on construction equipment"; **i.** Ibid.; **j.** Kelly, K., "A dream marriage turns nightmarish," *Business Week* (April 29, 1991), pp. 94–5; **k.** "Caterpillar"; **l.** "Komatsu throttles back on construction equipment".

INTERNATIONAL
C   A   S   E

"FORTE'S FORTÉ"

The largest hotel chain in the UK and the eighth-largest in the world is Britain's Forte PLC.[a] Chairman Rocco Forte's Italian immigrant father started the family business as a milk bar on London's Regent Street in 1935. After the Second World War, the business expanded rapidly after it won the contract food business for Heathrow Airport and the rights to operate roadside service areas on Britain's emerging highway system. The shift into the hotel business didn't begin until 1958, with the acquisition of the Waldorf Hotel in central London.[b]

Today, the Forte PLC empire consists of hotels and food service establishments that serve almost every segment of their respective markets. From the most luxurious hotels and restaurants to the most economical roadside chains, Forte has established a strong international presence, especially in Europe and North America. On the upper end of the market, its holdings include some of the world's oldest and most famous hotels, such as Brown's in London, the Savoy group (Forte owns 68 percent of these old-world luxury hotels), and New York's Plaza Athenée. At the lower end, it includes the economy TraveLodge and Forte Posthouse chains. This diversity, however, did not translate into strong earnings in the early 1990s.[c]

According to some long-time company employees, it would be hard to overestimate the impact Rocco Forte has had on corporate strategy.[d] He became chairman in 1992 after his father stepped aside. At the time, recession and the Gulf War had severely squeezed profits, which shrank from £185 million to £60 million (US$362 million to $107 million) between 1991 and 1992. Another difficulty was the increase in interest rates just at the time Forte increased its borrowing for acquisitions (at variable rates). This left the Forte group with greater debt-servicing obligations than it felt comfortable with. It was obvious that the new chairman faced some difficult strategic challenges as he took over the helm.[e]

Since then, Forte's number one priority has been to perceivably improve the quality of service at all Forte hotels and restaurants. In 1995, the company began testing a quality improvement plan and a system for measuring its success. Another step toward increased quality was divestiture of businesses in which the public was not the customer. For example, the customers of Alpha, the airport food chain, were airlines and airport facilities. Forte performs better when it has more direct contact with the customers who actually experience its products and services. In addition, management decided to sell several other "non-core" interests like its 50 percent stake in Kentucky Fried Chicken (Great Britain). These two divestitures alone raised £193 million (US$289.5 million), giving the company the cash necessary to fuel expansion and better control debt.[f]

Next, Forte has been interested in pushing the company into new markets with recognized brand names. In addition to a strong British foundation, the company has a significant presence in the rest of Europe and America, with such names as Harvester, Posthouse, and TraveLodge. In 1994, Forte reached a £214 million (US$321 million) agreement to purchase Meridien, the widely recognized French hotel chain. The acquisition included 54 hotels, of which 44 are management contracts rather than outright ownership. Forte hopes to consolidate many of its premium hotels under the Meridien name. Rocco Forte feels, "the important thing is to lock into your customers, find out what they want, and clearly define your brands."[g]

One way Forte is achieving this goal is through its computerized guest-recognition system at its luxury properties. Guests can rest assured that they will find their favorite champagne and preferred flowers without having to retrain the staff. Forte makes the simple assertion, "If people like what you give them and they're comfortable, they're loath to change."[h]

Rocco Forte appears determined to develop the Forte group into the number one international hotel business. He is quick to note that Sheraton, Hilton, and Inter-Continental have about 50,000 rooms each, while Forte has only 25,000 rooms (including Meridien). This does not mean that the company is about to go on a shopping spree. Instead, it is likely to continue with its corporate strategy of acquisitions and divestitures. Also, Forte will consider management agreements and other possible alliances that will help it achieve its ambitions.[i]

The latest figures show that business is strong in the key London market, but it is still a long way back to the record high levels of the 1980s, when pre-tax profits topped £200 million (US$350 million). However, it is a sign that the company is on the right road back.[j]

Forte's pre-tax income for the fiscal year ending January, 1996 was £190 million (US$300 million), up 65 percent from the previous year. After following a strategy of acquisitions and divestitures, Forte itself became the target of an acquisition in 1996 by the Granada Group, a UK-based consumer services group.

Discussion Questions

1   How is Forte coordinating its divestiture and acquisition strategy to deliver more value to its customers?

2   Branding has become an important issue in the hotel industry. How could a brand name like TraveLodge or Meridien give an advantage to Forte?

3   An acquisition strategy usually means the integration of two or more organizations. What obstacles must be overcome in order to achieve a successful integration?

Sources: **a.** Moskowitz, M., "Trusthouse Forte," *The Global Marketplace* (1987), p. 609;   **b.** Martin, J., "Trusthouse Forte, PLC," *Company Histories* (1988), p. 106;   **c.** "Forte, PLC", *Inves Text*, Lehman Brothers Limited (August 4,1995);   **d.** Davidson, A., "Sir Rocco Forte," *Management Today* (February, 1995), p. 40;   **e.** Ibid.; **f.** "Hotels pay a price for luxury," *Institutional Investor* (November, 1994), p. 53;   **g.** Davidson, A., "Sir Rocco Forte," p. 40;   **h.** "Hotels pay a price for luxury," p. 53;   **i.** Davidson, A., "Sir Rocco Forte," p. 40;   **j.** Ibid., p. 41.

NOTES

1 Thompson, A. A. Jr and Strickland, A. J. III, *Strategy and Policy: Concepts and Cases*. Plano, TX: BPI (1981).

2 Prahalad, C. K. and Hamel, G., "The core competence of the corporation," *Harvard Business Review* (May–June 1990), pp. 79–91.

3 "How Wal-Mart outdid a once-touted Kmart in discount-store race," *Wall Street Journal* (March 24, 1995), p. A1.

4 "Service is our only product," in *1995 European Quality Award Special Report*. Brussels: European Foundation for Quality Management (1995), pp. 62–8.

5 "NationsBank," in *Value Line Investment Survey*. New York: Value Line (March 10, 1995), pp. 21–8.

6 Peters, T. J. and Waterman, R. N., *In Search of Excellence*. New York: Harper and Row (1982).

7 Bettis, R. A. and Hall, W. K., "Diversification strategy: accounting determined risk and accounting determined return," *Academy of Management Journal*, 25(2) (1982), pp. 254–64; Pitts, R. A. and Hopkins, R., "Firm diversity: conceptualization and measurement," *Academy of Management Review*, 7 (1984), pp. 620–9.

8 Ramanujam,V. and Varadarajan, P. R., "Diversification and performance," *Academy of Management Journal*, 30(2) (1987), pp. 380–93.

9 Amit, R. and Wernerfelt, B., "Why do firms reduce business risk?" *Academy of Management Journal*, 33 (1990), pp. 520–39.

10 Bettis, R. A., "Modern financial theory, corporate strategy, and public policy: three conundrums," *Academy of Management Review*, 3(8) (1983), pp. 406–15; Venkatraman, N. and Camillus, J., "Exploring the concept of fit in strategic management," *Academy of Management Review*, 9 (1984), pp. 513–25.

11 "Hanson ventures into power business, acquiring Eastern Group for $4 billion," *Wall Street Journal* (August 1, 1995), p. A3.

12 Markides, C., "Diversification, restructuring and economic performance," *Strategic Management Journal* (February 1995), pp. 101–18.

13 Smith, G. D., Arnold, D. R. and Bizzell, B. G., *Strategy and Business Policy: Cases*. Boston: Houghton Mifflin (1986).

14 "Knowing your place in the supply chain: how Milliken delivers quality and learned to say thank you," *European Quality*, 1(1) (1994), pp. 38–43.

15 Harrison, J. S., Hall, E. H. Jr and Caldwell, L. G., "Assessing strategy relatedness in highly diversified firms," *Journal of Business Strategies*, 7(1) (Spring 1990), pp. 34–46.

16 Siehl, C., Smith, D. and Omura, A., "After the merger: should executives stay or go?" *Academy of Management Executive*, 4(1) (1990), pp. 50–60.

17 "Godzilla Bank: huge Japanese merger could help revitalize the financial sector," *Wall Street Journal* (March 29, 1995), p. A1.

18 "Do mergers really work?" p. 90.

19 Porter, M. E., "From competitive advantage to corporate strategy," *Harvard Business Review* (May–June, 1987), p. 43.

20 Berg, S. and Friedman, P., "Corporate courtship and successful joint ventures," *California Management Review*, 22 (1980), pp. 85–91.

21 Stahl, M. J., *Strategic Executive Decision*. New York: Quorum (1989).

22 "GM mulls tough call in Toyota venture," *Wall Street Journal* (June 10, 1988), p. 1.

23 "Telecom firms scramble for foothold in Europe," *International Herald Tribune* (August 29, 1995), p. 11.

24 "2 Japan automakers join stampede to start up production in Vietnam," *International Herald Tribune* (September 8, 1995), p. 15; "Show is on the road in Vietnam," *International Herald Tribune* (September 28, 1995), p. 17.

25 O'Neill, H., "Restructuring, re-engineering, and rightsizing: do the metaphors make sense?" *The Academy of Management Executive*, VIII(4) (November 1994), pp. 9–11.

26 Pearce, J. and Robbins, D., "Restructuring remains the foundation of business turnaround," *Strategic Management Journal*, 15(5) (June 1994), pp. 407–417.

27 Iacocca, L., *Iacocca: an Autobiography*. New York: Bantam (1984).

28 "Alcatel embarks on $2 billion reorganization," *International Herald Tribune* (September 28, 1995), p. 13.

29 Alder, H. S., "The thorough way to approach divestment," *Management Focus* (May–June, 1981), pp. 3–7.

30 Nees, D., "Increase your divestment effectiveness," *Strategic Management Journal*, 2 (April–June, 1981), pp. 119–30.

31 Hayes, "New emphasis on divestment opportunities," *Harvard Business Review* (July–August, 1972).

32 Alder, H. S., "The thorough way to approach divestment"; Cohen, R. and Slatter, S., "How to divest" *Management Today* (May 1983), pp. 92–5.

33 Brooks, B., "Some concerns find that the push to diversity was a costly mistake," *Wall Street Journal* (October 2, 1984), p. 37.

NOTES CONT.

34 Stahl, *Strategic Executive Decisions*.

35 "Tokyo panel advises breakup of NTT," *International Herald Tribune* (October 4, 1995), p. 23.

36 "It'll be a hard sell: getting Campeau's creditors to agree could take years;" *Business Week* (January 29, 1990), p. 30.

37 "Lessons for Campeau: it's not easy being a Chapter II retailer," *Wall Street Journal* (January 30, 1990), p. 1.

38 "European Quality Award Criteria," in *1995 European Quality Award Special Report*. Brussels: European Foundation for Quality Management (1995), p. 34.

39 "Chinese corporations bulk up to take on the world," *Wall Street Journal* (July 5, 1995), p. A6.

40 Coyne, K. P., "Sustainable competitive advantage – what it is, what it isn't," *Business Horizons* (January–February, 1986), pp. 54–61.

41 Ghemawat, P., "Sustainable advantage," *Harvard Business Review*, 64(5) (1986), pp. 53–8.

42 Gale, B., *Managing Customer Value*. New York: Free Press (1994), p. 18.

43 "How Wal-Mart outdid a once-touted Kmart in discount-store race," *Wall Street Journal* (March 24, 1995), p. A1.

44 "Wal-Mart," in *Value Line Investment Survey*. New York: Value Line (February 23, 1996), p. 1665.

BUSINESS-LEVEL STRATEGY:
COMPETITIVE STRATEGY

LEARNING OBJECTIVES

After reading this chapter, you should be able to accomplish the following.

1 *Describe the differences and similarities between corporate and business levels of strategy.*

2 *Compare and contrast the three generic competitive strategies described in the text.*

3 *Analyze an industry with Porter's five forces model of industry competition.*

4 *Discuss the importance of the six market entry barriers described in the text.*

5 *Explain the relationship of TQ to competitive strategy.*

A firm usually decides at the corporate level in which business(es) it wishes to operate. Then it decides how to enter the chosen business. These decisions are in the realm of corporate-level strategy.

Once the corporate-level strategy has been set, the firm's executives must *decide how to operate in the chosen business*. These latter decisions comprise the *business-level strategy*. This level of strategy, how to compete in the chosen business, and the impact of TQM on strategy[1] are the subjects of this chapter.

Business-level Strategy

This section examines an important business-level strategic question. How should the firm compete in its chosen business?

Competing within the chosen industry

This level of strategy has received increasing attention in many companies due to the intensity of global competition. The intensity of that competition is appparent in the World Competitiveness Scoreboard for the years 1993 and 1994 (see figure 6.1).[2] According to IMD in Switzerland, World Competitiveness combines two primary components: (a) the statistical indicators of competitiveness as recorded by international organizations and national institutes; and (b) the perceptions of business executives on the competitiveness of their countries drawn from the yearly Executive Opinion Survey. For the first time in 1994, separate ratings of industrialized and industrializing countries were combined into one overall global rating.

In 1994, the USA and Singapore were rated as more competitive than Japan. This marked the end of an eight-year span in which Japan had been rated as the world's most competitive economy. The USA had been rated as most competitive in the early 1980s. Although the international ratings had not been compiled prior to 1980, many would have rated the USA as the most competitive world economic power after the Second World War for about forty years. History and the data indicate that global competition has become more intense in the recent past, with leadership changing and many more international competitive players.

Managers need to ask if their firm can build on a competitive advantage of their country. In an analysis of Britain's competitive advantage, Kay noted that the quality of Japan's manufactured goods is better; the USA is more innovative; scientific and technical education is better in Germany; and Italian designers are more skilled. "Britain's greatest strategic asset is the English language. This feeds directly into British competitive advantages in publishing . . . all kinds of audio-visual media, and tertiary education."[3] Recognition of national competitive advantage is an important ingredient in leveraging a corporate competitive strategy as a firm decides how to compete.

Prior to intense global competition, many managers thought that it was not necessary to pay attention to competitive strategy. Many thought that strategy was the province of the most senior executives in the firm. The speed of global competitors' moves has changed such thinking. Now managers throughout the

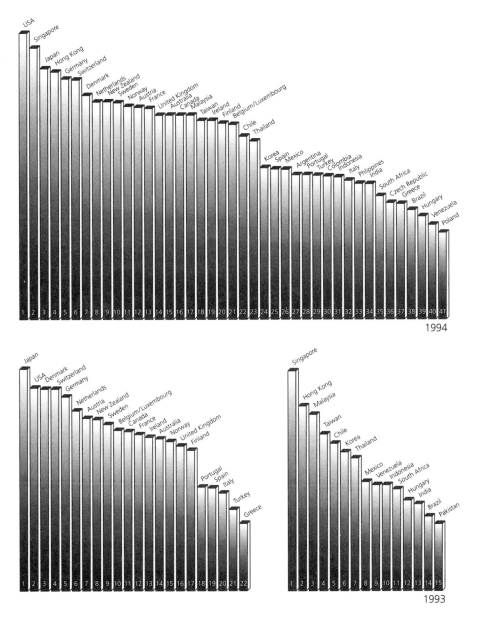

Figure 6.1 The world competitiveness scoreboard.
Source: The World Competitiveness Report. Lausanne: IMD (1994), p. 2.

firm must think in terms of the competition and competitors' moves relative to the firm's customers.

Although competitive strategy has its drawbacks, it does help the manager to think externally to the firm. Competitive strategy provides a framework for the manager to think about external issues, particularly competitive moves.

Even if the firm has operated in that industry for some time, the executives must address the question of how to compete. With the exception of monopolies, all companies compete by virtue of their daily operations. Therefore, they have a *de facto* competitive strategy. If they do not understand the competitive forces shaping their industry and respond with an explicit competitive strategy, then they leave their success to chance.

Relationship to corporate strategies

As described earlier, corporate-level strategy is a choice of which business(es) in which to operate. Competitive business-level strategy is a choice of how the firm competes in the chosen business(es). Now we examine the relationship between the two choices.

The strategic planning process and the SWOT analysis discussed earlier argue for consistency in the strategic plan if the plan is to be implementable and successful. Porter showed that a major difference between successful and failed acquisitions was the consistency between the corporate and competitive levels of strategy.[4] He contended that if a company has developed expertise in one competitive strategy at the business level, then it should enter future businesses in which that same competitive strategy is important. For example, if a firm in the consumer products industry is skilled at competing through advertising of branded products, that firm should stick to such a competitive strategy. The firm probably does not have the core competency to compete in a business in which low cost through large capital-intensive plants for standardized products is required. Therefore, the firm should enter and compete only in those businesses in which it can compete based on advertising of branded products.

Expertise in a particular competitive business-level strategy helps to determine the kinds of other businesses to enter. Thus, competitive business-level strategy influences corporate-level strategy. This link stresses the corporate-level strategies of concentration or related diversification.

The sustainability of a core competency in a type of competitive strategy must be considered.[5] Sustained competitive advantage is likely if the company is committed to a particular kind of competitive strategy throughout all of its operations.[6]

An example of a firm having a sustained competitive advantage due to a particular competitive strategy is the Compaq Computer Company. Compaq wrote the book on how to compete by offering low-priced personal computer clones to IBM computers. In 1991, Compaq seemed to lose its sense of strategy and lose market share, and fired its president, Rod Canion. In 1991, Compaq was no longer the low-price leader and was no longer profitable. In the first half of 1992, it rediscovered its low-price strategy and set the computer industry ablaze with a PC price war so that it could regain market share. Compaq introduced new products early and increased production to recognize learning curve effects and lower prices. Its low-price strategy was so successful that Compaq had trouble satisfying the demand for its low priced computers.[7] After Compaq increased production, it outsold all others in 1994 in PC sales. In 1994, Compaq sold 2,290,000 PCs versus 1,620,000 for IBM.[8]

Porter's Generic Competitive Strategies

Porter is one of the most influential writers in the area of competitive strategy. He described three separate generic strategies applicable in a variety of industries: cost leadership, differentiation, and focus.[9]

Cost leadership

Cost leadership means the lowest cost of operation in the industry. Cost leadership, *not* price leadership, is the generic strategy. A firm could be the lowest-cost producer yet not offer the lowest-priced products/services. That firm would enjoy profitability above the average in the industry. However, cost leaders often do compete on price and are very effective at such a form of competition with their low-cost structures.

Cost leadership is easier said than done. To achieve it, there must be an organization-wide commitment to achieving a low-cost structure. This commitment must be pursued without ignoring quality and other features needed by the customer. Cost leadership is pursued through low cost of quality, workforce productivity, economies of scale, experience, low wages, buyer bargaining power, etc. *Economy of scale* refers to using huge physical assets to lower the unit production cost.

A good example of cost leadership through economies of scale in the beer industry is Anheuser-Busch. Anheuser-Busch builds immense breweries with large productive capacity. This procedure spreads fixed costs over large quantities of production. In such a fashion, the unit cost of production is lower than that of competitors with smaller plants, due to Anheuser-Busch's economies of scale in water processing, refrigeration, and packaging.

Some South Korean firms used economy of scale as a way to achieve cost leadership in the manufacture of computer memory chips in the early 1990s. At a time when the Japanese economy was in severe recession and large capital Japanese investments were nearly impossible, some South Korean firms were betting billions of dollars in new chip plants to lower the cost of chip production. Samsung Electronics, Hyundai Electronics, and LG Electronics should be formidable competitors in this industry for years to come. South Korean firms controlled more than one-third of the global memory chip market in 1995, with forecasts that their worldwide market share would grow.[10]

Wal-Mart is the cost leader in the discount retail market. It has achieved this cost leadership position through a variety of means, like most cost leaders. Wal-Mart uses buyer bargaining power from large volume purchases. The firm has a very efficient, computer-intensive distribution system linked to some of its major suppliers. Wal-Mart makes use of economies of scale with extremely large strategically located distribution centers. The corporation also pays careful attention to store location. Wal-Mart is also the price leader in its industry. Thus, Wal-Mart was beating the competition in the 1990s.

There is a risk in seeking cost leadership through economies of scale and large capital investments. If demand for the product declines dramatically in a short time period, the large capital investment could become a relic. Dramatic declines in demand in a short time period are often due to a substitution effect. For example, in the 1980s, due to a fashion fad in which it was stylish to wear denim in several different ways, demand for denim skyrocketed. Whereas denim had been used primarily to make jeans for younger people and for work, denim was suddenly popular for the additional uses of jeans for men and women of a variety of ages, for denim skirts, denim jackets, and denim coats. An automobile manufacturer even upholstered the interior of a special edition automobile in denim. Consequently, the textile industry expanded productive capacity to meet the demand created by the denim fashion fad. After the fad waned, demand for denim fell. Several large denim producing plants with significant capital investment were obsolete.

Differentiation

As a competitive strategy, *differentiation* refers to a product or service that is different or somehow unique as perceived by the customer. A firm can achieve differentiation for its products or services in a number of different ways. The company can build a brand image through extensive advertising. The firm might design extra features into the product/service to make it different from competing products/services. The company could provide extra customer service with the product/service. It could operate an extensive dealer network for repair and distribution. The firm could be perceived as distributing only very high quality items. It could offer a continuous stream of new products/services and be known as an innovator. The firm might be the first to market with new products/services.

Differentiating firms assume that customers will pay extra for an item if the customers perceive that it is different. Such firms also assume that the nature of the difference is valued by the customer. However, there is a limit to how much of a premium customers will pay for a differentiated product/service.

Advertising frequently plays a large role in differentiation strategies because customers must be convinced that there is something different about the product/service. For example, Merrill Lynch spends millions of dollars advertising on television. The ads try to convince us that they have insight into financial investments that few others have.

Differentiating firms typically employ substantial consumer research efforts to identify changing consumer tastes. With such data, the firms can be the first to market with a new differentiated product. IBM and Procter & Gamble are two examples of differentiators using large consumer research efforts. Additionally, both firms advertise substantially to persuade customers that their products/services meet customers' tastes.

Glaxo Wellcome, the world's largest prescription drug company, differentiates itself by concentrating on the discovery and marketing of new drugs. To reinforce that strategy, Glaxo recently completed a billion dollar (US) science complex 30 miles north of London to house 1,500 scientists and support staff searching for new drugs. Glaxo has chosen not to diversify into healthcare in general as several of its competitors have in the 1990s.[11]

Federal Express is a good example of a firm employing a differentiation strategy. It uses superior service, including guaranteed delivery next day, tracking of the package's location, and security of the package. Land's End and L. L. Bean both provide superior service through quick delivery, a variety of sizes, stylish clothing, very high quality of merchandise, and no-hassle returns.

The Caterpillar Company differentiates itself with a broad list of quality machines, and an extensive dealer network for parts and repair. "Cats" usually do not break, but if they do, many firms know that they can get them fixed quickly. Throughout the world, many construction firms willingly pay a price for such a supply and repair service. For them, the alternative is the high cost of a delayed construction project due to broken, idle construction equipment.

Focus

Focus means concentrating on serving a particular target group, segment, or market niche. The focusing firm attends closely to the needs of the target segment, even more closely than the cost leader or differentiator. Focus refers to the narrowness of the market served, or market niche, rather than the characteristics of the product/service.

When concentrating on the market niche, cost focus or differentiation focus are two alternatives. In *cost focus*, the focusing firm offers a product/service to a market segment at a lower price than competitors. In *differentiation focus*, the focusing firm offers a product/service which is more differentiated than all competitors' comparable products/services to a market segment.

A good example of differentiation focus is a Ferrari automobile. That sports car, with its extreme attention to performance and image, with an extremely high price, is targeted at a very narrow market segment. Revco's senior citizen discounts on prescription drugs is an example of cost focus.

Stuck in the middle

Porter argued that there is a fourth, *de facto* strategy in business-level competitive strategy, which he identified as "stuck in the middle."[12] It is not an *a priori*, purposeful strategy *per se*. "Stuck in the middle" is the result of not successfully pursuing any of the three generic strategies.

Maybe the firm is not sure which of the three generic strategies is the best strategy for an industry. Sometimes the company is unwilling to commit the necessary financial resources to a market to achieve cost leadership through economy of scale. Maybe the firm is not able to achieve differentiation with unequaled quality or dealer networks. By not having the lowest costs, by not being really differentiated in the minds of the consumer, or by not successfully targeting a market segment, the firm usually experiences weak profits and limited market share.

Mercedes was stuck in the middle in the mid-1990s. Due to competition from several other luxury car makers, like Lexus, Mercedes was no longer the most differentiated car in the luxury class. However, Mercedes's prices were considerably higher than several others. In the mid-1990s, the German firm was scrambling to redesign its products and lower its costs, partly by building cars in the USA and other European countries. Such international sourcing was new for the firm as it sought to battle competition.

In the early 1990s, Kmart apparently recognized that it was stuck in the middle. It was not the lowest-priced mass merchandise retailer. Many recognized that Wal-Mart was. Nor was Kmart differentiated, as many of its stores were old and in less than desirable locations. As Kmart had difficulty lowering its costs, it was still stuck in the middle in the mid-1990s. Its chairman was replaced by the board of directors in early 1995, partly due to stockholder satisfaction with lackluster performance. It usually takes considerable work and time for large firms to change competitive strategies in the minds of consumers, as noted in the Xerox story.

INTERNATIONAL EXHIBIT

QUALITY, INTERNATIONAL COMPETITION AND THE CUSTOMER AT XEROX

In 1960, Xerox shipped its first copiers. Over the next 15 years, Xerox ruled an entire new industry it had invented.[a]

After 15 years of absolute industry dominance, Xerox became complacent and out of touch with its customers. In the late 1970s, the company produced unacceptable quality products and services at high prices. Xerox had become "stuck in the middle". It lost dramatic market share to Japanese competitors like Canon, Minolta, and Sharp. Xerox's market share tumbled from more than 90 percent in the early 1970s to less than 15 percent in the early 1980s.[b] The butt of many office jokes became the phrase: "Copier temporarily in order."

To regain customers and market share lost to the Japanese competitors, Xerox, under the leadership of David Kearns, launched its Leadership through Quality Strategy.[c] "We redefined quality as meeting the requirements of our customers. It may have been the most significant strategy Xerox had ever embarked on. Quality actually decreases costs by reducing rejects, eliminating excessive inspections and field service, and most importantly, by diminishing the cost of business lost to competitors."[d]

As a measure of the dramatic improvement, Xerox won the Malcolm Baldrige National Quality Award in 1989 and the European Quality Award in 1992. As of 1991, Xerox reported the following results. "We have reduced our average manufacturing cost by over 20 percent despite inflation. We have reduced the time it takes to bring a new product to market by up to 60 percent. We have decreased our defective parts from 8 percent to less than three-hundredths of 1 percent. We are the first American company in an industry targeted by the Japanese to regain market share without the aid of tariffs or protection of any kind."[e]

Quality, in terms of meeting customer requirements, had become an effective international competitive strategy for Xerox. The strategy yielded lower costs, quicker new products, and fewer defects, and regained customers.

Source: a. Kearns, D., "Leadership through quality," Academy of Management Executive (May 1990), p. 86–9; **b.** Kearns, D. and Nadler, D., Prophets in the Dark: How Xerox Reinvented Itself and Beat Back the Japanese. New York: Harper Business (1992), p. xiv; **c.** Osterhoff, R., Locander, W. and Bounds, G., "Competitive benchmarking at Xerox," in M. J. Stahl and G. M. Bounds (eds), Competing Globally through Customer Value. Westport, CT: Quorum Books (1991), p. 788; **d.** Kearns, "Leadership through quality"; **e.** Kearns, D., "Foreword," in Stahl and Bounds, p. ix.

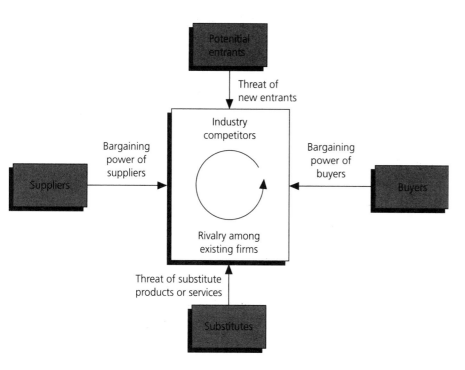

Figure 6.2   Forces driving industry competition.

Source: Reprinted with permission of The Free Press, a division of Simon & Schuster from Porter, M. E., *Competitive Strategy: Techniques for Analyzing Industries and Competitors*. New York: The Free Press (1980). Copyright © 1980 by The Free Press.

Porter's Five Forces Model

As the world economy has been engulfed by strong international competition, Porter argued that strategy equates to how the firm competes against other firms in its business. Porter argued that strategy is not just a series of models at the corporate level of strategy. He noted that strategy includes analyzing potential entrants, suppliers, buyers, substitutes, and competitors.[13]

Porter described the competitive forces shaping an industry in his five forces model of industrial competition. The model (figure 6.2) has been one of the most widely used models in strategic management. By analyzing the five forces, one can assess the forces driving competition in an industry and evaluate the odds of a firm successfully entering and competing in an industry. Thus, one can measure the industry's attractiveness for entry or exit, analyze competitive trends, and plot future strategy. The five forces are: potential entrants with their threat of entry; buyers with their bargaining power; suppliers with their bargaining power; substitutes with their threat of substitute products or services; and industry competitors with their rivalry among existing firms.

Buyers and bargaining power

Buyer power is the capability of buyers, purchasing agents, and customers of the industry to influence the price and the terms of the purchase. If buyer power is high, then the profit margins of incumbent firms tend to be low. If there are only a few buyers, or if the buyers are well organized, then buyer power may be high. The industry is unattractive to potential entrants who are considering entry if buyer power is high. Buyer power in the retail clothing industry is limited, as the buyers are so numerous. It is hard to exact price concessions from the retailer when there are numerous customers for the retailer.

Potential entrants and entry barriers

The subject of creating and maintaining market entry barriers has received considerable attention from executives. If the incumbent firms in the industry can keep potential entrants at bay and dissuade them from ever entering the industry, the entire subject of competition and its impact on incumbent firms' profits becomes moot. The threat of new firms to enter an industry is low if the incumbent firms have high power to influence prices, control resources, and shape the nature of competition within the industry.

Harley-Davidson offers an example of the effect of potential entrants. In the 1970s, many Harley executives thought that the barriers to entry into the upscale American motorcycle industry were too high because of the capital requirements and customer loyalty. Consequently, they viewed the competition in terms of other American firms and paid little attention to potential Japanese entrants. They did not regard the Japanese motorcycle companies as serious competitors partly because the Japanese entered at the low-priced end of the market. The American firms took the Japanese firms seriously after the Japanese firms had made dramatic sales inroads into the higher-end American motorcycle market with both low price and high quality.

Incumbent firms often spend substantial resources designing and building market entry barriers. Substantial entry barriers limit the competition and can yield high profitability for the incumbents. The opposite is also true. In the retail clothing industry, entry barriers tend to be low, and consequently profit margins are limited. Entry barriers are low because there are few sustainable cost advantages to incumbents, only limited financing is required to lease retail store space, and it is difficult to differentiate the product. As potential entrants can enter readily, the potential limits prices and profits.

Of all the entry barriers that have been studied, the three most important market entry barriers are cost advantages of incumbents, product differentiation of incumbents, and capital requirements.[14] Cost advantages of incumbents accrue from a variety of sources, including economies of scale, experience effects, proprietary product or process technology, favorable access to raw material, favorable location, and low cost of quality. Sony lost a cost advantage for Japanese based production of television sets when the yen appreciated dramatically in the early 1990s. In response, Sony stopped exporting TVs made in Japan in 1996. Japanese consumer electronics makers shifted about 70 percent of the production of their products abroad in the early 1990s.[15] Product differentiation of incumbents refers to the brand identification and customer loyalties associated with the incumbent firm's existing products/services. The need to invest large amounts of financial resources creates a barrier to entry called capital requirements.

3.23

4.10

Suppliers and bargaining power

Supplier power is the capability of vendors or suppliers to decide the price and the terms of supply. Suppliers include vendors of labor, raw materials, and capital goods. If supplier power is high, then the profit margins of incumbent firms in the industry tend to be low. Such low profit margins make an industry less attractive to potential entrants evaluating an entry decision. A rough measure of supplier power is the number of suppliers in the industry. The existence of many suppliers typically indicates low supplier power, and vice versa.

Supplier power in the steel industry is formidable for the large, mature steel companies, like Bethlehem Steel and Republic Steel. The United Steel Workers Union has near monopoly supplier power on the supply of labor to the steel industry. The concentrated supplier power keeps the labor cost of large, mature, domestic steel firms high. To get around such high supplier power, several small mini-mills, like Nucor Steel, have been started within the recent past with non-union lower-cost labor. Thus, the mini-mills are able to keep their labor cost low and compete with low priced Japanese and Korean steel imports.

Substitute products and services

The availability of substitutes for an industry's products and services alters the power of incumbent firms. As the availability of substitutes rises and as the ease of substitution increases, the power of incumbent firms to control prices and the terms of the business declines. A good example of a competitive force arising from a substitute product is the substitution of aluminum for steel in many uses. "I'll grant that steel makes a good railroad rail," says David Reynolds, retired chairman and son of the founder of Reynolds Metals Co., "but anything else we've got a shot at."[16] Such substitution was partly responsible for the growth of the aluminum industry and the shrinkage of the steel industry in the 1980s and the 1990s, when both were faced with global competition. In 1995, Alcoa announced that it was building a plant in the upper midwest to make structural aluminum components for automobiles. This further encroached upon the historical market of the steel industry.

Competitors and rivalry

Competitive rivalry among existing firms in an industry is the extent to which firms respond to competitive moves of other incumbent firms. In some industries, an implicit "gentleman's agreement" seems to exist in which firms respect one another's market niches and follow a "live and let live" strategy. In other industries, a "dog eat dog" idea prevails, cutthroat competition is the rule, and competitive moves are vigorously countered.

A good example of competitive forces shaped by the rivalry among incumbent firms is the soft drink industry. The soft drink industry is infamous for its "Cola Wars," in which millions of dollars in advertising are spent to protect a market share. So that one did not gain a competitive lead over the other, both Coca-Cola and Pepsi were each experimenting with iced tea in the early 1990s.[17] In almost every situation, the two firms aggressively matched each other's moves.

Porter's five forces model offers a way to analyze the competitive dynamics in

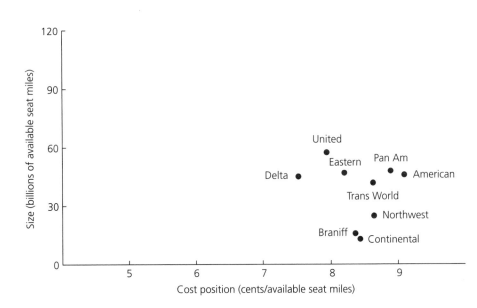

Figure 6.3 Competitive group map of the airline industry, 1981.
Source: *Moody's Transportation Manual*. New York: Moody's Investor's Service (1982).

an industry. After such an initial analysis, competitive group analysis can help with market entry and product positioning decisions.[18]

Competitive group analysis

Competitive group analysis is an important way to analyze the competitive structure in an industry. By plotting how the major firms in an industry compete along two competitive dimensions, an executive starts an analysis concerning positioning the firm and its products/services.

There are several steps involved in the analysis and graphical presentation of competitive groups. First, identify the important competitive dimensions in the industry. *Competitive dimensions* are the specific factors the firms are using to compete within the industry. Competitive dimensions are more specific, like quality, size of market served, number of products, dealer network, etc., than the generic competitive strategies in the industry. For example, in the 1990s, one might argue that a primary competitive strategy in the airline industry is differentiation. However, to conduct a strategic group analysis, a specific description of differentiation via number of markets served is required. The second step is to construct two dimensional plots of the competitive dimensions with the positions of the competitors. The third step is to analyze the firm's position relative to competitors.

Examples of competitive groups from the US airline industry in 1981 and 1989 are contained in figures 6.3 and 6.4. Those dates are chosen because they show the massive movement associated with deregulation in the 1980s. Cost and size of the airline are the important competitive dimensions. Size is a proxy for how many

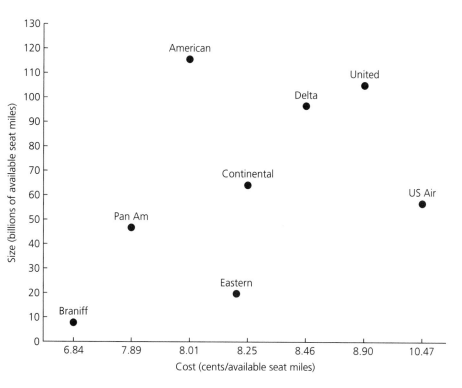

Figure 6.4 Competitive group map of the airline industry, 1989.
Source: Annual reports of the eight airlines, 1989.

different destinations the traveler can reach without switching airlines. Airline size is measured by available seat miles (ASM). Cost is measured by operating expense per ASM, a commonly used measure of airline cost structure.[19]

In 1981, the major airlines operated with similar costs. This was associated with the government's regulation of prices, which provided little incentive for the airlines to reduce costs. As has been demonstrated in many industries, regulation of prices encouraged competition on bases other than price. Price competition became very relevant only after the industry had been deregulated. Then, costs became very important. The 1989 plot of airline competitive groups in figure 6.4 shows the different positioning of the airlines once cost assumed importance.

It is quite common to see a diagonal pattern in a strategic group map like the 1989 plot if one of the dimensions is cost/price, and the other dimension is a specific form of differentiation. For many products/services, the customer demands more of the differentiated dimension or feature as the price increases. Many would argue: "You get what you pay for." It is the off diagonal positions that may present unique opportunities for market entry or product/service positioning.

Market entry and product positioning

Competitive group analysis shows the soundness of current competitive strategy, the need for repositioning in that industry, the wisdom of entering the industry, and how to position new products/services. A competitive group plot can help a firm to decide where on the diagonal to position itself and anticipate average profitability for the industry. If the firm can achieve an off-diagonal position connoting greater differentiation at lower cost/price, the firm may realize above average profitability for the industry. Off diagonal high-value positions can be achieved by different or proprietary technology; or high-quality products/services that also lower the firm's costs; or more differentiated products/services at the same cost.

Total Quality and Competitive Strategy

Before the study of competitive strategy, little attention was paid to business-level strategy. Many firms, like British Airways, GM, Harley-Davidson, Mercedes, and Xerox, rue the time when they ignored or underestimated their competitors, especially in the intense internationally competitive arena in which many firms operate. But let us recognize some risks associated with competitive strategy.

Competitors or customers?

By definition, competitive strategy involves concentrating on the firm's competitors. Competitors are at the heart of Porter's generic competitive strategies, are at the center of Porter's five forces model in figure 6.2, and are analyzed in competitor group analysis. Such a concentration on competitors frequently comes at the expense of concentrating on the customer.

The best competitive strategy is a customer value strategy. By concentrating on exceeding customer requirements in a TQ mode, the firm will be in a better position than its competitors to retain current customers and win new customers.

Concentration on competitors' current products and services usually results in the firm pursuing a follower mentality. Such followership results in imitation rather than innovation. By definition, a firm cannot be the early market entrant with new products/services if the firm merely imitates the competition. In an era in which customers are constantly demanding new products and services with the latest technology, late market entrants pay a stiff penalty in ignoring customers.[20] In studying the impact of slow product introduction in the PC industry, *The Wall Street Journal* reported: "Introducing a new generation of PCs just three months behind schedule can cost a company 40 percent to 50 percent of the gross profit it had planned to make on the new line."[21]

Under a TQ banner, firms benchmark competitors primarily for the best processes and systems. Firms develop new products and services through intense examination, understanding, and projection of customers' future requirements. Understanding competitors' current products is *not* the key to the design of new products or services. Customers are important for new product/service design *and* competitors are important for process/system design, in that order.

Buyers or customers?

The use of the term buyer versus customer is unfortunate because it connotes a near adversarial exchange. It certainly does not connote a partnering relationship.

The background of the five forces model in industrial economics connotes the near adversarial exchange based upon the bargaining power idea. It suggests that if there is some way to weaken the bargaining power of the buyer, then all is well and the firm need not worry about exceeding or even satisfying customer requirements.

Suppliers or partners?

In today's competitive world, which demands zero defect production and delivery, many firms recognize their suppliers as partners in their system.[22] The idea of supplier power based in industrial economics connotes the adversarial mentality described in the preceding section. GM recently forced its suppliers to compete more based on price. This caused many writers to wonder how such a move would impact the quality of the products.[23] Some view the willingness to treat suppliers as partners as an acid test in the commitment to continuous quality improvement.[24]

Cost leadership and differentiation through total quality

A reading of Porter's generic competitive strategies suggests that most firms typically achieve only one of the generic competitive strategies. Some firms never achieve even one of the three strategies and remain "stuck in the middle."

Two separate analyses of Porter's generic competitive strategies argued that cost leadership and differentiation are simultaneously achievable. Both may be required to achieve sustained competitive advantage in the industry. High quality, innovation, learning effects, and economies of scale were mentioned as some conditions for achieving both generic competitive strategies.[25]

Mintzberg, the noted strategist, recently offered an alternative to Porter's three generic competitive strategies.[26] Mintzberg's list of strategies specifically included differentiation by quality as a generic strategy. Mintzberg also included differentiation by image, design, price, and support, as well as undifferentiated, to complete his list of six strategies. A recent comparison of Porter's and Mintzberg's lists of generic strategies offered support for Mintzberg's list.[27]

Several writers have contended that flawless quality, and the systems that produce it, are the principal ways to simultaneously achieve both low cost and differentiation.[28] This is a chief idea of TQ stressed throughout this book. Cost leadership is associated with low cost of quality, high workforce productivity, flat organizational structures, and short response times. Differentiation is associated with dedication to providing flawless quality and value to customers.

This TQ strategy seems to have been employed successfully by many Japanese firms in several industries, including consumer electronics and automobiles.[29] D2D, P&G, TNT Express, Texas Instruments Europe, Xerox, and Warner-Lambert are some of the growing number of firms who have used quality to achieve both low cost and differentiation.[30] In the 1990s, customers demand affordable quality due to choices from international competition.

A good example of a British firm using quality to achieve both low cost and differentiation is TNT Express, which won the first UK Quality Award in 1994.[31] The logistics and transport company started its total quality initiative in 1989. Through 1993, profit increases have been achieved every year; profit margins have increased from 5.3 to 9.7 percent; the unit cost per shipment has decreased by 20 percent; TNT has been the first choice carrier among UK business each year since 1991; on-time deliveries have risen from 94 to 97.8 percent; and, the customer base has expanded from 62,000 in 1989 to 105,000.

▮ Summary ▮

The relationship between the corporate and business levels of strategy is reviewed. The two levels of strategy should be consistent. The firm should compete at the business level in ways in which the firm has skill. This further supports concentration or related diversification as corporate strategies.

As a generic business-level competitive strategy, cost leadership means production of the product/service at the lowest cost in the industry. Differentiation means the offering of a product/service that is perceived by the customer as somehow unique or different. As a competitive strategy, the focuser serves a specific target group, segment, or market niche, and serves it well.

Porter modeled how firms compete in an industry with his five forces model of industry competition. Those five forces are: potential entrants with their threat of entry; buyers with their bargaining power; substitutes with their threat of substitute products or services; suppliers with their bargaining power; and, industry competitors with their rivalry among existing firms.

One of the five forces measures entry barriers as a way to preclude competition in an industry. The three most important entry barriers reviewed are cost advantage of incumbents, product differentiation of incumbents, and capital requirements. Two of these entry barriers (cost leadership and differentiation) are especially important because they are two of Porter's three generic competitive strategies.

Competitive group analysis is an important way to analyze the competitive structure in an industry. By plotting how the major firms in an industry compete along two competitive dimensions, an executive starts an analysis concerning positioning the firm and its products/services.

Shortcomings of competitive strategy are reviewed. The concentration on the competitors, not the customers, is a shortcoming. Total quality is a primary way to achieve both low cost and differention to offer affordable quality to customers.

DISCUSSION QUESTIONS

1 Compare and contrast corporate and competitive levels of strategy.

2 How does competitive strategy influence acquisitions?

3 Give one example each of a computer company or division of a computer company that primarily follows one of the three generic competitive strategies.

4 How should Mercedes exit its stuck in the middle spot?

5 Analyze the soft drink industry with Porter's five forces model of industry competition.

6 Analyze entry into the brewing industry in terms of the market entry barriers discussed in the text.

7 Relate competitive strategy to total quality.

8 Discuss the utility of a single competitive strategy in an era in which customers demand affordable quality.

KEY TERMS

Business-level strategy	consists of the decisions on how to operate in the chosen business.
Buyer power	is the capability of buyers, purchasing agents, and customers of the industry to influence the price and the terms of the purchase.
Competitive dimensions	are the specific factors the firms are using to compete within the industry.
Competitive rivalry	among existing firms in an industry is the extent to which firms respond to competitive moves of other incumbent firms.
Cost leadership	means the lowest cost of operation in the industry.
Cost focus	means the focusing firm offers a product/service to a market segment at a lower price than competitors.
Differentiation	refers to a product or service that is different or somehow unique as perceived by the customer.
Differentiation focus	means the focusing firm offers a product/service that is more differentiated than all competitors' comparable products/services to a market segment.
Economy of scale	refers to using huge physical assets to lower the unit production cost.
Focus	means concentrating on serving a particular target group, segment, or market niche.
Supplier power	is the capability of vendors or suppliers to decide the price and the terms of supply.

Plumley Companies Uses Quality and Strategic Alliances to Compete Internationally

QUALITY CASE

"GET LOST!" That is what the Buick Automobile Company told Plumley Companies in 1983. The Paris, Tennessee, based maker of rubber hoses and ducts and silicone gaskets for automobiles and small engines had just lost a major customer due to poor quality. Competitors were offering higher quality.

That was the wake up call the firm needed to prosper in the quality oriented competitive world of auto parts. Mike Plumley, Chairman and CEO of the privately held company founded in 1967 that bears his family name, had certainly heard the wake up call. "Losing a major customer like Buick really told us that we had to change our ways or we were going to lose them all."

He then launched a massive long-term quality improvement effort to reduce defects and reduce the cost of poor quality. Plumley started training its workers in statistical process control (SPC). But the firm soon realized that many of its workers lacked the math and literacy skills needed to properly use SPC and other continuous improvement tools. So Plumley launched an education program on language and math skills. Those that needed to complete their high school diploma were eligible for company-sponsored education to get that diploma. As Mike Plumley remarked, "Our education program was not part of a grandiose vision. It came out of need." Now the employees spend over two hours a month on a variety of concepts including variation, SPC, stable processes, self-directed teams, and continuous improvement, among others.

Plumley instituted an innovative gainsharing program as a modification of its compensation system. In the program, plant employees typically increase their pay over their base wages by about 10 percent, and can achieve up to 20 percent. These payments arise from accomplishing goals concerning quality, waste reduction, *kaizen* (continuous improvement), productivity, and safety.

The company also works toward quality certification with its major customers. Plumley proudly displays the numerous quality awards it has won from major customers and government agencies. Those awards include Total Quality Excellence from Ford, Targets for Excellence from GM, Quality Excellence and Pentastar from Chrysler, Quality Master from Nissan, Certificate of Achievement Award from Toyota, the Japan Export/Quality Target Achievement Award, and the Tennessee Quality Award. As of late 1994, Plumley Companies was only one of 17 suppliers to have won the TQE Award from Ford, and was in the top 1 percent of GM's suppliers to have won their TFE Award.

Plumley is convinced that quality starts with customer requirements. To communicate the priority of the customer in its quality efforts, the company uses an organization chart with customers at the top.

To provide more value to customers, Mike Plumley offered extensive engineering services by investing in expensive computer-aided design facilities to design the hoses, ducts, and gaskets for its customers. Plumley also augments common carrier trucking with its own fleet when necessary, to insure the customer that deliveries are timely and are handled a minimum number of times.

Recognizing that the automobile industry was changing, Plumley concluded that it could not base its future just on the Big Three domestic producers in Detroit. Plumley now deals with all the Japanese transplants in the USA and supplies parts to automobile firms in Japan, Europe, Australia, and Mexico.

Its initial efforts were frustrating. It took four years of trying to win a sale with a Japanese transplant before Mike Plumley landed his first such contract in 1987. It was a US$350,000 contract to provide fuel-filler tubes to Nissan's plant in Smryna, Tennessee. "That order hangs on my wall, because it's the only order that I had to work four years to get." As a measure of improvement, Plumley sold $14 million of parts to Japanese transplants in 1993.

A key to learning how to do business with Japanese firms was a joint venture Plumley entered into with a Japanese auto parts company, Marugo Rubber Industries. Plumley sells hoses and Marugo sells motor mounts and shock absorbers to the same customers. Each partner is winning something valuable from the joint venture: Plumley received access to Japanese customers and Marugo received access to US customers.

Plumley's quality and international investments have been paying rich dividends. In 1994, Plumley's sales were $107 million and the joint venture of Plumley–Marugo Ltd added sales of $12 million for a total of $119 million. Since the late 1980s, this represents a 10 percent annual growth rate in a time when many automobile suppliers shrunk. It appears that Plumley has learned how to compete internationally.

On February 1, 1995, the Dana Corporation of Toledo, Ohio, acquired Plumley Companies by buying all of its stock. This was a way to continue to fuel Plumley's growth, which required substantial amounts of cash.

Mike Plumley said of the Dana–Plumley alliance, "We are very excited about the opportunities this alliance brings to Plumley. Given our companies' respective capabilities, resources and cultures, we believe this partnership will increase our mutual growth." Mike Plumley will join Dana and remain in management of Dana's new Plumley subsidiary.

The Dana Corporation engineers, manufactures and distributes drivetrain components, engine and chassis parts, structural components, fluid power systems and industrial power transmission products. Dana is a *Fortune* 100 company with facilities in 27 countries, 36,000 employees, and sales of about US$6 billion in 1994.

Discussion Questions

1 Discuss the future of Plumley Companies if it had not chosen to compete on the basis of quality.

2 Discuss the importance of Plumley Companies selling to all the Japanese transplants in the USA and automobile firms in Japan, Europe, Australia, and Mexico.

3 Discuss the advantages and disadvantages of the joint venture with Marugo Rubber Industries.

4 Discuss the advantages and disadvantages of the acquisition of Plumley Companies by the Dana Corporation.

Sources: "Japan's gung-ho US car plants," *Fortune* (January 30, 1989), pp. 98–108; "Supply world success story," *Automotive News Insight* (June 11, 1990), pp. 10i–14i; "Foreign joint ventures need constant 'tuning'," *International Herald Tribune* (November 21, 1989), p. F1; "Plumley feasts on Japanese business," *American Shipper* (October 1993), pp. 73S–76S; "Japanese auto makers buy more US parts," *Wall Street Journal* (August 24, 1993), p. A1; "Quality," *Business Week* (November 30, 1992), pp. 66–72; "Dana expands technology leadership in sealing products with acquisition of Plumley Companies, Inc.," Dana Corporation News Release, Toledo, Ohio (February 1, 1995).

LIQUID ASSETS AT GUINNESS PLC

INTERNATIONAL

C   A   S   E

Battling tough odds to please customers is not an unusual challenge for Guinness PLC, which opened as a brewery at St James Gate on Dublin's famed James Street in 1759. The founder, Arthur Guinness, was confident he could brew a better beer than the approximately seventy other breweries located throughout Dublin. At that time in Ireland, there was almost no interest in beer outside of larger cities like Dublin. In rural areas, whiskey, gin, and poteen were the traditional libations. Much to the chagrin of friends and relatives, the 34 year old Arthur embarked on a new venture and signed a 9000 year lease for £45 per year (about US$28 today)!

Guinness began to brew beer according to an English recipe not well known in Ireland, that contained roasted barley, an ingredient that gave the beer a characteristically dark color. This type of beer had become known as "porter" because of its popularity with the porters and stevedores of Covent Garden and Billingsgate in London. Arthur brewed an extra stout porter beer so well that he eventually ousted all the English imports and captured a share of the English market. By 1825, the beer was known just as "stout" and was available internationally.[a]

Today, Arthur Guinness would be elated by the success his company has enjoyed. Guinness Original Stout is now brewed in 35 countries around the world, and Guinness produces three of the top four most widely distributed beer brands in the UK. It would probably surprise Arthur that Guinness's spirit subsidiary accounts for almost 36 percent of the world's name-brand Scotch whisky market, and 75 percent of Guinness's net profits. The company has grown to include a portfolio of top-selling spirits, such as Johnnie Walker Black Label (the world's number one whiskey), Dewar's White Label (the USA's best-selling Scotch), and top brands in Australia, Japan, and the United Kingdom. The company owns Guinness Publishing, publisher of the famous *Guinness Book of Records*.

When Sir Anthony Tennant became Chairman of Guinness in 1987, the company was experiencing tough times. Guinness had been involved in financial wrongdoing surrounding the 1986 takeover of Distillers (renamed United Distillers), which tarnished the company reputation, resulting in the departure of the former chairman and the former finance director. Despite the controversy, Guinness got to work managing the newly acquired spirit brands that were to generate new profits for the company.

The marketing skill Tennant had acquired at Ogilvy & Mather told him the United Distillers (UD) products had been underpriced, undermarketed, and, in the case of Dewar's Scotch, overproduced. They had been treated as high-volume beverages, which ignored the demand of the market. Tennant explains, "We are dealing with international, well-known brand names. A bottle of Scotch is something a man buys and keeps on his shelf for weeks. It says something to visitors, friends, and business associates."[b] This was a fact that UD had lost sight of as the company had expanded into 12 autonomous companies that used hundreds of distributors worldwide and produced dozens of sometimes competing products.

Tennant's first job was to restructure the company to create centralized control of national markets grouped into four regions: Europe, North America, Asia Pacific, and the rest of the world. The key strategy was to reduce the number of brands to an appropriately small mix for each market, and to differentiate each brand in the minds of the consumers. This strategy not only led to increased sales, but also allowed Guinness to price its products in accordance with their upscale images, thereby increasing profits.

During the 1980s, for example, Dewar's had been slowly losing market share in the USA, the world's largest Scotch market. In response, Guinness first bought control of its North American distribution for £418 million (US$732 million). The company then launched an ad campaign for Dewar's depicting the Scottish hills, mists, and old fashioned British red phone booths that renewed the brand's positioning as a drink for the sophisticated, relaxed drinker. Although Guinness has not reversed the decline of Scotch in this mature market, it has improved the quality of sales as measured by unit sales.[c]

At the same time, Guinness aggressively relaunched Johnnie Walker Red Label, the number three Scotch, to appeal to the "young, extroverted, sociable drinking man"[d] (75 percent of Scotch is consumed by men). The best known ad shows a female jogger in a bikini saying to her jogging companion, "He likes me for my mind. And he drinks Johnnie Walker." In response to feminist objections, Guinness responded with good humor and showed a new ad showing a male jogger saying to his companion, "She likes my cooking. And she drinks Johnnie Walker."

By 1991, appealing to the twenty-something consumer, with top brands positioned to meet the needs of important market segments, UD successfully boosted Dewar's market share from 15 to 17.5 percent. At the same time, Johnnie Walker's 9.5 percent market share approached the 10 percent share of the number two brand, J&B. More recent attempts to attract younger drinkers include giving away free mixed Scotch drinks at trendy bars. Dewar's margaritas and Dewar's sours were especially popular, but would probably cause traditional Scotch lovers to pass out in indignation.[e]

While UD enjoyed great success, Guinness Brewing did not remain still. It was one of only a few truly international beers (Heineken, Carlsberg, Fosters, and Guinness Stout) in a world market that was highly fragmented and localized in nature. In order to achieve significant growth rates, Guinness had to be flexible and innovative. It sought business deals worldwide. As Guinness Brewing Worldwide managing director, Brian Baldock, stated, "We'll look at any sort of deal – if it's the right market, the right price, the right structure, or the right partnership with the right partners, we'll consider it." In one case, Guinness combined its stout breweries in

Malaysia and Singapore with local lagers, Anchor and Tiger. It then licensed the right to sell Heineken in the two countries, and offered shares of Guinness Asia on the Singapore stock exchange, becoming a 50 percent owner of the new company. With the attractive product mix, this company is enjoying annual growth of 20 percent.

Among other ventures, Guinness Brewing bought a Spanish brewery, a Mexican distributorship, and the distribution rights to Pilsner Urquell, the original Pilsner beer from Plzen in the Czech Republic.[f] One indicator of this success is the fact that Guinness Stout is the nineteenth best-selling brand in the world by sales, the twelfth largest by volume, and the fourth largest by total Guinness Brewing profits.[g]

Overall, results from 1984 to 1994 were outstanding. Sales grew to £4.7 billion (US$7.3 billion) from £924 million (US$1.6 billion), reflecting a 15 percent annual growth rate. Net income grew 32 percent annually, rising to £641 million (US$1.0 billion) from £38 million (US$67 million).[h]

According to a 1995 study conducted by *Financial World* magazine, two of Guinness's brands are the top two best-managed alcoholic beverage brands in the world and among the top 20 best-managed brands overall. The number one alcoholic beverage, with a brand value of US$2.8 billion, is Johnnie Walker Black. Guinness Stout is number two, with an estimated brand value of US$2.318 billion.[i]

A list of other Guinness accomplishments is equally impressive. Guinness is the number one exporter of American bourbon to Japan, the number three importer of foreign lager into the USA, the number one exporter of draft beer to Germany, the number one distiller of German premium brandy, and the leading brewer of Spanish lager.[j] "It is an advantage in today's international arena to be based in a small, relatively insignificant country," says Tennant, "because if you can't see beyond your own shores, then you're really in trouble."[k]

Just as in 1759, Guinness demonstrates that it can produce a distinctive premium alcoholic beverages for the times, price them accordingly, and deliver customer satisfaction to win market share from competitors. With less than 3 percent of Arthur's original lease expired, the success at Guinness shows that a flexible, long-term competitive business strategy is one way to achieve superior results and deliver exemplary customer value.

Discussion Questions

1 How does Guinness's business strategy of making high-quality products at premium prices differ from other consumer products?

2 Why was it important for Guinness to produce the right mix of spirits for each of its international markets?

3 Why did Guinness Brewing concentrate on partnerships and joint ventures rather than just intensifying its marketing efforts for Guinness Stout?

Sources: **a.** Kiersey, C. O., "Guinness," Guinness Page, World Wide Web (October 12, 1995); **b.** Ferry, J. "In high spirits: the other Guinness story," *The Sunday Times Magazine* (UK) (November 11, 1991), p. 20; **c.** "Guinness Company Report," Panmure Gordon & Co. Ltd. *InvesText* (March 27, 1995); **d.** Ibid, p. 20; **e.** Flynn, J. and Berry, J., "Skol, dude: spirits get hip," *Business Week* (May 30, 1994), p. 97; **f.** "Pilsner Urquell beer has survived seven centuries," *Accountancy* (June, 1995), pp. 38–9; **g.** Ferry, J. "In high spirits: the other Guinness story," p. 22; **h.** "Guinness, PLC," *Hoover's Handbook of World Business* (1995–6), pp. 240–1; **i.** Badenhausen, K., "Brands: the management factor," *Financial World* (August 1, 1995), p. 54; **j.** "Stout thrives in the land of lager," *Fortune* (November 28, 1994), p. 20; **k.** Ferry, J., "In high spirits: the other Guinness story," p. 22.

NOTES

This chapter was influenced by Karakaya, F. and Stahl, M. J., *Market Entry and Exit Barriers*. Westport, CT: Quorum Books (1991); Porter, M. E., *Competitive Strategy*. New York: Free Press (1980) and *Competitive Advantage*. New York: Free Press (1985); Stahl, M. J. and Bounds, G. M., *Competing Globally through Customer Value*. Westport, CT: Quorum Books (1991); and Stahl, M. J. and Grigsby, D. W., *Strategic Management for Decision Making*. Boston: PWS-Kent (1991).

1 Schonberger, R. J. "Is strategy strategic? impact of total quality management on strategy," *Academy of Management Executive*, 6(3) (August 1992), pp. 80–7.

2 *The World Competitiveness Report, 1994*. Lausanne, Switzerland: IMD (1994), pp. 1–2.

3 Kay, J., "Is there a competitive advantage of nations?" *Siemens Aktiengesellschaft* (May, 1995), p. 39.

4 Porter, M. E., "From competitive advantage to corporate strategy," *Harvard Business Review* (May–June 1987), pp. 43–59.

5 Coyne, K. P., "Sustainable competitive advantage–what it is, what it isn't," *Business Horizons* (January–February 1986), pp. 54–61.

6 Ghemawat, P., "Sustainable advantage," *Harvard Business Review*, 64(5) (1986), pp. 53–8.

7 "Compaq can't cope with demand for Pro Linea PCs," *Wall Street Journal* (July 10, 1992), p. B1.

8 "IBM tries, and fails, to fix PC business," *Wall Street Journal* (February 22, 1995), p. B1.

9 Porter, *Competitive Advantage*.

10 "Chipmakers gamble on inexpensive production," *International Herald Tribune* (September 26, 1995), p. 16.

11 Osborn, A., "Glaxo Wellcome: creating the world's largest drug company," *Europe* (October, 1995), pp. 18–19.

12 Porter, *Competitive Advantage*.

13 Ibid.

14 Karakaya and Stahl, *Market Entry and Exit Barriers*.

15 "Sony will halt export of TVs made in Japan," *International Herald Tribune* (October 6, 1995), p. 21.

16 "Aluminum producers, aggressive and agile, outfight steelmakers," *Wall Street Journal* (July 1, 1992), p. 1.

17 "The Cola kings are feeling a bit jumpy," *Business Week* (July 13, 1992), p. 112.

18 Porter, *Competitive Strategy*; Cool, K. O. and Schendel, D., "Strategic group formation and performance," *Management Science*, 33(9) (1987), pp. 1102–24; Oliva, T., Day, D. and DeSarbo, W., "Selecting competitive tactics: try a strategy map," *Sloan Management Review*, 28(3) (1987), pp. 5–15.

19 Bailey, E. E., Graham, D. R. and Kaplan, D. P., *Deregulating the Airlines*. Cambridge, MA: MIT Press (1986).

20 Wilson, C., Kennedy, M. and Trammell, C., *Superior Product Development*. Oxford, UK: Blackwell (1995).

21 "IBM tries, and fails, to fix PC business," p. B1.

22 Mariotti, J., *The Power of Partnerships*. Oxford, UK: Blackwell (1995).

23 "GM tightens the screws," *Business Week* (June 22, 1992), p. 30.

24 "Shrinking supplier bases," *The Wall Street Journal* (August 16, 1991), p. B1.

25 Hill, C., "Differentiation versus low cost or differentiation and low cost," *Academy of Management Review*, 13 (1988), p. 401.

26 Mintzberg, H., "Generic strategies: toward a comprehensive framework," *Advances in Strategic Management*, 5 (1988), pp. 1–67.

27 Kotha, S. and Vadlamani, B., "Assessing generic strategies," *Strategic Management Journal*, 16 (January 1995), pp. 75–83.

28 Bowles, J. and Hammond, J., *Beyond Quality*. New York: G. P. Putnam's Sons (1991); Deming, W. E., *Out of the Crisis*. Cambridge, MA: MIT Press (1986); Garvin, D. A., *Managing Quality: the Strategic and Competitive Edge*. New York: Free Press (1988); Griffiths, D., *Implementing Quality with a Customer Focus*. Milwaukee: Quality Press (1990); Stahl, M. and Bounds, G. (eds), *Competing Globally through Customer Value*.

29 Ishikawa, K., *What Is Total Quality Control? The Japanese Way*, Englewood Cliffs, NJ: Prentice-Hall (1985).

30 Kearns, D. T., "Leadership through quality," *Academy of Management Executive*, 4 (May 1990), pp. 86–9; Locander, W. and Saxton, W., "Application to P&G," and Judge, W. et al., "Application to Capsugel," both in Stahl and Bounds, *Competing Globally through Customer Value*; "European Quality Award Criteria," in *1995 European Quality Award Special Report*. Brussels: European Foundation for Quality Management (1995), p. 34.

31 "Explosive growth at TNT Express as the quest for perfection goes on," *UK Quality* (December 1994), pp. 8–9.

BUSINESS-LEVEL STRATEGY: TOTAL QUALITY AND CUSTOMER VALUE STRATEGY

LEARNING OBJECTIVES

After reading this chapter, you should be able to accomplish the following.

1 Explain how high quality and low cost can go together.

2 Describe the importance of management systems, especially customer value systems, in producing high quality.

3 Describe the importance of the customer and customer value in business-level strategy.

4 Discuss the role of benchmarking in quality improvement.

5 Relate the ideas of customer value and best net customer value to the idea of quality.

6 Describe the importance of customer value determination systems in organizations.

7 Describe the importance of quality function deployment and new product development systems in organizations.

8 Explain why quality is at the heart of the rebirth of industrial competitiveness.

9 Discuss the payoff from total quality management.

As described in chapter 6, business-level strategy is concerned with how the firm operates in its chosen business. One way to view business-level strategy is through the model of competitive strategy (chapter 6). Another way to understand the subject of business-level strategy is through the model of total quality and customer value strategy.

How should the firm provide value to customers in its chosen business(es)? This is not a trivial business-level question, since some argue that this question is even associated with corporate-level strategy concerning the choice of business. In a recent book on customer value, Gale argues that to be successful today, "Companies enter and invest only in businesses where they can be quality and value leaders."[1] Before addressing these issues, we need to understand how high quality and low cost can go together.

A Systems Model of Quality

How can managers and their organizations yield superior quality at low cost? For many firms to embrace the idea of delivering superior quality to their customers as a business strategy, the firms first needed an answer to this question. It was important to link superior quality and low cost in order for such a business strategy to be sustainable, as Saturn proved. (See quality case at the end of this chapter.)

Quality *and* low cost

Philip Crosby, W. Edwards Deming, Armand Feigenbaum, Kaoru Ishikawa, and Joseph Juran made a lasting contribution to business strategy and practice when they showed how high quality *and* low cost can go hand in hand.[2] Crosby popularized the idea with his book, *Quality Is Free.*[3]

Historically, economists had argued that quality, or any feature of a product, costs money. The more quality in a product, the higher was the cost of the product according to many economists.[4] Since many managers relied on inspection after production to achieve high quality, the economists were correct that quality costs money. But it does not need to be that way.

With the logic in figure 7.1, we see how high quality leads to lower costs. For this logic to hold, quality cannot be inspected in at the end of the production process. Rather, quality is a strategy that must permeate an organization throughout its activities. "Cease dependence on inspection to achieve quality. Eliminate the need for inspection on a mass basis by building quality into the product in the first place."[5]

The idea that high quality could be achieved at low cost was a watershed in business operations. Now firms pay attention to designing the product to eliminate recurring defects in production. Firms also design manufacturing processes so that operations occur without errors, and firms manage systems to eliminate the cause of defects. Then they continuously improve the products/services and the processes to yield even greater value to customers. Organizations pay attention to the cost of quality, or the cost of poor quality.

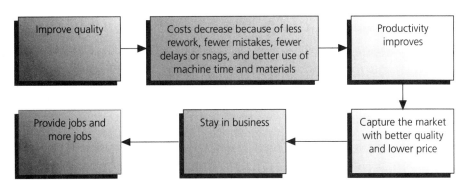

Figure 7.1   The pervasive role of quality.
Source: Deming, W. E., *Out of the Crisis*. Cambridge, MA: MIT Center for Advanced Engineering Study (1986), p. 3. Reproduced by permission.

The cost of quality

As noted in chapter 1, the cost of quality refers to those costs incurred due to producing poor-quality products and services. Included in the cost of quality are the costs of scrap, rework, warranty repair, inspection, and quality related maintenance.[6] These costs are sometimes expressed as a percentage of cost of goods sold. In an earlier era, many firms experienced a cost of quality of 15–30 percent.[7] Firms that implement TQ often experience declines in the cost of quality of 90 percent or more over a few years. Through continuous improvement of the critical cross-functional processes, some firms relentlessly drive the cost of quality toward zero. Then, affordable quality becomes a realizable goal. With lower costs and higher quality, the firms can provide more value to customers as their prime business level strategy.

Capsugel, as a division of Warner-Lambert, makes hard gelatin capsules for the worldwide pharmaceutical industry. The firm has plants in Belgium, China, France, Japan, the UK and the USA. Capsugel has been lowering their cost of quality by one-half every five years. It does this primarily by qualifying suppliers, continuous process improvement, and eliminating inspection after production. In an earlier process, the firm employed over 100 inspectors per plant to inspect the product *twice*. Redesign of the systems, including selecting a few suppliers based on quality, continuous process improvement, training of new behavior, and attention to customer requirements, helped them accomplish the reductions in the cost of quality.[8]

Management systems and processes

Total quality attempts to closely link strategies and systems. Those systems and processes require a primary focus on external customers, and cross-functional horizontal spans.[9]

Per chapter 1, cross-functional systems are activities and resources linked to providing value to customers that span at least two functions of design, production, marketing or finance. The cross-functional systems typically include personnel and resources from several functional activities, like design, production, marketing, and finance.[10] Such cross-functional systems are associated with horizontal structures and flatter organizations with fewer levels of management, less direct supervision, cross-functional teams, and more employee training.

Two cross-functional systems are briefly described in this chapter, since both relate to a customer value strategy. One cross-functional system is the customer value determination system and the other is the new product development system. The managerial implications of horizontal processes and systems are explored in greater detail in the strategy implementation chapters.

Global competition and customer choices

Why not stick with the old managerial systems and ignore customers who demand both high quality and low cost? Are such demanding customers in the minority?

As chapter 3 showed, deregulated global competition has offered customers choices in many industries. If the customer does not like a Lincoln, the customer could choose among Cadillac, Mercedes, BMW, Lexus, and Infiniti. Thirty years ago, the only relevant US choice may have been a Cadillac. If the customer does not like a Xerox copier, the customer can choose among Sharp, Minolta, and Canon. Twenty years ago, the only choice may have been Xerox. If the customer does not like Caterpillar, the customer can choose Komatsu and Deere. If a UK customer does not like DHL or Federal Express, the customer can choose TNT Express. The choices seemingly have no end. In such an environment, customers demand high quality, new technology, low price, and more as indicated later. International competition taught companies in many countries that they must deliver superior value to customers in order to retain them as customers.

Managers must heed the customer in this new internationally competitive era or face bankruptcy. In the summary of a recent international quality study, the American Quality Foundation made the following bold statement concerning the importance of quality as a business strategy. "Quality improvement is the fundamental business strategy of the 1990s. No business without it will survive in the global marketplace."[11]

It appears that governments and companies in a number of countries understand the importance of quality as a business strategy. As indicated earlier, the Baldrige National Quality Award, the Deming Prize, and the European Quality Award are given annually in the USA, Japan, and Europe, respectively, to recognize outstanding accomplishments in total quality.[12] About thirty states in the USA have separate annual quality awards. Annual quality awards are also given in Belgium, Bulgaria, Denmark, Finland, France, Germany, Greece, Iceland, Ireland, The Netherlands, Norway, Poland, Portugal, Russia, Slovakia, Slovenia, Spain, Sweden, and the United Kingdom.[13] In a survey, 71 percent of the respondents from the UK indicated that their employers had introduced a formal quality management campaign.[14]

Total Quality as a Business Strategy

Total quality is a business strategy in that it shows managers how to operate within a business by focusing primarily on customers.[15] As we will see later in this chapter, once managers focus on customers, then different managerial systems are needed to deliver value to customers.

Customers

As a business strategy, TQ focuses first and foremost on consistently improving value to customers and thereby delighting customers.[16] The primary focus is the customer, not the competitor as in competitive strategy (chapter 6).[17] This is a major strategic difference between customer value strategy and competitive strategy. Under customer value strategy, the firm retains current customers and attracts new customers by delivering best customer value. By focusing on customers, the firm grows market share, and competitors lag.

A recent analysis of the impact of TQM on strategy listed 19 key ideas associated with TQM. The first and most important key idea listed is "Get to know the next and final customer."[18]

The reader may recall from chapter 1 that the customer is at the core of the definition of TQ. How pervasive is this idea of a focus on customers? *Business Week* reported survey results showing that about 90 percent of firms using quality strategies reported that they focused on customer satisfaction.[19] A recent survey in the UK showed that an increased focus on customers was the greatest benefit of using the UK Quality Award criteria for corporate self-assessments.[20] A 1995 review in Canada showed that customer focus was one of the critical factors in TQ implementations in manufacturing, service and government examples.[21]

After watching Xerox nearly go bankrupt and then regain customers from the Japanese with its "Leadership through Quality" strategy, David Kearns, former Chairman of Xerox, offered an eloquent description of failure in a handbook for decline. The first chapter for decline reads as follows. "Assume you own the customer, that you know what he wants better than he does and that he will remain loyal to you no matter how much you abuse him. The chapter also advises you not to waste time measuring customer satisfaction and definitely not to pay attention to or respond to customer complaints."[22]

In a service business, it is sometimes too easy to take customers for granted because they are always there. Yet British Telecommunications (BT) Northern Ireland won the Irish Quality Prize in 1994. One of its key business lessons follows. "Listen to your staff and your customers. You'll be surprised how much they know."[23]

Midland Bank, a 150 year old bank in the UK with 46,000 employees and a 1700 branch network, has recently been positioning itself as "the listening bank." Andy Stephens, Midland's service quality director, described the major changes associated with being "customer-led." "So we have a major structural change developing around the customer. We are backing that up with training, with new job objectives and service standards and we are making our reporting management information (MI) much more customer focused. Whereas, being a bank, we used to report on financial results, we now report on customer retention, recruitment, cross-sales and complaints. Service quality and customer focus must be consistently projected as a strategic strand of the business, backed up by unequivocal and visible support from the top of the organization."[24] Around the time of the interview with Mr Stephens, Midland reported an 11 percent increase in annual operating profits.

Robert Galvin was the Chairman of Motorola when it won a Baldrige National Quality Award. He seemed to understand the centrality of customers to the success of Motorola. In a description of Motorola's strategy, Galvin described Motorola's foremost goal of total customer satisfaction.[25] For his leadership in the quality arena, Galvin received the American Society for Competitiveness Award for Outstanding Private Contributions to Competitiveness.

Satisfying the diverse needs of customers throughout the world is a huge, never-ending undertaking. Yet, as Procter & Gamble (P&G) derived most of its US$33 billion revenue in 1995 from international sources, P&G is committed to quality, value and customer satisfaction. A good example of how P&G delivered value to consumers internationally may be found in China. Although some argued that there was limited potential for consumer goods in that country because of relatively low levels of income, P&G observed that dandruff stands out in a nation of black-haired people. Few Chinese shampoos were effective against dandruff. So P&G introduced three shampoos with antidandruff formulas and now sells more shampoo in China than anyone.[26]

**INTERNATIONAL
EXHIBIT**

PROCTER & GAMBLE: A STATEMENT OF PURPOSE

We will provide products of superior quality and value that best fill the needs of the world's consumers.

We will achieve that purpose through an organization and a working environment which attracts the finest people; fully develops and challenges our individual talents; encourages our free and spirited collaboration to drive the business ahead; and maintains the Company's historic principles of integrity, and doing the right thing.

Through the successful pursuit of our commitment, we expect our brands to achieve leadership share and profit positions and that, as a result, our business, our people, our shareholders, and the communities in which we live and work, will prosper.

These are the principles that guide our actions as a Company and our attitudes about our employees:

- *We will employ, throughout the Company, the best people we can find without regard to race or gender or any other differences unrelated to performance. We will promote on the same basis.*
- *We recognize the vital importance of continuing employment because of its ultimate tie with the strength and success of our business.*
- *We will build our organization from within. Those persons with ability and performance records will be given the opportunity to move ahead in the Company.*
- *We will pay our employees fairly, with careful attention to the compensation of each individual. Our benefit programs will be designed to provide our employees with adequate protection in time of need.*
- *We will encourage and reward individual innovation, personal initiative and leadership, and willingness to manage risk.*
- *We will encourage teamwork across disciplines, divisions and geography to get the most effective integration of the ideas and efforts of our people.*
- *We will maximize the development of individuals through training and coaching on what they are doing well and how they can do better. We will evaluate Procter & Gamble managers on their record in developing their subordinates.*
- *We will maintain and build our corporate tradition which is rooted in the principles of*

personal integrity; doing what's right for the long-term; respect for the individual; and being the best in what we do.

These are the things that will enable us to achieve the category leadership that is our goal in every business in which we compete:

- *We will develop a superior understanding of consumers and their needs. This is the foundation and impetus for generating the superior benefits and value consumers seek in other brands.*
- *We will develop strategies and plans capable of giving us the competitive advantage needed to meet our business objectives.*
- *We will create and deliver product and packaging on all our brands which provide a compelling advantage versus competition in bringing consumers superior benefits that best satisfy their needs. To do this we will be the world leader in the relevant science and technology.*
- *We will seek significant and sustainable competitive advantages in quality, cost and service in our total supply and delivery systems so as to meet our business objectives.*
- *We will have superior, creative marketing on all our brands. We will have enduring superior copy, and promotion programs distinguished by their creativity, effectiveness, and efficiency.*
- *We will develop close, mutually productive relationships with our trade customers and our suppliers. We will work with these partners in ways that are good for both of our businesses.*
- *We will promote a sense of urgency and a willingness to try new things. This will enable us to get better ideas working in the market ahead of competition.*
- *We will follow the principles of Total Quality to achieve continual improvement in everything we do. Whatever level of performance we have achieved today, we know that we can and must improve upon it tomorrow.*

Source: *Procter & Gamble, Cincinnati, Ohio (1993).*

Total customer satisfaction and delight

Customer satisfaction is the customer's positive or negative feeling about the value received from using a firm's product/service.[27] Meeting customer requirements and satisfying customers is one level of customer commitment. Striving to satisfy customers by meeting their expectations may imply a reactive system to provide to customers what they request of the firm. Such a reactive mode is different from striving for total customer satisfaction, customer delight, or exceeding customer expectations. The latter three expressions show that the firm may go beyond what customers demand today to keep them as customers tomorrow. For example, Eastman Chemical expresses its vision as "To be the World's Preferred Chemical Company by focusing on exceeding customer expectations."[28]

Ford figures it costs five times as much to attract a new customer as it does to retain an old one.[29] Such a commitment may mean providing better value than all other competitors and is associated with growing market share through retaining old customers and winning new customers.

Whirlpool, the world's leading manufacturer of white goods, has been building market share in Europe through customer satisfaction since it acquired a 53 percent stake in Philips's appliance business for about US$500 million in 1989. "Our vision is to achieve global leadership in the appliance industry and related businesses. As we satisfy our customers, they will prefer our products and services over others in the marketplace."[30]

Land's End, the high-performing, high-quality mail order clothing retailer,

Table 7.1 Percentage of businesses indicating the importance of customer satisfaction as a primary criterion in the strategic planning process

	Past three years	Current	Next three years
Canada	20	44	80
Germany	10	22	59
Japan	30	42	80
USA	18	37	69

provides an example of the primacy of the customer. Land's End's Principles of Doing Business reflect their dedication to the customer. "We do everything we can to make our products better. We improve material, and add back features and construction details that others have taken out over the years. We never reduce the quality of a product to make it cheaper. Our products are guaranteed. No fine print. No arguments. We mean exactly what we say: GUARANTEED. PERIOD."[31]

In different countries, an increasing percentage of firms are using information on customer satisfaction as a criterion in their strategic planning process. Table 7.1 shows the increasing percentage of firms in Canada, Germany, Japan, and the USA who have used, currently use, and in the future expect to use such information on customer satisfaction.[32]

Shareholders and owners

What about the needs of the shareholders? Are not the purposes of management and companies to maximize the wealth of the owners? Does the primacy of the customer detract from owner needs?

A growing body of evidence shows that TQM, with its focus on the customer, is the way in a globally competitive marketplace to produce superior long term financial value for owners.[33] From 1988 to 1993, winners of the Baldrige National Quality Award have outperformed the stock market by nearly three to one, according to *Business Week*. Over that time, the average Baldrige winner yielded a cumulative gain of 89 percent, whereas the Standard & Poor's 500 stock index delivered 33 percent.[34] Thus, some investors now speak of a "Baldie Play".

Three recent empirical studies have shown the superior business results associated with implementing quality as a business strategy. In 1991, The US General Accounting Office reported to the Congress on a study of 22 companies who were finalists for the Baldrige National Quality Award in 1988 and 1989. According to the report: "Companies that adopted quality management practices experienced an overall improvement in corporate performance. In nearly all cases, companies that used TQM practices achieved better employee relations, higher productivity, greater customer satisfaction, increased market share, and improved profitability."[35]

Easton and Jarrell compared the performance of 108 firms who had implemented TQ to varying degrees from 1981 to 1991 with over 300 firms with no

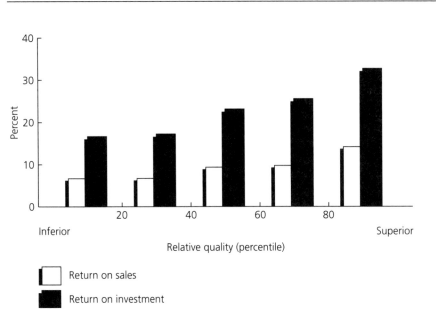

Figure 7.2 The relationship between quality and profit.
Source: Reprinted with the permission of The Free Press, a division of Simon & Schuster from Buzzell, R. D. and Gale, B. T., *The PIMS Principles*. New York: Free Press (1987), p. 107. Copyright © 1987 by The Free Press.

evidence of TQ implementation of comparable size in the same industries. The researchers reported: "The findings indicate that performance, measured by profit margin, return on assets, asset use efficiency, and excess stock returns, is improved for the sample of firms that adopted TQM. For firms with more advanced TQM systems, the improvement in financial performance is notably and consistently stronger".[36]

In a large-scale data analysis of the relationship between quality and profit, Buzzell and Gale found that the higher the quality, the higher was the profitability.[37] This positive relationship between quality and profitability was true for both measures of profitability tested – return on sales and return on investment. Figure 7.2 shows the positive relationship between quality and profitability.

Competitors

Chapter 6 discusses the importance of the competitor in the formulation and implementation of business strategy. The chapter closes by noting some disadvantages of focusing on competitors. Principally, by concentrating on competitors, it is easy to lose sight of customers. This flies in the face of what business strategy should be concerning serving customers' real needs.[38]

By following the competitors, the firm is destined to pursue a follower strategy. By never being first to market with a new product, the firm is destined to realize below average financial returns. However, the competitor is relevant to help the firm understand ways to improve processes and systems in an activity known as benchmarking.

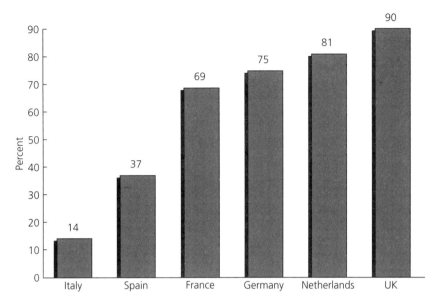

Figure 7.3 Benchmarking Royal Mail reliability (percentage of first class letters delivered next day).
Source: Heller, R., *TQM Quality Markers: the Leaders and Shapers of Europe's Quality Revolution*. St Gallen: Norden (1993), p. 244.

Benchmarking

Functional benchmarking is studying and maybe even emulating the best processes and systems in the world, whether in the firm's industry (a competitor) or in any industry. The Xerox corporation developed benchmarking to a fine business practice, and Camp documented those practices in an entire book.[39] If Xerox benchmarked L. L. Bean's order entry and billing system, such a practice would be called functional benchmarking.[40]

Competitive benchmarking refers to analyzing what the best competitor or leading companies in the industry are doing to discover the products, processes, and practices that satisfy customer needs. For example, if IBM studied and emulated how the Microsoft Company designed new software for PCs, such a practice would be known as competitive benchmarking. As part of Customer First (the TQ process for the Royal Mail), the Royal Mail in the UK benchmarks mail reliability in the Netherlands, Germany, France, Spain, and Italy.[41] Figure 7.3 graphically shows that international reliability benchmarking.

Competitive benchmarking of processes is the prime area for focusing on competitors. As this chapter emphasizes, managers should focus on customers to understand their value requirements as the first step in designing, improving and distributing products/services. Figure 7.4 describes the focus of managers between customers and competitors. The dangers of an internal focus are described in the earlier chapters in this book. Market focus combines high competitor focus for competitive benchmarking of processes, and high customer focus for customer

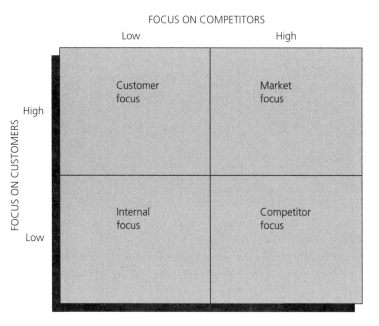

Figure 7.4 Managerial focus on competitors and customers.

value determination. Market focus is the preferred quadrant in describing managerial focus between competitors and customers.

Customer Value

Providing value to customers is much more than just eliminating defects. Customer value has many dimensions and must be systematically reflected in the firm's products and services. If the firm's core systems, like the customer value determination and new product development systems, can continuously determine and deliver superior customer value, then the firm will have a sustained competitive advantage.[42]

Multidimensional

Deming, Juran, Feigenbaum, Ishikawa, Crosby, and others taught the business world that it could deliver high quality and low price to the customer simultaneously. That finding started an era of paying attention to multiple dimensions of customer value. Quality no longer means just number of defects, or adherence to an internal engineering specification. Quality means delivering value to customers in accord with their expectations.

Schonberger presented a list of 12 dimensions of customer value. His list appeared after Garvin's list of eight items. The dimensions are reproduced below. Obviously, quality is more than the presence or absence of a defect.

1 Conformance to specifications.*
2 Performance.*

3 Quick response.

4 Quick-change expertise.

5 Features.*

6 Reliability.*

7 Durability.*

8 Serviceability.*

9 Aesthetics.*

10 Perceived quality.*

11 Humanity.

12 Value.

Note: the 12 items are from Schonberger and the eight items with asterisks are from Garvin.[43]

Value realized and value sacrificed

Value can be either positive or negative, because value can be realized, or value can be sacrificed. *Realized value* is value that the customer receives. It can include comfort, image, ease of use, reliability, consistency, enjoyment, and a host of other characteristics. *Sacrificed value* is value that the customer gives up. It can include time, money, energy, frustration, worry, and a number of other components. Thus, a two-dimensional view of customer value is appropriate. *Customer value* is the customers' perception of what they want to have happen with the help of a product/service, in order to accomplish a desired goal.[44]

If customers realize high value and sacrifice little, and thereby accomplish their desired goals, then the customers should be successful and return again for future purchases. This is apparent with industrial customers like those who purchase equipment from Caterpillar. If those customers receive high value and accomplish their goals, then they should return in the future to Caterpillar when they have future needs for such equipment.

It has been estimated that a satisfied customer will tell three other potential customers of his or her satisfaction. However, a dissatisfied customer will tell seven other potential customers of his or her dissatisfaction. Therefore, it is important for managers to pay attention to the value sacrificed by customers that could lead to dissatisfaction.

Best net value

Understanding both positive and negative dimensions allows one to form the difference between value realized and value sacrificed. The difference is called *net customer value* or simply *net value*. Then, it is easy to compare the net value for all competitive firms in the industry. The *best net value* becomes apparent from such a comparison.[45] This gives the firm a target. The business objective is to move the firm's customers to a position of higher value realized and lower value sacrificed, so that the best net value in the industry is offered.

Many view Federal Express as providing the best net value in US rapid small package delivery. It charges a moderate price for consistent, next day, secure delivery after pick-up of the package at the sender's place of work by courteous

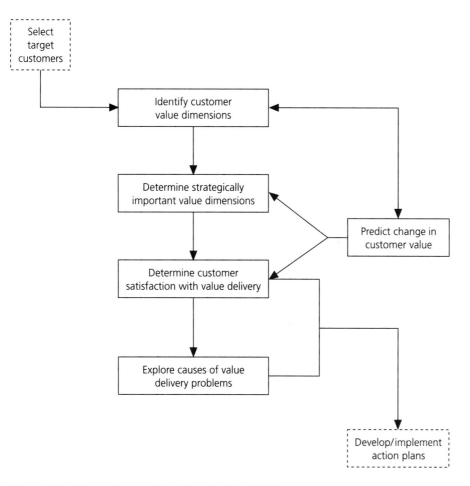

Figure 7.5 The customer value determination (CVD) process.
Source: Woodruff, R. and Gardial, S., *Know Your Customer*. Oxford: Blackwell (1996), p. 14.

employees. Sacrifice to the customer is minimized and value realized is substantial. The US Post Office does not yield such net value to customers.

Customer value determination systems

Providing best net value implies that particular attention is paid to determining customer requirements. Such an important task requires managers in several functions to fully understand value realized and value sacrificed. Such a cross-functional system needs to be formalized to pay it proper attention.

Figure 7.5 shows some of the key steps in the customer value determination process. Data collection includes interviews and focus groups on the front-end, large-scale surveys when measuring satisfaction, and small, scale in-depth follow-up when exploring problems. Together, the steps involve much data collection from many customers over time.

A good example is the worldwide customer satisfaction measurement system that Capsugel has in place. The system collects data from customers on a worldwide basis to determine what their requirements are and if they are being met by Capsugel. Managers are then held accountable to the customer satisfaction data. Sometimes, customers are impressed just because the firm cares enough to ask if they are satisfied.

At its Wixom, Michigan, Lincoln plant, Ford workers and managers review customer satisfaction/dissatisfaction data twice a month. "'We are very customer-driven', says Mr Nolan, noting that meetings are held twice a month in the plant's large conference room to go over the results of Ford's competitive new-vehicle-quality studies, which provide detailed reports on what customers liked or didn't like about the Wixom-made cars."[46] These data help them to continuously improve the product and the manufacturing process to yield even greater value to customers.

New product development systems/quality function deployment

New product development systems in TQM firms are good examples of cross-functional systems to invent and deliver value to customers. The new product development systems frequently contain personnel from most of the functional areas in the company who work together on the design of the new product. At Corning Laboratories, teams with representatives from research and development, manufacturing, and marketing guide prototypes from the labs to market.[47] Sometimes, customers are on the teams.

It appears that many Japanese and German firms understand the importance of including customer expectations in the design of new products/services. However, a worldwide survey showed that many US firms had not yet adopted this business practice when the survey was done in the early 1990s.[48]

Quality function deployment (QFD) is a technique being used more often today to insure that the design of new products or services is based upon customer criteria. QFD starts with customer criteria, translates them into product/service requirements, and then translates them into product/service requirement measures. *Quality function deployment* is a customer-driven design system that attempts to get early coupling between the requirements of the customer, marketing, and design engineering.[49]

For example, in the design of a personal computer, customer requirements might be expressed as ease of use, portability, quality of graphics, affordability, and speed. The product requirements might then be expressed as menu-driven commands, open architecture, lightweight unit, compact size, high-resolution screen, medium price, and fast microchip. The product requirement measures might then be expressed as lightweight unit (less than 10 pounds, or 4.5 kg), compact size (20 by 16 inches, or 50 by 40 cm, maximum outside dimensions), and medium price (greater than US$2,000, but less than $3,000 per unit).[50]

Purchasing and Supplier Partnering for Total Quality

There has been a change in many organizations concerning relationships with suppliers. Part of the reason for the change is the Japanese concept of *keiretsu*.

Keiretsu fosters long-term relationships with a few key suppliers versus short-term relationships with many suppliers. These long-term relationships are important since many firms recognize that suppliers have a profound impact on the value delivered to the firm's customers.

Low bid contracting versus partnering

In the past, a primary way to deal with suppliers was through low bid contracting. Whichever supplier bid the lowest, that was the supplier that received this year's contract. Unfortunately, that form of contracting encouraged any supplier who needed the business to shave a little off the bid to get the work. Sometimes, to get the contract with a low bid, the supplier cut down on quality in an attempt to hold down costs rather than to improve the system of production to lower costs and defects. This old way of contracting resulted in large numbers of suppliers, with high turnover in supplier relationships.

Partly due to the Japanese idea of *keiretsu*, many firms today are establishing long-term partnering relationships with suppliers. Rather than turn over a good supplier because some other supplier bids a few percent lower on a new contract, customers are sticking with suppliers as partners and working with them for long-term cost reduction and quality enhancement. This partnering even includes training of the supplier by the customer, especially in improvement of quality management systems. The Caterpillar Quality Institute and Motorola University conduct substantial supplier training.

Large number of suppliers versus single suppliers

This partnering relationship with suppliers is reducing the number of suppliers at many firms. Some firms have cut their supplier numbers by 90 percent.[51] Based upon a relationship of trust and long-term mutual interest, many customer firms are now willing to invest in a few key suppliers rather than requiring several suppliers to constantly bid against each other. Very high levels of quality make such partnerships possible as one firm can now trust another and bypass incoming inspection.

Acceptance sampling versus no incoming inspection

Under the low bid, competitive mentality of the past, it was assumed that the supplier would not be responsible for the quality of the supplied parts. Therefore, it was necessary for the customer to inspect incoming shipments from the supplier for defects to see if the shipment was good enough. **Acceptance sampling** refers to making a decision to accept or reject a shipment based upon the percentage or number of defects in an inspected sample from the shipment.

Today, rather than inspect the product, many customers are certifying the operations process of the supplier. Once the supplier's processes have been certified, the customer can eliminate incoming inspection. This facilitates a just-in-time system in which the incoming parts are immediately integrated into the customers operations. Many firms operating in this way have a formal designation for qualified suppliers.

Just-in-time inventory and production

A *just-in-time (JIT) inventory system* orders materials to arrive at the point of use exactly when they are needed. The result is that the inventory level approaches zero. Thus, the inventory holding cost approaches zero. A JIT system works only in cases where the process is in control, the managers know exactly when to order, and the orders arrive as scheduled with no variance. Such a finely tuned operations system works like clockwork when all the parts are coordinated, but if one part of the system introduces variance, the system shuts down quickly.

The Saturn Corporation works with a well tuned JIT system. When there was a strike at a parts supplier in 1992, the production system at Saturn ground to a halt in a few days. Saturn had no buffer inventory. To its credit, rather than laying off employees when there was no production, Saturn used the down time for training.

Sometimes, JIT systems are referred to as zero inventory or Japanese *kanban* inventory systems. JIT is also referred to as a *demand pull system* because each station or worker produces its output only when the next workstation or worker up the line says it is ready to receive more input. This contrasts with a *push inventory system*, in which large numbers of parts are made independent of when the next workstation can use them. The result is batches of unused inventory throughout the plant. Perhaps the most notorious push inventory system known was the Chrysler inventory system of the late 1970s. The company produced cars to inventory independent of whether they were selling. Chrysler was forced to rent warehousing space in abandoned fields to store unbought cars so they could sit there and rust. Such push inventory systems are seldom used today.

The Payoff from Total Quality

Per chapter 3, global commerce is marked by intense global competition today. Some old industries were decimated in the 1980s. Some companies lost customers, retrenched into smaller sizes, or moved manufacturing to low-cost countries. However, there has been a rebirth of US and European competitiveness in some industries and companies under the banner of TQM. This industrial renaissance is noted by high quality, low costs, short cycle times, regained market share, and increased profitability.

Improved operating performance

The most comprehensive study to date concerning the results of TQ firms is a 1991 US GAO study of 22 companies who were finalists for the Baldrige National Quality Award in 1988 and 1989. The firms reported average annual improvements from 5 to 12 percent in reliability, on-time delivery, order-processing time, defects, product lead time, inventory turnover, and costs of quality.[52]

High quality

The quality gap is the gap relative to many international competitors that has been most noticeably closed by US firms who have embraced TQM. The average decline in defects was about 10 percent per year for the Baldrige finalists in the US GAO study.

One of the most noticeable industries reporting improved quality is the auto industry. A 1990 survey of over 1,000 consumers shows that most thought the quality of US cars was almost as good as the quality of Japanese models. Although there are substantial differences among some auto makes in terms of quality, Saturn was ranked third in the J. D. Power Customer Satisfaction Survey within two years of its startup.

Xerox, a 1989 Baldrige Quality Award winner and a 1992 European Quality Award winner, credits its Leadership through Quality efforts with the dramatic improvement in quality. Xerox has improved designs, upgraded the quality of both internal and external suppliers, and improved manufacturing processes with dramatic declines in defect rates and costs.

The Corning, New York, plant of Corning, Inc. produces ceramic filters to purify molten metals such as iron and steel. As part of its quality strategy, the plant has implemented several changes in organization, management and personnel policies. The changes include the abandonment of shift supervisors, and of inspection after production. There is also greater reliance on cross-functional teams, including the use of production teams with engineering and maintenance personnel, the location of sales and marketing in the plant to improve responsiveness to customers, and cross-training so that workers can rotate among jobs. Defect rates have dropped from 1,800 to just 9 parts per million over a three-year period.[53] Corning won a Baldrige Award in 1995 partly because of the way it focuses on providing customer value.

Low cost

As Deming forecast, when quality goes up due to process improvements, then costs come down. Many firms have reported lower costs associated with such quality efforts. Thus, affordable quality has become the reality in many markets.

Primarily due to high costs, Texas Instruments (TI) shifted production of low-priced calculators to the Far East in 1982. With some determined people who wanted to prove that they could manufacture low-priced, high-quality calculators in the USA, and the encouragement of a major customer (Wal-Mart), the Lubbock, Texas, plant of TI regained the manufacturing. They designed the product and manufacturing process concurrently with engineers and manufacturing personnel by designing the product for ease of assembly with only seven components. Thus, the TI-25 calculator had the fewest parts of any scientific calculator in the world in 1990. TI selected top quality suppliers, eliminated wasteful steps in the manufacturing process, and used a continuous flow manufacturing process. Although TI did not publish the exact cost of manufacture, it apparently achieved its low-cost goal since it priced the line of TI-25 calculators from US$5 to $10, and scheduled production of 2,000,000 units in 1990.[54]

Short cycle times

One advantage of simplifying processes and focusing on providing customer value is reduced cycle time. *Cycle time* refers to the length of time required to complete the operation. For a new product/service, this includes the time to design a new

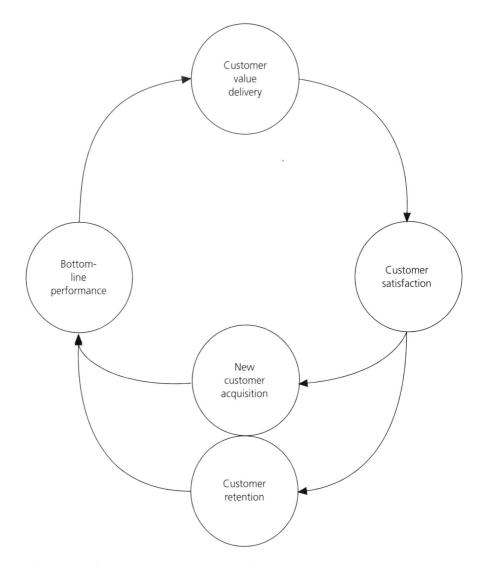

Figure 7.6 The customer responsiveness cycle.
Source: Woodruff, R. and Gardial, S., *Know Your Customer*. Oxford: Blackwell (1996), p. 6.

product/service and deliver it to the customer. For an existing product/service, cycle time refers to the time it takes to fill a customer's order.

A good example of reduced cycle time in auto design is the Chrysler Corporation. Chrysler reorganized its staff into platform teams: groups representing all departments that work on one car or truck from start to finish. The team is able to resolve conflicts early and prevent a hard-to-build car or unreliable design from ever reaching production. Chrysler has also developed a Japanese-style cooperative relationship with suppliers, recognizing that suppliers are part of its cross-functional team.[55] With its cross-functional teams and supplier partnering,

Chrysler has cut US$3 billion from yearly costs, and it can bring a car to market as fast as the best worldwide competitors. Chrysler has shortened its new car development cycle in the past five years from 54 months to 39 months and has done it with a smaller staff.

A good example of reduced cycle time in manufacturing is Motorola's Boynton Beach, Florida, plant that produces customized pagers. The plant uses a simultaneous engineering effort in which the pager was redesigned for robotic assembly. It shrunk the supplier base to 22 "best-in-class" sole-source suppliers, chosen for their extremely high quality levels. It also uses "real-time" computer statistical process control that attempts preemptively to avoid quality problems rather than just count mistakes. The plant can begin producing customized pagers *in lot sizes of one* within 20 minutes after a salesman enters an order via computer at Motorola's headquarters in Schaumburg, Illinois. Production of the pagers, customized to the proper radio frequency, takes less than two hours, including manufacture of printed circuit boards, final assembly, testing, and packaging.[56]

Regained market share and improved financial performance

In addition to the preceding examples of improved operating performance, the longer-term issues of increased sales, market share, and financial performance must be considered. In two separate studies, Shetty and Stratton each showed that companies furnishing quality products can charge more for their products, with resulting higher profit margins.[57] Figure 7.6 shows how customer value delivery yields business results.

Besides operating performance, the 1991 GAO study of 22 companies who were finalists for the Baldrige Quality Award in 1988 and 1989 collected data on market share increases, sales per employee, return on assets, and return on sales. All four outcomes increased, with the most noteworthy increase being the 13.7 percent average annual increase in market share.[58]

Business Week recently published a special issue on quality, titled "The Quality Imperative: What it Takes to Win in the Global Economy." In the introduction, the editors wrote: "Quality may be *the biggest competitive issue* of the late 20th and early 21st centuries."[59] Echoing that sentiment, Joseph Juran, one of the founders of the quality movement, recently remarked: "The twenty-first century will be the Century of Quality."[60] It appears that a number of firms throughout the world are realizing the quality imperative.

▌ Summary ▌

To operate in a chosen business, the firm's executives decide how to provide value to customers in that business. This decision is central to total quality and customer value strategy.

Crosby, Deming, Feigenbaum, Ishikawa, Juran, and others taught us that high quality and low cost can go together. More inspection after the fact of production and more cost are not the way to achieve higher quality in a competitive era. For higher quality to happen, there must be improvements in horizontal systems and processes.

Quality is much more than defect elimination. As a business strategy, TQ is focused primarily on the customer and the idea of providing customer value. Customer value is multidimensional and consists of value received and value sacrificed. Customer value determination systems attempt to discover what the customer values and does not value. Best net customer value refers to the greatest difference between value received and value sacrificed among all competitors.

Customer value systems that determine what the customer values, and design new products to fulfill those customer values, are crucial in quality improvement. Quality function deployment is a new product development system that explicitly incorporates customer value in the design and the design process.

Benchmarking refers to analyzing the processes and systems of the best "in class" firms to improve processes and systems.

Although severely battered by international competition in the late 1970s and throughout the 1980s, some American and European firms have been experiencing a rebirth with TQ. Those who have implemented many TQ ideas have recognized higher quality, lower costs, shorter cycle times, increased market share, and greater profitability.

DISCUSSION QUESTIONS

1 Explain how high quality and low cost can go together.

2 Explain the importance of management systems, especially customer value systems, in producing high quality.

3 Explain the importance of the customer and customer value in business level strategy.

4 How are benchmarking and quality improvement related?

5 How are the ideas of customer value and best net customer value related to the idea of quality?

6 Describe the importance of a customer value determination system in a technological firm with rapidly changing technology.

7 Relate the demands of customers to the demands of shareholders/owners in a TQ firm.

8 Is TQ a matter of national competitiveness? Explain.

KEY TERMS

Best net value	is the strongest net value among all competitive firms in the industry.
Competitive benchmarking	refers to analyzing what the best competitor or leading companies in the industry are doing to discover the products, processes and practices that satisfy customer needs.
Customer satisfaction	is the customer's positive or negative feeling about the value received from using a firm's product/service.
Customer value	is the customers' perception of what they want to have happen with the help of a product/service, in order to accomplish a desired goal.

Cycle time	refers to the length of time required to complete the operation.
Functional benchmarking	is studying and maybe even emulating the best processes and systems in the world, whether in the firm's industry (a competitor) or in any industry.
Net customer value or simply **net value**	is the difference between value realized and value sacrificed.
Quality function deployment	is a customer-driven design system that attempts to get early coupling between the requirements of the customer, marketing, and design engineering.
Realized value	is value that the customer receives.
Sacrificed value	is value that the customer gives up.

Saturn Regains Customers Lost to Japanese Auto Makers with Great Quality, Prices, and Dealers

Since the early 1970s, US auto manufacturers, and GM in particular, watched as Japanese auto manufacturers took more customers. GM's market share went into a tailspin and its annual loss in 1992 was US$23.5 billion, the largest ever recorded by a US firm.

GM's European operations under the Opel nameplate were not infected with such severe problems at the time. It remains to be seen why there were such large differences between the US and European operations of GM.

What would it take to regain customers from Honda, Nissan, and Toyota? How do you convince US customers, who have been burned repeatedly by poor quality, high prices, and high pressure dealers from Detroit, that a new era has arrived in autos?

The problems were so ingrained in its own systems of management and labor relations in the USA that GM decided to answer such a crisis with a whole new company, called Saturn. By starting Saturn, GM hoped to do what no US auto maker had accomplished in the two decades of the 1970s and 1980s. Saturn hoped to profitably build high-quality, low-priced small cars that regained customers and market share from Japanese models.[a] Saturn's specific mission was to "Market vehicles developed and manufactured in the US that are world leaders in quality, cost and customer satisfaction through the integration of people, technology and business systems, and to transfer knowledge, technology and experience throughout General Motors."[b]

This was a costly, ambitious, and risky undertaking. The GM investment to build Saturn was $5 billion. No one knew for sure if a US firm, even a brand new one, could wean consumers from the high-quality Japanese cars they had grown to love.

Saturn's business strategy for acceptance by customers in the fiercely competitive auto marketplace was based on a simple idea – customers would perceive more value in a low-priced, high-quality Saturn than in competing models. Saturn's quality was world class, its prices were low, and its dealers treated customers well with no-haggle pricing.

The commitment to delivering such value to customers was extraordinary in GM, as GM's plummeting market share showed.[c] GM had been accused by many of short-term profit thinking for the sake of maximizing current earnings. However, the $5 billion investment in Saturn was made with the expectation that profits would not be made until the mid-1990s.[d] In this case, the customer was first, and short-term profits were second.

Saturn's quality was not an accident. Saturn's workers were part of teams with previously unheard of levels of involvement in decision making, and very high levels of worker training

Table 7.2 J. D. Power customer satisfaction ratings for top five autos, 1994

Auto make	Customer satisfaction rating
Lexus	176
Infiniti	171
Saturn	155
Acura	150
Audi	148
Industry average	135

Note: The higher the number, the more satisfied customers were.
Source of data: "Saturn satisfaction is better than most luxury makes." *J. D. Power and Associates Special Report* (September 1994), p. 2.

by industry standards.[e] All workers were on salary and part of their pay was tied into reaching quality goals.[f] As part of a horizontal system of management, suppliers and dealers were integral parts of the Saturn team.[g] Saturn had one of the tightest just-in-time (JIT) inventory systems in North America, in which parts were delivered from suppliers just as they were needed for use in the assembly process. This JIT system revealed the source of quality problems, so they could be solved immediately. The team that designed the car included manufacturing personnel with experience in assembly and manufacturing processes. Their input helped design a car that was easier to assemble with fewer chances for manufacturing errors.[h]

Saturn's sales approach to no-haggle pricing started a marketing revolution among auto dealers. Ford, Chrysler, and other parts of GM experimented with no-haggle pricing because of Saturn's success in this area.[i]

Within two years of its late 1990 startup, Saturn had become a visible success. Its cars were ranked third in the world in the 1992, 1993, and 1994 J. D. Power Customer Satisfaction Surveys and number one among US makes. Saturn's rankings were based largely on their nearly impeccable quality, low prices and no-haggle pricing by dealers. The prices of some of the other cars in the top five were three or four times greater than Saturn's prices. Customer satisfaction ratings from the 1994 J. D. Power Customer Satisfaction Survey for the top five autos are in table 7.2.

Saturn's dealers were selling an average of 100 cars each month, more than any other brand sold in the USA[j] Saturn dealerships were ranked by auto dealers as the most valuable dealership to own in 1993.[k] Six weeks before the 1992 model year was officially over, the Saturn dealers sold out of cars.[l] In the spring of 1992, Saturn started to ship cars to Taiwan. Starting in 1993, Saturn was operating near capacity with three shifts and was producing nearly 300,000 cars per year from its one plant in Tennessee.[m] In early 1994, Saturn reported its first profit and lobbied General Motors for funds to start another plant.[n] Rumors were rampant in 1995 that another plant would be started to dramatically increase output.[o] In an outpouring of customer loyalty, 42,000 Saturn owners traveled to the plant in Spring Hill, Tennessee, for a "Saturn homecoming" in the summer of 1994.[p]

Saturn showed that GM could produce cars in the USA to global standards of quality, price, and customer satisfaction, and regain customers who had been lost to Japanese competitors. Also, Saturn showed that it takes long-term, executive-level commitment to superior customer value, and system-wide team approaches with suppliers, dealers, and workers to be world class.

Discussion Questions

1 How was Saturn's business strategy of very high quality and low prices different from other parts of GM?

2 Why was it important for Saturn to implement team concepts in the design and production of the cars?

3 Why was it important for GM to establish a new company rather than just start a new model in an existing GM plant?

Sources: **a.** "At Saturn, what workers want is . . . fewer defects," *Business Week* (December 2, 1991), pp. 117–18; **b.** Saturn Mission, Spring Hill, TN: Saturn Corporation, 1993; **c.** "Labor's days at GM," *Wall Street Journal* (September 4, 1992), p. A1; **d.** "Saturn: GM finally has a real winner," *Business Week* (August 17, 1992), pp. 86–91; **e.** Solomon, C. M., "Behind the wheel at Saturn," *Personnel Journal* (June 1991), pp. 72–4; **f.** "Saturn: GM finally has a real winner," pp. 86–91; **g.** "Saturn does right by customers; when will it make money?" *Automotive News* (June 3, 1991), p. 12; **h.** "Saturn: GM finally has a real winner," pp. 86–91; **i.** "Saturn's success breeds low-pressure copycats," *Wall Street Journal* (July, 31, 1992), p. B1; **j.** Ibid; **k.** "Honda: the dangers of running too lean," *Fortune* (June 14, 1993), pp. 113–14; **l.** "Fulfilling buyers' wishes, Saturn's well runs dry," *USA Today* (August 18, 1992), p. B1; **m.** Ibid.; **n.** "GM Saturn unit trumpets profit turned in 1993," *Wall Street Journal* (January 6, 1994), p. A4; **o.** "Saturn experiment is deemed successful enough to expand," *Wall Street Journal* (April 18, 1995), **p.** B1; p. Bemowski, K., "To boldly go where so many have gone before: Saturn Corp. sought to, and did, separate itself from the field," *Quality Progress* (February 1995), p. 32.

"PHILIPS ELECTRONICS NV USES QUALITY AS A WORLDWIDE STRATEGY"

INTERNATIONAL

C A S E

Philips Electronics NV, based in Eindhoven, the Netherlands, is the world's 31st largest industrial corporation, with 1995 worldwide sales of US$33.5 billion. It is also the world's eigth largest global electronics supplier, the world's largest manufacturer of color televisions, and one of the world's largest manufacturer of computer monitors.[a] The top seven global electronics suppliers are Hitachi, Matsushita, General Electric, Samsung, Siemens, Sony, and NEC, in that order. Sixty percent of Philips's sales are in Europe, 22 percent in the USA, 10 percent in Asia, 5 percent in Latin America, 2 percent in Australia and New Zealand, and 1 percent in Africa.

Philips is a true international firm with over 250 factories worldwide in over 40 countries. Some of its factories were noted for early attempts at job design to humanize the work.[b] It employs an international workforce of 240,000 and has sales and service outlets in 150 countries. The firm has nine product divisions: lighting, consumer electronics, Polygram (music), domestic appliances and personal care, components, semiconductors, communication systems, medical systems, and industrial electronics. In order to concentrate on its core competencies in electronics, Philips sold its home appliances division and its defense division in 1990.[c]

Philips is widely known for a strong technology base, as it spends 6–7 percent of sales on R&D, has research labs in five countries, and 60,000 patents to its credit. The firm created the audio cassette, video cassette, compact disc, and laser disc. However, it has not always been the most successful at commercializing its technology. In a globally competitive electronics industry, consumers demand additional user-friendly features, zero defects, and continually lower prices. In a competitive retail environment, retailing customers demand what consumers demand, plus just-in-time delivery of merchandise to prevent excess inventories and stockouts. How could Philips transform itself from a technology-driven company to a customer-driven company in such a world?

At its world headquarters in Eindhoven, Philips decided to use quality as a worldwide strategy. It modeled its efforts after the Baldrige and European Quality Award Criteria, and tailored its

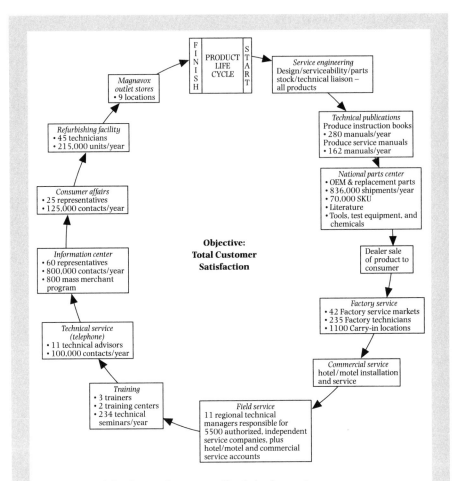

Figure 7.7 Philips Service Company quality circle of competence.
Source: Philips Consumer Electronics Company (1995).

own Total Quality processes, which it refers to as Philips Quality Award (PQA) 90. In 1995, all of its US and many of its European operations had implemented PQA 90.

Philips Consumer Electronics Company (PCEC) is a US$2 billion subsidiary based in Knoxville, Tennessee. It is one of the USA's leading full line marketers of consumer electronics under a leading brand name. It sells under the name of Magnavox and under the name of Philips. As of 1995, PCEC had sold more than 40 million color television sets in North America (i.e. the USA, Canada, and Mexico). PCEC also sold video, audio and disc technologies. Not only had PCEC qualified on PQA 90, but its manufacturing facilities were certified to ISO 9000 criteria, and it had won the Tennessee Quality Award in 1993 in recognition of its advances in quality. Its commitment to the customer and quality was signified by the gold pins formed in the shape of a capital "Q" that employees wore on their clothing, and by the centrality of total customer satisfaction, as shown in figure 7.7.

Robert Minkhorst, President of PCEC, described the firm's biggest challenge in the latter half of the 1990s. "We must change the mindset of the total organization from technology pull to customer pull."[d] Minkhorst recognized that there were two major classes of customers: large retailers, like Wal-Mart and Circuit City, who purchased the items from Philips, and the end use consumer.

To understand the requirements of the retailers, Philips was partnering with them. Some of the retailers, like Wal-Mart and Kmart, used non-selling floors in their stores, where the item was on display without a salesperson to explain the product to the consumer. To help explain the product to the consumer, Philips printed descriptive color ads on the sides of the boxes to perform some of the function of the traditional salesperson. Randy Mitchell, Vice President, Quality, noted that PCEC was trying to provide additional value to the retailers by growing the product line to include several other electronic products like caller i.d. and telephones. Then, the retailer could partner with fewer vendors.[e]

To understand the requirements of consumers, PCEC was conducting focus groups with consumers and creatively using a toll free 1–800 number. Mike Johnston, Vice President, Customer Service, described the function of the 1–800 number. "We receive 3,000 calls per day from across the US, Canada and Mexico into our customer center in East Tennessee. By having trained, empowered customer service representatives and technicians on the phone, we are able to delight the vast majority of consumers and customers who call here. One out of every four callers has a question on hookup. By helping the consumer understand how to hookup our product with another vendor's electronic component, we delight the consumer and prevent an unnecessary, costly service call, or warranty claim. Analysis of the call data also helps us to design products and manuals for the future."[f]

The other major process the firm is using to provide increased value to its customers and consumers is the logistics process. F. Joseph Brang, General Manager, US Operations, described some of the features driving the logistics process. "We have partnered with key, qualified suppliers and gone sole source with them in a very big way. Nearly all (97 percent) of our parts are sole sourced. If we do not sole source from the best in the world, then we are doing business with second best suppliers. Second best is simply not good enough for our customers."[g]

Philips has also dramatically reduced its manufacturing cycle time to reduce defects and deliver products to customers just in time. Lisa Deans, Quality Manager at the Greenville, Tennessee, TV manufacturing plant, indicated that whereas it had taken 15 days in the past to manufacture a TV set, it now takes three hours.[h] Such a reduced cycle time allows Philips to fill customer orders much more quickly than in the past.

What has been the payoff of such a commitment to total customer satisfaction? Although prices continued to erode at 2 percent per year in the worldwide competitive consumer electronics market, profits were up dramatically from 1991 to 1995. Sales were up and large projection TV sales were growing at 25 percent annually. PCEC planned to export large projection televisions to Europe starting in 1997. Total customer satisfaction survey results had improved significantly from 71 percent in 1991 to 90 percent in 1994.[i] It appers that the transformation to a customer-led company was well under way.

Discussion Questions

1 Describe the danger of being a technology-driven company in a competitive world.

2 Describe the importance of the logistics process to achieving total customer satisfaction.

3 How can a toll free number be used to help design the products of the future?

Sources: **a.** "Global 500", *Fortune* (1995); **b.** Hofstede, G., "Work structuring at Philips," in *Uncommon Sense About Organizations: Cases, Studies, and Field Observations*. London: Sage Publications (1994), pp. 93–114; **c.** "Philips Electronics", *Value Line Investment Survey* (May 19, 1995), p. 1565; **d.** Interview, Robert Minkhorst, Knoxville, TN (May 24, 1995); **e.** Interview, Randy Mitchell, Knoxville, TN (May 24, 1995); **f.** Interview, Mike Johnston, Jefferson City, TN, (March 22, 1995); **g.** Interview, F. Joseph Brang, Greenville, TN (May 10, 1995); **h.** Interview, Lisa Deans, Greenville, TN (May 10, 1995); **i.** "Philips Story," Philips Consumer Electronics Company, Knoxville, TN (1995).

NOTES

1 Gale, B., *Managing Customer Value*. New York: Free Press (1994), p. 18.

2 Crosby, P., *Quality is Free* New York: New American Library (1979); Deming, W. E., *Out of the Crisis*. Cambridge, MA: MIT Press (1986); Feigenbaum, A. "Engineering quality as a world marketing strategy," *Professional Engineer* (June 1982), pp. 12–17; Ishikawa, K., *What is Total Quality Control?* Englewood Cliffs, NJ: Prentice Hall (1985); Juran, J. M., *Managerial Breakthrough*. New York: McGraw-Hill (1964).

3 Crosby, P., *Quality is Free*.

4 Cole, W. and Mogab, J., *The Economics of Total Quality Management: Clashing Paradigms in the Global Market*, Oxford, UK: Blackwell (1995).

5 Deming, W. E., *Out of the Crisis*, p. 23.

6 Cole, W. and Mogab, J., *The Economics of Total Quality Management*.

7 Schonberger, R. J., *Building a Chain of Customers: Linking Business Functions to Create the World Class Company*. New York: The Free Press (1990), p. 77.

8 Judge, W., Stahl, M., Scott, R. and Millender, R., "Long- term quality improvement and cost reduction at Capsugel/Warner-Lambert," in Stahl, M. J. and Bounds, G. M. (eds), *Competing Globally through Customer Value*, pp. 703–9.

9 Garvin, D. A., *Managing Quality: The Strategic and Competitive Edge*. New York: The Free Press (1988), p. 49.

10 Stahl, M. J. and Bounds, G. M., *Competing Globally through Customer Value*, p. 2.

11 American Quality Foundation and Ernst & Young, *International Quality Study*. Cleveland: Ernst & Young (1991), p. 1.

12 Easton, G., "The 1993 state of US total quality management: a Baldrige examiner's perspective," *California Management Review*, 35(3) (1993), p. 32–54.

13 "Annual Report of European Organization for Quality," *European Quality*, 1(3) (1994), pp. 56–94.

14 Wilkinson, A., Redman, T. and Snape, E., "New patterns of quality management in the United Kingdom," *UK Quality*, 2(2) (Winter 1995), p. 39.

15 Powell, T. C., "Total quality management as competitive advantage," *Strategic Management Journal* (January 1995), pp. 15–37.

16 Bowles, J. and Hammond, J., *Beyond Quality: How 50 Winning Companies Use Continuous Improvement*. New York: G. P. Putnam's Sons (1991), p. 193; Cole, W. and Mogab, J., *The Economics of Total Quality Management*; Hackman, J. R. and Wageman, R., "Total quality management: empirical, conceptual, and practical issues," *Administrative Science Quarterly*, 40 (1995), pp. 309–42; Powell, T., "Total quality management as competitive advantage: a review and empirical study," *Strategic Management Journal*, 16 (January 1995), pp. 15–38; "Special Issue: Total Quality Management," *California Management Review*, 35, (Spring 1993); "Special Issue: Total Quality Management," *Canadian Journal of Administrative Sciences*, 12 (June 1995); "Total Quality Special Issue," *Academy of Management Review*, 19 (July 1994).

17 Day, G., "The capabilities of market-driven organizations," Journal of Marketing, 58 (October 1994), pp. 37–52; Flynn, B., Schroeder, R. and Sakakibara, S., "A framework for quality management research and an associated measurement instrument," *Journal of Operations Management*, 11 (1994), pp. 339–66.

18 Schonberger, R. J., "Is strategy strategic? Impact of total quality management on strategy," *Academy of Management Executive*, 6 (August, 1992), pp. 80–7.

19 "The quality imperative: what it takes to win in the global economy," *Business Week* (October 25, 1991), p. 38.

20 "Membership survey," *UK Quality* (September 1995), pp. 38–9.

21 Harris, C., "The evolution of quality management," *Canadian Journal of Administrative Sciences*, 12(2) (1995), pp. 95–105.

22 Kearns, D. A. and Nadler, D. A., *Prophets in the Dark: How Xerox Reinvented Itself and Beat Back the Japanese*. New York: Harper Business (1992), p. 270.

23 "Winning lines," *UK Quality* (March 1995), p. 6.

24 "Midland pays attention," *European Quality*, 2(4) (1995), pp. 28–31.

25 Galvin, R. W., *The Idea of Ideas*. Schaumburg, IL: Motorola University Press (1991), p. 68.

26 "Cleaning up: P&G viewed China as a national market and is conquering it," *Wall Street Journal* (September 12, 1995), p. A1.

27 Woodruff, R. and Gardial, S., *Know Your Customer*. Oxford, UK: Blackwell Publishers (1996), p. 95.

28 Eastman Chemical, *Strategic Intent*. Kingsport, TN (1993).

29 "Now quality means service too," *Fortune* (April 22, 1991), p. 100.

30 "Centrifugal force," *European Quality*, 1(1) (1994), p. 32.

31 Lands' End, Inc., *Annual Report*. Dodgeville, WI (1992), p. 2.

NOTES CONT.

32 American Quality Foundation and Ernst & Young, "International quality study," pp. 18–19.

33 Copulsky, W., "Balancing the needs of customers and shareholders" *Journal of Business Strategy* (November–December 1991), pp.44–7.

34 "Betting to win on the Baldie winners," *Business Week* (October 18, 1993), p. 8; Helton, B. R., "The Baldie Play," *Quality Progress*, 28(2) (February 1995), pp. 43–6.

35 US General Accounting Office, "Management practices: US companies improve performance through quality efforts," (May, 1991) GAO/NSIAD-91–190, p. 1.

36 Easton, G. and Jarrell, S., "The effects of total quality management on corporate performance: an empirical investigation," *Journal of Business* (1996).

37 Buzzell, R. D. and Gale, B. T., *The PIMS Principles*. New York: The Free Press (1987), p. 107.

38 Ohmae, K. "Getting back to strategy," *Harvard Business Review* (November–December 1988), pp. 149–56.

39 Camp, R. C., *Benchmarking: the Search for Industry Best Practices that Lead to Superior Performance*. Milwaukee, WI: ASQC Quality Press (1989).

40 Osterhoff, R., Locander, W. and Bounds, G., "Competitive benchmarking at Xerox," in Stahl, M. J. and Bounds, G. M. (eds), *Competing Globally through Customer Value*, p. 792.

41 "Delivering quality – is on time possible every time?" *UK Quality* (November 1994), pp. 8–10.

42 Coyne, K. P., "Sustainable competitive advantage–what it is, what it isn't," *Business Horizons* (January–February 1986), pp. 54–61; Ghemawat, P., "Sustainable advantage," *Harvard Business Review*, 64(5) (1986), pp. 53–8.

43 Schonberger, R. J., *Building a Chain of Customers*, p. 83; Garvin, D. A., *Managing Quality: the Strategic and Competitive Edge*. New York: The Free Press (1988), p. 49.

44 Woodruff, R. and Gardial, S., *Know Your Customer*. Oxford, UK: Blackwell Publishers (1996), p. 54.

45 Carothers, G., Bounds, G. and Stahl, M., "Managerial leadership," in Stahl, M. and Bounds, G. (eds), *Competing Globally through Customer Value*, p. 78.

46 "America's best plants: Ford Motor," *Industry Week* (October 15, 1990), p. 52.

47 "Corning laboratories," *Business Week* (October 25, 1991), p. 158.

48 American Quality Foundation and Ernst & Young, "International quality study," p. 21.

49 Band, W. A., *Creating Value for Customers*. New York: John Wiley and Sons (1991), pp. 168–169; Akao, Y., *Quality Function Deployment: Integrating Customer Requirements into Product Design*. Cambridge, MA: Productivity Press (1990).

50 Band, W. A., *Creating Value for Customers*, p. 168–9.

51 Mariotti, J., *The Power of Partnerships*. Oxford, UK: Blackwell (1995).

52 GAO, pp. 22–3.

53 "America's best plants: Corning," p. 40.

54 "America's best plants: Texas Instruments," p. 30.

55 "Chrysler on the road to recovery," *USA Today* (March 6, 1992), p. B1.

56 "America's best plants: Motorola," p. 62.

57 Shetty, V. K., "Product quality and competitive strategy," *Business Horizons* (May–June, 1987), pp. 46–52; Stratton, B., "The value of implementing quality," *Quality Progress* (July 1991), pp. 70–1.

58 GAO, p. 27.

59 "The quality imperative: what it takes to win in the global economy" (October 25, 1991), p. 4.

60 Juran, J., "Made in the USA.: a renaissance in quality," *Harvard Business Review* (July–August 1993), p. 47.

FUNCTIONAL STRATEGY

LEARNING OBJECTIVES

After reading this chapter, you should be able to accomplish the following.

1 Explain the desired relationship among corporate-level, business-level, and functional-level strategies.

2 Explain how technology contributes to customer value.

3 Discuss the international competitive nature of technology.

4 Discuss the information needs of external and internal customers.

5 Describe the customer value role of a management information system.

6 Explain the importance of product and service design to operations management.

7 Discuss the link between customer value strategy and products/services.

8 Relate the firm's decisions on customer value to the other marketing management decisions.

9 Describe the importance of consistency among the financial strategy decisions.

10 Explain the importance of training of human resources, and the importance of reward systems.

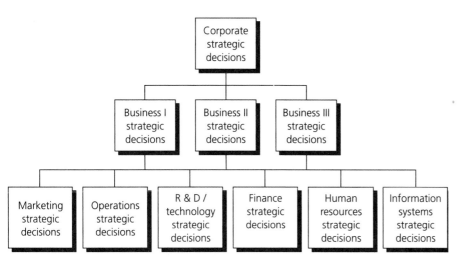

Figure 8.1 The hierarchy of strategic decisions.

Source: Stahl, M. J. and Grigsby, D. W., *Strategic Management: Formulation and Implementation*. Boston: PWS-Kent (1992), p. 104.

This chapter deals with the strategic decisions made within each of the business functions. These strategic decisions, made within the functions of operations, marketing, finance, human resources, research/development and technology, and information systems, are referred to as functional-level strategic decisions. These functional strategies are used to complement the customer value and competitive advantage sought by the business-level strategy.

Consistency of Functional Strategies

In all of the functional strategies reviewed in this chapter, we repeat two themes of consistency for successful performance of the organization. There needs to be consistency between the business-level and the functional strategies. There also needs to be consistency among the functional strategies.

Figure 8.1 attempts to show that consistency. Figure 8.1 shows a firm with three different businesses. The hierarchy of strategic decisions would be more complex if there were more businesses, or more simple if the firm was only in one business.

In the vertical direction, we look for consistency between the business-level and the functional strategies. If the firm primarily follows the business-level strategy of competitive strategy (chapter 6), then the functional strategies need to be designed and implemented with that competitive strategy in mind. If the firm primarily follows the business-level strategy of customer value (chapter 7), then the functional strategies need to be designed and implemented with the customer and customer value strategy in mind. Because of the increasing number of firms throughout the world pursuing customer value strategy, we use customer value strategy as the integrating business-level strategy for the various functional strategies. Some argue that TQ, with its emphasis on horizontal processes that span functions to focus on customer value, is the glue tying functions together.[1] If the particular firm is principally following competitive strategy, then that should be the guiding light that integrates the functional strategies.

In the horizontal direction, we also look for consistency among the functional strategies. Organizational performance will obviously be hampered if there are contradictions among the various functions. For example, mayhem will result if finance shrinks the capital budget so as to increase the amount of funds for a stock buyback program, while operations has decided to increase new plant construction by 200 percent to meet growing demand for new products developed by R&D.

R&D, Technology and Technological Change

We emphasize that technology is a tool to help managers deliver greater value to customers and thereby win increased market share and profits for their efforts. *Technology* is the sum of knowledge, tools, techniques, and processes used to transform organizational inputs into outputs.[2] *Technological change* refers to changes in any of these technological factors. For decades, the technology used to transform inputs into outputs changed slowly. However, in the past few decades, the pace of change in science and engineering has exploded. Such new technological knowledge has found its way into the globally competitive marketplace. Technology is now being used as a competitive weapon to gain new customers.[3]

The USA is a global leader in the development of new technology. However, some international competitors, especially Japan, have been implementing new technology at a faster pace to yield new products for customers. Herein lies the challenge for managers: managers must implement new technology at a faster pace to yield new or improved products and services for customers.

Management of technology

The *management of technology* (MOT) includes how the organization uses technology to yield value to customers. As such, the management of technology (MOT) concerns itself not only with many strictly managerial tasks, but also with many technical subjects from engineering and science. Management intersects with engineering and science to yield MOT.[4]

For example, a research scientist at a pharmaceutical company like Merck in the USA, or Glaxo Wellcome in the UK, may be interested in the reaction of Alzheimer's disease to a new drug. That scientist may be pursuing the issue strictly from the scientific side. A manager at the pharmaceutical company involved with the project may need to work through the maze of federal activities to win approval to distribute the new drug. The manager may also need to work with banks to gain financing for the new plant to produce the drug, with industrial engineers to design the production process, and with an advertising agency to launch the new product. Those managerial activities are referred to as the management of technology.

Rules of competition in an industry

Many firms use technology to improve their competitive positions. Managers can either develop the new technology or borrow it from others if it is not proprietary. *Proprietary technology* is technology held by one firm and not shared with other firms. Proprietary technology held by one firm in an industry can change the rules of competition in that industry, as Porter noted. "Technology affects competitive advantage if it has a significant role in determining relative cost position or differentiation."[5]

A chemical company developing a new chemical process that lowers the cost of production by 35 percent can become the lowest cost producer. Competitors in the industry can try to differentiate their products, or they can exit the business, or they can stay in the business and suffer losses.

Contribution to customer value

New technology is expensive in terms of the money involved and the disruption to the organization to introduce it. Personnel must be retrained, equipment needs to be replaced or modified, and productive output is often disrupted. Therefore, managers should not introduce new technology just for the sake of having the latest new technological toys in the industry.

New technology should be introduced for its contribution to customer value. Whether the increased customer value is in the form of reduced cycle time, lower cost, or higher quality, technology is a means to improved customer value.

Continuous improvement of products can extend the maturity phase of the life cycle (chapter 2). By improving and adding new value to the product/service, the firm can extend the time until customers switch to other products/services. This continuous improvement tactic is counter to the old tactic of "milking" the product for profitability with little new investment.

A way to offer value to customers is to offer the new product/service to customers earlier. In many markets, customers demand the latest in new technology in products/services without delay. By shortening product development cycle times, the firm can be the first to market with the new product/service. *Product development cycle time* is the time from conception of the idea for a new product, through the product development phase, until the new product is first offered to the customer.

Good examples of shortened product development cycle times are in the automobile industry. Toyota's product development cycle time is three years, whereas the comparable number for some Detroit firms is five years. Within Detroit, Chrysler has dramatically shortened its new product development cycle time, from 54 to 39 months.[6]

The cost of being late to market can be huge. Just three months' "slip" in the

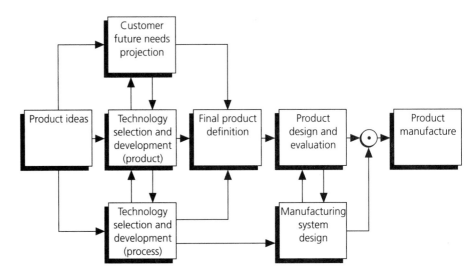

Figure 8.2 A superior product development process for an innovative product.
Source: Wilson, C., Kennedy, M. and Trammell, C., *Superior Product Development: Managing the Process for Innovative Products*. Oxford: Blackwell (1996), p. 17.

schedule to new product introduction can cost 50 percent of the gross profits in a fast-moving industry like personal computers.[7]

An obvious area for the application of new technology is in cost reduction. Cost reduction may be the most frequently used factor to justify new technology. The steel industry has been replacing obsolete open hearth furnaces with basic oxygen furnaces. New basic oxygen furnaces produce a ton of steel at much lower cost than from old open hearth furnaces.

Another good reason to introduce new technology is to reduce the variance of production and thereby improve quality. Sometimes robots are used to yield consistent quality. Training in statistical process control is a good example of the use of technology to improve quality and reduce variance.

Product development

Product development is the phase of the technological life cycle where most of the organization's investments in new technology occur. There are many variables that should be considered in the development of new products. The most important is the link to customer value.

As figure 8.2 indicates, product development is tied into a projection of customer future needs and the selection of technology for the product and the process. Customer needs must be projected into the future because of long lead times to develop the technology and develop the product.

The product development cycle time for new automobiles is three or four years depending on the manufacturer. To offer airbags or anti-lock brakes on new automobiles, the manufacturer must project the demand for those products three or four years into the future. After such long-range projections, the manufacturer can decide to start product development.

This section stresses that technology should be selected for its contribution to customer value. The selection of the technology should be tied into satisfying projected customers' future needs. In a portable personal computer, do customers want color displays or low price? The answer to such a question helps the manager to pick the product and process technology.

Technological leadership or followership

As a matter of policy, some firms are technological leaders. *Technological leadership* means being the first to market with new technology. By communicating that policy to customers, the firm hopes that customers will know that the firm's products have the latest technology available. Being a technological leader can be very rewarding if customers like the latest technology. The technological leader frequently retains market share leadership because it has set the standard for the market. The policy can also be very risky if customers do not like the unproven technology. Porsche automobiles usually had the latest technological innovations. Some customers bought their Porsches because they thought they were buying something unique.

Some firms have a policy of being a technological follower. *Technological followership* is letting other firms introduce new technology into the marketplace first and then copying or modifying the proven technology. Being a follower can be less risky in terms of original financial outlay, but the policy usually means that the follower will not become market dominant. IBM was not the first firm to offer personal computers in the early 1980s. IBM waited to see if customers were interested in the personal computers offered by Apple.

International dimensions of technology

Technology is increasingly being used by international competitors as a way to compete. Some countries, notably Japan and Germany continue to invest in technology at a faster rate of growth than does the USA. Both countries dramatically increased the rate of investment in R&D during the 1970s and the 1980s.[8]

In a recent international survey, Japanese firms were more than twice as likely as US firms to use technology to provide value to customers. "Japanese manufacturers place much more importance on flexibility by targeting variety, innovation, and technological superiority."[9]

Many Japanese firms have relative ease in translating new technology into products for customers. One reason is the more holistic thinking in the Japanese culture relative to Western managers, which makes it more natural for people of different functions in Japanese organizations to work together in new product development.[10]

Japanese firms continue to receive more patents in the USA than US firms. Japanese firms headed the list of US patent awards for the seventh year in a row in 1992. Canon, Toshiba, Mitsubishi, and Hitachi held the top four slots. General Electric Co. was the highest ranking US firm at fifth.[11]

Management Information Systems

Management information systems (MISs) are used for internal organizational purposes and for external customer value purposes. A *MIS* is a set of computer hardware and software that gathers, organizes, summarizes, and reports information for use by managers, customers, and others. Thus, the design and operation of a MIS is a key system that can provide value to customers so that they can accomplish their goals.

The roles of management information systems

In the past, MISs were used to make internal operations faster, more accurate, and more efficient. Today, the more exciting uses of MISs are those that provide additional value for external customers and help the firm gain market share. An MIS can serve at least four different roles for the organization. The first two roles (transaction/bookkeeping and strategic planning) have a traditional, internal focus. The last two roles (competitive weapon and customer value) have a more recent external focus.

Transaction/bookkeeping role

An MIS can be used to record, store and report transactions. In this role, the MIS serves a bookkeeping role. This traditional role of a MIS is the least exciting and least imaginative. The awesome power of the MIS is used for the functions of recording, storing, summarizing, and reporting on transactions. The transactions are usually recorded and summarized in financial terms. In this role, the MIS serves primarily as an internal tool – although a fast, accurate, and expensive one. When using an MIS only in this capacity, managers take a cost-centered view of MIS: since the MIS is an expense with little direct role in providing value to customers, costs of the MIS are to be minimized.[12]

Many banks have used large computers to record, summarize, and report to customers on checking accounts at the end of the month. The banks have used the information internally as a way to track cash flow. This expenditure to clear and record millions of check transactions was large, because the MIS usually required mainframe-sized computer power. Little value was provided to the customer except for an end of the month statement. Not until the customer could access his or her account through automatic teller machines, which are computer terminals, was much value provided to the customer. By tying into the bank's MIS, ATMs provide a quick, 24-hour, seven-day, local banking service.

Strategic planning role

A MIS can be used as an integral part of the strategic planning process. The MIS is used to collect, analyze and report information concerning demographic, regulatory, economic, marketplace, and competitive trends that are useful in strategic planning. Computers may be tied into industry databases to track sales of competitors by kind of product, product features, and price. It is not unusual to find corporate computers tied into several large external databases involving industry, marketplace, and demographic trends of all kinds. The explosive growth of the Internet has strengthened this use.[13] Computers are often used in strategic planning to perform computerized simulations of alternative strategies and their results. The MIS may be viewed as a strategic decision support system and as a strategic intelligence system.[14]

Competitive weapon role

The view of MIS as a competitive weapon is recent.[15] A problem with this view is that it may ignore the changing needs of the customer. A firm may have a MIS to accurately track levels of internal inventories relative to competitors' sales. However, the MIS says nothing about the desirability of the products by the customer. Accurate tracking of buggy whips is of little value to customers with autos. Peter Drucker, the often cited management theorist, reminds us that firms must become information based and deliver more value to customers with information.[16]

By focusing on the current competition, the firm may also ignore new competitors. General Motors collected reams of information on Ford and Chrysler. For a dangerously long time, GM assumed that the Japanese were not worth worrying about.

Customer value role

Where the MIS is viewed in the customer value role as a way to help customers achieve their goals, the value of the information merges with the value of the product/service of the firm. The information itself becomes a service alongside the other products and services of the organization. Banks that transfer funds electronically provide value to customers in terms of speed and security in addition to the actual transmission of the funds. Some auto service stations offer credit card payment at the pump, providing additional customer value of speed and convenience. Financial services firms, like Merrill Lynch, are delivering more financial products and information to customers by being tied into multiple electronic financial markets. Financial services brokers and bankers can quote interest rates on many kinds of investment because they are linked to many financial markets.

At the Boeing Company, computers were used extensively to design the company's latest airplane – the 777. Boeing hopes to lower the cost of design, lower the cost of maintenance, and lower the number of design defects to be fixed after initial production with its computer-aided design (CAD). Boeing is gambling billions on the 777 and using a radical CAD. The CAD enables Boeing to skip the usual paper drawings and full-scale mockup, and go straight from computer images to fabrication and assembly. Over 200 "design/build" teams, with cross-functional membership from customers (the airlines), mechanics, salespeople, engineers, and assemblers, are integrated by the CAD.[17]

Some organizations use their MIS to construct a customer profile by analyzing customer data concerning customers' buying behavior and their needs. Some airlines provide value to customers through their MIS, as in the international exhibit.

INTERNATIONAL AIRLINES, MIS AND CUSTOMER VALUE

Some international airlines are providing value to their customers by entering into joint ventures, linking their management information systems together, and advertising the combined benefits to the public. The linked MISs provide more combined flights throughout the world, make reservations easier to complete, and offer transferable frequent flyer points from one airline to another for future free travel.

In 1994, Delta Airlines had joint ventures with KLM, Lufthansa, Swissair, Japan Airlines, and Air New Zealand. By including the schedules of those five international joint venture partners in its computerized reservation system, Delta spanned the world for its customers, even though Delta aircraft did not fly to many of the international destinations that some of its partners did. The schedules offered many more flights and easier reservations. Transferable frequent flyer points were also earned from flying on one of the international partner airlines and transferred to the customer's Delta frequent flyer account. If a customer took an Air New Zealand flight from the USA to New Zealand and return, and earned 16,000 frequent flyer points on Air New Zealand, those points were transferred to the customer's Delta frequent flyer account for future free travel on Delta. The frequent flyer points were credited in Delta's MIS automatically.

The information needs of external and internal customers

This section highlights the most obvious information needs of external customers in an era of information technology. However, remember that these now obvious needs were not apparent in the recent past when computers first became popular. Firms that discover still newer ways to provide value to customers through a MIS will increase their market share. Internal customers have information needs like external customers. All organizational members who use a MIS are internal customers of the information systems department that designed and implemented the MIS.

Accessibility

Information must be accessible to customers to be of value to them. If customers cannot achieve ready access to information when they need it, the information has little value. A classic example of providing value to customers through accessibility of information is the American Airlines Sabre reservation system. American found a way to deliver a different dimension of value to customers than its rival, United Airlines. United's reservation system exclusively listed United's flights. American's reservation system provided all airlines' schedules, so that agents would use its system all the time. However, American listed its own flights first, with the result that many agents never looked further. By making all the flight schedules accessible, American provided additional value to customers, and thereby gained additional customers.[18]

Timeliness

Information is of little value to customers if it is not timely. They need current information to make timely decisions. Indeed, customers frequently need *real time information*, which is information that immediately reflects the underlying reality. American Hospital Supply Company designed a computerized way to provide real time information to its customers on purchasing inventory. AHSC's customers are purchasing agents for hospitals and clinics. By placing a computer terminal in each customer's office, AHSC's system provided order entry, invoicing and billing, inventory control, and shipping with a high degree of timeliness and accuracy. Since AHSC could now deliver computer-ordered hospital supply items within 24 hours, customers were able to reduce their inventory stock levels from 75 to 30 days. Purchasing and inventory financing costs declined considerably.[19]

User-friendliness

Information must be understandable to be of value to customers. *User-friendly* means that the user of the information can use the MIS with little difficulty due to ease of following instructions. National Car Rental's Smart Key System for renting cars uses a touch screen operated system with just a few options per screen. The system is quick and easy for customers to operate.

Security

Customers have a need for secure information if the information concerns their own assets and their own behavior. Automatic teller machines need to display information in such a way that only the customer has access to the information. Personal identification numbers (PINs) are meant to give access only to the owner. Recently, Fidelity Investments, the USA's largest mutual fund company, tried to make access easier to its customers so that they could easily conduct business over the phone. However, Fidelity discovered that it had made access too easy, as anyone with a push-button phone could gain access to the accounts of Fidelity customers. Fidelity fixed this security issue by requiring callers to have a PIN *and* Social Security Number to gain access to their accounts.[20]

Accuracy

Information quality is the degree to which information accurately portrays reality. Just as external customers demand accurate information to make decisions, internal customers need the same accuracy in information for decision making purposes. USAA is one of the USA's largest auto insurers. When customers call in to check or change information in their auto insurance policies, the USAA agent must have an accurate information data base.

Effects of MISs on global competition

Management information systems that have no national boundaries are a means of enhancing international competition. In the airline industry, firms with computerized worldwide airline reservation systems can offer value to customers that others cannot, as described in the international exhibit.[21] In the financial services industry, firms electronically linked to the world's major financial markets in New York, London, Frankfurt, Tokyo, and Hong Kong can provide real time financial information to customers needing to deal in international currencies.

The MIS can tie together internationally dispersed resources of the firm as if they were in the next building.[22] At some international firms, the power of MISs is speeding new product development by eliminating distances and borders. Designers and engineers around the world in Texas Instruments (TI) now send

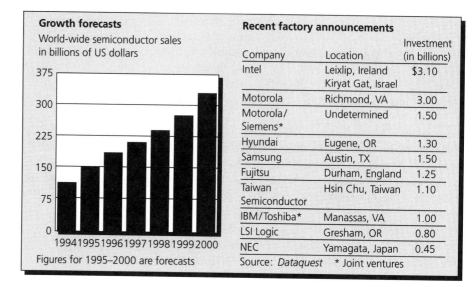

Recent factory announcements		
Company	Location	Investment (in billions)
Intel	Leixlip, Ireland	$3.10
	Kiryat Gat, Israel	
Motorola	Richmond, VA	3.00
Motorola/ Siemens*	Undetermined	1.50
Hyundai	Eugene, OR	1.30
Samsung	Austin, TX	1.50
Fujitsu	Durham, England	1.25
Taiwan Semiconductor	Hsin Chu, Taiwan	1.10
IBM/Toshiba*	Manassas, VA	1.00
LSI Logic	Gresham, OR	0.80
NEC	Yamagata, Japan	0.45

Source: *Dataquest*   * Joint ventures

Figure 8.3   International semiconductor sales and new production.
Source: The Wall Street Journal (October 30, 1995), copyright © 1995 Dow Jones & Co., Inc. All rights reserved worldwide.

detailed designs instantly over the computer network so that TI employees anywhere can work on them simultaneously. The time needed to develop a calculator shrank by 20 percent as soon as TI began sending drawings electronically in 1989.[23]

The number of firms recognizing the growing uses of information systems technology has led to an explosion in the worldwide sales of semiconductors. Figure 8.3 shows the forecast growth in the worldwide sales of semiconductors through the year 2000. To meet that demand, a number of semiconductor firms in Germany, Japan, Korea, Taiwan, the USA, and the UK have announced plans to build expensive new semiconductor plants throughout the world. The figure also shows a joint venture between Motorola, a US firm, and Siemens, a German firm, as well as a joint venture between IBM, a US firm, and Toshiba, a Japanese firm.

Operations Management

Whether in hard goods manufacturing of a durable item like an automobile or an aircraft, or service operations in a hotel or bank, operations management is at the core of many organizations.

Operations, manufacturing and service management

Operations management is the process of managing the production of goods and services. Thus, operations management is a broad term that includes both manufacturing and service management. Manufacturing management is the process of managing the production of tangible goods, but does not include services. Whether it is of autos, motorcycles, soft drinks, aircraft, or chemicals, there is tangible output in manufacturing. *Service management* is the process of producing non-tangibles with customer involvement and consumption at the point of delivery. Whether NationsBank, Fidelity Investments, Delta Airlines, FedEx, UPS, TNT Express, or the British Royal Mail, service organizations deliver their non-tangible services at the point of production. As services consume a growing part of our economy, the broader term of operations management is preferable.

Many of the steps in product and service operations are identical. There are common concepts on plant layout, purchasing of materials from suppliers, and training of employees in both product and service operations. A distinction between product and service operations is that services are consumed by the customer at the point of generation. Therefore, there is no inventory function for finished goods. In a bank, loans are generated at the point of servicing the customer. Loans are not held in inventory. Haircuts are not held in inventory in a barber shop.

Many firms recognize the need to integrate processes across design, operations, and quality control. Figure 8.2 shows the importance of product design to manufacturing. Product/service design needs to be fully integrated with operations management to deliver superior value to customers.

Today, many firms recognize the critical importance of operations management to the ability of the firm to provide consistent value to customers.[24] However, in the mid-1980s, there was a disturbing trend in American industry to deemphasize the importance of operations management. The term *hollow corporation* arose to describe a firm that did not manage its own operations. Many US manufacturers were exiting manufacturing and turning themselves into marketers for foreign producers.[25] In the 1990s, that trend was reversed.

The experience at Xerox of almost giving up its business to Japanese firms slowed the growth of the hollow corporation trend. In describing Xerox's near bankruptcy, the ex-chair of Xerox, David Kearns, offered a Handbook for Decline. The list of what *not* to do included: "Deemphasize Manufacturing. Don't pay too much attention to how the product is made, to improvements in the manufacturing process, or to the relationship among design, development, engineering, and production. Keep anyone with manufacturing experience well away from the executive suite. The true secret of success is to completely get out of the business of producing things yourself."[26]

Translating customer value strategy into products/services

In customer value strategy, firms take responsibility for providing value to their customers. Thus, firms must be involved in some kind of operations. Whether those operations involve tangible products or intangible services, the operations translate the raw inputs into outputs with value for the customers. Figure 8.4 contains an example of such a transformation function. The product or service is the means of transmitting value to the customers. That is why it is so important for an organization to be in control of its operations. Radio Shack is a retailer. Its operations are primarily retailing in its stores and do not include much manufacturing activity. Alternatively, Panasonic's operations are primarily in manufacturing, with little activity in retailing. Although the two organizations differ in

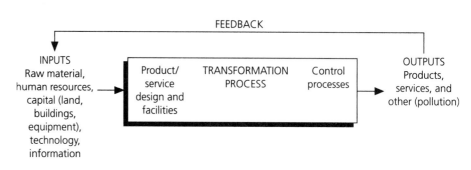

Figure 8.4 The operations management system.

terms of principal operations, each organization is in control of its principal operations that deliver value to its customers.

In the early 1980s, Chrysler neared bankruptcy. The firm nearly left design and manufacturing to others, and became an assembler and retailer of Japanese cars. It nearly lost control of its destiny as it became a hollow corporation. Since then, Chrysler has regained control of its design and manufacturing and recaptured market share in the 1990s.

Designing operations and processes

Figure 8.2 shows the importance of simultaneous product and process design for the product manufacture, known as *concurrent engineering*. Designing operations is a broader term than designing the manufacturing system, as the former includes services operations as well as product manufacturing.

There are several decisions that must be made to complete the design of operations. Decisions must be made on what is to be produced (product/service planning), how (process technology selection), how many (capacity planning), where (facility location planning), how work flows (layout planning), and who does what (job design). These decisions must be consistent with each other to yield a consistent operations strategy that reinforces the business strategy.

Unchallenged international facility locations can nearly guarantee the success of international operations. In the mid-1990s, as other auto producers regained their footing and wanted to produce cars for Southeast Asia, some Japanese carmakers argued for continued governmental protection of their Southeast Asian locations. "Japanese carmakers, who dominate the Southeast Asian market under generous protection, fear that a free-trade plan being debated by the Asia-Pacific Economic Cooperation Forum might introduce fiercer competition more quickly than they can handle. An official at one of Japan's largest carmakers said: 'We are worried that these countries may open their markets only to let South Korean, European and US companies destroy their industry through exports of manufactured cars.'"[27] In 1995, Japanese companies held 90 percent of the Southeast Asian car market, estimated at about one million cars annually in Thailand, Indonesia, Malaysia, and the Philippines.

Today, processes are increasingly being seen as the way to organize in firms, versus by function. One of the biggest advantages of focusing on processes, rather than functions, is that processes enable the organization to focus on the customer. Viewing the materials transformation process as those activities tied into transforming material into value for the customer is a process view. Such a view examines inventory in terms of customer values, not internal economics.

Process reengineering is the redesign of the process by which a product or service is created and distributed. Process reengineering means the perpetual search for ways to improve procedures and methods for products and services.[28] Reengineering is covered in greater detail in the next chapter under a contrasting approach to organizational design.

Marketing Management

Consistency among the functional areas, particularly between operations and marketing, is a necessary condition for continued corporate success. Sometimes attempts to suboptimize in marketing by building market share, or increasing profitability, cause the firm to lose sight of the customer and customer requirements.

Figure 8.5 shows one model of ways to improve performance in marketing. Some of the market penetration, product development, and market development decisions under the banner of increasing sales volume can be in conflict with some of the decisions taken to improve profitability. As with all the functional decisions, consistency is a necessary condition for success. One way to insure such consistency is to start the design of the marketing strategy with a definition of the customer and customer value requirements.

Defining the customer and customer value requirements

Who are the target customers? That is a question that every firm should be able to answer without hesitation. Just as importantly, who are the future targeted customers? Different answers to the two questions can have profound implications for changes in marketing strategy and changes in the entire firm.

A megatrend in Germany, Japan, and the USA is the "graying" of those populations as the post-Second World War baby boomers reach maturity and senior citizen status (figure 2.1). Different products need to be designed and marketed to meet such a trend. Per *Business Week*, "By 2020 almost one-third of the US population will be 55 or older. The field of designing products to meet the needs of an aging population is about to explode."[29]

Philips Consumer Electronics Company (see chapter 7) defines its customers differently from its consumers. For PCEC, the customer is a retailer, like Wal-Mart and Kmart. The consumer is the individual who buys one of its Magnavox televisions. The customer and the consumer have different requirements. PCEC must be responsive to both, but if it does not delight its customers, the consumer may never even see its Magnavox TVs.

Chapter 7, on customer value strategy, describes customer requirements as the start of the entire TQ process.[30] A section in this chapter on managing technology

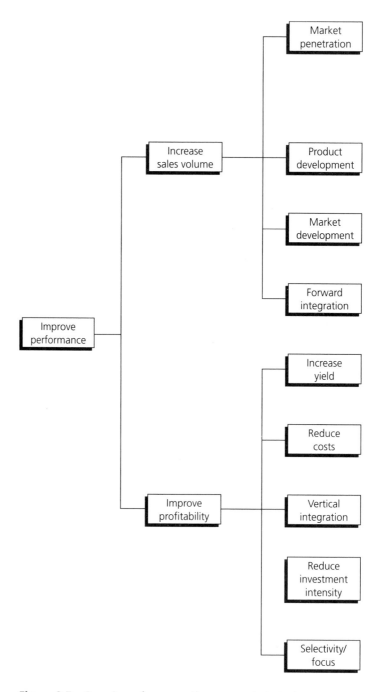

Figure 8.5 Generic performance improvement strategies.

Source: Reprinted by permission from Day, G. S., *Strategic Market Planning: the Pursuit of Competitive Advantage*, p. 103. Copyright © 1984 West Publishing Company. All rights reserved.

starts the product design process with customer requirements. By definition, no product can be a quality product if it does not meet customer requirements. The most perfectly manufactured horse drawn wagon is of little use in an era when people buy and drive autos.

The importance of the product in delivering value to customers is covered in chapter 7, and the product development sections in this chapter. Besides the product, there are three other decisions in marketing strategy that should flow from defining customer requirements: price, place/distribution, and promotion/advertising.

Price

Some analysts argue that pricing decisions are the least understood and least consistent strategic decisions made in organizations.[31] Indeed, pricing decisions are strategic because they communicate to the firm's competitors and customers whether the firm is competing on the basis of price leadership or differentiation. The firm needs to communicate whether it is offering a nondifferentiated commodity-like product that should be purchased because of its low price, or a differentiated product that deserves to be purchased at a premium price.

A firm wishing to increase sales volume and penetrate markets might lower its prices. But the firm must ask itself if such price cuts would be consistent with a differentiation strategy. If the firm wishes to improve profitability, it might increase price. Again, the firm must ask itself if such price hikes would be consistent with a price-leadership strategy.

Cost-plus pricing, which is a fixed add-on to actual cost, is a strategy that can cause a firm to lose sight of its competition and ignore the messages sent to customers about price leadership or differentiation. The firm's cost of manufacture may be independent of competitors' cost of manufacture, as described by learning curves or the existence of market entry barriers. Distribution inefficiencies may further cloud the cost picture. Pricing decisions should *not* be made on the basis of cost-plus. Rather, pricing decisions should be strategic decisions that reinforce business-level competitive decisions and customer value decisions. For example, if the corporate level stresses market share growth, a pricing decision might be biased on the low side to encourage sales.

Place/distribution

In terms of distribution strategy, the firm must consider whether it will use its own or outside distribution paths. *Distribution channels* are the paths and means the firm uses to get its products/services into the hands of customers. Firms must make this decision on every product they offer, whether they have distribution channels in place or not. Even though IBM had one of the best-developed distribution channels in place when it introduced its personal computer in the early 1980s, the firm decided to use independent distributors to distribute its personal computers. This decision was made in part to reach customers different from those involved with IBM's existing distribution system.

The existence of a well-developed distribution channel is a corporate asset that helps a firm decide to market new products. It appears that Anheuser-Busch's distribution channel for beer had something to do with its decision to market snack foods through the same channel.

The firm also must decide whether the proper incentives are in place for its own channels. This problem occurs sometimes when new products or classes of products are introduced. What kind of incentive could IBM offer its sales force to sell personal computers compared to the incentive it offered to sell mainframe computers?

Place also includes the geographic distribution of facilities. A firm must have distribution facilities in place to serve the customers alluded to in its mission statement. In the 1970s, the Coors Brewing Company was concentrating primarily on the western USA. After Coors decided to become a national firm in the 1980s, it took years to open distribution facilities throughout the rest of the country.

Promotion/advertising

Few areas in marketing receive as much attention as promotion or advertising. Questions of ethics or truth in advertising, method of promotion, effectiveness, and use of in-house or outside promotional forces must be considered.

The issues of method and effectiveness are especially important in attempting to create an image for a product that may not be a differentiated product to start with. The many blind taste tests of beer that have been conducted seriously question whether there are identifiable taste differences within a class of beers. Yet beverage firms spend millions of dollars on advertising per year to convince consumers that there are differences. Some of the advertising budgets and sales suggest that the consumers are indeed convinced that there are differences.

Some firms prefer to contract out their promotional activities rather than conduct them with in-house resources. If the firm decides on such an approach, it must be careful to ensure that the resultant promotional campaign fits the firm's competitive business strategies and the targeted market. Procter & Gamble (P&G) ran an ad campaign for marketing Camay soap in Japan. After sales flopped, P&G discovered that the translation of the television ads indicated "bad manners" between the man and woman in the ad due to cultural differences in interpreting a bath scene.[32] After that experience, the firm decided to hire foreign nationals in marketing and other areas to understand cultural differences.

Financial Management

There are few functional-level strategies besides finance in which decisions can be as counterproductive for the entire corporation if they do not mesh.[33] The consistency of the financial strategy with the corporate- and business-level strategies and the consistency of the many financial decisions are critical. Decisions on profitability can run counter to decisions on sales growth, which can run counter to decisions on financial leverage. A firm may decide on massive doses of leverage as a takeover defense, thereby incurring such large debt service as to hurt profitability. Or a firm may accept marginal credit risks as customers to accomplish a sales target, but hurt profitability due to some poor credit risks.

Financial objectives and strategies

There is a critical need in the financial area for the objectives and strategies to be clearly stated. An objective of "improved profitability" is dramatically different from an objective of "improved return on equity by at least one-half of 1 percent per year for each of the next five years." The case analysis guide (chapter 2) presents the formulas for the ratios in this section.

Some industries prefer one financial ratio or group of ratios to others. The nature of the business may suggest the kinds of ratios that are preferable. Capital-intensive industries such as steel may prefer return on investment as a profitability ratio. Retailers such as grocers may prefer sales-based measures such as return on sales as a profitability ratio.

Many financial ratios are measures of objectives. The firm's objectives should be quantitative enough to suggest the choice of ratios. Whichever financial ratios the firm prefers, it should consistently indicate over time which ratios it is using.

Financial ratios, or measures of objectives, should always be compared with the firm's own past experience and with industry averages, if possible. This relative comparison should be undertaken in the strategy formulation phase to indicate what is possible. The comparison should also be done in the evaluation and control stage to indicate possible reasons for differences between planned and actual numbers.

In all cases involving financial objectives, integrity and truth in reporting are absolutely necessary conditions to insure investor confidence. That integrity is especially important in international financial issues, as there may be limited available information. Daiwa Banks of Japan allegedly hid extensive losses of about US$1.1 billion in bond trading in the mid-1990s. When that alleged fraud became public information, confidence in Daiwa Banks was shaken. The markets sold its stock and the US Federal Reserve revoked Daiwa's charter and forced Daiwa to end all activities in the USA by early 1996.[34]

Profitability

Many have asserted that an emphasis on maintaining stock value leads to short-term decision making on the part of managers, as they fail to undertake long-term projects. This assertion, however, is not supported by empirical evidence. Wool-ridge documented the positive response of stock prices to long-term strategic decisions, even if the strategic decisions have a small short-term profit.[35] Making the long-term profitability decisions is a sign of a strong, mature management team.[36]

Liquidity and cash management

Liquidity ratios define the ability of the firm to cover debt. Whatever ratio(s) the firm prefers based on industry averages and the firm's own past history, stability is important. Substantial variance in these numbers questions the firm's ability to meet its short-term financial obligations.

Cash management usually refers to the balancing of cash inflows with out-flows. Many firms prepare a cash budget or a cash-flow budget to insure that there will be adequate amounts of cash for short-term needs. Some have speeded up accounts receivable and slowed down accounts payable to improve cash positions. When cash flow becomes that critical, one must ask how long before the bankruptcy or the divestiture occurs.

Leverage and capital management

Few financial strategic decisions have received as much attention in the recent past as leverage.[37] *Leverage* is the amount of debt relative to equity. In a recent survey of corporate executives, 47 percent responded that they felt that American companies were carrying too much debt.[38] Because of LBOs, with their bias toward debt, and corporate raiders, who encourage firms to keep their debt levels high, there are new biases toward debt.

This leverage question must be addressed in the broader context of corporate strategy and corporate control. As *Business Week* pointed out, "The driving force behind most increases in leverage is management's desire to stay in charge.[39]

Asset management

Asset management, which refers to how intensely the firm is using its assets, offers little disagreement concerning the appropriate levels of the measures. As long as the firm is protected against inventory stock-outs, then the more intensely the assets are worked the better. Whereas some of the other financial decisions have advantages and disadvantages relative to the corporate- and business-level objectives, there are few drawbacks to working the firm's assets or inventory more intensely. Perhaps the only limits are technology and industry comparisons.

The collection period for receivables may be the only activity measure in which higher-level strategy may indicate that more is not better. As the ratio is formed by a division of accounts receivable by annual credit sales, the measure could be reduced by shrinking the numerator of accounts receivable. Shrinking accounts receivable could result in lost sales. If other strategies are aimed at increasing sales, such a cut of the collection period would be counterproductive. This is another case in which consistency among strategies needs to be addressed.

Investment ratios

Management of investment ratios is definitely an area in which the other relevant strategies, and even the issues of corporate control and ownership, must be considered. Low price–earnings ratios have been known to encourage corporate raiders. The firm may wish to keep the ratio high through stock buybacks or through a series of decisions to reduce the volatility of earnings.

Low or volatile dividend payouts or common stock dividend yields have been known to anger investors. The result may be a lower stock price than otherwise, due to investors' sales of stock or investors' attempts to terminate the firm's top executives. Therefore, the executives may pursue a series of decisions to stabilize the dividend stream. Dividend policy is a serious matter at many directors' meetings, as considerable information concerning future profitability is inherent in dividend decisions.[40] Stable or growing dividends communicate confidence in future profitability. Volatile dividends communicate uncertainty concerning future profitability.

Figure 8.6 The human resource process.

Human Resource Systems

Human resources are not just the skills and the number and kinds of people in the organization. Managers increasingly recognize that systems must be designed to maximize the potential of the organization's current and future human resources.

Human resource processes and systems

This section treats the HR system from the process perspective. The HR sub-processes and the flow of human resources in the organization through the various sub-processes are examined. This includes HR planning, recruitment, selection and hiring, training and development, performance appraisal, and rewards. For effective performance, these processes must be consistent with each other and the business-level strategy. The goal of these sub-processes is longevity of a high-performing individual. Figure 8.6 shows this process view.

Viewing human resources from the process perspective helps managers in at least two ways. First, it helps managers understand the integrated systems nature of many HR activities. Saturn refers to its HR processes as "people systems". Some organizations have viewed HR activities as isolated functions, in which some functions are not consistent with others. Sometimes managers conducting the recruiting and hiring do not integrate their activities with those managers designing the reward system. The result may be that one kind of talent is hired, while another kind of behavior is rewarded.

The systems view also helps the manager to see HR problems as defects in the system, not necessarily the fault of any one manager. This view also recognizes that a person's problematic behavior may be salvageable through training and appropriate rewards. For example, failure to properly serve the customer may be the result of inadequate training. An incident of alleged sexual harassment may be due to a failure in the selection process or in the training process.

Human resource processes

As noted in figure 8.6, human resource planning is the first step in the HR process. *HR planning* involves forecasting staffing needs and the steps needed to fulfill those needs.

Once the organization has decided to hire employees to fill certain positions, then managers need to attract applicants to those positions. *Recruiting* is the process of attracting individuals to apply for jobs.

Selection is the process of determining the applicants' qualifications and choosing the best applicant for the job. In an increasing number of TQ organizations, the selection process is conducted by peers in the work team.[41]

Training and development is the process of developing knowledge, skills, and behaviors in people that will enable them to better perform their jobs. Many managers recognize that human resources are the only appreciating asset. With education, training, and experience, human resources can increase in value over time. As resources, people are to be valued, not viewed as dispensable parts. Other assets, such as buildings and equipment, depreciate over time no matter how well they are maintained. R. Galvin, the Chairman of Motorola, described the importance of training under the heading, "Welcome heresies of quality." Included was an Old Truth: "Training is overhead and costly." That view was replaced by a New Truth: "Training does not cost."[42] Obviously, there is an out-of-pocket cost for training. However, many managers recognize training as a way to gain future customer satisfaction and reduce future costs by training employees how to do it right the first time. Backing up Galvin's New Truth, Motorola estimated that it has earned US$30 for every $1 it has invested in quality training.[43] Many organizations are spending 5–7 percent of payroll on training today. That figure compares with the era of Galvin's Old Truth, when organizations spent less than 1 percent of payroll on training. In the past, training and development had stressed functional, technical and specific job-related skills. Today, many organizations stress a broad range of cross-functional and quality issues, and teaming, diagnostic and problem solving skills.[44] The kinds of team-based skills and behaviors needed are covered in greater detail in chapter 9.

Performance appraisal is an important process in organizations because it signals to members the kinds of behaviors that subsequently might be rewarded. *Performance appraisal* is the process of evaluating how well individuals and teams are performing their jobs. In many traditional organizations, performance appraisal was based on supervisory review of individual goal accomplishment tied into financial performance. In many organizations today, performance appraisal is based on customer, peer, and supervisory review of team goal accomplishment tied into improvements in quality and customer value delivery.[45]

Reward processes have changed in organizations. A recent review of traditional reward systems characterized them as based on competition for individual merit increases. In contrast, TQ based reward systems consisted of team/group based rewards, including financial rewards and non-financial recognition.[46] Several organizational quality transformations have failed because of the inability to redesign the reward system to support the values of customer focus and teaming.[47] Old reward systems that reinforce old forms of individual behavior may be hard to change. Even as IBM was losing billions of dollars in the early 1990s, it still lavished millions of dollars on annual "Golden Circle" celebrations for its top salespeople.[48] What was the message about the importance of team behavior?

For effective performance, all these HR processes must be consistent with each other and the business-level strategy. The hoped for result of the entire HR process is the continuation of high-performing employees in the organization. If the firm retains those employees, then its HR processes are effective and the organization has a competitive advantage. If too many valued employees quit, or if too many low performers must be terminated, then managers need to ask how the HR system can be improved.

Labor relations

The prior sections in this chapter assume that management is interacting directly with employees. However, a substantial number of employees interact with management through unions.

Many managers prefer not to deal with unions because union contracts restrict the freedom of managers to deal with employees over issues of wages, benefits, working conditions, and other HR issues.[49] *Labor-management relations* refers to the process of dealing with employees who are represented by a union.

Unions were very popular and powerful in the USA in the early and mid twentieth century. They have been declining dramatically in the past few decades, with membership in several unions down by one-third in the past two decades.[50] Many workers have decided that they do not need unions, given the protection provided by laws. In some countries, where employment law is not developed or is not favorable to the worker, unions may be quite strong.

▌ Summary ▌

The strategic decisions made within the functions of operations, marketing, finance, human resources, research/development and technology, and information systems are referred to as functional-level strategic decisions. These functional strategies are used to complement the customer value and competitive advantage sought. There needs to be consistency between the business-level and the functional strategies. There also needs to be consistency among the functional strategies.

Technology is the knowledge, tools, techniques, and processes used to transform organizational inputs into outputs. Technological change refers to changes in any of these factors. The management of technology includes how the organization uses technology to yield more value to customers. Reduced cycle time, reduced cost, reduced variation, and quality improvement are all ways in which new technology adds value to customers. Product development is the process where most of the organization's investments in new technology pay off. The most important factor in the development of new products is the link to customer value. Some firms are technological leaders; others choose to be technological followers. New technology is a hot area in international competition. Japanese and Germans were investing in new technology at a higher rate of growth than US firms. Such high levels of investments in technology are consistent with the strategy of using technology to deliver value to customers.

Management information systems (MISs) have served several different roles in their brief post-Second World War history. Many systems were introduced into organizations to serve a transaction or bookkeeping role. Where the purpose of the MIS was to cut costs, improve speed, process greater volume, and increase accuracy. In a strategic planning role, the MIS is used to collect, analyze, summarize, and disseminate information dealing with external changes and forecast changes that may effect the future of the firm. In a competitive weapon role, the MIS is used to track competitors and their products and actions to help managers decide on competitive responses. In a customer value role, the MIS is used to provide customers with timely, accurate, accessible information that has value to the customer. The information needs of both external and internal customers include accessibility, timeliness, accuracy, user-friendliness, and security. Those managers who find new ways to provide these values to customers will gain new customers.

Operations management is the process of managing the production of goods and services. Many firms today recognize the critical importance of operations management to the ability of the firm to provide consistent value to customers. Products or services are viewed as delivery mechanisms to deliver value to customers. Operations managers today recognize the importance of process control. Stable, in-control processes yield products and services of consistent quality. Process reengineering is the continuous improvement of the process by which a product or service is created and distributed.

Defining customers and customer value requirements are the first steps in marketing strategies. The major decisions in marketing strategy concern the product/service, price, place/distribution, and promotion/advertising. These elements must be consistent with each other and with what operations can deliver.

Financial strategies concern profitability, liquidity and cash management, leverage and capital management, asset management, investment ratios, and financial planning and control. Inconsistency among the financial decisions can prohibit accomplishment of corporate and business level strategies.

This chapter treats the HR system from the process perspective, which includes HR planning, recruitment, selection and hiring, training and development, performance appraisal, and rewards. The hoped for result of these sub-processes is longevity of high-performing people. This HR process view helps managers in at least two ways. First, it helps managers to understand the integrated systems nature of many HR processes. Second, the systems view also helps the manager to see HR problems as defects in the system, not necessarily the fault of any one manager. Human resources are the organization's only appreciating asset.

DISCUSSION QUESTIONS

1 Explain the desired relationship among corporate-level, business-level, and functional-level strategies.

2 Explain how technology contributes to customer value. Give an example from the health care and insurance industries.

3 Compare and contrast the different roles of management information systems. Explain which role will assume even greater importance in the future.

4 How is the customer value strategy of the firm related to its products and services?

5 Why is product design so critical to operations?

6 Describe the two different bases for pricing decisions.

7 How do the firm's decisions on customer value relate to the other marketing management decisions?

8 Why is consistency among the financial strategy decisions important?

9 Describe the conditions that make human resources an appreciating asset.

KEY TERMS

Asset management	is how intensely the firm uses its assets.
Concurrent engineering	is simultaneous product and process design for the product manufacture.
Cost-plus pricing	is a fixed add-on to actual cost.
Distribution channels	are the paths and means the firm uses to get its products/services into the hands of customers.
A hollow corporation	is a firm that does not manage its operations.
Human resource planning	involves forecasting staffing needs and the steps needed to fulfill those needs.
Information quality	is the degree to which information accurately portrays reality.
Labor–management relations	refers to the process of dealing with employees who are represented by a union.
Leverage	is the amount of debt relative to equity.
Liquidity ratios	define the ability of the firm to cover debt.
The management of technology	includes how the organization uses technology to yield value to customers.
A management information system	is a set of computer hardware and software that gathers, organizes, summarizes, and reports information for use by managers, customers, and others.
Manufacturing management	is the process of managing the production of tangible goods, but does not include services.
Operations management	is the process of managing the production of goods and services.
Performance appraisal	is the process of evaluating how well individuals and teams are performing their jobs.
Process reengineering	is the redesign of the process by which a product or service is created and distributed.
Product development cycle time	is the time from conception of the idea for a new product, through the product development phase, until the new product is first offered to the customer.
Proprietary technology	is technology held by one firm and not shared with other firms.
Real time information	is information that immediately reflects the underlying reality.
Recruiting	is the process of attracting people to apply for jobs.
Selection	is the process of determining the applicants' qualifications and choosing the best applicant for the job.

Service management	is the process of producing non-tangibles, with customer involvement and consumption at the point of delivery.
Technology	is the sum of knowledge, tools, techniques and processes used to transform organizational inputs into outputs.
Technological change	refers to changes in any of these technological factors.
Technological followership	is letting other firms introduce new technology into the marketplace first and then copying or modifying the proven technology.
Technological leadership	is being the first to market with new technology.
Training and development	is the process of developing knowledge, skills, and behaviors in human resources that will enable them to better perform their jobs.
User-friendly	means that the user of the information can use the MIS with little difficulty due to ease of following instructions.

Federal Express and UPS Place Bets on Technology

US industrial corporations have invested heavily to improve quality in production and design. This quality revolution now extends far into the service functions of many corporations. One way to achieve superior quality is through the application of information technology. Companies with the highest levels of service quality typically have developed information systems that greatly enhance their ability to collect and disseminate useful information that is valued by the customer.

Competition based on functional expertise in technology is clearly profiled in the "express delivery wars" between Federal Express (FedEx) and United Parcel Service (UPS), the two leading express mail companies. Both companies have come to rely on state-of-the art technology to serve their customers better, faster, and less expensively than ever before. Overnight delivery that was unusual a decade ago is now a routine service, but the battle is far from over. These rival companies are battling to increase their share of this US$18 billion-a-year industry. FedEx's chief information officer, Dennis Jones, sums up the industry necessity well: "We have to create new technological capabilities so we never become a standing target." The latest services offered by both companies reveal the truth of this statement.[a]

UPS has invested over US$150 million to develop its TotalTrac service, a global cellular network that gives the company the ability to receive "real time" information about all shipments and deliveries around the world. After a package delivery or pickup is made, data are scanned by the newest generation of a handheld unit. When the employee returns to the vehicle, the unit is inserted into an electronic holster, and a short burst of information is transmitted to world headquarters.[b] This wireless technology already plays an important role in a new service called "Early AM," which delivers shipments by 8:30 a.m.[c] UPS promises this to be only the first of several new product offerings in 1995.

FedEx shipped customers over 30,000 of its newly released FedEx Ship software packages in the first two months of 1995. This software runs on a PC and makes it easy for customers to place pickup orders, print shipping labels, and track delivery without having to invest in special hardware for their mailrooms. Internet users can track when deliveries are made and who signed for them without FedEx Ship software.[d] With this service, FedEx helps customers to reduce costs by giving them fast service and accurate information without ever touching the telephone.

Although FedEx currently holds 45 percent and UPS 25 percent of the market, both companies know that business is very price sensitive. Customers are not going to be loyal for very long if switching will make a difference in their earnings without sacrificing quality. Price-based competition between 1989 and 1994 drove profit margins down from 12 to 8 percent, a trend that will continue.[e]

These rivals invest in technology to remove waste and lower costs. They recognize that computers are able to place orders, identify shipments, select routes, track and trace packages more efficiently than humans.[f] Computers at FedEx continually track the performance of the service from the time an order is placed until a delivery is made. Not only errors, but the type and severity of errors, are recorded and analyzed. This information allows both management and employees to follow their weekly performance. The data are then used as a basis to mobilize the organization to eliminate the problem. The importance of this type of information is also apparent at UPS. In fact, Chief Executive Officer Kent Nelson stated: "We realized that the leader in information management will be the leader in international package distribution – period."[g]

One significant fact that may give FedEx an advantage over UPS is the company's exceedingly strong employee relations. Frederick W. Smith, Founder, Chairman, and Chief Executive Officer of FedEx, has often emphasized the importance of people: "Customer satisfaction begins with employee satisfaction. When people are placed first, they will provide the highest possible service, and profits will follow."[h] That emphasis helped the firm to be the first in the service category to win the prestigious Malcolm Baldrige Award in 1990. This success is partly due to the innovative application of technology to human resource management. FedEx developed PRISM, a human resource system that demonstrates another way in which information systems can contribute to competitive advantage. PRISM empowers both managers and employees. Employees throughout the world can examine their personnel data, update their address and phone number, change benefit options, access training records, participate in on-line training sessions, examine wage schedules, and apply for jobs available anywhere throughout FedEx's worldwide operations.[i] Although UPS also enjoys a very good reputation as an employer, difficult disputes with unionized labor contrasts with the exceptional culture at FedEx. This threat of strikes puts UPS at a competitive disadvantage.

FedEx and UPS are on the leading edge of technological strategy in the world. The exciting aspect of the situation isn't what technology can do for sales, transportation, human resources, or any other functional area. The real impact will come from the ways in which information systems integrated across many functional areas create value for the consumer.

Discussion Questions

1 Describe the value provided to customers of each firm.

2 What roles do information systems and human resources play in the value provided to customers of each organization?

3 Forecast the impact that other advances in information systems technology, like electronic mail and the World Wide Web, might have on these two firms.

Sources: a. Greising, D., "Watch out for flying packages: FedEx and UPS step up hostilities in express delivery," *Business Week* (November, 1994), p. 40;   b. Tausz, A., "UPS: tracking parcels over the airwaves," *Computing Canada* (September 14, 1994), p. 16;   c. "UPS international business leads air volume surge," UPS Press Release (October 19, 1994);   d. "Federal Express," in *Value Line Investment Survey*. New York: Value Line Publishing, Inc. (December 23, 1994), p. 259;   e. *Business Week* (November 14, 1994), p. 40;   f. Stahl, M., "UPS," in *Management: Total Quality in a Global Environment*. Cambridge, MA: Blackwell Publishers (1995), p. 461. g. Ibid.;   h. Stahl, M. "Federal Express's people first environment helps win a Baldrige," in *Management: Total Quality in a Global Environment*. Cambridge, MA: Blackwell Publishers (1995), p. 336.   i. Greengard, S., "Federal Express makes its workflow automation package work," *Personnel Journal* (July, 1994), p. 32N.

QUANTIFYING THE VALUE OF STRATEGY AT BRITISH PETROLEUM

British Petroleum (BP) is well known as an international, London-based oil company, but in the early 1980s it had diversified into businesses such as chemicals, coal, gas, minerals, and nutrition. This diversification strategy led to problems in allocating investment resources between the different divisions and projects of the large conglomerate.

In 1992, BP suffered losses of US$624 million, demonstrating that the company could not successfully compete in the fiercely competitive international oil business while also trying to compete in other businesses. Because oil prices are very volatile, BP turned to a financial tool to help it to accomplish its strategic goals. As BP began to concentrate primarily on the oil business, problems of fitting corporate decisions into both the strategic and financial framework of the company were difficult to resolve. It became clear that strategic and financial planning processes were based upon different theories that sometimes contradicted each other.

Finding useful financial tools to make informed investment decisions has traditionally been the realm of corporate financial officers. The most widely accepted techniques focus primarily on a narrow range of internal variables, quantitative information, shorter-term results, control processes, and techniques to determine specific risks. The "unit of analysis" is a specific project that the company is considering. The actual "object of analysis" is known as the expected cash flow, not accounting profits. The value of all expected cash flows is adjusted (discounted) to reflect the company's cost of investing in the projects (known as cost of capital). Essentially, the financial officer recommends accepting only projects expected to produce increased cash flows for the company. These techniques appear to account principally for tangible areas of investment. Few companies have extended this approach to appraise less tangible areas of investment like the strategic planning process.

Linking the value of a business strategy to that of an individual project has proven difficult. How to handle interdependencies among projects and the impact of longer-term risks is not yet fully understood. Naturally, this makes the value of a business strategy difficult to define in terms of financial assumptions.

Attempting to bridge the gap between financial appraisal and strategic planning led the top management of BP to begin to recognize the value of cross-functional processes as early as 1989. Executives searched for a better way to allocate corporate investment among their businesses. Traditional methods made them uncomfortable because they did not reflect the creation of value, mainly because the methods were backward- rather than forward-looking. Paradoxically, managers were expected to make decisions based on future cash flows, but they were rewarded based on measures of historical accounting information. To address these problems, top management implemented an approach called value-based management (VBM) in four broad phases.

In phase one, BP worked with external consultants to estimate the net present value (NPV) of its portfolio of businesses, appraise the projected results of business strategies, and identify where value might be created or lost. Some activities were found to create less value than previously thought. In one instance, analysis showed that BP had no competitive advantage in a market only loosely related to its core businesses. This caused BP to change its view about where value was created. It began to consider BP's competitive position and the attractiveness of the market in making the investment decision.

Phase two is best characterized as a learning process. BP discovered that VBM was not a magic formula, but a discipline that required intelligence to apply its principles to different situations.

Applying VBM engaged managers in an ongoing learning process about how value is created and how the tools are applied. This always leaves room for continuous improvement. One challenge was to carefully manage high expectations to give the new process the necessary time to establish itself, gain acceptance, and produce results.

Phase three extended VBM to BP's international businesses. The leader of this project, Simon Woolley, summarized the experience of managers: "At first managers expected an absolute answer to an imprecise problem – measuring value creation. As they learned more about VBM they began to realize that the value of VBM lies not so much in absolute measurement but in its ability to make comparisons . . . It enables you to benchmark your performance relative to your competition." Again, there was the realization that VBM was more than a technique – it was a gradual process of sustained learning.

The last phase involved setting up control and reward systems in line with VBM. Strategic and financial planning processes were linked to management targets and rewards. In addition, periodic review of VBM has provoked healthy debate that continuously leads to an improved ability to interpret the effectiveness of VBM against a changing background.

This and other changes to the strategic planning process led quickly to a complete remaking of the company. BP divested itself of more than US$6 billion of noncore operations, like the nutrition and mineral businesses. In addition, the company cut its staff and pursued cost efficiencies that are the best in the industry. By 1994, just two years after its huge losses, BP generated more profits per barrel of oil than any other oil company. As the low-cost producer of oil, BP enjoys a significant advantage in the competitive international oil industry. Company management expects this success to continue as it strives to reach the goal of being the best in all 11 of its remaining businesses.

The experience at BP reveals that different functions can be coordinated at different levels into a single system. It no longer makes sense to BP's top management to engage in the strategic planning process without understanding and integrating functional areas like financial appraisal, measurement, and human resources. Realizing the advantages of integrated strategic planning was a key factor in the turnaround of BP.

Although BP was not the first oil company to aggressively pursue changes, it acted more swiftly and decisively to achieve the best results in the industry. BP successfully spread the teamwork approach throughout the organization and challenged them to contribute to the succeess of the corporation in a more focused way. In 1995, BP made a net profit of US$2.9 billion. The management feels ready to consider using its competitive advantage to expand its global market into Latin America, Southeast Asia, and China.

Discussion Questions

1 Explain the reasons why a company like BP would need to integrate functions that had previously been kept separate.

2 Describe how the use of value based management might lead to overly simplistic strategic planning.

3 Discuss what relationship BP sees between the creation of value, market position, and competitive advantage. How did the divestiture of noncore assets play a role?

Sources: *Planning* (UK) (June 1993), pp. 87–94; Grundy, T., *Corporate Strategy and Financial Decisions.* London: Kogan Page (1992), pp. 159–67; "BP comes back even as oil prices sink", *Wall Street Journal* (September 8, 1995), p. A6; "BP after Horton", *The Economist* (UK) (July 4, 1992), p. 59.

NOTES

1 Harrington, H. J., *Business Process Improvement: the Breakthrough Strategy for Total Quality, Productivity, and Competitiveness*. New York: McGraw-Hill (1991), p. 9.

2 Rosseau, D. and Cooke, R., "Technology and structure," *Journal of Management* (1984), pp. 345–61.

3 "Special Issue – Technological Transformation and the New Competitive Landscape," *Strategic Management Journal*, 16 (Summer 1995).

4 Boulton, W., *Resource Guide for Management of Innovation and Technology*. St Louis: American Assembly of Collegiate Schools of Business, National Consortium for Technology in Business, and Thomas Walter Center for Technology Management at Auburn University (1993).

5 Porter, M., *Competitive Strategy*. New York: Free Press (1985), p. 169.

6 "Chrysler on the road to recovery," *USA Today* (March 6, 1992), p. B1.

7 "IBM tries, and fails, to fix PC business," *Wall Street Journal* (February 22, 1995), p. B1.

8 "What the US can do about R&D," *Fortune* (October 19, 1992), p. 75.

9 "Brace for Japan's hot new strategy," *Fortune* (September 21, 1992), p. 63.

10 Koizumi, T. "Management of innovation and change in japanese organizations," in Prasad, S. (ed.), *Advances in International Comparative Management*. London: JAI Press (1989), pp. 245–54.

11 "Business bulletin," *Wall Street Journal* (February 4, 1993), p. A1.

12 King, W. R. "Strategic planning for information resources," *Information Resource Management Journal* (Fall 1988), pp. 2–3.

13 "The Internet: how it will change the way you do business" *Business Week* (November 14, 1994), pp. 80–8.

14 Camillus, J. C. and Lederer, A. L., "Corporate strategy and the design of computerized information systems," *Sloan Management Review* (Spring 1985), p. 35.

15 Porter, M. and Millar, V., "How information gives you competitive advantage," *Harvard Business Review*, 63(4) (1985), pp. 149–59.

16 Drucker, P., "The coming of the new organization," *Harvard Business Review* (January–February 1988), pp. 45–53.

17 "Betting on the 21st century jet" *Fortune* (April 20, 1992), p. 102.

18 Stahl, M. J. and Grigsby, D. W., *Strategic Management for Decision Making*. Boston: PWS-Kent (1992), p. 95.

19 Ibid.

20 "Getting personal: at Fidelity Investments, computers are designed to make the company seem more human," *Wall Street Journal* (April 6, 1992), p. R19.

21 "Race for computerized booking systems is heating up among European airlines," *Wall Street Journal* (December 1, 1988), p. B3.

22 "The new realism in office systems," *Business Week* (June 15, 1992), p. 128.

23 "Who's winning the information revolution?" *Fortune* (November 30, 1992), p. 116.

24 Flynn, B., Sakakibara, S. and Schroeder, R., "Relationship between JIT and TQM: practices and performance," *Academy of Management Journal*, 38(5) (October 1995), pp. 1325–60; Dean, J. and Snell, S., "The strategic use of integrated manufacturing," *Strategic Management Journal* (1996).

25 "The hollow corporation," *Business Week* (March 3, 1986), p. 57.

26 Kearns, D. T. and Nadler, D. A., *Prophets in the Dark*. New York: Harper Business (1992), p. 271.

27 "Japanese carmakers apply brakes," *International Herald Tribune* (November 16, 1995), p. 17.

28 Harrington, H. J., *Business Process Improvement: the Breakthrough Strategy for Total Quality, Productivity, and Competitiveness*. New York: McGraw-Hill (1991), p. 9.

29 "Gray expectations," *Business Week* (April 11, 1988), p. 108.

30 Hurley, R., "TQM and marketing," *Quality Management Journal* (July 1994), pp. 42–51.

31 Rao, R. C., and Bass, F. M., "Competition, strategy, and price dynamics: a theoretical and empirical investigation," *Journal of Marketing Research*, 22 (1985), pp. 283–96.

32 "After early stumbles, P&G is making inroads overseas," *Wall Street Journal* (February 6, 1989), p. B1.

33 Donaldson, G., "Financial goals and strategic consequences," *Harvard Business Review* (May–June 1985), pp. 57–66.

34 "Investors punish Daiwa Bank," *International Herald Tribune* (September 28, 1995), p. 13; "In a signal to Japan, US bars Daiwa Bank, indicts it and officials," *Wall Street Journal* (November 3, 1995), p. A1.

35 Woolridge, J. R., "Competitive decline and corporate restructuring," *Journal of Applied Corporate Finance* (1988), pp. 26–36.

NOTES cont.

36 Ehrhardt, M., *The Search for Value: Measuring the Company's Cost of Capital.* Boston: Harvard Business School Press (1994).

37 Sandberg, C. M., Lewellen, W. G. and Stanley, K. L., "Financial strategy: planning and managing the corporate leverage position," *Strategic Management Journal*, 8 (1987), pp. 15–24.

38 "The view from the executive suite," *Business Week* (November 7, 1988), p. 143.

39 "Learning to live with leverage," *Business Week* (November 7, 1988), p. 141.

40 Ang, J. S., "Do dividends matter: a review of corporate dividend theories and evidence," *Monograph Series in Finance and Economics*, 2 (1987).

41 Blackburn, R. and Rosen, B., "Total quality and human resource management," *Academy of Management Executive* (August 1993), p. 51.

42 Galvin, R., *The Idea of Ideas.* Schaumburg, IL: Motorola University Press (1991), p. 100.

43 Blackburn, R. and Rosen, B., "Total quality and human resource management," *Academy of Management Executive*, p. 56.

44 Ibid., p. 51.

45 Cole, R., "Introduction – Special Issue on TQM," *California Management Review*, 35 (Spring 1993), p. 8; Ghorpade, J. and Chen, M., "Creating quality driven performance appraisal systems," *Academy of Management Executive* (February 1995), pp. 32–41.

46 Blackburn, R. and Rosen, B., "Total Quality and Human Resource Management," p. 51.

47 Cole, R., "Introduction – Special Issue on TQM," p. 8.

48 "As IBM losses mount, so do the complaints about company perks," *Wall Street Journal* (October 27, 1993), p. A1.

49 Heckscher, C., *The New Unionism.* New York: Basic Books (1988).

50 "What us worry? Big unions' leaders overlook bad news, opt for status quo," *Wall Street Journal* (October 5, 1993), p. B1.

CHAPTER
9
NINE

STRATEGY IMPLEMENTATION:
STRUCTURE AND TEAMS

LEARNING OBJECTIVES

After reading this chapter, you should be able to accomplish the following.

1 Explain the difference between formal and informal organization structures.

2 Compare and contrast the various structural forms and their advantages and disadvantages.

3 Describe the major differences between an organizational focus and a process focus.

4 Discuss the importance of cross-functional integration and describe two important cross-functional systems.

5 Compare and contrast the role of managers in a flat organization and the role of teams in such organizations.

6 Relate self-managed teams to customer value strategy.

7 Describe the three team issues of involvement, empowerment, and self-management.

Some argue that a principal *the* role of managers is to implement or install strategy. Thus, managers should design and continuously improve the organization structure, team processes, corporate culture, and behavioral processes that implement strategy. Strategy implementation is so important that we devote two separate chapters to it. We start with structure and teams.

What Is an Organization?

Ever since people have joined together to accomplish goals, they have wondered about the best way to organize themselves.

Purpose: goal accomplishment

Chandler offered the following definition of structure. "*Structure* can be defined as the design of the organization. The design has two aspects. It includes, first, the lines of authority and communication between the different offices and officers, and, second, the information and data that flow through these lines of communication and authority."[1]

Few would argue with Chandler's definition of structure. However, there is some disagreement as to whether strategy causes structure or structure causes strategy.[2] We do not resolve the disagreement, but we argue that strategy and structure must be consistent if successful implementation of strategy is to occur and facilitate goal accomplishment.

Inappropriate structure can also prevent reaching goals. *Fortune* analyzed problems for the automobile industry and was particularly interested in the disastrous effect of the 1984 reorganization at General Motors. When Jack Smith moved in as President in April 1992, he set about undoing the reorganization that GM undertook eight years before. "It's tough to operate when the structure isn't right. It just stops you cold."[3] Many people inside and outside the company blame the reorganization for many of the problems that afflicted GM in the 1990s. Instead of flattening the organization and getting closer to the customer, the reorganization did just the reverse.

Sometimes organizational structures are so out of touch with customer needs that firms start new organizations removed from the old organization. Witness Saturn. GM wanted to prove to the world that it could design, manufacture, and market high-quality, reasonably priced small cars that would be preferred over imports. Rather than trying to achieve such a formidable goal in an existing division of GM, a whole new company was started in Tennessee, 500 miles away from the corporate level of GM in Detroit.

Diversity of organizational types

Figure 9.1 describes alternative structural forms. The more divisionalized the organization becomes, the more complex is the structure. One way to understand the consistency between strategy and structure is to observe evolutions in structure as organizations grow more complex. As the strategy becomes more complex, then the structure becomes more complex.[4] The various forms are defined later.

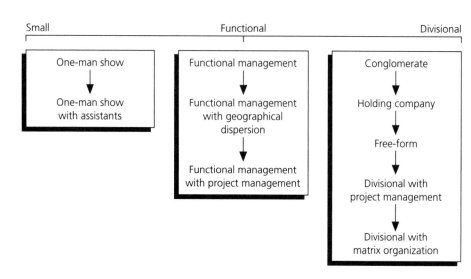

Figure 9.1 Alternative structural forms.

Source: Shirley, R. C., Peters, M. H. and El-Ansary, A. I., *Strategy and Policy Formation: a Multifunctional Orientation*. New York: John Wiley & Sons (1981), p. 239. Copyright © 1981 John Wiley & Sons. Reprinted by permission.

Formal and informal structure

There are at least two types of structure in organizations that reflect the grouping of resources, as well as the flow of work and information. There is the formal or explicit organization, and there is the informal or implicit organization.

Formal

The *formal organization* is the structure specified in the organization chart. The *organization chart* diagrams the functions, departments, or positions in the organization and shows how they are related in patterns of formal authority. Generally, formal authority starts at the top of the organization and can be traced throughout the organization.

The vertical dimension of an organization chart shows the number of reporting or hierarchical levels. Each vertical level describes another level of management. For example, a tall organization chart might have eight layers of management.

The horizontal dimension refers to the breadth of supervision and is measured by the number of employees supervised, called the *span of control*. Small spans of control denote much control and supervision. The Roman military was based upon the number 10 as the basis for spans of control. Today, spans of control are growing larger as employees are more highly trained and work in different teams.

Informal

The informal organization is not explicitly drawn or formally communicated. The *informal organization* is reflected in the patterns of communication and influence associated with flows of information, activities, and social activities of organizational members. Wise managers learn to use the informal, as well as the formal organization to get work done.

Structural Forms

Mechanistic and organic structures are two broad categories of organizations described before we discuss specific structures.

Mechanistic and organic structures

Burns and Stalker noted that mechanistic organizations occur in environments with stable technology and stable demands from customers.[5] In *mechanistic designs*, tasks are fractionated and specialized. There is little emphasis on clarifying the relationship between tasks and organizational objectives. The structure of control, authority, and communication is primarily vertical between superior and subordinate.

Organic organizations are suitable for changing technological environments requiring innovation with trained workers. In *organic designs*, tasks are more interdependent. There is more emphasis on relevance of tasks and organizational objectives. Control, authority, and communication are varied. Communication is vertical and horizontal, depending upon where needed information resides.

Functional

One of the most common organizational forms is the functional form. It is frequently found in firms pursuing a strategy of concentration or high relatedness. Like activities or like functions are grouped together in a *functional structure*. Accounting activities are grouped together, as are operations, marketing, and design. If the organization becomes large, a significant corporate staff may emerge that reports directly to the executive office in a staff or advisory capacity.[6]

Advantages. The functional form is appropriate if the firm is pursuing a concentration or relatedness strategy with stable products/services (chapter 5). With a single product or only a few highly related products, the functional structure is appropriate. It allows for maximum specialization of effort and economy of scale. For example, if a firm is in the business of designing, manufacturing and marketing only mainframe computers, then a functional structure may be appropriate.

Disadvantages. In the functional organization, coordination across the functions becomes increasingly difficult as the number of products, number of markets, or kinds of customers grow.[7] In such situations, a more complex structure becomes appropriate.[8] In the mainframe computer example, if the firm starts designing, manufacturing, and selling personal computers in addition to its mainframe business, then a more complex structure may be needed.

Geographic

As the firm grows in geographic coverage, the simple functional form often evolves into a *geographic structure*. Like functions are grouped together within each geographic area but not across geographic areas. There may be separate divisions for Europe, North America, and the Pacific Rim.

Advantages. In a geographic structure, the organization can focus on the needs of the customers in each geographic segment. In the insurance industry, customers in different parts of the country may have different needs due to different lifestyles.

Disadvantages. Duplication and coordination of activities across geographic areas can be expensive and lead to an added layer of management.[9] For example, design and production of insurance policies can occur and be duplicated in more than one geographic area. If such design, production, and marketing activities become too customized to the customers in a specific area, then the image of the firm in the minds of customers may become blurred. It may be hard to conduct a national advertising campaign if the products and services are customized by region.

Product/division

The *product or division structure*, in which separate manufacturing, sales, and accounting activities are grouped together around products, is a logical evolution of the functional form. Another functional organization is added in duplicate to the existing functional organization for the second product.

In the computer example, it is like having a separate company (division) for mainframe computers and a separate company (division) for personal computers. Even though common activities like manufacturing are found in both divisions, they are segregated by product as the basis for the divisional grouping.

Advantages. As with the functional form, there is a high degree of specialization of effort. There may also be substantial economies of scale if the volume in each of the divisions is large enough to justify the separate facilities and workforces.

Disadvantages. Coordination across divisions becomes exceedingly difficult. The degree of specialization causes personnel in one division to lose sight of customers and problems in the other division. If customer needs evolve, the degree of specialization makes it difficult for employees to evolve to the new needs. For example, the mainframe people may not be able to think of the needs of customers in small organizations who need an intermediate sized minicomputer.

Customer

In a *customer organization*, activities, personnel, and resources are grouped by common types of customers. In the computer example, all activities associated with industrial customers are grouped together, all activities associated with educational customers are grouped together, and likewise for home customers.

Even if the organization does not go so far as to group resources and personnel by common type of customer, the organization can still focus activities around a customer, especially in a service organization. Karolinska Hospital in Stockholm, Sweden, reorganized work at the hospital around patient flow, instead of around its functional departments. Instead of bouncing a patient from department to department, the hospital viewed the move from illness to recovery as a process focused on the patient, with stops in admission, surgery, recovery, and other departments. Since moving to the patient-focused model, the hospital has cut waiting times for surgery from six or eight months to three weeks. Also, three of the hospital's 15 operating rooms have been closed, with associated cost savings, yet

3,000 more operations are performed annually, a 25 percent increase. The hospital received the commitment of physicians when it showed the advantage to them of the new focus, including less time on administrative issues like scheduling.[10]

Advantages. In such a customer-focused organization, the needs of the customer can be well served. Since all activities associated with a customer segment are grouped, all functional activities (e.g. production, marketing, finance) are targeted at specific kinds of customers.

Disadvantages. If the customer group has varied needs, then the activities in a division can be varied. For example, in the industrial division of the computer company, activities associated with the design, manufacture, and sales of mainframe, minicomputer, and personal computers are all grouped together. There is also duplication of activities and personnel across divisions as design, manufacture, and sales of personal computers are also conducted in the educational and home divisions.

Holding company

Holding companies are conglomerations or collections of separate seemingly unrelated groupings of businesses or divisions called strategic business units, or SBUs. Within each SBU or division there is some common important strategic dimension. Across SBUs, there may be little commonality. Thus, a holding company is like a multiple divisional organization with an added layer of management. It is as if there were separate companies within the company. The function of management at the holding company or corporate level is to loosely oversee a number of nearly autonomous companies. There are few functional specialists centralized at the corporate level.

Advantages. The greatest advantage of such a structure is diversification of risk.[11] It is assumed that the unrelated SBUs operate on different cycles and have different cash flows. Therefore, in a year when one SBU is experiencing weak profits, the other SBUs may be having offsetting positive cash flows. In such a fashion, the risk to the investor is limited.

Disadvantages. There are several disadvantages associated with a holding company structure. Coordinating the independent SBUs is difficult. Since SBUs are unrelated in their core businesses, there is no expectation of positive fit. Budgeting and allocation of resources among such unrelated businesses can be difficult, since the corporate executives must compare apples and oranges. Financial control and operational control can be difficult, since the SBUs function on different cycles. Overlapped staffs and functions at the various levels are also problems.

Matrix

The *matrix organization* is an overlay of businesses or projects on functional groupings. This structure coordinates activities and resources across functions associated with a specific business while retaining functional specialization. The various businesses do not completely "own" the functional resources as in a SBU structure. In a matrix, the businesses or product lines "borrow" the functional resources from the functions. Matrix forms evolved in the aerospace and construction industries with the development of separate projects.[12]

Advantages. The matrix structure helps managers to deal with a number of new products or businesses. Since the functions remain with their human and other resources, managers can dedicate resources to new products or businesses quickly. The matrix may be less expensive than duplicating the functional resources for each new product. Thus, a matrix structure may be appropriate in high-technology industries or industries with frequently changing new products. Aerospace, computers, and electronics industries with streams of new products are examples where matrix organizations are used. The Boeing Company uses a matrix organization when it starts a new aircraft.

Disadvantages. Matrix forms have coordination problems even though increased coordination is the desired goal.[13] There may be recurring battles among the business/product managers and the functional managers. Matrices are expensive to operate because of the extra layer of management, and may be counterproductive in stable organizations with few products. Communications arising from two directions may be confusing. Some people have trouble reporting to more than one boss.

Contrasting Approaches to Organizational Design

In the choice of an organization structure, there are at least five different approaches to designing organizations.

Classical approach
The classical approach focuses organization design efforts on patterns of authority and specialization of tasks to produce efficiency. However, such an approach leaves to chance the integration of activities to deliver value to the customer. This approach focuses on the inside of the organization and pays little attention to customers or competitors.

Environmental approach
The environmental approach argues that an organization should stay in touch with opportunities and threats in the external environment. See chapter 2.

A classic study by Burns and Stalker reported on the relationship of the kind of environment and the required organizational structure.[14] They found that a loose, flexible structure is best suited to a changing environment. Tight, stable structures are more appropriate in stable environments. Due to fierce international competition and rapidly changing technology, most environments today are uncertain and changing.

Task-technology
Woodward reported on a classic study linking the kind of manufacturing technology and the required organizational structure. She found that there were three kinds of manufacturing technology.[15] *Small batch production* refers to the production of items in batches of one, or a few, designed to customer orders. *Mass*

Table 9.1 Manufacturing technology and organizational structure

Structural feature	Small batch	Mass production	Continuous
Formalization	Low	High	Low
Centralization	Low	High	Low
Written vertical communication	Low	High	Low
Verbal Lateral communication	High	Low	High
Overall structure	Organic	Mechanistic	Organic

Source: Woodward, J., *Industrial Organizations: Theory and Practice*. London: Oxford University Press (1965). Reprinted by permission of Oxford University Press.

production is the production of many items with the same specification. *Continuous process production* refers to nonstop production of the flow of work.

Her findings on appropriate structure are contained in table 9.1. As mass production gives way to smaller batch production today, fewer firms follow the formalized, centralized, vertical, mechanistic organization described in the middle column.

Balanced power approach

Mintzberg described the design of organizational structure as an exercise in balancing the power of different groups. He described the cast of organizational power players as consisting of the external coalition and the internal coalition (see figure 9.2).

The relative amount of power of various groups should be reflected in the design of the organization. As external customers gain more influence in the twenty-first century due to alternatives associated with international competition, Mintzberg's view suggests that more emphasis will be placed on designing organizations to serve customers.[16]

Cross-functional systems and processes

Many of the problems associated with traditional, hierarchical organizations suggest that a process view of organizations is needed because the process is the problem, not the employees.[17] The process focus has the twin themes of improvement and teaming to provide value to customers. Unfortunately, the organizational focus has the twin themes of assigning fault to individual employees in the pursuit of the bottom line. For example, the *Harvard Business Review* reported on a paper company that shifted emphasis from problem assignment to fixing the process that caused the problem. Positive results were forthcoming: "Six months out, customers were beginning to notice a marked difference in quality."[18]

A process view has spread to include the legal profession. A law firm in Tennessee described its mission, strategy, and organizational design in a one-page document. "Structure. The business process is managed through empowered individuals and teams to provide service and value to our clients. Each individual takes ownership of responsibilities, with the support and encouragement of the rest of the team."[19]

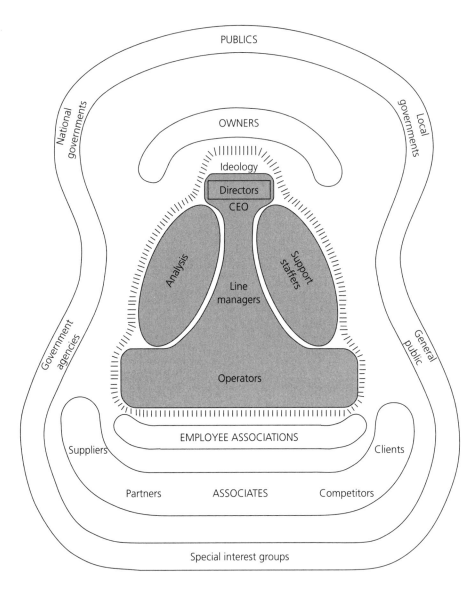

Figure 9.2 The cast of organizational power players.
Source: Mintzberg, H., *Power in and around Organizations*. Englewood Cliffs, NJ: Prentice Hall (1983), p. 29.

Figure 9.3 shows a systems view of an organization which focuses on delivering value to consumers. Note the cross-functional systems associated with design and redesign, distribution (including suppliers and customers), and consumer research. Harrington noted that a typical organization's business processes might include: new product development; materials management; and customer needs analysis.[20] Those processes are similar to those in figure 9.3.

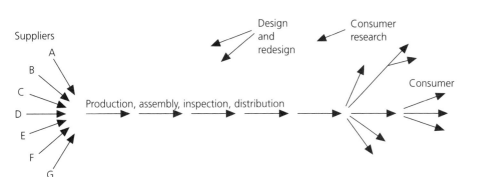

Figure 9.3 The new way to view an organization: the system.
Source: Adapted from Deming, W. E., *Out of the Crisis*. Cambridge, MA: MIT Press (1986), p. 4.

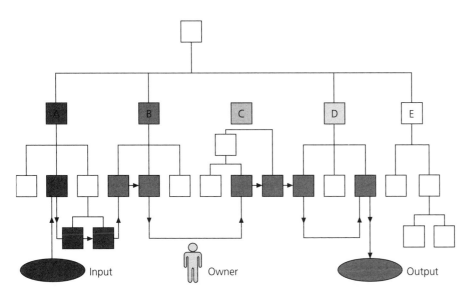

Figure 9.4 Interrelation between "vertical" functions and "horizontal" processes.
Source: Juran, J. M., *A History of Managing for Quality: the Evolution, Trends, and Future Directions of Managing for Quality*. Milwaukee, WI: ASQC Quality Press (1995), p. 590.

Juran showed how the horizontal processes are interrelated with the functions in an organization (see figure 9.4). Such an approach requires specific identification of the output, usually value to the customer.[21] The organization resembles more of a flat rectangle than a pyramid. If all the key horizontal processes were drawn and there were few intersections with function E, then a manager would ask if function E was needed in the organization. Process owners carry titles different from functional heads. For example, GE Medical Systems has a "vice president of global sourcing and order to remittance."[22] This key horizontal process is generically known as the logistics and materials system and is covered in greater detail later.

Because of their centrality to most businesses, there are at least four cross-functional systems that should exist in most business organizations. These four common cross-functional systems are: the customer value determination system; the new product design and development system; the logistics and materials system; and the information flow system.

The customer value determination system

This system is the one that is arguably the most important, yet the most frequently ignored in many organizations. In large organizations, there is a tendency to take customer requirements for granted. Comments like the following are often the prelude to organizational decline. "We understand the customer. Otherwise, we would not have grown to our current large size." Elements of this cross-functional system are discussed in chapter 7.

The new product design and development system

In this internationally competitive era, with rapidly advancing technology, customers are demanding the latest in new products and services. Firms need systems to take customer requirements and rapidly mix them with the latest technology to deliver new value. This system often involves partnerships with suppliers.[23] The system is covered in detail in chapter 8.

The logistics and materials system

Organizations need to cross-functionally manage the acquisition, transformation and distribution of material. This system includes supplier/purchasing functions, the materials transformation/manufacturing functions, and distribution functions. Suppliers are part of this system.[24] The supplier and operations management aspects of this system are covered in detail in chapter 8.

A good example of this system may be found in Wal-Mart. Sam Walton's obsession with automated logistics was key to Wal-Mart surpassing Kmart in retailing. "He invested tens of millions of dollars in a companywide computer system linking cash registers to headquarters, enabling him to quickly restock goods selling off the shelves. He also invested heavily in trucks and distribution centers, around which he located his stores. Besides enhancing his control, these moves sharply reduced costs."[25]

A slightly more encompassing definition of this system was used by GE Medical Systems, which makes magnetic resonance imaging machines. The plant defined the order-to-remittance process as the activities from when an order is received through manufacturing through shipment to payment. Through a focus on that process and the elimination of two layers of management, the process time was cut by 40 percent over a three-year period.[26]

Information flow

Information technology is having a dramatic impact on the design of organizations. Old structures were characterized by division of labor and task specialization. Today's principles are integration and cross-functional unification. Due to networks of computers, company departments are fusing. Organizations are

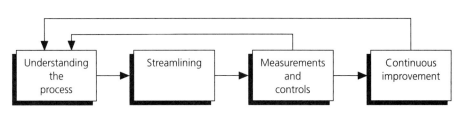

Figure 9.5 Process reengineering.
Source: Adapted from Harrington, H. J., *Business Process Improvement: the Breakthrough Strategy for Total Quality, Productivity, and Competitiveness*. New York: McGraw-Hill (1991), p. 23.

growing so closely allied with customers and suppliers that organizational boundaries between them are dissolving.[27]

A good example exists with some international airlines. Swissair and Singapore Airlines moved accounting, bookkeeping, and ticketing operations to Bombay, India. The move was made possible by tightly woven information systems.[28] This integration due to information flow is dealt with in greater detail in chapter 8.

Reengineering

Per chapter 8, reengineering is the redesign of the process by which a product or service is created and distributed.[29] This means the perpetual search for ways to improve procedures and methods for producing and distributing products and services. Figure 9.5 represents a model of reengineering. It became popular as a way to improve organizations in the 1990s.[30] When reengineering was done with the focus on improving value to customers, some organizations made quantum jumps in their ability to better serve their customers.

When reengineering was done without the focus on improving value to customers, it became an excuse for firing people as a way to take costs out of the organization.[31] Such a "slash and burn mentality" left some firms demoralized and without the needed resources for future growth. "Corporate anorexia" described the condition of some firms after such cuts. The *Wall Street Journal* reported that of the firms that reported downsizing between 1989 and 1994, 86 percent noted diminished employee morale and 30 percent noted diminished worker productivity.[32] For example, Deutsche Bank in Germany is a giant, with US$450 billion in assets. It had a history of self-confidence. Recently, it has seen a dramatic decline in employee morale and an increased turnover of senior employees after announcing plans to cut costs, eliminate an entire level of management, and reduce 15 percent of its workforce associated with more reliance on electronic banking.[33]

Key Contingencies for Structural Design

Several criteria must be considered in designing structure.

Strategy

As mentioned earlier, strategy and structure should be related. After the Second World War, the primary US manufacturing strategy was long production runs of

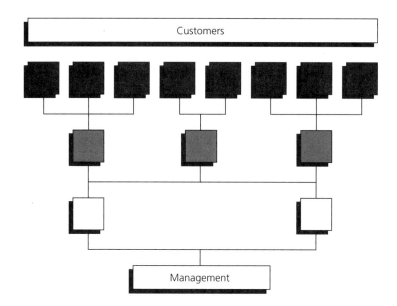

Figure 9.6 KLM organization chart.
Source: Vrakking, W. J., "Customer orientation within the organization," in Mastenbroek, W., *Managing for Quality in the Service Sector*. Oxford: Blackwell (1991), p. 68.

standardized products, which suggested a functional grouping. Today, the model is shorter production runs of specialized products with changing technology, which suggests a systems and process framework.

Customer requirements

The single most important requirement for organizational design concerns responsiveness to customer requirements. If the current organizational structure precludes organizational members from focusing on customers, then the organization needs to be changed. Unfortunately, many pyramidal, functional structures that focus on their internal system of authority and division of labor are hampered in their attempt to focus on the customer.

The decade of the 1990s may be remembered in business as the decade of the customer. As chapter 3 describes, customers on a global basis are demanding, as they have many alternatives from which to choose. Due to advances in quality and technology, many of the choices are affordable. In such an era, organizations must be responsive, or they might lose their customers, as firms like GM, Harley-Davidson, and Xerox have found out in earlier times. Cross-functional customer value determination systems will become increasingly important for the survival of organizations.

KLM Airlines in Europe depicts the importance of being customer driven even in its organization chart (figure 9.6). It shows customers, at the top, being served by non-managerial employees, who are supported by mid-level managers, with top-level management at the bottom.[34] KLM has inverted the traditional command and control pyramid that had top management ruling the organization.

Federal Express uses a similar inverted pyramid with the external customer at the top, served by front-line employees, with support from mid-level managers, and top-level management at the bottom.[35]

In both organizations, there is a realization that the structure exists to deliver value to the customer. Both structures also recognize that customer value information and customer value delivery flow from the customer and those employees closest to the customer.

Since both firms are in service industries, this may be an area where service firms are able to implement a TQ concept more readily than manufacturing firms. Service firms are in direct perpetual contact with external customers. Manufacturing firms might not be. Therefore, it may be easier for some service firms to depict the customer driven feature of their structures than for some manufacturing firms.

Technological change

A key contingency for organizational design is technological change. As the pace of such change increases, organizations need to be more flexible and adaptive. Since technological change is expected to intensify, the future may hold mostly organic organizations with horizontal work and communication flows.

Partly to deal with technological change, a modular or virtual design approach is sometimes used in which some activities of the organization are outsourced. The outsourcing may vary as the demands of technological change vary. Figure 9.7 shows an example of a modular type of organization with predominantly horizontal flows of work. Since 1984, Hewlett-Packard (H-P) has sold more than 15 million laser printers that use a motor made by Canon of Japan. Canon developed the motor and sold it to H-P, which performed the assembly, sales, and service. In other technological areas at H-P, like ink jet printers, the outsourcing is different and H-P and Canon are fierce competitors.[36]

International competition

International competition increases the demands on the organization structure. Because of the international competition, customers are more demanding that they receive the latest technological products and features. This increases the need for the organization to operate with reduced cycle times to deliver value to customers. Horizontal and matrix organization structures are best suited for such a task. *Business Week* noted that, in a global economy, rigid structures will be swept away and corporations that can adapt will thrive.[37]

Size

The size of the organization is associated with its design. Small organizations are easier to integrate due to the proximity of the people and the general nature of many people's tasks. Conversely, large firms have special integration problems. A trend in organizational design in the 1990s is *downsizing*, which is the purposeful shrinking of organizations. GM and IBM are two good examples of large organizations that have shrunk by tens of thousands of employees in the recent past.

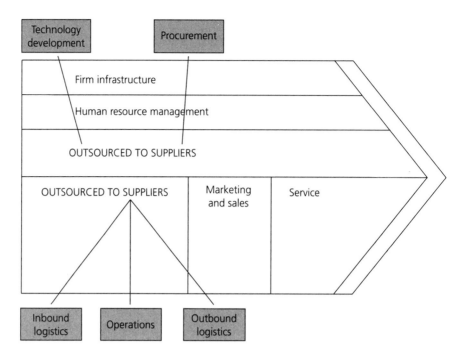

Figure 9.7 A horizontal, modular organization.

Source: Dess, G., Rasheed, A., McLaughlin, K. and Priem, R., "The new corporate architecture," *The Academy of Management Executive* (August 1995), p. 9.

Diversification of products and services

A holding company structure is an appropriate organization design for a series of diversified products. Such products may be unrelated and/or they may be in unrelated markets. Today the trend is to concentrate on product lines and do those products very well to provide the best value to customers. Thus, the holding company form should become increasingly rare.

Technology interdependence

Technological interdependence can influence structure. *Interdependence* is the degree to which organizational units depend on each other for resources to perform their tasks. There are three types of interdependence that influence structure. *Pooled interdependence* means that each unit is relatively independent because work does not flow among units. Fast food restaurants are good examples. *Sequential interdependence* means that the output of one unit becomes the input of another unit. There is much more interdependence and sharing of resources in this form. A good example is a computer assembly line. *Reciprocal interdependence* means that the output of unit one becomes the input for unit two, which transforms the input and sends it back to unit one as its input. Colleges in a university are a good example in which students take courses in one college and then return to another college for higher-level courses.

Information processing requirements

The needs of the organization concerning the amount and the frequency of information processing influence the organizational design. Limited sampling of external information can be associated with an inwardly focused organization. A prison may have limited information needs and an inward focus.

The number of organizations which do not need frequent external information is limited and growing smaller. Frequent sampling of information is associated with many ties and mechanisms that are in touch with the external world, especially markets and customers. For example, an airline needs much information from the outside world to understand customer's needs. Information flow is often a key cross-functional process.

Teams are often used to operate cross-functional processes.

Teams in Organizations

Some cross-functional teams have the same problems as individual integrators, such as special assistants, coordinators, facilitators, and integrators: they are band aid approaches to a structural design issue. Some teams, such as councils, committees, task forces, and problem solving teams, are temporary. Thus, their ability to influence real work is limited. Some cross-functional teams are long-lived and are serious attempts to integrate activities in recognition of the horizontal work flow.[38] Titles like project teams and cross-functional teams suggest long-lived attempts to perform the integration role of cross-functional systems and the role of focusing on the customer.[39]

A *team* is a collection of two or more people who interact regularly to accomplish common goals.[40] Teams have been around as long as organizations have been around. Wherever people regularly interact to accomplish goals, whether in formal or informal settings, teams exist. Assembly teams in Saturn work together to assemble cars. Surgical teams in a hospital work together to complete complicated surgeries. The terms team and group may be used almost interchangeably. In many organizations today, the term team is more frequently used for at least two reasons. First, because of the cross-functional nature of many teams, the term "cross-functional team" arose. Second, it is possible to discuss teamwork as a spirit and as a corporate cultural value.

The role of teams

Teams have been praised as the key in some organizations to focus on cross-functional issues. The quality case on Motorola is such an example, where widespread adoption of cross-functional teams has helped the organization on its quality journey. In forecasting the organization of the twentieth century, *Business Week* recently advised: "Build for speed and flexibility. Flatten hierarchies. Use Teams to chase new opportunities and ensure cross-fertilization."[41]

In other organizations, the wholesale adoption of teams without managerial leadership to yield value to customers has been associated with the death of the quality journey. Florida Power and Light (FPL) implemented hundreds of teams in the name of quality improvement. The firm was even the first in the USA to win the Deming Prize, which previously had been awarded in Japan only to Japanese firms for outstanding quality progress. However, FPL's quality journey was halted when the cost of the program could no longer be justified relative to the value it provided to customers.[42] A recent study in Canada found that 80 percent of the study participants had reward/compensation systems focused on individual, not team, performance".[43]

Cross-functional teams are essential to yield increased value to customers as the teams go hand-in-hand with flattened organizational structures. Jack Welch, CEO of General Electric and leader of its rebirth in the 1980s and 1990s, has become a spokesperson for organizational change. He described the critical importance of cross-functional teams and project teams in the new flattened architecture of GE with fewer layers of management.[44] In Germany, Daimler-Benz, the parent of Mercedes autos, eliminated two tiers of management and introduced teamwork. It reported that productivity rose by 30 percent in the ensuing two years.[45]

The Thermos Corporation designs, manufactures and markets leisure products. It recently replaced its bureaucratic culture with flexible interdisciplinary teams, which included customers and suppliers, to yield an award winning design for a new electric grill. Without the interdisciplinary team, Thermos guessed that it would have produced a modification of an existing gas grill, rather than the revolutionary electric design that won awards.[46] Managers designed the system for new product design and development, which was implemented by teams.

What is the role of management in such an organization? Managers design systems operated by teams and individuals. Deming addressed this as one of his 14 points in describing the work of managers. "Break down barriers between departments. People in research, design, sales, and production must work as a team, to foresee problems of production and in use that may be encountered with the product or service."[47]

There are several different kinds of teams in organizations. Some customer-relevant teams are cross-functional, some are within a discipline. Some teams are permanent, some are temporary. Many teams have the common characteristic today that they contain members from a variety of areas in the firm.

Cross-functional teams

A *cross-functional team* is a team with members from at least two functions of design, production, marketing or finance. A cross-functional team may be drawn as a matrix organization. Such teams are usually horizontal with members from equal levels in different functions, or they may be diagonal teams with members from slightly different levels in differing functions.

Cross-functional teams implement and operate the cross-functional systems described earlier in this chapter. Some refer to cross-functional teams as interdisciplinary teams. In describing its "Statement of Purpose", Procter & Gamble listed the eight principles that guide its actions as a company, including a teamwork principle. "We will encourage teamwork across disciplines, divisions and geography to get the most effective integration of the ideas and efforts of our people."[48]

It would be difficult to imagine organizations today without cross-functional teams. Motivated, trained, and integrated cross-functional teams make it possible to deliver greater value to customers, at lower cost, with less supervision, and flatter organizational structures.

In 1994, GTE Directories, which produces the yellow pages in many phone books, won a Baldrige National Quality Award in the service company category, partly because of the way the firm used teams to improve. Ninety-six percent of its employees are involved in quality teams. There are 13 permanent process teams charged with continual improvement of those 13 key processes.[49]

By focusing on customers' needs for a small, stylish, inexpensive new car, and bringing together key personnel from all the functions in a cross-functional design team, Chrysler designed and produced the Neon in 31 months. Other cars designed with a typical functional approach consumed 47 months.[50]

Committees and task forces are two common cross-functional teams. A *committee* is a long-lasting team, usually cross-functional, designed to deal with activities that recur. A college admission committee usually has members from several disciplines in the college to add breadth to the admission process. A *task force/problem solving team* is a temporary team, usually cross-functional, designed to deal with unique problems. A task force is usually formed to investigate the cause of an aircraft accident, with members from several government agencies, the airline, the pilots' association, and the aircraft producer.

Formal and informal teams

A *formal team* is a team officially created by the organization as part of the formal organization structure. Formal teams, sometimes referred to as formal groups, may appear on organization charts. An X-ray department in a hospital and a loan department in a bank may be thought of as formal teams.

An *informal team* is a voluntary team not officially sanctioned by the organization. Informal teams form because they have common interests, such as recycling, or for social reasons. Experienced managers often work with informal teams as communication and influence networks. Managers must be attentive that their actions do not cause informal teams to grow that are in opposition to management.

Employee involvement teams

Employee involvement teams are teams formed to increase the participation and involvement of employees in their jobs in order to increase the value provided to customers. Suggestion groups and quality circles are good examples. Quality circles and many other employee involvement teams do not have the power to make changes to the work or the system. Thus, such teams are basically study groups that recommend changes to managers.[51] This suggests a traditional approach to organizations, with "managers" holding the power to make and implement decisions.

Employee involvement is considered an early step toward using the full capability of employees in organizations.[52] To further tap the capabilities of teams to continuously improve and deliver value to customers, teams must be empowered. Quality action teams at FedEx implemented recycling programs that earned the firm nearly US$200,000 annually at one site.[53]

Empowered teams

Empowerment refers to the sharing of power and authority to make and implement decisions with non-managerial employees.[54] By sharing power with employees to operate systems, managers are free to work on improving systems and providing more value to customers. John Sculley, the former Chairman and CEO of the Apple Computer Company, commented on the importance of empowering employees. "Our old, ineffective, hierarchical model will need to be replaced by the new empowerment model of putting critical thinking and decision-making skills into the hands of a fully educated work force."[55]

Empowerment is a partner of a flattened organization with few layers of managers. Thus, there is little direct supervision of employees. The organization implementing empowerment also fosters a participative culture that values employees. A flat organization, empowerment, and a participative culture are complementary. Eastman Chemical Company described the ten principles that constitute its quality policy, including the empowerment principle. "Create a culture where people have the knowledge, skills, authority, and desire to decide, act, and take responsibility for results of their actions and for their contribution to the success of the company."[56]

Self-managed work teams

Self-managed work teams have the power to make the operating decisions and operate the systems designed by managers. Such teams plan, set priorities, organize, coordinate with others, measure, take corrective action, solve problems, and deal with team personnel issues.[57] As a team, they act as traditional managers in hierarchical organizations. Self-managed work teams require a high level of training and a high level of trust from management.[58] Although some refer to self-managed work teams as autonomous teams, they are not autonomous since they are tied into systems designed by managers.

A good example exists at the Saturn Corporation, in which the teams plan and control much of the work, including work methods, quality improvement, and personnel decisions. Some Milliken textile plants that have no "supervisors" in the plant on second and third shifts are another good example of self-managed work teams.

The relative amount of power possessed by different kinds of teams is shown in figure 9.8. As more organizations evolve to a more horizontal organization to emphasize cross-functional processes, there will be more emphasis on cross-functional teams. *Fortune* recently described the key elements in the evolving knowledge of the horizontal organization. "Teams will provide the foundation of

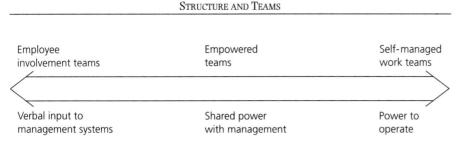

Figure 9.8 Spectrum of teams and power in organizations.

the organization design. They will not be set up inside departments, like marketing, but around core processes, such as new-product development. Process owners, not department heads, will be the top managers."[59]

The amount of power in those teams will be partly a function of the centrality of the customer, and the need to retain or share power by managers. We forecast that as increased international competition improves the primacy of the customer, more organizations will move to empowered and/or self-managed teams to operate and improve the cross-functional processes. The challenges in changing an organization from a top-down hierarchically centered culture to a horizontal, process focused culture are reviewed in chapter 10.

INVOLVEMENT THROUGH TEAMWORKING IN THE UK

This case study is concerned with the operation of team working at one plant of a large American-owned multinational, codenamed Qualchem. The company has outlets all around the world, and it sells high-quality specialty chemicals for use in both the domestic and commercial markets. It is one of the leaders in its market, and the major change over the past decade has been the continuing challenge of Japanese companies and products. Indeed, one of the major influences on corporate strategy in recent years, as well as employment policy, has been the perceived threat of Japanese import penetration into the USA plus the more competitive markets in other countries.

Over 100,000 people are employed by Qualchem worldwide, of whom nearly 8,000 work in the UK across a number of sites in different parts of the country. The bulk of these are employed at the head office and principal production site, including a sizable research division and distribution department. Two other sites employ smaller numbers of staff, who are engaged on production of raw materials and products for use in the main factory; in all cases, products are sold in both British and European markets. The site which forms the basis of this case study is the smallest unit in the company in Britain, with just over 200 staff, but the policies which it implements are broadly in line with those adopted at other sites. If anything, however, it is slightly further down the team working road because of its size and the nature of the technology employed at the site.

The parent company, Qualchem – like many others in the chemical industry – publishes a set of corporate principles which is distributed to all employees. The preface to this is written by the UK Chairman, and it states that the booklet "is an expression of the way in which we intend to manage the company taking account of the external influences which are crucial to our business interests." He continues by asking employees to "help make these statements a living commitment, by developing the beliefs into plans for continuous improvement."

Qualchem's mission comprises five goals, of which two are particularly relevant for this case: (a) recognize that our people are our most important asset; and (b) adopt quality as a way of life. The "people" policies and practices are fairly typical of this kind of progressive organization, and include commitments to the best health and safety standards, equity of treatment, effective channels of communication, a superior employment package, stability of employment, and high performance standards from staff.

The "quality" policies refer to visible and reinforced managerial commitment to quality, an emphasis on customers (both external and internal to the organization), quality as a measure of performance, and clarity of employee goals and objectives. The final point has a clear relevance for Employee Involvement; it states that "we will create an environment that encourages quality by ensuring that the contribution of all employees to the quality process is maximized by training, teambuilding, leadership, and ensuring individuals are responsible for their own processes."

Teamworking is one part of Qualchem's World Class Manufacturing Strategy, the other two parts being performance management and statistical process control (SPC). SPC is a key part of the quality improvement programme, and this aims to provide the teams with a mechanism for assessing the quality of production, as well as a methodology which will help them to overcome problems. Ultimately, all operators will be trained in the use and meaning of statistical techniques which are relevant to their part of the operation.

Performance management is a system designed to seek and achieve continuous improvement in the key aspects of each individual's or team's work, and it operates according to "reinforcements of good behavior". These reinforcements can be either tangible or social (e.g. visits organized for the team, a contribution to a local charity, a beer bust, a badge, a word of thanks from the plant manager). The crucial point is that they are meant to reinforce actions which management defines as good for the business (section, department, plant). This appears to have been well received in the US plants, but they are less sure about its general application in Britain – despite some evidence that it has gone down well with certain shopfloor teams – because of differing cultures and traditions.

The third strand of world class manufacturing is the team working concept, and this is being extended across the whole company. This has developed well at the case study site, particularly with process operators on the chemical plants who are now covered by a single grade.

The move towards world class manufacturing has been bolstered by two further employee relations practices. First, the company aims to devote 5 percent of each employee's time (on average each year) to training and development, and this includes not only technical skills training but also teambuilding exercises as well. An example of the former would be the provision of specific packages, often delivered in conjunction with local technical colleges, for different grades of staff – say multiskill training for craftworkers, or simple maintenance skills for process operators. Another would be training in how to interpret controls on the plant, their meaning and significance, and their relevance for quality. An example of the latter would be outward bound courses designed to develop team spirit and decision making within groups, and to reduce barriers between different grades of staff. While these sorts of exercises have become more common for managers over the past decade, at Qualchem these have been extended to manual workers as well.

The second element which underpins team working, and appears necessary for it to work effectively, is a revamped pay package which drastically reduces the number of grades on the shop floor. Under the new system, there are four principal grades: ancillary worker/laborer, process operator, craftworker, team leader. Each grade has a "start" and "established" rate, although variations are possible due to shift allowances and other fringe benefits. Pay levels for a process operator on shifts are high, not only for the industry but also compared with average wages for many white collar and managerial staff in other sectors.

Source: Marchington, M., Managing the Team: a Guide to Successful Employee Involvement. *Oxford, UK: Blackwell (1992), pp. 123–6.*

▍ Summary ▍

The primary purpose of an organization is to accomplish goals, preferably customer-relevant goals. There are at least two kinds of organization that the manager can use to accomplish work. One is the formal organization that is described on organization charts. The other is the informal organization that consists of the patterns of communication and influence among employees.

The organization chart is the picture of the formal organizational structure. The chart has both vertical (number of layers) and horizontal (span of control) dimensions.

Several organizational forms are reviewed. Functional organizations group similar tasks. Geographic organizations repeat the structure in each major location. Product or division organizations group activities associated with common products. Customer organizations group activities associated with types of customers. Holding companies have strategic business units (SBUs) that are collections of divisions with commonality within the SBU and little commonality across the SBUs. Matrix organizations overlay product or business organizations on a functional structure.

There are different approaches to designing organizations including classical, environmental, task-technology, and systems/process approaches. Systems and process approaches are most closely tied to designing the work to provide value to customers.

A process and systems approach groups activities associated with the provision of customer value. Alternatively, an organizational approach is concerned with authority, reporting relationships, and control independent of the customers.

The need to integrate across functions has become increasingly important due to several changes in the business world. Increased international competition has been associated with customer demands for affordable quality. Rapidly changing technology has been associated with shortened cycle times.

There are at least four cross-functional systems common to many organizations. The customer value determination, new product design and development, logistics and material, and information flow systems are common to many organizations attempting to provide greater value to customers. These systems are usually implemented by cross-functional teams.

Organizations are becoming increasingly customer-focused, with reliance on customer value determination systems. Organizations are also becoming smaller by downsizing themselves, as it is easier to stay in touch with customers when smaller. Structures are becoming flatter as cross-functional teams are assuming many of the functions previously performed by managers. Organizations are also becoming more flexible and adaptable as customer needs change rapidly. This may take the form of matrix and cross-functional systems organizations with decreased emphasis on vertical, hierarchical forms.

A team is a collection of two or more people who interact regularly to accomplish common goals. Managers create and improve systems operated by individuals and teams. A cross-functional team is a team with members from at least two functions of design, production, marketing or finance. Thus, cross-functional teams are usually horizontal, with members from equal levels in different functions, or they may be diagonal teams with members from slightly different levels in differing functions. Cross-functional teams operate cross-functional systems.

Committees and task forces are two common cross-functional teams. A committee is a long-lasting team, usually cross-functional, designed to deal with activities that recur. A task force/problem solving team is a temporary team, usually cross-functional, designed to deal with unique problems. A formal team is a team officially created by the organization as part of the formal organization structure. An informal team is a voluntary team not officially sanctioned by the organization. Experienced managers often work with informal teams as communication and influence networks.

Employee involvement teams are teams formed to increase the participation and involvement of employees in their jobs in order to increase the value provided to customers. Quality circles were an early form of employee involvement teams. Empowerment refers to the sharing of power and authority to make and implement decisions with non-managerial employees. Empowered cross-functional teams share the power with managers to operate the cross-functional systems designed by managers. Empowerment is a partner of a flattened organization with few layers of managers. Thus, there is little direct supervision of employees. Self-managed work teams have the power to make the operating decisions and operate the systems designed by managers. Such teams plan, set priorities, organize, coordinate with others, measure, take corrective action, solve problems and deal with team personnel issues.

DISCUSSION QUESTIONS

1 Describe the principal purpose of organizations.

2 Discuss the pros and cons of the various structural forms.

3 Discuss the different approaches to designing organizations.

4 Forecast the future of the process focus.

5 How will customer requirements and international competition impact structural design in the future?

6 List the four main cross-functional systems common to many organizations. Describe their purposes.

7 Discuss the educational and training needs of people who work in teams versus those who do not.

KEY TERMS

A committee	is a long-lasting team, usually cross-functional, designed to deal with activities that recur.
Continuous process production	refers to nonstop production of the flow of work.
A cross-functional team	is a team with members from at least two functions of design, production, marketing, or finance.
In a customer organization,	activities, personnel, and resources are grouped by common types of customers.
Downsizing	is the purposeful shrinking of organizations.
Empowerment	refers to the sharing of power and authority to make and implement decisions with non-managerial employees.
Employee involvement teams	are teams formed to increase the participation and involvement of employees in their jobs in order to increase the value provided to customers.

The formal organization	is the structure specified in the organization chart.
A formal team	is a team officially created by the organization as part of the formal organization structure.
Like activities or like functions	are grouped together in a **functional structure**.
In a geographic structure,	like functions are grouped together within each geographic area but not across geographic areas.
Holding companies	are conglomerations or collections of separate seemingly unrelated groupings of businesses or divisions called strategic business units, or SBUs.
The informal organization	is reflected in the patterns of communication and influence associated with flows of information, activities, and social activities of organizational members.
An informal team	is a voluntary team not officially sanctioned by the organization.
Interdependence	is the degree to which organizational units depend on each other for resources to perform their tasks.
Mass production	is the production of many items with the same specification.
The matrix organization	is an overlay of businesses or projects on functional groupings.
Mechanistic designs	are structure in which tasks are fractionated and specialized.
Organic designs	are structures in which tasks are interdependent.
The organization chart	diagrams the functions, departments, or positions in the organization and shows how they are related in patterns of formal authority.
Pooled interdependence	means that each unit is relatively independent because work does not flow among units.
In a product (or division) structure,	separate manufacturing, sales and accounting activities are grouped together around products.
Reciprocal interdependence	means that the output of unit one becomes the input for unit two which transforms the input and sends it back to unit one as its input.
Self-managed work teams	have the power to make the operating decisions and operate the systems designed by managers.
Sequential interdependence	means that the output of one unit becomes the input of another unit.
Small batch production	refers to the production of items in batches of one, or a few, designed to customer orders.
The span of control	is the number of employees supervised.
Structure	is the design of the organization.
A task force/problem solving team	is a temporary team, usually cross-functional, designed to deal with unique problems.
A team	is a collection of two or more people who interact regularly to accomplish common goals.

Motorola's Six Sigma Total Quality Process Emphasizes Processes and Teams

Motorola was founded in 1928 by Paul Galvin. He led the company until his death in 1959. His son, Robert Galvin, was CEO from 1959 until 1990, and continued on the Motorola board in the 1990s. His son, Christopher Galvin was Assistant COO prior to being named as President in 1993.[a]

The company had about 120,000 employees and US$27 billion in sales in 1995. International business accounted for about 60 percent of sales.[b] All of its products and services were in the area of electronics, including mobile radio and paging systems, semiconductors, integrated circuits, cellular phones, space communications, and computers.

In the early 1980s, Motorola stressed quality improvement, with a goal of a ten times improvement in quality in five years. In 1986, Motorola chose a formal total quality process that it labeled as Six Sigma. Six Sigma refers to a defect rate of no more than 3.4 per million. Its total quality process won Motorola one of the first Malcolm Baldrige National Quality Awards in 1988. The six steps in Motorola's Six Sigma Process follow.[c]

- Identify the work you do (your "product").
- Identify who your work is for (your "customer").
- What do you need to do your work, and from whom (your "supplier").
- Map the process.
- Mistake-proof the process, and eliminate delays.
- Establish quality and cycle time measurement and improvement goals.

The Six Sigma Process is implemented in the context of the Motorola culture. Motorola's fundamental objectives, key beliefs, goals, and initiatives have been translated into 11 languages for Motorola's worldwide operations and are printed on a small card for employees to carry. The card's contents are shown in figure 9.9.

What does empowerment for all mean in such a large organization, with over 100,000 employees? What is the role of teams in such a process?

Quality has become a way of life at Motorola. It is a key driver – driven not only by management, but also by teams of employees at every level throughout the company, a team process begun in the 1960s.

In 1990, the team process was formalized as a total customer satisfaction, problem solving team competition. During that year, more than 2,000 teams were formed. Training was made available on analytic techniques and judging criteria were announced. By 1992, the number of teams had increased to 3,700; 24 teams competed at the corporate level for the gold. The panel of judges for the final selection was – and continues to be – the senior management of the company. The criteria are:

- teamwork;
- results;
- project selection;
- institutionalization;
- analysis techniques;
- presentation;
- remedies.[d]

All those teams must function within the context of a quality plan or mayhem will result. The competition is among teams from all over the world. By winning an annual team competition held at corporate headquarters, the "Road Runners" team from the Land Mobile Products sector in Malaysia reinforced the importance of teams in Motorola's global TQ process.

(Side 1)

OUR FUNDAMENTAL OBJECTIVE
(Everyone's Overriding Responsibility)

Total Customer Satisfaction

(Side 2)

KEY BELIEFS – *how we will always act*

Constant Respect for People
Uncompromising Integrity

KEY GOALS – *what we must accomplish*

Best in Class
• People
• Marketing
• Technology
• Product: Software, Hardware and Systems
• Manufacturing
• Service

Increased Global Market Share
Superior Financial Results

KEY INITIATIVES – *how we will do it*

Six Sigma Quality
Total Cycle Time Reduction
Product, Manufacturing and Environmental Leadership
Profit Improvement
Empowerment for All, in a Participative, Cooperative and Creative Workplace

Figure 9.9   Motorola's objectives, beliefs, goals, and initiatives.

Understand customer's needs

Evaluate and improve processes to meet needs

Develop measurement systems to track progress

Educate, reward, communicate

Set reach-out goals

Figure 9.10   Top-down commitment and involvement.

The importance of quality will continue to intensify as Motorola approaches the twenty-first century. Customers are continually raising the bar of excellence. A simplified plan for quality improvement at Motorola is shown in figure 9.10.

Motorola continues to set reach-out goals. A goal is a ten times reduction in defects every two years. Metrics have changed from parts per million to parts per billion.

Now, as throughout its history, there has been a drive to do better, an aim for *renewal* strongly supported by senior management, but also pervasive throughout the entire organization. In a way, quality breeds quality. The Six Sigma Process and renewal seem to be working as Motorola's earnings and sales were growing close to 20 percent per year in the mid 1990s. Motorola's stock had more than sextupled in the seven years from the time it won the Baldrige Quality Award in 1988.[e]

Discussion Questions

1 If Motorola is already at Six Sigma, how can it achieve a goal of ten times reduction in defects every two years?

2 Describe the problems and opportunities of reinforcing its Six Sigma Quality Process in the USA, Europe, and China.

3 How important are emphases on processes and teams in Motorola's Six Sigma Process?

Sources: a. Galvin, R. W., *The Idea of Ideas*. Schaumberg, IL: Motorola University Press (1991), p. 215;
b. "Motorola", in *Value Line Investment Survey*. New York: Value Line Publishing, Inc. (January 27, 1995), p. 1068;
c. Buetow, R., *The Motorola Quality Process*. Schaumberg, IL: Motorola, Inc. (January 15, 1987), p. 9;   d. *Quality Renewal*. Schaumberg, IL: Motorola, Inc. (1989), p. 4; e. *Value Line* (January 27, 1995), p. 1068.

INTERNATIONAL CASE

MAKING CENTS AT SAINSBURY'S

The newly wed John James and Mary Ann Sainsbury opened the doors of their small London dairy in 1869, hoping to eventually have enough stores for each of their future sons. The store drew customers because of its remarkable cleanliness and efficiency, a stark contrast to the mostly dirty London shops of the day. Right from the start, Sainsbury began to build its business by offering the highest quality products at the lowest price.[a]

Although the Sainsburys had six sons, the business grew much faster than their family. By 1900, the Sainsbury family owned 48 stores. Today, J. Sainsbury PLC has become Britain's leading retail grocery chain, with 355 stores, over 130,000 employees, and £12 billion (US$19 billion) in revenue.[b] Its most widely recognized competitive advantage rests on its "Sainsbury's"-labeled products, which account for over 65 percent of sales. Not to be confused with lower quality private labels, Sainsbury's products have consistently earned higher quality ratings than their branded counterparts, not to mention better service and competitive prices.[c]

Sainsbury attributes its continuing success to qualities instilled by the founders: clear direction, attention to detail, and a willingness to innovate to remain on the forefront of the grocery industry. To attain this efficiency, Sainsbury found that it worked best as a functional organization. The three main functions are trading, retailing, and distribution. Each has its own operational hierarchy, planning, and direction setting capabilities. Operational policies and joint goals were determined centrally through both informal and formal processes. A key role is played by teams comprised of members of Sainsbury's unusually active board, many of whom gather weekly in response to market and operational issues.[d]

The firm's capacity for innovation has been proven in the way it has been able to accomplish tasks that transcend functions. This was most notable in 1989, when Sainsbury reviewed and renewed its commitment to the integration of new information technology within the company. Implementation of an information strategy developed in the 1970s was largely complete. In order to move ahead and maintain a competitive advantage, Sainsbury recognized that it needed a new strategy for the 1990s.[e]

Instead of the conventional approach of hiring a specialist to analyze internal needs and make recommendations, a participative approach was used. Teams of employees from all functional areas within the company worked together to make their own analysis of Sainsbury, supported by a process facilitator. Since employees knew the company better than outsiders, Sainsbury found that the inclusive approach gave more insight into how information flows could be made more useful to managers at all levels of the company. The first task was to identify the most important decisions made within the company and determine how they could be supported with information technology.[f]

This team approach to the information technology project was designed to produce a strategy that "fit" Sainsbury as an organization and to include a high level of commitment throughout the company, from top to bottom. Four teams were formed with distinct responsibilities and varying scope: (a) the steering committee, (b) the task force, (c) the advisory group, and (d) the project team. During the four phases of the project, the number of participants increased or decreased to include as much of the organization as necessary for each task. The final product was not so much a prescribed blueprint for action as it was a departure point for "initiatives" that would lead to a new information system. Since the board was involved in every phase of the project, buy-in was practically assured. This was helped by the five guiding principles developed by Sainsbury employees for this project. These principles were:

1   The learning principle: strategy and planning is an organizational learning process.
2   The interpretive principle: it is management's task to state and develop interpretation of the company and its environment.
3   The participatory principle: the active participation of management is essential to give commitment and ownership.
4   The pluralist principle: divergent interests between groups have to be accommodated.
5   The adaptive principle: organizations are complex, open, and adaptive systems.[g]

Since 1989, Sainsbury has implemented a high-tech information system that has halved the average time it takes to get a product from the supplier to the consumer. The impact has not only been on the Sainsbury organization, but also on other organizations within the retail food supply chain. According to Angus Clark, the Sainsbury director responsible for systems and distribution, bar-code scanning at the checkout counters has changed the whole supply-chain operation from a "push" system to a "pull" system. Historically, forecasts dictated what was pushed down the supply chain to each retail outlet, but scanning has allowed Sainsbury to capture demand data the instant a sale is made. Now, production and distribution can be calibrated to levels of real demand.[h]

The astonishing difference this change makes in terms of reduced inventory expenses, logistics, and transportation costs, and increased responsiveness to consumer demand may not be immediately apparent. However, when this technology is fully implemented, it is expected to cut £18.9 billion (US$30 billion) of costs out of the entire retail food supply chain. It is no wonder that Sainsbury has striven to be an industry leader in information technology.[i]

As more companies within the retail food supply chain invest in the latest information technology, it is also having a broad effect on company structure. Not only does this technology demand intra-organizational teamwork to implement, it requires inter-organizational teamwork in order to achieve the benefits of an instantaneous flow of information from the point of sale to manufacturers to raw material suppliers.

As the benefits of this new technology become more apparent, many more organizations will make the investment to upgrade their information systems. Although there has been much progress already, the industry is still in the infancy stage of making the changes necessary to integrate this technology both internally and across organizations. Based on Sainsbury's innovative record and current success, it can be counted on to be the industry's transformational leader.

Discussion Questions

1 How does a functionally organized company like Sainsbury's build successful teams?

2 What different skills does a manager in a cross-functional company need that are not required in a functionally organized company?

3 Sainsbury and other companies are increasingly able to gather more and more detailed information about consumers. What advantages and disadvantages do improved information systems provide to customers?

Sources: **a.** "Sainsbury's company history," J. Sainsbury, World Wide Web (November, 1995); **b.** "J. Sainsbury PLC," *Compact Disclosure* (November, 1995); **c.** "J. Sainsbury PLC," *Company Histories* (1988), p. 657; **d.** "Ormerod, R., "Putting soft OR methods to work: information systems strategy development at Sainsbury's," *Journal of the Operational Research Society* (1995), p. 282; **e.** Leonard, L., "Is there a place for frozens in ECR's promised land," *Frozen Food Age* (May 1995), p. 1; **f.** "Ormerod, R., "Putting soft OR methods to work: information systems strategy development at Sainsbury's," p. 280; **g.** Ibid, p. 285; **h.** Brown, M., "Sainsbury's star act," *Management Today* (April, 1994), p. 78; **i.** Leonard, L., "Is there a place for frozens in ECR's promised land," p. 1.

NOTES

1 Chandler, A. D. Jr, *Strategy and Structure*. Cambridge, MA: MIT Press (1962), p. 16.

2 Hall, D. J. and Saias, M. A., "Strategy follows structure," *Strategic Management Journal* (1980), p. 156.

3 "US cars come back," *Fortune* (November 16, 1992), p. 58.

4 Galbraith, J. R. and Nathanson, D. A., *Strategy Implementation*. St Paul: West Publishing Co., (1978), chapter 8.

5 Burns, T. and Stalker, G., *The Management of Innovation*. London: Tavistock (1961).

6 Galbraith, J. R. and Nathanson, D. A., chapter 8.

7 Mitroff, I., Mason, R. and Pearson, C., "Radical surgery: what will tomorrow's organizations look like?" *Academy of Management Executive*, 8 (May 1994), pp. 11–21.

8 "The search for the organization of tomorrow," *Fortune* (May 18, 1992), p. 95; "The horizontal corporation," *Business Week* (December 20, 1993), p. 76.

9 Shirley, R. C., Peters, M. H. and El-Ansary, A. I., *Strategy and Policy Formation*. New York: Wiley (1981), pp. 238–50.

10 "The struggle to create an organization for the 21st century," *Fortune* (April 3, 1995), pp. 98–9.

11 Hax, A. C. and Majluf, N. C., *Strategic Management* Englewood Cliffs, NJ: Prentice Hall (1984), pp. 383–99.

12 Cleland, D. I. and King, W. R., *Systems Analysis and Project Management*, 3rd edn. New York: McGraw-Hill (1983).

13 Cleland, D. I. and King, W. R. (eds), *Project Management Handbook*, 2nd edn. New York: Van-Nostrand Reinhold (1988).

14 Burns, T. and Stalker, G., *The Management of Innovation*.

15 Woodward, J., *Industrial Organizations: Theory and Practice*. London: Oxford University Press (1965).

16 Mintzberg, H., *Power in and around Organizations*. Englewood Cliffs, NJ: Prentice Hall (1983).

17 Harrington, H. J., *Business Process Improvement: the Breakthrough Strategy for Total Quality, Productivity, and Competitiveness*. New York: McGraw-Hill (1991), p. 9.

18 Sirkin, H. and Stalk, G., "Fix the process, not the problem," *Harvard Business Review* (July–August 1990), p. 30.

19 Andersen, McClintock and Range, "Statement of mission and vision," Memphis, TN (1992), p. 1.

20 Harrington, H. J., p. 35.

21 Juran, J., "A history of managing for quality in the united states" in Juran, J. (ed.), *A History of Managing for Quality*. Milwaukee: ASQC Quality Press (1995), pp. 553–602.

22 "The struggle to create an organization for the 21st century" *Fortune* (April 3, 1995), p. 91.

NOTES CONT.

23 "Manufacturers use suppliers to help them develop new products: they save big as vendors do much of the engineering but lose some control," *Wall Street Journal* (December 19, 1994), p. A1.

24 "Some companies let suppliers work on site and even place orders," *Wall Street Journal* (January 13, 1995), p. A1.

25 "How Wal-Mart outdid a once-touted Kmart in discount-store race," *Wall Street Journal* (March 24, 1995), p. A1.

26 "The struggle to create an organization for the 21st century" *Fortune* (April 3, 1995), pp. 96–8.

27 Bowles, J. and Hammond, J., *Beyond Quality*. New York: G. P. Putnam's Sons (1991), p. 159.

28 "Airlines going global to trim costs," *International Herald Tribune* (April 8–9, 1995), p. 9.

29 Cross, K., Feather, J., and Lynch, R., Corporate Renaissance: the Art of Reengineering, Oxford, UK: Blackwell (1994), p. 4.

30 Hammer, M. and Champy, J., *Reengineering the Corporation*. New York: HarperCollins (1993).

31 O'Neill, H., "Restructuring, re-engineering, and rightsizing," *Academy of Management Executive* (November, 1994), pp. 9–11.

32 "Some companies cut costs too far, suffer 'corporate anorexia'," *Wall Street Journal* (July 5, 1995), p. A1.

33 "Long highly praised, Deutsche Bank finds itself in some trouble," *Wall Street Journal* (November 16, 1995), p. A1.

34 Vrakking, W. J., "Customer orientation within the organization," in Mastenbroek, W. (ed.), *Managing for Quality in the Service Sector*. Oxford, UK: Blackwell (1991), p. 68.

35 *Blueprints for Service Quality: the Federal Express Approach*. New York: AMA Membership Publications Division (1991), p. 17.

36 "More and more firms enter joint ventures with big competitors," *Wall Street Journal* (November 1, 1995), p. A1.

37 "Reinventing America," *Business Week* (Special Issue, 1992), p. 60.

38 "Staying power: Motorola illustrates how an aged giant can remain vibrant," *Wall Street Journal* (December 11, 1992), p. A1.

39 Spencer, B., "Models of organization and TQM," *Academy of Management Review*, 19(3) (1994), pp. 446–71.

40 Larson, C. and LaFasto, M., *Teamwork*. Newbury Park, CA: Sage (1989).

41 "Tearing up today's organization chart," *Business Week* (Special 1994 Bonus Issue: 21st Century Capitalism), p. 82.

42 Evelyn, J. J. and DeCarlo, N., "Customer focus helps utility see the light," *Journal of Business Strategy* (January/February 1992), pp. 8–12; Wood, R., "A hero without a company," *Forbes* (March 18, 1991), pp. 112–14.

43 Koze, S. and Masciale, E., "Why teams don't work and how to fix them," *Canadian Manager* (Spring 1993), pp. 8–9.

44 "Revolutionize your company," *Fortune* (December 13, 1993), pp. 114–18.

45 "Corporate Germany revamps operations: Daimler-Benz leads the way," *Wall Street Journal* (April 7, 1995), p. A1.

46 "Payoff from the new management," *Fortune* (December 13, 1993), pp. 103–10.

47 Deming, W. E., *Out of The Crisis*. Cambridge, MA: (1986), p. 24.

48 *A Statement of Purpose*. Cincinnati, OH: P&G (1993), p. 2.

49 Nadkarni, R., "A not-so-secret recipe for successful TQM," *Quality Progress*, 28(11) (November 1995), pp. 91–6.

50 "Why buy Chrysler?" *USA Today* (April 4, 1995), p. B1.

51 Dale, B. and Cooper, C., *Total Quality and Human Resources*. Oxford, UK: Blackwell (1992), pp. 111–12.

52 Marchington, M., *Managing the Team: a Guide to Successful Employee Involvement*. Oxford, UK: Blackwell (1992), pp. 115–23.

53 *Blueprints for Service Quality: he FedEx Approach*, pp. 72–3.

54 McFarland, L., Senn, L. and Childress, J., *21st Century Leadership*. New York: The Leadership Press (1993), p. 64.

55 Ibid., p. 63.

56 *Eastman Quality Policy*. Kingsport, TN: Eastman Chemical Company (1993).

57 Band, W. A., *Creating Value for Customers*. New York: Wiley (1991), p. 189; Godfrey, A. B., "Ten areas for future research in TQM," *Quality Management Journal* (October 1993), p. 57.

58 Bowles, J. and Hammond, J., *Beyond Quality: How 50 Winning Companies Use Continuous Improvement*. New York: Putnam (1991), p. 98.

59 "The struggle to create an organization for the 21st century," *Fortune* (April 3, 1995), p. 91.

STRATEGY IMPLEMENTATION:
CULTURE AND BEHAVIOR

LEARNING OBJECTIVES

After reading this chapter, you should be able to accomplish the following.

1 Relate Schein's three levels of organizational culture to each other.

2 Discuss the importance of symbols, stories, heroes, slogans, and ceremonies in communicating and reinforcing culture.

3 Describe the kinds of organizations that would favor adapters, rebels, good soldiers, and mavericks.

4 Describe why it takes so long to change organizational cultures.

5 Describe the differences between management and leadership.

6 Explain the differences between formal and informal leaders.

7 Describe the role of a transformational leader.

8 Relate the concepts of leaders as empowerers, and self-managed work teams, to traditional concepts of leadership.

9 Compare and contrast motivation and leadership.

10 Compare and contrast formal and informal communication, as well as vertical and lateral communication.

This chapter also deals with strategy implementation. To implement strategy, managers should design and continuously improve the organizational culture and behavioral processes of leadership, motivation, and communication.

Organizational Culture and Change

As the managers at Toyota and NUMMI have known (see quality case), organizational culture is a key means to reinforce appropriate behavior and the goals of the organization. We consider the nature of organizational culture; how managers can reinforce culture; and the importance of cultural change.

Organizational culture

Organizational culture is intangible and thus difficult for some to deal with. Yet organizational culture can be one of the most powerful levers for managers to use when implementing strategy.

Observable and not observable

Organizational culture consists of the key values and beliefs that are shared by organizational members. As such, culture may not be readily observable. However, there are signs and symbols of culture that are observable.

A noted writer in the area of organizational culture is Schein. He argued that there are observable and not observable levels of culture. Schein speaks of values and beliefs, and the underlying assumptions in the not observable part of culture.[1]

The values and beliefs are core to the definition of culture and are at the center of organizational culture. Values and beliefs are not necessarily observable. However, in some organizations they may be written and widely communicated, as in the Johnson & Johnson and Motorola cases in chapters 4 and 9. If the values and beliefs are not directly observable, they can be inferred from how organizational members explain their behavior.

Another part of culture that is not observable consists of the underlying assumptions beneath the values and beliefs. These assumptions are the very foundation of the firm's culture. The assumptions may be so widely shared by organizational members that they are unaware of them.

The observable part of culture in all organizations consists of the artifacts and the behavior of its members.[2] *Artifacts* are the signs and products of culture. Although this part of culture is readily observable, it may be hard to interpret without knowledge of the underlying values and beliefs. For example, some may consider it awkward for Motorola employees to carry a card stating the primacy of customers. However, the Motorola value concerning the primacy of customers described on the card explains the nature of that behavior.

The observable part of organizational culture builds on the not observable parts. Those three parts and the building block idea are represented in figure 10.1.

The artifacts and behavior may take several noteworthy forms, including symbols, awards, stories, heroes, slogans, and ceremonies that signify organizational values. A *symbol* is usually an object that conveys meaning to others. Organizational awards are usually symbols of the behavior that the organization is trying to reinforce.

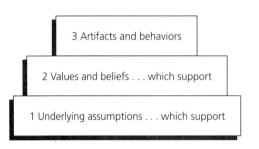

Figure 10.1 Three dimensions of organizational culture.
Source: Based on Schein, E., *Organizational Culture and Leadership*. San Francisco: Jossey-Bass (1985), p. 14.

Stories are descriptions of actual organizational events that characterize the values of the organization. To symbolize the cooperation between management and the union at Saturn, members tell stories of how a team of 99 managers and union members studied and traveled together for nearly a year to design the new corporation.

Heroes are individuals who personify the culture of the organization. Bill Gates, founder and CEO of Microsoft, with his hard working, risk taking, innovative ways, is a god-like hero at Microsoft. That firm has grown into the world's largest software firm partly because of his vision and actions.

A *slogan* is a short saying capturing a key organizational value. Land's End captures much of its organizational culture with its slogan: "GUARANTEED. PERIOD."[3] The corporation feels so strongly about the saying that it repeats it in most of its advertising. Land's End has even registered the saying in its unique form of all capital letters and a period after each word with the US government to protect it. Caterpillar has a slogan of "24-hour parts service any where in the world." This communicates its corporate value concerning meeting the customer's needs.

Ceremonies are special activities that communicate organizational values. Graduation ceremonies at universities are meant to communicate the importance of learning on a campus.

In his work on cross-cultural differences, Trompenaars noted that individualism versus collectivism is a key dimension describing cultural diversity in business around the world. In collecting data from 15,000 managers throughout the world, Trompenaars posed the following question. "Two people were discussing ways in which individuals could improve the quality of life. A. One said: 'It is obvious that if individuals have as much freedom as possible and the maximum opportunity to develop themselves, the quality of their life will improve as a result.' B. The other said: 'If individuals are continuously taking care of their fellow human beings the quality of life will improve for everyone, even if it obstructs individual freedom and individual development.' Which of the two ways of reasonong do you think is usually best, A or B?" Figure 10.2 shows the differences in many countries throughout the world. This key value impacts the way business people in different cultures behave.

Percentage of respondents opting for individual freedom (answer a)

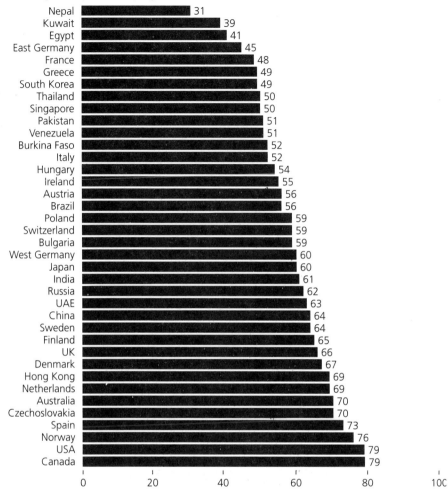

Figure 10.2 The quality of life.

Source: Trompenaars, F., *Riding the Waves of Culture: Understanding Cultural Diversity in Business*. London: Economist Books (1993), p. 48.

Managerial reinforcement actions

Given the above description of organizational culture, the manager needs to know the key levers and mechanisms to use to develop and reinforce the desired culture. Schein offered such a five part discussion after he had established the above descriptions of the dimensions of culture. Those five actions are:

1. The behaviors leaders measure and control.
2. Leaders' reactions to crises.
3. Modeling and coaching of expected behaviors.

4　Criteria for allocation of rewards.
5　Criteria for selection, promotion, and termination of employees.[5]

These actions send powerful signals concerning what is valued by the organization. The levers concerning the reward system and the hiring and termination system send powerful and long lasting signals concerning the organization's culture. As discussed in a later section, changing the culture can be difficult because these levers are so long lasting in the signals they send to organizational members.

When two organizations merge or one acquires another, differing organizational cultures can cause conflict. Michael Schulhof, President of Sony Corp. of America, was forced to resign that post in late 1995 after having been the only US executive ever to achieve such a visible and powerful job in a Japanese company. This termination and Matsushita's divestiture of MCA are symptomatic of the dangers of trying to bridge Japan's formal corporate world of long-term planning with Hollywood's freewheeling style. When differing corporate cultures clash, terminations or divestitures are common.[6]

Purposes of organizational culture

Organizational culture serves several important purposes in the life of the organization and its members. Culture is a way for new members to learn what is important in the organization and to guide their behavior. Culture also communicates values to customers and other external stakeholders.

Socialization

New organizational members undergo a learning process concerning organizational life called socialization. *"Organizational socialization* is a process by which a new member learns and adapts to the organization that he or she has joined."[7] In socializing new members, organizations create a series of events designed to undo non-conforming old values the individual may hold, and prepare the new member to learn the new organizational values. Training, communication, and reward systems play a substantial part in organizational socialization activities.

In addition to the formal organizational socialization process, there is also an *informal socialization*, which is the process by which a new member learns and adapts to the informal organization. The primary source of informal socialization is the work group/team which can exert powerful standards for work behavior and output on its members. This is such an important topic that it is treated·in the prior chapter on teams.

The organizational and informal socialization processes may be complementary with each other or they may be in conflict. Wise managers insure that they are complementary.

Behavioral conformity

A prime purpose of organizational culture is behavioral conformity. The organization is interested in the member behaving in ways that further organizational goals. Faced with such pressures for conformity in values and behavior, the member has at least four choices.[8] The individual can conform or not conform to

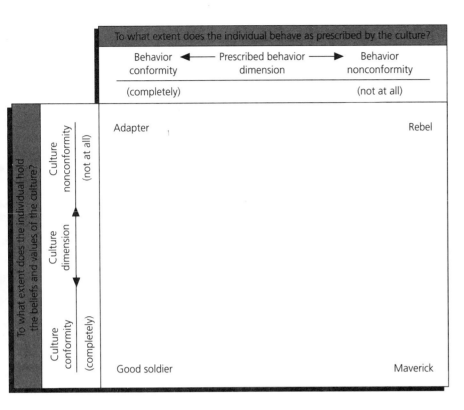

Figure 10.3 Cultural and behavioral conformity.

Source: Sathe, V., "Implications of corporate culture: a manager's guide to action," *Organizational Dynamics* (Autumn 1983), p. 15. Reprinted by permission of American Management Association, New York. All rights reserved.

the values and beliefs of the organization, and the individual can conform or not conform to the behavior prescribed by the culture.

Figure 10.3 describes the four different combinations of cultural and behavioral conformity. Rebels probably will not be in the organization for too long, as they reject both the organizational values and the appropriate behavior. The military and other rigid hierarchies like good soldiers because they conform on both dimensions. Some organizations highly value mavericks because they preserve the culture and values, while adding diversity to the behavioral menu of employees. Adapters are of less value because they do not further the culture of the organization in the long term.

Organizational fit with environment

The corporate culture described in Toyota and NUMMI was deliberately designed and communicated to relevant stakeholders early in the life of the organizations. The executives designed the culture to fit the organizations' environments. Whether newly designed or evolving over time, managers must ask if their organization's culture fits the environment.[9]

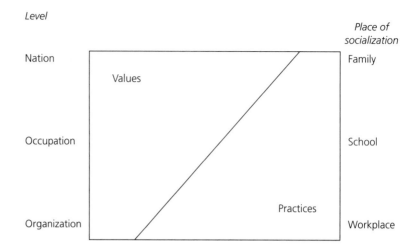

Figure 10.4 The nature of cultural differences: the national, occupational, and organizational levels.

Source: Hofstede, G., *Cultures and Organizations*. London: McGraw-Hill (1991), p. 182. Copyright © 1996 Geert Hofstede.

Different environments give birth to different cultures. Hofstede noted that cultural differences can be observed at national, occupational, and organizational levels.[10] Figure 10.4 shows those levels of cultural differences and the source of socialization. The manager needs to be aware of these various sources of cultural differences and recognize what the manager can and cannot change in the workplace.

Recently, the Japanese government's Fair Trade Commission (FTC) has been trying to break up a number of Japanese cartels with their price-fixing behavior that limits competition. The FTC is finding that business collusion remains deeply ingrained in Japan's way of doing business, as about half of its manufacturing industry still engages in some sort of price-fixing. "Cartels are a cultural tradition dating back to the 1600s so there is a lingering tendency to tolerate or even encourage anticompetitive behavior", says Ushio Chujo, a Keio University economist.[11] Companies from countries without a cultural tradition of cartels may find it hard to break into such Japanese industries.

Notice the different values between the two countries in the international exhibit. Those different environments influence the operations of the firms.

INTERNATIONAL EXHIBIT

UNION CARBIDE'S MIC PLANTS IN THE UNITED STATES AND FRANCE

One of the most famous industrial accidents in the twentieth century happened on December 3, 1984, when a tragic toxic gas leak of methyl isocyanate (MIC) occurred at a Union Carbide plant in Bhopal, India, killing at least 1750 people and leaving thousands of others sick and incapacitated. That plant was closed and never reopened. In subsequent litigation, US District Judge John F. Keenan called the case "the most significant, urgent, and extensive litigation ever to arise from a single event."

Although its own internal inspections and reports had warned of potential problems in controlling reactions and failures both in India and at a similar plant at Institute, West Virginia, Union Carbide took the position that potential problems had been handled and that both plants were operated in accordance with proper safety standards. It suggested sabotage as a likely, but not conclusive, explanation of the "accident" in India, and sharply criticized the way Indian supervisors had loosely implemented the company's safety standards.

Subsequent investigation indicated that there had been more than 70 generally small MIC leaks at the Institute plant from 1980 to 1984. That plant was closed for a five-month period after the Bhopal disaster, but reopened after presumably thorough inspections by Union Carbide, the State of West Virginia, the Environmental Protection Agency and the Occupational Safety and Health Administration. Before reopening the plant, Union Carbide put in place US$5 million in new safety equipment, introducing new safety monitors and a new cooling system that was thought to "solve" the problems that arose in India.

A year later, on April 1, 1986, Union Carbide was fined US$1.3 million by the US Labor Department for 221 safety violations at the Institute plant. This was the largest such fine in history. OSHA inspectors charged that Union Carbide had intentionally underreported the number of injuries at the plant and maintained defective safety equipment. Secretary of Labor Brock said the findings show a "laissez-faire attitude" toward worker safety. However, none of these violations involved the MIC unit, and no one had died. No units were closed.

Less well-discussed and investigated is a semi-obscure Union Carbide facility in Beziers, France, that uses large quantities of MIC in order to produce an insecticide. Beziers is in a region of France that has one of the highest unemployment rates in that country. The French are well aware of the safety concerns that have arisen about Union Carbide facilities. However, workers have made it clear that they are much more concerned about losing their jobs than they are about injury from toxic gases. Shortly after Bhopal, Environment Minister Huguette Bouchardeau had the plant inspected and declared it safe. Local officials have made it clear that jobs at this facility are critical to the area's economic viability. Bouchardeau further noted that, "in France, there are at least 300 companies that present comparable risks. If we reacted emotionally to the catastrophe [in India], there would be an industrial disaster in France."

Source: Beauchamp, T. and Bowie, N., Ethical Theory and Business, 3rd edn. Englewood Cliffs, NJ: Prentice Hall (1988), pp. 253–4.

Cultural change

As the speed of environmental change increases, organizational cultures must also change. Yet many of the cultural changes are painfully slow.

The need for cultural change

As environments change, the organizational cultures must adapt. Yet, corporate cultures are enduring. They require several years to change and only with much effort.[12] Throughout all its recent turmoil signaling that IBM needed to change dramatically, the firm continued to be known for its rigid bureaucracy and rules.

Many firms have recognized the importance of changing corporate culture as they launch new strategies. New strategies based on quality may conflict with old strategies that have valued schedules and productivity. Xerox and Harley-Davidson are two examples of firms that took years to change corporate cultures to a greater emphasis on quality. Even after years of change, including winning a Malcolm Baldrige National Quality Award and regaining market share from Japanese competitors, Xerox's culture is still changing. David Kearns, former Chair of Xerox, describes the change process as "a race with no finish line".[13]

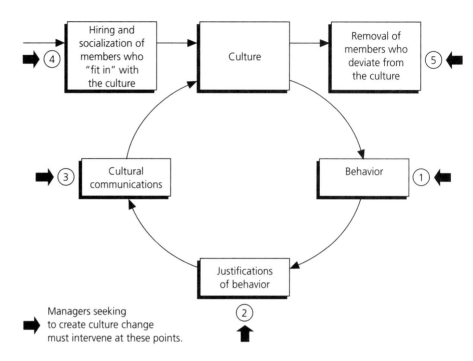

Figure 10.5 How culture perpetuates itself.

Source: Sathe, V., "Implications of corporate culture: a manager's guide to action," *Organizational Dynamics* (Autumn 1983), p. 18. Reprinted by permission of American Management Association, New York. All rights reserved.

Crisis and cultural change

Frequently it takes a survival crisis, or a near death experience, to energize an organization to change its culture from one set of values to another set of values. As noted in the Harley-Davidson case, Harley had lost over two-thirds of its market share and millions of dollars before it changed its culture to value quality. Xerox saw its market share go from nearly 100 percent to less than 15 percent before it changed its values.[14]

Culture and the status quo

There are several processes at work to keep corporate cultures stable and resistant to change. Figure 10.5 is a model of some of the stabilizing and reinforcing factors that act to keep culture in a status quo situation.

Sathe, the author of figure 10.5, argued that managers attempting to change culture are most successful if they change in the order listed in the figure.[15] The first thing to change is people's behavior. Through direction, reward, training, or other means, the manager must change the behavior of the organization's members. Training takes time, and it takes years to change reward systems because there are too many stories in the organization of the old behaviors that had been rewarded. Then, there must be cultural justifications for the behavior. New rituals, new stories, and new heros are needed to justify the new behaviors.

To change the status quo and move the culture to a new level, some organizations heavily invest in training. Wainwright Industries won a Baldrige Award in 1994 in the small business category. Wainwright invests 7 percent of its payroll in training, which is seven times the average in the USA. Motorola University employs 300 in-house and 600 out-of-house consultant teachers, with an annual budget of US$120 million.[16]

These new cultural artifacts, stories, symbols, and rituals need to be widely and consistently communicated. Procter & Gamble (P&G) managers often repeat the story of a P&G production line worker who called a customer and investigated the amount of time and the temperature at which the customer had baked a Duncan Hines angel food cake in order to solve a quality issue.[17] This story emphasizes how production line workers get involved in quality improvement, not just corporate executives.

The fourth step that a manager must take to impact culture concerns the hiring and socialization of members who match the culture. If new managers and employees are hired who already have the desired values, there are few time lags for training and socialization before the new employee can act on those values.

Lastly, a way to reinforce a culture is to remove those organizational members whose behavior deviates from the cultural values. Their removal reduces the variance in behavior and sends powerful signals to those in the organization concerning appropriate behavior. Today, termination is viewed as a last resort, as it is increasingly difficult to terminate employees and organizations have substantial investments in human resources. Many firms would prefer to pursue the other four steps first.

Organizational culture and total quality

A TQ culture has distinct organizational values and beliefs. Some describe TQ as a shift in thinking and organizational culture.[18] Transforming an organizational culture that is not based on customer value, continuous improvement, and cross-functional processes to one based upon these TQ values is a large-scale, multi-year task. The new culture needs to focus on customers and processes that yield improved value to customers.

An inwardly focused company needs to become primarily customer focused. Shortly after Lou Gerstner took over as CEO at IBM in 1993, he remarked: "I have never seen a company that is so introspective, caught up in its own underwear, so preoccupied with internal processes. Some dealings required 18 signatures. It was bureaucracy run amok."[19] From 1986 to 1993, IBM had taken US$28 billion in writeoffs and in 1993 its stock was off 75 percent from its peak in 1987.[20]

The Ritz-Carlton Hotel won a Baldrige Award in 1992 in the service company category. It reinforces its focus on the customer in a number of different ways. Employees are thoroughly trained in the hotel's Gold Standards: the hotel's credo, employees' motto, three steps of service, and 20 Ritz-Carlton Basics. To provide personalized service, computerized profiles of repeat guests' room and service preferences are maintained. About 95 percent of hotel guests leave with the impression of "a memorable visit."[21]

The concepts of organizational learning and continuous improvement (*kaizen*) are part of a TQ culture.[22] Learning about customers so that the organization can improve is key to the customer value determination system discussed in chapter 7, on customer value strategy. In many organizations, the idea of a continuous stream of small improvements is alien to the idea of "If it's not broke, don't fix it." Per figure 10.5, recognizing that the old culture is broke may take time, especially if the organization had been successful with its old culture.[23]

Leadership

What do Lee Iacocca, Ronald Reagan, Adolf Hitler, Winston Churchill, and Martin Luther King all have in common? Although they had differing motives, all were strong leaders. All had a strong influence on followers. This section examines leadership because leadership is so important in organizational life.

Importance of leadership

Just how important is this thing called leadership? Leadership is especially important in total quality organizations because TQ involves dramatic change to a new and improved way of doing business and managing operations. It takes influencial leaders to cause followers to change.

There are no known cases of firms sustaining strong TQ strategies and practices throughout the organization without the vocal and personal leadership of the firm's executives. A recent US review of the elements of success of transforming organizations along TQ lines stressed the primary role of leadership in helping an organization and its employees to make that transformation.[24] Similar findings were observed in Europe: "Of Europe's top 500 companies which are implementing TQ, interviews with the Chief Executives have shown that 90 percent believe they must lead the TQM process."[25] Leadership is a crucial factor in the Malcolm Baldrige Quality Award and the European Quality Award.

As an act of leadership, Roger Milliken, CEO of Milliken and Company, taught quality courses. Likewise, David Kearns, when he was CEO of Xerox, taught quality courses. When Robert Galvin was CEO at Motorola, he placed quality at the top of the agenda for executive meetings.[26]

Managers: leaders or administrators

Recall that management focuses on delivering customer value. Management is not strictly internally focused administration.

Administration is the operation of internal systems. Therefore, in bureaucratically administered organizations, administration can be completely divorced from the customer. Thus, an administrator in a government agency may be a bureaucratic administrator who consistently follows the rules, but ignores the customer.

Leadership is influencing people toward the accomplishment of goals. Leadership is associated with the determination of goals, a vision for the future, and change to reach the goals and the future. Leadership is about helping people to do things they would not normally do.

Formal versus informal leadership

Formal leadership is associated with those who have the explicit designation from the organization as the leader. Whether elected or appointed, the formal leader has a position as the leader of the group.

Often within a group, *an individual emerges as the informal leader*, who influences group members even without the formal designation. Formally designated leaders are wise to partner with the informal leader to help influence organizational members. This is particularly true in TQ organizations that have empowered individuals to work on systems improvement to deliver greater value to customers. Entire levels of formally designated managers may be eliminated and replaced by trained leaderless groups. Self-managed teams without a formally designated leader may operate to serve the customers' needs.

Organizational leadership versus interpersonal leadership

Leaders are found in organizations and in interpersonal situations. The biggest difference is the establishment and communication of the goals. An organizational leader will spend considerable effort to formulate and articulate the goals to be implemented. The formulation and articulation of the goals establishes the direction for change. By articulating the goals, the organizational members can buy into the goals or reject them. For example, executives at Saturn ask the workers to buy into the notion of producing high-quality cars in self-managed groups.

An interpersonal leader may try to influence others for the sake of his or her individual needs and personal goals. Gang leaders are examples of interpersonal leaders who sometimes influence others to exhibit socially unacceptable behavior.

Transformational/charismatic leadership and total quality

Individuals who have exceptional impact on their organizations and its people are called charismatic or transformational leaders.[27] *Transformational or charismatic leaders* are leaders who through their personal vision, energy and values inspire followers and thus have a major impact on organizational success. Charismatic leaders articulate a vision or higher-level goal that captures followers' commitment and energies. They lead by their own example and are careful to behave in accord with the values they espouse for the followers.

Mother Theresa, Martin Luther King, Winston Churchill, and Mahatma Gandhi are examples of transformational or charismatic leaders. Unfortunately, Adolf Hitler and Mussolini were also charismatic leaders. The power of the charismatic or transformational leader is independent of the "goodness" of the vision articulated by the leader.

When he took over as CEO at Xerox in 1982, it would have been easy for David Kearns to maintain the status quo. However, in an act of transformational leadership, he helped the organization and its members to recognize that they must change dramatically and quickly to deliver quality to the customer in order to survive and grow.[28] He helped them see that they were in a new era of global competition from several Japanese copier firms, like Canon, Minolta and Sharp, that had targeted Xerox. Since Xerox could no longer take its customers for granted,

Xerox had to reinvent itself and find new ways to deliver value to customers. Kearns also influenced US universities to change in a TQ direction when he started the TQ Fora series of meetings between industry and academia on the subject in 1989. Kearns left the well-paying and highly respected job as CEO of Xerox to become Under Secretary of Education so that he could help improve the quality of the US educational system.

Leadership, empowerment, and self-managed work teams

The very role of managers as leaders as defined in this chapter is increasingly being questioned. An increasing number of organizations recognize that the role of the manager is to establish, stabilize, and continuously improve the system and processes of work for employees.

Such a concept of management suggests that managers work on the systems. Once the processes have been established, managers concentrate on training employees to enable them to operate the processes. Managers should also empower employees to solve problems in real time rather than refer all problems to managers. Such an empowerment role is less directive than several traditional leadership models. Flatter organization structures with broader spans of control further limit the interaction and direction of the "leader" with the subordinates.[29]

In 1993, Honda of America used a slight downturn in production as a way to intensify further its commitment to worker training. Honda doubled the amount of technical training for workers from 5,000 hours to 10,000 hours in the first quarter of 1993 in its Ohio plant.[30] The technical training included study of the jobs of co-workers. In such a fashion, Honda increased the ability of the workers and co-workers to function without direction from a formal leader. This practice of using slow downs in production to increase training contrasts with the United Automobile Workers Union and the Big Three from Detroit, who use slow downs to give workers time off with pay.

Some organizations are training subordinates so thoroughly in cross-functional teams that the traditional role of managers as leaders has evolved. Since self-managed work teams have the power to make the operating decisions and operate the systems, managers need not supervise as in the past. Milliken and Company reported that some of its plants operate second and third shift without managers in the plant. Saturn is structured so that self-managed groups of employees perform most of the traditional managerial/supervisory functions. Nordstrom Department Stores publishes a rule for its employees: "Rule no. 1: Use your good judgment in all situations. There will be no additional rules."[31] These trends limit the role of traditional formal leadership in organizations, and underline the importance of continual employee training. Teams and empowerment are so important that chapter 9 explores those topics in detail.

Motivation

One of the most often used terms among managers is the word "motivation". It is a misunderstood term that has been used to praise some managers ("Coach Holz is a great motivator"), and to explain poor performance ("I was just not motivated").

This section defines motivation, recognizes the importance of motivation for the individual and for managers, and reviews the role of individual motivation in system performance.

Motivation defined

There are several different definitions of motivation. Some are concerned with the source of motivation. Is motivation an internal state, or is motivation externally reinforced and controlled by others? Can managers motivate others by linking rewards to desired work outcomes in a process of motivation?

Since managers cannot observe a state inside an individual, motivation is defined such that it is observable. *Motivation* is the amount of energy and direction of energy displayed by an individual.[32] An individual can be greatly motivated in one setting, but poorly motivated in another. Thus, it makes no sense to make an overall statement about the person's motivation without knowing the amount and the direction.

A college student can display high motivation to perform on a football team. He may practice football vigorously, and consistently lift weights to increase his strength. Yet the same student may display poor motivation to perform in the classroom. Without being forced by the coach to attend classes and study hall, the student may display no effort to perform academically. So it is necessary to describe the direction of the effort and energies to fully describe the motivation.

Importance of motivation

Motivation is critical to understanding job performance. When motivation is mixed with the individual's ability, then the manager can forecast the individual's performance. Many organizations invest heavily in training to increase the ability of employees to perform their jobs. If the person's ability is non-existent, then the resulting performance can be disastrous no matter how high the motivation is. For example, a person may be highly motivated to fly a jet aircraft. But a crash may result if the person does not have the ability from training.

Motivation and ability interact to yield high individual performance. The interaction is described as a multiplicative effect, i.e. performance = motivation × ability. If either motivation or ability is zero, then the performance is zero.

Motivation and system effects

What is the role of the system in determining performance? Noting that systems are the responsibility of management, Deming estimated that 94 percent of problems are due to the system.[33] To attain the best performance from motivated employees, they must work in a consistent system that allows them to perform highly.[34]

One of a manager's prime functions is to design and improve the system that employees operate. Managers need to design stable processes with the right activities and the right resources at the right time for employees to perform well. The combination of motivation, ability, and the system yields job performance, as depicted in figure 10.6. Performance provides feedback information which impacts subsequent motivation.

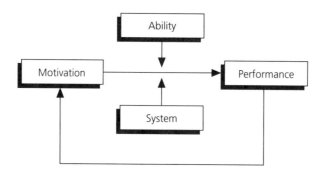

Figure 10.6   Motivation and system effects on performance.

Part of the systems management work is the design and consistent operation of rewards and incentives systems tied to desired behavior. These systems reinforce motivation and channel motivated behavior in the desired directions. It often takes years for an organization to change its reward system from one based on individual performance to one based on team performance. It is also a long-term change to switch from rewarding short-term financial results to rewarding customer value. Federal Express won a Baldrige Award partly because it understands the role of motivated people in a service business.

Individuals from different ethnic backgrounds and different countries may have different needs. Thus, managers need to be aware of the differing needs of their workers and not assume that they will all respond uniformly.

The Communication Process

Communication is the process by which information is shared and understood by two or more people. In this section, we stress the process of understanding the information as new communication patterns arise in changing organizations.

Organizational communication
In today's organizations, communication processes extend throughout the organization in a number of different ways. The formal and the informal, the vertical and the horizontal must all be used in concert by the effective communicator in a multi-pronged communication network throughout the organization.

Formal communication
Formal communication flows along the lines of the organization prescribed by management. Years ago in a hierarchical organization, this had meant top-down communication. In many organizations today, this means top-down, bottom-up, and horizontal communication in accord with designated cross-functional systems and processes.

Formal communication flows horizontally in a hospital, following a patient as the patient moves across departments from chemotherapy, to diet and nutrition, to physical therapy. Such horizontal communication is as legitimate as communication within the physical therapy department. Similarly, formal communication flows laterally in the Chrysler Design Center, including design, manufacturing, and marketing in the development of a new car. Such horizontal communication is as valid as communication within the design department.

Informal communication

Informal communication flows in the organization independently of the structure prescribed by management. Nearly every organization has an informal communication network, sometimes known as a grapevine, that is independent of the formal structure and formal communication channels. Cafeterias, mail rooms, break rooms, wellness clubs, and other places where employees gather are places where informal communication networks are found. The wise manager is not only aware of such communication networks, but uses them as part of the communication process.

Vertical communication

Vertical communication flows upward or downward in the organization. Many managers are good at issuing communications to lower levels in the organization and thus have come to regard vertical communication primarily as top-down communication. However, effective managers also recognize the importance of upward communication and will reinforce bottom-up communication. Such upward communication is a recognition of feedback and the value of a two-way communication process. Sometimes, upward communication is not pleasant for managers because it may reveal that all is not well in the organization. Nonetheless, the manager committed to continuous improvement recognizes that feedback from lower organizational levels is needed to uncover problems as a prelude to system improvement. Managers who do not encourage upward communication are akin to the ostrich with its head in the sand.

Lateral communication

As process improvement thinking has spread throughout organizations, the use of cross-functional teams to design and improve horizontal processes has exploded. As much work is done horizontally, so flows much communication. New product design and development teams at Xerox, which include members from most functional areas, are rich in horizontal communication processes. Not only is there lateral communication within the team, there is also lateral communication with the functional home offices in production, marketing, finance, etc. In such a fashion, a large part of the organization is kept abreast of the development of the new products.

Communication networks

The effective communicator uses formal and informal communication processes together, as well as vertical and horizontal communication processes. All the communication processes are used in concert in a multi-pronged communication network throughout the organization. By criss-crossing the entire organization in a number of ways, effective communication is reinforced. By using both vertical communication processes and horizontal processes through teams, managers at NUMMI span the organization with a communication network.

Communication processes are spread throughout organizational life. People are constantly transmitting information, and hopefully meaning, to others. The importance of good communication only grows as organizations become more diverse. As organizations become international in their scope of operations and in their personnel, clear communications become critical. The case on NUMMI shows the importance of good communication between people of different nationalities and different experiences. The case also shows the importance of lateral communication processes in an organization using cross-functional teams.

McDonald's has a limited number of wholly owned subsidiaries throughout the world. To insure clear communications, they have staffed with locals. In Beijing, Chinese staff the McDonald's.[35]

Communication and total quality

In many organizations, TQ is a change from traditional ways of doing business with an internal and profit focus. Focusing on the customer requires new ways of operating and behaving. Leadership pointing to a new vision of the future requires extensive and multidimensional communication of that vision to all concerned. Managers, employees, and suppliers must understand the importance of customers to the organization before they can commit themselves to such a vision.

The importance of communication in TQ

TQM is an abbreviation for total quality management. However, some refer to TQM as total quality mayhem when executives and employees are out of sync. This caused the authors of a book on quality to remark: "Until consensus is reached between executives and employees about how to go about achieving quality, there will be a great deal of wasted effort – or no effort at all."[36]

Communications are important in all organizations. However, they are especially important in customer-focused organizations because of the importance of horizontal processes involving people of varied organizational allegiances. Marketing personnel may have the same allegiance, speak the same language, and use similar assumptions. Production personnel may have their own set of assumptions, allegiances, and technical jargon. In an organization with cross-functional teams, communication is even more important to help personnel to deal across those different sets of jargon, assumptions, and allegiances.

Bowles and Hammond offered the Ten Commandments of Continuous Improvement, including a commandment on communication. They urged managers to discuss the undiscussibles.[37] In some corporate cultures that have had a history of success, breeding arrogance, it is near heresy to admit that quality needs to be improved. It would be unspeakable to admit that the firm needs an enterprise-wide, indefinite commitment to redesigning horizontal processes and refocusing on the customer.[38] That is why some TQ efforts take years in the birthing. Like an alcoholic who must admit that he or she has a problem before recovery can begin, an organization in need of a commitment to the customer and quality first must admit that the organization needs to improve the quality of its products and services.

Total quality communication guidelines

Communication is so important to a TQ process that recent lessons from Baldrige winners included "steps for developing a communication strategy." These include stating quality objectives in the business plan in the same way that cost and schedule are included. They also include requiring each unit to prepare an annual communication plan in support of the organization's implementation plan.[39]

Some advise selecting a name for the firm's total quality effort.[40] It is interesting to observe how many organizations have followed this communication advice and selected a custom name for their corporate total quality effort. To name a few, Alcoa refers to "Excellence through Quality"; Allied Signal refers to "Total Quality Leadership"; IBM refers to "Market Driven Quality"; Procter & Gamble refers to "Total Quality"; and Xerox refers to "Leadership through Quality". Each firm must brand a title to fit its own unique history and culture.

▮ Summary ▮

Organizational culture consists of the key values and beliefs that are shared by organizational members. As such, culture may not be readily observable. In addition to values and beliefs, another part of culture that is not observable consists of the underlying assumptions beneath the values and beliefs. These assumptions are the very foundation of the organization's culture. The assumptions may be so widely shared by organizational members that they are unaware of them.

The observable part of culture in organizations consists of the artifacts and the behavior of its members. The artifacts and behavior may take several noteworthy forms, including symbols, stories, heroes, slogans, and ceremonies that signify the organizational values. A symbol is usually an object that conveys meaning to others. Stories are descriptions of actual organizational events that characterize the values of the organization. Heroes are individuals who personify the culture of the organization. A slogan is a short saying that captures a key organizational value. Ceremonies are special activities that communicate organizational values.

Managers need to know the key levers and mechanisms to use to develop and reinforce the desired culture. These managerial actions include: the behaviors leaders measure and control; the leaders' reactions to crises; modeling and coaching of expected behaviors; the criteria for allocation of rewards; and the criteria for selection, promotion, and termination of employees.

New organizational members undergo a learning process concerning organizational life, called socialization. It is a process by which a new member learns and adapts to the organization that he or she has joined.

A prime purpose of organizational culture is behavioral conformity. The organization is interested in the member behaving in ways that further organizational goals. Faced with such pressures for conformity in values and behavior, the member has at least four choices. The individual can conform or not to the values and beliefs of the organization, and the individual can conform or not to the behavior prescribed by the culture.

As environments change, the organizational cultures must change. Yet corporate cultures are enduring. They require several years to change and only with much effort. Frequently it takes a survival crisis to energize an organization to change its culture from one set of values to another set of values.

Leadership is influencing people toward the accomplishment of goals. Those goals can be organizational goals or the personal goals of the leader. Some of the world's nastiest leaders, like Adolf Hitler, had great influence over followers.

Formal leadership is associated with those who have the explicit designation from the organization as the designated leader. Whether elected or appointed, the formal leader has a positional or formal designation as the leader of the group. Often within a group, an individual emerges, known as an informal leader, who influences group members even without the designation as leader. Formally designated leaders are wise to partner with the informal leader to influence organizational members.

Transformational or charismatic leaders are leaders who, through their personal vision, energy and values, inspire followers and thus have a major impact on organizational success. Many TQ journeys start and are sustained by transformational leaders who have an unyielding vision of the importance of serving the customer. The concepts of leaders as empowerers and self-managed work teams observed in many total quality organizations challenge traditional concepts of leadership.

Motivation is the amount of energy and direction of energy displayed by an individual. Motivation is critical to an understanding of job performance. When motivation is mixed with the individual's ability, then the manager can forecast the individual's performance.

Communication is the process by which information is shared and understood by two or more people. Organizational communication today takes many paths and forms. The effective communicator recognizes that both formal and informal communication processes can be used to increase the odds of effective communication. As many organizations become flatter, with more cross-functional teams, lateral communication processes grow in importance along with upward communication processes. The effective manager recognizes that downward vertical communication is just one form of communication. Communication is especially important in organizations making a shift to a TQ strategy because of the change involved. The change means that organizational members must be informed, lest chaos result. Executives should show by their non-verbal communication, i.e. their behavior, that they are committed. To communicate the link between the firm's culture and TQ, it is not unusual for each organization to invent its own unique label.

DISCUSSION QUESTIONS

1 Why should managers focus on the values and beliefs part of organizational culture rather than just behavior?

2 How do reward systems and hiring and termination systems reinforce corporate culture?

3 Describe the kinds of organizations that would favor mavericks over good soldiers.

4 Explain why cultural change takes so much time.

5 Describe the importance of informal leaders in TQ organizations.

6 Relate the concepts of leaders as empowerers and self-managed work teams to traditional concepts of leadership.

7 How do motivation, ability and the system all interact to yield performance?

8 What are the roles of formal and informal communication in a communication network?

9 How can a manager strengthen informal communication flows?

KEY TERMS

Administration	is the operation of internal systems.
Artifacts	are the signs and products of culture.
Ceremonies	are special activities that communicate organizational values.
Communication	is the process by which information is shared and understood by two or more people.
Formal leadership	is associated with those who have the explicit designation from the organization as the leader.
Heroes	are people who personify the culture of the organization.
The informal leader	influences group members, even without the formal designation.
Informal socialization	is the process by which a new member learns and adapts to the informal organization.
Kaizen	is the Japanese concept of continuous improvement.
Leadership	is influencing people toward accomplishing goals.
Motivation	is the amount of energy and direction of energy displayed by an individual.
Organizational culture	consists of the key values and beliefs that are shared by organizational members.
Organizational socialization	is a process by which a new member learns and adapts to the new organization that he or she has joined.
Slogans	are short sayings that capture key organizational values.
Stories	are descriptions of actual organizational events that characterize the values of the organization.
A symbol	is usually an object that conveys meaning to others.
Transformational or charismatic leaders	are leaders who, through their personal vision, energy and values, inspire followers and thus have a major impact on organizational success.

The *Kaizen* Culture at Toyota and NUMMI

Toyota struggled to produce passenger cars beginning in the late 1930s, but the Japanese military hampered these efforts and demanded trucks to support the coming war effort. After the Second World War, the company again attempted to enter the passenger vehicle market, with limited success. In 1950, thirteen years after entering the market, Toyota had produced a total of 2685 cars. In comparison, Ford's famed Rouge manufacturing facility was producing 7,000 cars per day.[a] No one could have predicted that Toyota would become the world's third largest automaker, with over US$94 billion in sales by 1995.[b]

As a young Toyota engineer in 1950, Eiji Toyoda (a member of the founding family) visited Ford's Rouge plant for three months and wrote back to headquarters that he thought "there were some possibilities to improve the production system."[c] Together, he and Toyota's top engineer, Taiichi Ohno, began to develop the revolutionary new Japanese-style Toyota production system that eventually came to be known as "lean" production, which contrasted to American-style "mass" production.

Importing American production techniques was not possible because of the relatively tiny scale of Japanese production. Post-war Toyota could not afford to run the large batches and store the huge inventories of finished parts that the Americans did. Instead, the company needed to produce small batches just before they were assembled on to automobiles and to eliminate the need to carry large amounts of inventory. One way this was accomplished was the flexible use of one production line to make several different parts. In order to do this, Ohno and Toyoda developed a method of changing the multi-ton dies used to stamp out parts that took only a few minutes and could be performed by the production workers. The impact of this innovation was enormous. It not only enabled Toyota to produce cars with many fewer press lines than Americans, it made it possible to identify mistakes almost immediately, eliminating wasteful production. The changes also required a highly skilled workforce that was trained to think about entire processes and solve problems.

Another innovation was the use of *kanbans*. *Kanbans* are simply cards that are used as signals that set a limit on the size of work-in-progress inventories, essentially the queues that build up in front of a production process. When no *kanbans* are available, enough parts have been made on the given line to satisfy the current production needs and work stops, but the workers don't. They use this idle time to perform die changes or maintenance, engage in problem solving, or help out somewhere else on the line. *Kanbans* promote the efficient use of time and eliminate the practice of building unneeded inventories just in case they are needed. This simple *kanban* idea was extremely difficult to implement because it practically eliminated the "safety-net" of inventories. It also required much more vigilance to anticipate problems before the entire production process ground to a halt.

More fundamental than *kanbans*, the principle of *kaizen* or continuous improvement is a way to get at the root causes of problems and fix them. Improvement is not obtained in quantum leaps forward, but in incremental improvements that help to improve the overall process. For example, workers analyzing all aspects of a problem may discover that it is due to a cause like poor scheduling, poor part design, or excess scrap. The worker's job would be to find a way to eliminate the problem by making changes to the schedule, redesigning the questionable part, or changing the process to eliminate scrap. Complete devotion to *kaizen* helped to propel Toyota quickly up the learning curve because improvements could be implemented faster.

Undoubtedly, characteristics of the Asian culture helped Toyota to achieve its success. Research on differences among 12 capitalist countries suggests the following differences between American and Japanese organizational views:[d]

American	Japanese
Analytic and reductive	Oriented toward larger integrated wholes
Focused on profit	Focused on well-being of stakeholders
Competition is crucial	Cooperation is crucial among businesses

These cultural differences may also help to explain why American automakers have traditionally seen themselves as a collection of different functions performed by individuals. Alternatively, Japanese automakers have tended to see their organization as a group of people whose functioning depends on social interaction. At a time when Ford delegated quality improvements to be the function of a department, Toyota considered *kaizen* to be the responsibility of every employee.

Today, Toyota is arguably the best automaker in the world. In the USA, it is the third biggest selling brand overall, and the biggest selling import brand, with 26 percent of the import market in 1995.[e] The *kaizen* culture instilled in workers throughout the company will continue to make Toyota a tough competitor in spite of unfavorable market conditions. Aggressive cost cutting has cut about US$700 off the cost of producing a car in Japan and shipping it to the USA, offsetting much of the decline of the dollar against the yen. Toyota claims it can cut more costs by further reengineering its factories and vehicles.

Clearly, culture can be the source of sustainable competitive advantage. Just as American innovativeness made the USA an industrial leader throughout most of the century, Japan's *kaizen* culture is proving to be an important source of industrial leadership for the next century.

General Motors was so impressed by Toyota, that GM launched a 50–50 joint venture with Toyota, referred to as New United Motor Manufacturing, Inc. NUMMI, which began production in late 1984, assembles smaller sized cars designed by Toyota. It is located in Fremont, California, and employs about 2,500 people. The plant receives components and parts from Toyota plants and suppliers in Japan and from suppliers in the United States. The cars it assembles are sold to marketing organizations belonging to each of its parent companies. GM hoped to learn from NUMMI and transfer those learnings to other GM sites.

NUMMI utilizes the "just-in-time" inventory system that Toyota developed in Japan. All components, parts, and sub-assemblies flow together in a continuous process paced by the main assembly line. Suppliers deliver their products to the NUMMI plant on a nearly continuous basis – in some cases, every few hours or so. There is minimal inventory and little testing or inspection of supplier-provided parts.

NUMMI works with qualified suppliers on a long-term basis. Cooperation among members of the supply chain is key. Suppliers work on the design and quality of their products, with substantial assistance from NUMMI when required. Purchase relationships are of indefinite duration. Suppliers know what is expected of them in terms of product schedule and quality. They also know that NUMMI will help them solve problems.

The Japanese concept of *kaizen*, or continuous improvement, has been successfully integrated into the NUMMI culture. The plant is a "living" institution. It is constantly learning and changing. Work teams focus on how to improve what they are doing. Job rotation and cross-training, which give workers a more complete perspective on the production process, are integral aspects of every worker's development.

It is important to note that there are really four partners in this joint venture, not just Toyota and GM. The United Automobile Workers (UAW) and the employees themselves are also very important partners. The UAW has been especially accommodative in developing "new" ways of doing things. For example, it has accepted non-traditional wage systems and pay classifications. The work environment at NUMMI is much less adversarial than that of its predecessor. The evidence is solid on this. At any given time five or six grievances (i.e. workers' complaints against management that allege a violation of the labor agreement) are usually outstanding at NUMMI. Yet a few years back, when the same plant was run by GM (and eventually shut down), the outstanding grievances typically totaled at least 1,000. Absenteeism at NUMMI is about 5 to 6 percent; it was 20 percent or more under the prior operator. Interestingly, about 80 percent of the workers now covered by the labor agreement at NUMMI also worked at the plant under the prior operator. NUMMI has been doing quite well in terms of its union–management relations. Moreover, the Toyota production system and methods of workforce organization have been implemented at NUMMI and are operating well. NUMMI is also doing quite well compared to Toyota plants in Japan. Product quality at NUMMI is as high as that at Toyota's plants in Japan. Worker efficiency is close to that of Toyota's plants in Japan and higher than originally expected.[f] It appears that the *kaizen* culture has been successfully transplanted and implemented as a competitive advantage.

Discussion Questions

1 What role did American production technology play in the development of new production methods at Toyota?

2 How important were the *kanban* and *kaizen* principles to quality improvement at Toyota?

3 What significance does culture play in the way American and Japanese managers approach business?

4 Describe the major cultural differences between the traditional US managerial system that had been practiced in a unionized plant, and Toyota's management approach at NUMMI.

Sources: **a.** Womack, J., Jones, D. and Roos, D., *The Machine that Changed the World*. New York: Harper (1990), p. 48;   **b.** "Toyota Motor", *Value Line Investment Survey* (March 17, 1995), p. 112;   **c.** Womack, J., Jones, D. and Roos, D., *The Machine that Changed the World*, p. 49;   **d.** Hampden-Turner, C. and Trompenaars, A., *The Seven Cultures of Capitalism*. New York: Currency Doubleday (1993), p. 32;   **e.** "Best-selling 10 auto imports," *The Market Share Reporter* (1995), p. 1028.   **f.** Grosse, R. and Kujawa, D., *International Business*. Chicago: Irwin (1992), pp. 344–8.

INTERNATIONAL

C   A   S   E

JARDINE MATHESON AND HONG KONG

Jardine Matheson (JM) is one of the oldest and largest trading companies in Asia. The company's business roots are in import/export services, but its diversified businesses include real estate, banking, financial services, insurance, retail establishments, supermarkets, restaurants, shipping, and hotels.[a] Sales in 1995 were US$10.6 billion and have averaged more than 16 percent growth over the previous five years.[b]

The current management under *taipan* ("big boss") Alaisdair Morrison is very cautious. JM hopes to continue conducting the bulk of its business (57 percent) in Hong Kong and China after the British colony is returned to Chinese sovereignty in 1997. Nevertheless, the company has taken measures to reduce the potential risks to its shareholders of conducting business under communist rule.[c]

JM's culture is intertwined with the history and culture of Hong Kong and trade with the Far East, especially China. It is impossible to understand the company's present situation without some knowledge of its tumultuous history in the region. One thing has remained constant in both good and bad times – JM has played a central role.

The European trading companies founded in the early seventeenth century were some of the earliest manifestations of multinational corporate capitalism. Organized by private investors, these companies were chartered to explore and exploit parts of the world. The Dutch East Indies Company, Hudson's Bay Company, and East India Company were created during this time. It was under the auspices of the East India Company in 1820 that two Scottish traders and adventurers, William Jardine and James Matheson, met in Canton, China. Their partnership led to the 1832 opening of the trading company that bears their names.[d]

JM's successes and failures in trade with China over the next 165 years were determined by the social, economic, and political forces in the area.

- Until 1842, JM and all "foreign barbarians" in China were restricted to Canton by the xenophobic Manchu government, which believed that China was the center of the universe and already possessed all things in abundance.[e]
- JM amassed a fortune in tea and silk exports, but the problem arose of how to pay the Chinese. JM found and shipped the one thing China didn't have in abundance – Indian opium.
- When the Chinese government tried to stop the opium trade by destroying 20,000 filled chests, JM called the British forces to defeat the Chinese in what is known as the First Opium War. The resulting 1842 Treaty of Nanking opened five Chinese ports and ceded Hong Kong (JM's new headquarters) to the British. Successive defeats opened the rest of China to trade.[f]
- JM became more than a trading company. It was a major force in building the economic infrastructure of China. JM opened silk factories, operated textile mills, sent the first steamships to China, built China's first railway, operated mines, published a newspaper, and introduced a sugar refinery. By 1872 it had exited the offensive opium trade.
- JM built a successful and cooperative relationship that continued as China developed its economy on its own. Shanghai became as important a center for JM as Hong Kong until Japan invaded China in 1937.
- When Japan invaded Hong Kong during the Second World War, JM suspended operations until after the war.[g]
- The *taipan* after the war, John Keswick, began to rebuild JM assets in China and remained neutral in the political struggle between nationalist and communist forces. Communist forces took over in 1949. By 1954, JM has written off its US$20 million worth of nationalized Chinese assets.[h]
- Trade with China has continued to the present through state-run trading houses, except during the 1966–9 "Cultural Revolution." Since 1972, JM has been allowed to open three offices in China. Although business on mainland China now accounts for only a small percentage of total sales, JM has never given up hope of again increasing business there.[i]
- Although it has been a public company since 1966, control of JM has largely remained with members of the Keswick family, descendants of William Jardine's nephew.[j]

JM's history in Hong Kong tells a different story. No company has enjoyed the almost symbiotic relationship with Hong Kong that JM has. It used to be a common saying that Hong Kong is run by Jardine Matheson, the Royal Hong Kong Jockey Club, and the colonial government – in that order.[k] Some of the important milestones are:

- The very idea of Hong Kong as a British colony from which traders could operate was the idea of a JM *taipan* after the first opium war. JM was the first company to purchase land on Hong Kong and locate its headquarters there.[l]
- JM organized or built much of the infrastructure of Hong Kong, beginning with the ports and ferry service to and from the island. Nine streets are named after JM *taipans*.[m]
- JM benefited from the explosive growth that transformed Hong Kong into an international hub for trade and commerce after the Second World War. Refugees from China poured into the colony, helping to increase the population to 5.5 million from 500,000 in the 50 years after the war.[n]
- Hong Kong's economy is often considered capitalism in its purest form. There are 128 banks and 32 airline services, and 20,000 ocean vessels call at the free port of Hong Kong each year.[o]
- As Hong Kong has grown, JM's influence has diminished. The power and wealth of Hong Kong and other Asian Chinese entrepreneurs have exceeded JM's.

- In 1984, Britain agreed to return Hong Kong to China in 1997.
- In an effort to protect shareholders from the eventual rule of the National People's Congress, JM was the first to move its corporate registration to Bermuda in 1984. In 1992, JM moved its stock listings to Singapore. Both moves angered China and the Hong Kong government.[p]

With this colorful history as the backdrop, and with corporate governance legally protected outside of Hong Kong, the conciliatory tone of the current *taipan*, Alasdair Morrison, makes sense. Although the Chinese government has prevented JM from receiving some large contracts,[q] Morrison would like to resolve their differences and build a reputation of sincerity. At a 1995 Chamber of Commerce meeting, Mr Morrison sounded almost apologetic when he said, "Some of Jardine's actions have caused offense in China in recent years. That is a matter of regret to us."[r]

Mr Morrison has strongly emphasized JM's faith in Hong Kong. He likens the changes in corporate governance to the hundreds of thousands of Hong Kongers who have obtained foreign passports, "not because they want to leave, but because they want to feel comfortable about staying on."[s] He is also quick to remind the Chinese that JM is still Hong Kong's largest employer, with a local payroll of 58,000 and a total of 220,000 worldwide. In addition, the majority of JM's profits continue to come from Hong Kong.[t]

If foreign investors shy away from doing business with China, the new government may be hard pressed for allies. In this context, JM's message is clear. It hopes that China would prefer to deal with the "foreign devils" it knows. No other company has traded with China for as long as JM, throughout the turns of history. No other company can offer China the unique cultural experience, the business expertise in Asia, the desire, and the ability to bridge the international gap between East and West. And few companies have US$1 billion in cash that they are willing to invest in Hong Kong.

Only time will tell if JM's cautious optimism and the *taipan*'s leadership will pay off. Uncertainty about Hong Kong's future has had a predictably negative affect on JM's earnings as 1997 approaches. Even though the times have changed tremendously, there is one JM tradition that hasn't changed for most of its history. JM still fires guns over Victoria Harbor daily at noon from the East Point site where it opened its office in 1842, celebrating its status as the original *hong* ("big company") of Hong Kong.[u]

Discussion Questions

1 How has the external culture and history of the region affected Jardine Matheson's relationship with the Chinese?

2 If Jardine Matheson wants to stay in Hong Kong and trade with the Chinese, why has the company moved its headquarters and stock listing out of Hong Kong?

3 Explain why hiring the new *taipan*, Alasdair Morrison, might be an important part of improving relations with China.

Sources: **a.** "Jardine Matheson Holdings Limited," *Hoovers Handbook of World Business*. Austin, TX: Reference Press (1995), p. 286; **b.** "Jardine Matheson Holdings Limited," *Compact Disclosure* (December 1995); **c.** Gargan, E., "Jardine Matheson's new humility," *International Herald Tribune* (December 2–3, 1995), p. 15; **d.** Moskowitz, M., "Jardine Matheson," in *The Global Marketplace*. New York: Macmillan (1987), pp. 308–9; **e.** "Jardine Matheson Holdings Ltd.," *Corporate Histories*. Chicago: St James Press (1988), p. 468; **f.** Moskowitz, M., "Jardine Matheson," p. 310; **g.** "Jardine Matheson Holdings Ltd.," *Corporate Histories*, p. 469; **h.** Ibid.; **i.** Moskowitz, M., "Jardine Matheson," p. 315; **j.** Ibid., p. 314; **k.** "Jardine Matheson Holdings Ltd.," *Corporate Histories*, p. 468; **l.** Moskowitz, M., "Jardine Matheson," p. 315; **m.** Ibid.; **n.** Ibid., p. 316; **o.** Ibid.; **p.** Karp, J., "Island hopping," *Far Eastern Economic Review* (April 7, 1994), p. 73; **q.** Lindorff, D., "A nasty little shoving match in Hong Kong," *Business Week* (October 3, 1994), p. 68; **r.** "The taipan and the dragon," *The Economist* (April 8, 1995), p. 62; **s.** Ibid.; **t.** Gargan, E., "Jardine Matheson's new humility," p. 15; **u.** Moskowitz, M., "Jardine Matheson," p. 315.

NOTES

1 Schein, E., *Organizational Culture and Leadership*. San Francisco: Jossey-Bass (1985), p. 14.

2 Ibid.

3 Land's End, Inc. *Annual Report*. Dodgeville, WI: Land's End, Inc. (1992).

4 Trompenaars, F., *Riding the Waves of Culture: Understanding Cultural Diversity in Business*. London: Economist Books (1993).

5 Schein, E., *Organizational Culture and Leadership*. San Francisco: Jossey-Bass (1985), pp. 223–43.

6 "Ouster of Schulhof leaves focus fuzzy at Sony Entertainment," *Wall Street Journal* (December 6, 1995), p. A1.

7 Schein, E., "Organizational socialization and the profession of management," in Boone, L. and Bowen, D. (eds), *The Great Writings in Management and Organizational Behavior*. Tulsa, OK: Penn Well Books (1980), p. 392.

8 Sathe, V., "Implications of corporate culture: a manager's guide to action," *Organizational Dynamics* (Autumn 1983), p. 15.

9 Deal, T. and Kennedy, A., *Corporate Cultures: the Rites and Rituals of Corporate Life*. Reading, MA: Addison-Wesley (1982).

10 Hofstede, G., *Cultures and Organizations*. London: McGraw-Hill (1991), p. 182.

11 "Japan's business cartels are starting to erode, but change is slow," *Wall Street Journal* (December 4, 1995), p. A1.

12 Lorsch, J., "Managing culture: the invisible barrier to strategic change," *California Management Review* (1986), pp. 95–109.

13 Kearns, D. and Nadler, D., *Prophets in the Dark: How Xerox Reinvented Itself and Beat Back the Japanese*. New York: HarperCollins (1992), p. 257.

14 Ibid., p. xiv.

15 Sathe, V., "Implications of corporate culture: a manager's guide to action," *Organizational Dynamics* (Autumn 1983), pp. 5–23.

16 Nadkarni, R. A., "A not-so-secret recipe for successful TQM," *Quality Progress* (November, 1995), p. 94.

17 "Procter & Gamble rewrites the marketing rules," *Fortune* (November 6, 1989), p. 91.

18 Waldman, D., "What is TQM research?" *Canadian Journal of Administrative Sciences*, 12(2) (1995), p. 91.

19 "Rethinking IBM," *Business Week* (October 4, 1993), pp. 88–9.

20 Ibid., p. 87.

21 Nadkarni, R. A., "A not-so-secret recipe for successful TQM," *Quality Progress* (November, 1995), p. 92.

22 Senge, P., *The Fifth Discipline: The Art and Practice of the Learning Organization*. New York: Doubleday (1990); Sitkin, S., Sutcliffe, K. and Schroeder, R., "Distinguishing control from learning in TQM," *Academy of Management Review*, 19 (July 1994), pp. 537–64.

23 Hatch, M., "The dynamics of organizational culture," *Academy of Management Review*, 18 (October 1993), pp. 657–93.

24 Cole, R., "Introduction," Special Issue on Total Quality Management, *California Management Review* (Spring 1993), p. 8.

25 Spenley, P., "TQ executive skills: the key to success or failure," A TQM Special Report, British Quality Foundation, London (1995), p. 8.

26 Nadkarni, R. A., "A not-so-secret recipe for successful TQM," *Quality Progress* (November, 1995), p. 92.

27 Tichy, N. M. and Ulrich, D. O., "The leadership challenge – a call for the transformational leader," *Sloan Management Review*, 26 (Fall 1984), pp. 59–68.

28 Kearns, D. T. and Nadler, D. A., *Prophets in the Dark: How Xerox Reinvented Itself and Beat Back the Japanese*. New York: Harper Business (1992).

29 Ebrahimpour, M. and Withers, B., "Employee involvement in quality improvement: a comparison of American and Japanese manufacturing firms operating in the US," *IEEE Transactions on Engineering Management*, 39 (May 1992), pp. 142–8; Harber, D., Marriott, F. and Idrus, N., "Employee participation in TQC: an integrative review," *International Journal of Quality and Reliability Management*, 8(5) (1991), pp. 24–34.

30 "Back to school for Honda workers," *The New York Times* (March 29, 1993), p. D1.

31 Peffer, J. "Producing sustainable competitive advantage through the effective management of people," *Academy of Management Executive*, IX (February 1995), pp. 55–72.

32 Steers, R. and Porter, L., *Motivation and Work Behavior*, 5th edn. New York: McGraw-Hill (1991).

33 Deming. W. E., *Out of the Crisis*. Cambridge, MA: MIT Institute for Advanced Engineering Study (1986), p. 315.

34 Barney, J. B. and Zajac, E. J., "Competitive organizational behavior," *Strategic Management Journal*, 15, Special Issue (Winter 1994), pp. 5–10.

NOTES CONT.

35 Maddox, R. C., *Cross-cultural Problems in International Business*. Westport, CT: Quorum Books (1993), pp. 43–4.

36 Townsend, P. and Gebhardt, J., *Quality in Action*. New York: Wiley (1992), pp. 18 and 96.

37 Bowles, J. and Hammond, J., *Beyond Quality: How 50 Winning Companies Use Continuous Improvement*. New York: G.P. Putnam's Sons (1991), p. 194.

38 "Dinosaurs: IBM, Sears, GM," *Fortune* (May 3, 1993), pp. 36–42.

39 Schmidt, W. and Finnigan, J., *The Race without a Finish Line: America's Quest for TQ*. San Francisco: Jossey-Bass (1992), pp. 268–9.

40 Schmidt and Finnigan, *The Race without a Finish Line*, pp. 272–9.

EVALUATION, CONTROL, AND PROCESS IMPROVEMENT

LEARNING OBJECTIVES

After reading this chapter, you should be able to accomplish the following.

1 *Compare and contrast intended, deliberate, unrealized, emergent, and realized strategies.*

2 *Describe how planning, evaluation, and control are linked.*

3 *Describe the traditional management control cycle steps.*

4 *Contrast corrective action and process improvement.*

5 *Relate common and special causes of variation.*

6 *Describe the role that statistical thinking plays in process improvement to yield better value for customers.*

7 *Relate process improvement and organizational learning.*

11

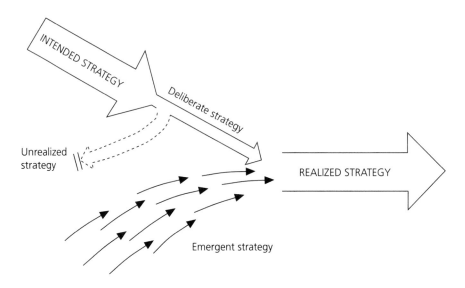

Figure 11.1 Intended and realized strategies.

Source: Mintzberg, H., "The strategy concept I: five P's for strategy," *California Management Review*, 30 (Fall 1987), p. 14. Copyright © 1987 by the Regents of the University of California. Reproduced by permission.

Once the strategic plan has been formulated and the strategies have been implemented, a strategic evaluation and control process needs to be installed. The organization needs to monitor performance and take corrective action if needed. *Strategic evaluation and control* is the process of evaluating strategic plans and monitoring organizational performance so that necessary corrective action can be taken. Today, it also includes process improvement to preclude out-of-control situations from occurring, and to continually provide greater value to customers.

Characteristics of Control and the Environment

Why does actual performance sometimes not match desired performance? Was the plan flawed in its formulation, or in its implementation? Were there uncontrollable factors?

Intended and realized strategies

Mintzberg tells us that no matter how well the organization plans its strategy, a different strategy may emerge. He described five dimensions of strategy: intended, realized, deliberate, unrealized, and emergent strategies. Mintzberg related the five dimensions as shown in figure 11.1: "(1) Intended strategies that get realized; these may be called deliberate strategies. (2) Intended strategies that do not get realized; these may be called *unrealized strategies*. (3) Realized strategies that were never intended; these may be called emergent strategies."[1]

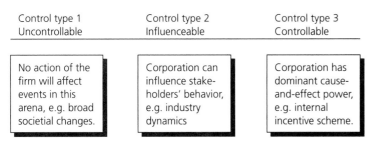

| Control type 1 | Control type 2 | Control type 3 |
| Uncontrollable | Influenceable | Controllable |

No action of the firm will affect events in this arena, e.g. broad societal changes.

Corporation can influence stake-holders' behavior, e.g. industry dynamics

Corporation has dominant cause-and-effect power, e.g. internal incentive scheme.

Figure 11.2   Control types.
Source: Reprinted by permission from *Strategic Market Planning*, by George Day. Copyright © 1986 by West Publishing Company.

There are a number of ways in which the realized strategy can become different from the planned or intended strategy. They may differ because of unrealistic strategies, poor views of the external environment, poor implementation, or uncontrollable changes in the external environment. These reasons highlight the importance of a strategic evaluation and control process.

Control types

Organizations face situations with different degrees of control.[2] Figure 11.2 describes control types and appropriate organizational action.

It is important for the organization to understand and classify the situation in terms of degrees of control so that it can implement appropriate corrective action. Even uncontrollable situations require a response from the organization if the situations affect the firm's strategies. For example, firms could not control the dramatic appreciation of the Japanese yen and German mark in 1995. However, impacted firms could alter their plant location and international production strategies in response. Indeed, Mercedes decided on more lower-cost production outside of Germany as part of its response to the appreciating German mark.[3]

Environmental changes

Organizational slack is unused capacity in the organization's resources. Deliberately leaving some slack can position the organization to respond to changes in the environment.[4] Organizational slack is not a substitute for strategic control. However, slack allows for dramatic, uncontrollable, unplanned changes in the environment.

An analysis of environmental changes classified by their speed and extent is in figure 11.3. The classification helps the firm to understand the amount of organizational slack appropriate for a situation. A firm operating in the upper left quadrant of figure 11.3, faced with slow and small environmental changes, does not need much slack. However, a firm operating in an environment with fast and large changes (lower right quadrant) may choose to maintain significant amounts of slack if it is to respond to those environmental changes. Manufacturing firms in cyclical industries, like automobile companies, often maintain considerable

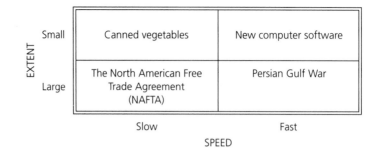

	Slow	Fast
Small	Canned vegetables	New computer software
Large	The North American Free Trade Agreement (NAFTA)	Persian Gulf War

EXTENT (vertical axis), SPEED (horizontal axis)

Figure 11.3 Speed and extent of environmental changes.
Source: Adapted from Sharfman, M., Wolf, G., Chase, R. and Tansik, D., "Antecedents of organizational slack," *Academy of Management Review*, 13 (1988), p. 605.

organizational slack to deal with fast and large environmental changes. The slack may take the forms of idle plants and billions of dollars (US) cash, so that the companies can respond to economic expansions and recessions.

Extent of evaluation and control

There is a difference between strategic evaluation and control systems and operational control systems. Strategic evaluation and control systems include evaluation of the appropriateness of the objectives and the strategies, as well as subsequent control of performance in accord with the plan. *Operational control* accepts the objectives and attempts to control operations in accord with the plan. Sticking with manufacturing cost-control objectives despite inflationary or currency exchange differences is an example of operational control. Revising profit objectives due to increased costs associated with the Persian Gulf War is an example of strategic control.

We focus on strategic as well as operational control since our interest is in evaluation of the strategic plan and control of organizational operations. Operational control should be consistent with strategic control. For example, if the firm has a goal of a 5 percent reduction in costs for the year, then it makes sense for a department to reduce travel expenses.

Managers are charged with improved quality, lowered costs, and increased speed for the products and services they offer to customers. This requires improvement in the systems that yield the products and services. Such improvements require proactive managerial actions in addition to the reactive managerial actions found in traditional management control systems.

Traditional Management Control

Controlling means ensuring that the organization is actually achieving its planned objectives. This control process has several steps. Unfortunately, this idea of control has always had the notion of corrective action after the product has been produced, or the service has been rendered.

Determine objectives

Planning and control are linked in the first step of determining objectives. Planning refers to deciding in advance what the organization's objectives ought to be and what its members ought to do to attain the organizational objectives. Thus, many managers speak of their planning and control system.

Objectives should be specific, measurable, time phased, and realistic. Specificity and realism are important goal characteristics so that the goals can be achieved. There is little positive motivational impact on employees, and there may even be negative motivational impact if the employees think they cannot achieve the goal.

The objectives express a hope for the future in terms of future goals. The objectives may be short-, medium-, or long-term goals. Although there is no single definition of goals relative to time, approximate guidelines are: short-term goals are less than one year; medium-term goals are one to five years; and long-term goals are more than five years.

Financial and economic measures

Goals should be measurable so that managers can determine if progress is being made toward accomplishing the goals. These goals are usually expressed with regard to output goals in economic and financial terms, such as an increase in total dollar sales or an increase in profitability.

Measurement often implies priority. Many managers have found that you get what you measure. If managers concentrate on measuring financial performance, then organizational members rightly conclude that financial goals are most important for the organization. This may also suggest that owners and stockholders are the most important stakeholders for the organization.

Measure performance

Once the goals have been set, and the measures determined, then managers must measure the actual performance. Obviously, there is a time lag between setting the goal and measuring the actual performance. If the goal is a long-term goal of five years, the time lags are often too long to take corrective action.

This is a problem with output-relevant goals. There is a considerable time lag between when the activities are performed and when the output, such as profitability, is measured.

Corrective action

If the actual performance is not in line with the objective, then corrective action is taken. Because of the time lags and the output orientation of many measures, it is rare that such corrective action treats the cause or source of the problem. The feedback of information may simply determine how realistic goals may be in

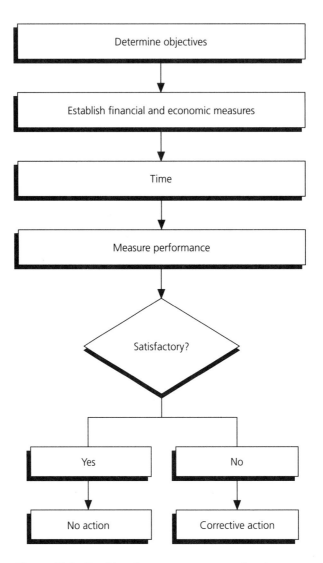

Figure 11.4 Traditional management control cycle.

the future. The steps in the traditional management control cycle are shown in figure 11.4.

Having "fixed" the problem, the manager typically advances to the next problem to be "solved". Here is the difficulty with much traditional management control. Without treating the cause of the problem, without improving the process that caused the problem, the problem will most likely reoccur. And another manager will be rewarded for "fixing" another problem.

A good example of the corrective action phase with an attempt to address some of the underlying problems is found in the Levi Strauss International Exhibit.

INTERNATIONAL
EXHIBIT

LEVI STRAUSS POLICES WORKING CONDITIONS IN INTERNATIONAL APPAREL MANUFACTURERS

In the past two decades, apparel manufacturers and retailers have been under intense international competition from low priced garments assembled in low wage countries. The flood of imports was so strong in the 1980s that US textile manufacturers started a patriotic-themed "Made in the USA" campaign using celebrities like Bob Hope. The ads argued that "it does matter" where the garment was made.

To help understand the structure of the industry, note that the textile manufacturer is the firm that makes the cloth. That operation is very capital intensive. Once the cloth is made, it is usually sold to an apparel manufacturer, who does the cutting and sewing of the cut pieces of fabric into a garment. The labor-intensive sewing is sometimes referred to as assembly. Despite some high-technology attempts to automate the sewing process with robots, most of those attempts have failed because of the flexibility of the fabric. The apparel operation is based on an individual operator, usually a relatively unskilled, patient, dexterous woman at a sewing machine.

The US government hastened the movement of apparel manufacturers offshore when it provided special tariff relief for garments assembled in the Caribbean. Under Section 807 of the tariff code, the US government ruled that no tariffs would be collected on the increased value associated with the labor added to a garment assembled in the Caribbean. This was part of an attempt to promote jobs, economic growth, and political stability in the Caribbean. Partly because of this initiative and the competition from low-wage countries, tens of thousands of apparel manufacturing jobs were lost in the United States. Even though such jobs historically had been low paying, with compensation not much more than US$7–8 an hour plus fringe benefits, it is hard to keep costs down when the wages in many developing countries are considerably less than US$1 per hour with few or no fringe benefits. In the late 1980s, some textile plants in the People's Republic of China paid a wage rate of US$0.22 an hour, and some apparel plants in the Caribbean paid a wage rate of US$0.80 an hour.

The US textile industry's "Made in the USA" campaign had limited success. Many customers were interested primarily in the cost and quality of the garment, and paid little attention to country of origin. So many large apparel firms had to decide between low-priced garments from low-wage countries, or lost sales due to higher prices of US sewn garments.

Liz Claiborne, the large women's apparel firm, contracted nearly all of its apparel manufacturing throughout the world. Wal-Mart advertised that most of its stores' goods were domestically manufactured, but there were several cases of internationally sourced goods. Land's End, the mail order retailer, indicated if its garments were domestically or internationally manufactured. Levi Strauss, the world's largest supplier of brand-name apparel, contracted much of its apparel manufacturing throughout the world.

An issue with contracting such manufacturing to low-wage countries is that labor practices are deplorable in some countries due to non-existent labor laws, or laws less stringent than those in the United States. Few low-wage countries have the multitude of laws covering equal employment opportunity, compensation and benefits, child labor, labor relations, and occupational safety and health that exist in the United States.

When such deplorable conditions become known, US public pressure against such practices can be quite heated. For example, US public pressure against apartheid in South Africa forced the withdrawal of most US firms from that country. Such public pressure can result in boycotts against the other country or the US company doing business with firms in the other country.

Deplorable working conditions in some low-wage countries raise an ethical dilemma for US firms that purchase garments from manufacturers in such countries. Are the US firms subsidizing such behavior?

Some US firms have tried to enforce certain labor standards on international suppliers from a stance of enlightened self-interest (chapter 4) because domestic customers wanted it. This raises a whole series of questions. Some have charged that the US firm's behavior is no less than meddling in the internal affairs of another country. Some have pointed out that by raising the cost of doing business in another company, the US firm is in effect pricing that company and its workers out of future work because some international competitor will undercut prices with less costly labor practices.

Amid these charges, Levi Strauss has tried to insure that its international garment contractors treat their workers well in their plants. In 1992, Levi became the first in its industry to promote a broad set of guidelines for its contract plants that covered labor and the environment. Levi said it would inspect plants and cancel contracts for violators.

Im Choong Hoe is an inspector for Levi who checks for health and safety hazards and abuses of worker rights in contract plants in Southeast Asia from Bangladesh to Indonesia. His main concern is worker safety and he frequently checks number of fire exits and extinguishers in plants in case of fire. He says that a fire would be disastrous in some crowded plants, killing many workers.

But if a contract is canceled, how does that help the welfare of the displaced workers? To solve such a dilemma, Levi has designed some innovative approaches to protect the workers. When a Levi inspector discovered that one of its contractors employed children, Levi continued to pay the children while they attended school at the factory rather than force the company to fire them and cause their families to lose needed wages.

As international joint ventures grow in importance and frequency, this ethical dilemma will be confronted by more managers. As more firms respond to public pressure, attention will be paid to working conditions in low wage countries.

Sources: *"Levi tries to make sure contract plants in Asia treat workers well,"* Wall Street Journal *(July 28, 1994), p. A1;* Vogel, D., *"Is US business obsessed with ethics?"* Across the Board *(December 1993), pp. 31–3; Grigsby, D., "Liz Claiborne, Inc.," in Grigsby, D. and Stahl, M. (eds),* Strategic Management Cases. *Belmont, CA: Wadsworth (1993), pp. 54–73; Singer, A., "Ethics: are standards lower overseas?"* Across the Board *(September 1991), pp. 31–4.*

Today's internationally competitive marketplace does not provide the luxury of waiting until a problem occurs and then "fixing" it. To preclude problems, managers must work to continuously improve the outputs of their processes. In today's organization, the block under "No action" in figure 11.4 needs to be modified to read "Process improvement". Managers need to understand kinds of variation in the process to improve it.

Control in the Presence of Variation

This section focuses on variation in outputs, systems, and processes, and the implications of that variation for managerial practice. Different kinds of variability in output have different implications for managerial behavior and the processes associated with yielding value for customers. Confusion concerning causes of variation can generate inappropriate managerial behavior.[5]

Statistical thinking

Statistical thinking stresses that all work activities are part of larger processes with variation. Statistical thinking recognizes that all processes have variability, and that variability can arise from two different causes (common cause and special cause). Deming commented on the importance of managers recognizing and reducing variation. "Understanding of variation, special causes and common causes, and the necessity to reduce constantly the variation from common causes, is vital."[6]

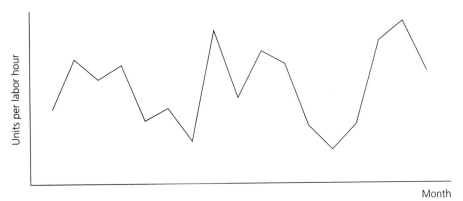

Figure 11.5 Common cause variation.

Source: Sanders, R. S., Leitnaker, M. and Ranney, G., "Managing in the presence of variation," in Stahl, M. J. and Bounds, G. M., *Competing Globally through Customer Value*. Westport, CT: Quorum Books, (1991), p. 255. Copyright © Greenwood Publishing Group, Inc. Reprinted by permission.

The major factors involved in many TQ failures were recently noted. These factors include: "The over-reliance on statistical methods; and the under-reliance on statistical methods."[7] Thus, statistical methods are very important, but they cannot be the sole feature of management.

Data are used to understand the variation and its causes in a process. Learning about variation in a process precedes improving the process. Reducing variation with data analysis is at the heart of systems and process improvement. Note how "statistical methods, process emphasis, and continual improvement" are some of the Principles in Eastman's Quality Policy in the quality case in this chapter.

Common causes of variation

Common causes of variation are those system sources that affect each and every result in a series.[8] All the data are within the boundaries of variation in the historical data. Common cause variation is always present in a system, although the assignable cause, or causes, may not be found. There may be many sources of variation or many causes of variation in the system. The result of these causes is predictable. There will be a predictable amount of noise or chance variation in the data.

Figure 11.5 is an example of common cause variation. Given the current system and processes behind the data, a certain amount of fluctuation in units produced per labor hour is predictable. The variation is within a certain predictable range.

Special causes of variation

Special causes of variation are present at isolated times to yield variation in addition to that produced by common causes.[9] As such, special cause variation is sporadic and not predictable. Although the data are not predictable, they can be linked with

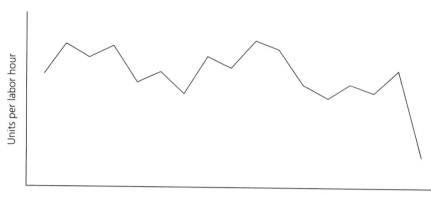

Month

Figure 11.6 Special cause variation.
Source: Sanders, R. S., Leitnaker, M. and Ranney, G., "Managing in the presence of variation," in Stahl, M. J. and Bounds, G. M., *Competing Globally through Customer Value*. Westport, CT: Quorum Books, (1991), p. 255. Copyright © Greenwood Publishing Group, Inc. Reprinted by permission.

an assignable event. Thus, special cause variation is also known as signal or assignable variation. The data associated with special cause variation are few in number.

Figure 11.6 is an example of special cause variation. The last data point in the series is not predictable from the range of the data before it. There is a special cause of variation in the last data point that requires further investigation to determine the assignable event.

This distinction between common and special causes of variation is crucial to system improvement activities. Frequently, confusion between these two sources of variation leads to mistakes in managerial attempts to improve the system, or to control the system. Deming reminded us of this confusion concerning these two sources of variation when he wrote about these two mistakes. "Mistake 1. To react to an outcome as if it came from a special cause, when actually it came from common causes of variation". "Mistake 2. To treat an outcome as if it came from common causes of variation, when actually it came from a special cause."[10]

Most variation in a system arises from common causes of variation. Knowledge of the system based on data and experience, combined with some of the quality improvement tools, will help the manager discover the common causes of variation. For example, month to month variation in monthly sales figures is usually due to common causes of variation. Managerial attempts to take corrective action due to common cause variation in the monthly sales figures by adding additional sales people, or offering special sales promotions, may only add additional variation and expense. Procter & Gamble found that it had been adding variation to its sales due to its use of coupons. Customers would buy extra quantities when the coupons were good and cutback purchases without the coupons. This added variation to the warehousing, inventory, manufacturing, and purchasing systems. Such variation increased costs and precluded the kinds of cost reductions customers demanded. To remove the variation, stabilize the system, and lower costs, P&G stopped using coupons and evolved to an everyday value-priced strategy in the early 1990s.

Customer-relevant measures

To improve the system, the manager should ask the question of what measures to follow. What data should be collected? If the system is not customer-relevant, then what is the purpose of the system? Examples of customer-relevant measures include sales, percentage growth in sales, quality, time to introduce new products, and market share. Customer-relevant service measures include service time and number of complaints. Examples of customer-relevant manufacturing measures include customer-relevant product characteristics (e.g. weight, dimensions, color, chemical composition), and percentage not meeting customer specifications. Customer relevant administrative measures include number of errors and time to complete the activity.

International Computers Ltd (ICL), a British computer firm, uses continuous improvement of processes to deliver more value to customers. ICL developed a continuous improvement process called dELTA, the aim of which is to "improve a thousand things by 1 percent rather than one thing by 1,000 percent."[11] Design to Distribution Ltd (D2D), an ICL wholly owned subsidiary in contract electronics manufacturing, won the European Quality Award in 1994.[12]

Process Control and Improvement

The culture of continuously improving the process, versus after the fact correction of output, are the important messages here. Statistical process control (SPC), or any of the other process improvement tools not covered here, are not the primary messages. Many managers today recognize that if they continuously improve the process, the output of the process should surpass customers' expectations. Then, the need for after-the-fact correction of output of the process will be lessened.

Many processes do not suffer the time lag that many output-relevant measures suffer. For example, "the fraction of customer service requests taking more than five days to answer" is a real time process measure. It does not have the time lag of measuring return on assets for the year.

Based upon statistical thinking, and a recognition of common and special causes of variation, SPC is the most frequently used tool to improve processes. *SPC is the application of statistical thinking and statistical analysis of data to control and improve processes.* SPC uses process data to understand stable and unstable processes, reduce variation, and improve the process.

Stable processes

A *stable process* is one in which the process measure shows no evidence of special causes of variation. A stable process is referred to as a *consistent* or *in-control process.*

There are several advantages of stable processes. The greatest is process predictability. Process performance, costs, and quantities are predictable with stable

Table 11.1   Frequency of use of process simplification to improve business processes (percentages)

	Seldom or never	Occasionally	Usually	Always or almost always
Canada	11	19	52	19
Germany	16	50	28	6
Japan	2	16	35	47
USA	12	42	35	12

processes. The second advantage is in terms of process improvement. Planned process improvements can be measured and evaluated with data.

A common way to improve processes is through process simplification. Table 11.1 shows the percentage of businesses indicating how often they use process simplification to improve business processes in Canada, Germany, Japan, and the USA. The data indicate that the use of this practice varied significantly across these nations when the data were reported in 1991.[13]

A stable process does not necessarily mean that the product or service will meet the customer's needs. "In-control" or "stable" only means that the process is predictable and consistent. For example, the drive-in system at a bank may consistently yield waiting times ranging from zero to 12 minutes, with an average of six minutes. However, customers may demand waiting times of less than two minutes.

Unstable processes

An *unstable process* is one in which the process measure shows evidence of special causes of variation. An unstable process is referred to as an *out-of-control or inconsistent process*.

Unstable processes are hard to control because the manager never knows when there will be a special cause of variation that will produce data beyond the range of experience. Process improvement is difficult in unstable processes because special causes of variation may mask the effects of the improvement.

Eliminating special causes is an important managerial action to move toward stable processes. Timely data are required so that special causes can be determined quickly. After the specific, temporary, or local problem has been corrected, the manager should prevent the special cause from recurring. Once the special causes have been eliminated and the process is stable, the manager can move to improve a stable process.

Capable processes

The purpose of process improvement is to yield processes that meet customers' requirements. A *capable process* is one that meets customers' requirements. Process capability is a process requirement in addition to process stability.

As increasing numbers of customers do not have the time to wait, a number of service organizations are focusing on dramatic reductions in service time. Although the service time at Avis was competitive, Avis recently simplified the process for renting a car to dramatically reduce the service time. Avis now stores relevant customer information to rent a car, including preferences and credit card information, in its computers and matches that information with a car reservation request. The information is printed on an Avis form and is waiting in the car to be rented before the customer arrives. Rather than wait in line at a counter to give the information, the customer goes directly to the rented car and simply shows a current driver's license to a guard to leave the Avis lot with the car. Thus, the service time for the customer has been reduced to near zero. By focusing on customers' needs not to wait, Avis simplified the process rather than just adding more clerks to reduce the waiting time somewhat.

Sea Ray Boats designs, manufactures and markets pleasure power boats ranging from 15 feet to about 40 feet (4.5 to 12 meters). Sea Ray uses process improvement to reduce the cost of quality (COQ) and thus lower overall costs.[14] A recent survey of nearly 900 UK managers revealed that about 45 percent of British manufacturing firms have goals for, and measure improvements in their Cost of Quality.[15]

Capsugel, a division of the pharmaceutical firm Warner-Lambert, manufactures and distributes two-piece, hard gelatin capsules to pharmaceutical companies worldwide. It has plants in the USA, Belgium, France, Japan, Mexico, Thailand, Brazil, and China. Capsugel uses process improvement to lower its cost of quality by one-half every five years. The use of SPC to improve processes helped to transcend international language barriers as statistics are language-free.[16]

Process improvement and organizational learning versus control

Process improvement to yield improved value to customers is the major difference between TQM and traditional management control that stresses corrective action after the fact. A theme of this book is the primary responsibility of managers to improve value for customers. SPC and other tools for systems and process improvement, important as they are, are not the primary message.

How important is this task of systems and process improvement for managers? Deming commented on the potential for payoff from managerial improvement activities when he estimated the percentage of problems associated with the system. "I should estimate that in my experience most troubles and most possibilities for improvement add up to proportions something like this: 94 percent belong to the system (*responsibility of management*), 6 percent special."[17] (Emphasis added.)

The common elements of success in many TQM efforts were recently noted. They include: "Systematically improving the quality of all business processes from an internal and (especially) external customer perspective."[18]

Process improvement aims to continually improve processes to yield continually improved value to customers before problems occur. In such a fashion, problems are prevented, rather than being corrected after they occur. Rather than inspection and repair after production and delivery, process improvement activities decrease the defect rate, lower the cost, and reduce the cycle time. As more organizations are structured in terms of their key processes (chapter 9), process improvement will take on increased importance. This improvement theme requires knowledge of kinds of variation in a process, and improvement of the process, rather than control of process output after the problem occurs.

The concepts of organizational learning and process improvement (*kaizen*) are closely related.[19] Learning about customers so that the organization can improve its processes is key to the customer value determination system discussed in chapter 7. Indeed, learning about customers is key to the entire strategic management process that attempts to match the firm's core competencies with customer requirements. The feedback of information concerning the value provided to customers is used to improve processes and thereby yield more value to customers in the future, and to formulate future strategies. As figure 1.2 shows, those feedback loops are at the core of the entire strategic management process as the organization interacts with its environment.

▪ Summary ▪

Frequently there are differences between intended and realized strategies. For a variety of reasons, including managerial shortcomings in formulation and implementation, there may be unrealized strategies. Due to external events beyond the control of managers, there may also be emergent strategies. As these may all combine to yield a realized strategy different from the intended strategy, the organization needs to evaluate and control its strategy and operations.

In implementing a strategic control system, managers distinguish among various control types, including controllable, influenceable, and uncontrollable. Controllable situations are under the direct cause and effect power of the organization to correct. Uncontrollable situations imply that no action of the firm will affect the situation because the firm is powerless in that situation. Influenceable situations may in some cases be controlled indirectly. These control types are viewed relative to the speed and extent of environmental changes. The organization is almost powerless to control fast, large changes in the short term. Slow, small changes leave the organization room to effect control action.

There is a problem with financial output goals of a considerable time lag between when the activities are performed and when the output, such as profitability, is measured. If the actual performance is not in line with the objective, then corrective action is taken. Because of the time lags and the output orientation of the financial measures, it is rare that such corrective action treats the cause or source of the problem. Here is the crux and fallacy of much traditional management control. Without treating the cause of the problem, the problem will most likely reoccur.

Systems improvement aims to continually improve the system and processes to yield continually improved customer value before problems occur. To continuously improve value to customers, managers should look for customer-relevant measures in deciding what to improve. Rather than inspection and repair after production, systems improvement activities decrease the chance that a defect or problem will occur. Thus, problems are prevented, rather than being corrected after they occur.

Statistical thinking stresses that all work activities are part of larger processes with variation. Variability can arise from two different causes (common cause and special cause).

Statistical process control (SPC) is the application of statistical thinking and statistical analysis of data to control and improve processes. SPC attempts to understand stable and unstable processes, reduce variation, and improve the process.

A stable, in-control, or consistent process is one in which the process measure shows no evidence of special causes of variation. Since stable processes are predictable, managers can proceed with process improvement. An unstable, out-of-control, or inconsistent process is one in which the process measure shows evidence of special causes of variation. Unstable processes are hard to predict. This makes process improvement difficult because the variation due to the special causes may mask the effects of the improvement.

Once the process is stable, process improvement changes features of the process that are always present. This usually requires managerial action for improvement because fundamental changes in the system are often required. As more organizations are structured in terms of their key processes (chapter 9), process improvement will take on increased importance.

DISCUSSION QUESTIONS

1 How are intended, deliberate, unrealized, emergent, and realized strategies related to each other?

2 How are planning, evaluation, and control linked?

3 How does a short-term orientation of some managers reinforce the idea of corrective action?

4 Relate the idea of process and systems improvement to the customer as the stakeholder.

5 Give an example of a common cause of variation and a special cause of variation associated with the length of time to receive treatment in a hospital emergency room.

6 How could the use of statistical thinking help you to improve the registration system at your college/university?

7 Relate process improvement and organizational learning. Is the linkage more important in industries with stable or rapidly changing technologies?

KEY TERMS

A capable process	is one that meets customers' requirements.
Common causes of variation	are those system sources that affect each and every result in a series.
Controlling	means ensuring that the organization is actually achieving its planned objectives.
Operational control	accepts the objectives and attempts to control operations in accord with the plan.

Organizational slack	is unused capacity in the organization's resources.
Planning	refers to deciding in advance what the organization's objectives ought to be and what its members ought to do to attain the organizational objectives.
Statistical thinking	stresses that all work activities are part of larger processes with variation.
Special causes of variation	are present at isolated times to yield variation in addition to that produced by common causes.
A stable process	is one in which the process measure shows no evidence of special causes of variation.
Statistical process control (SPC)	is the application of statistical thinking and statistical analysis of data to control and improve processes.
Strategic evaluation and control	is the process of evaluating strategic plans and monitoring organizational performance so that necessary corrective action can be taken.
Unrealized strategies	are intended strategies not realized.
An unstable process	is one in which the process measure shows evidence of special causes of variation.

Eastman Chemical Company Competes Globally with Quality and International Plants

Eastman Chemical Company (New York Stock Exchange symbol – EMN) had been a major division of Eastman Kodak Company. EMN was started in 1920 to provide chemicals to the parent company in the photographic business. On January 1, 1994, it was spun off from the parent firm and became a standalone company. Over the years, EMN had grown into a major international chemical company, with 1995 worldwide sales of about US$5 billion.[a] About 22 percent of those sales were from international operations.

Headquartered in Kingsport, Tennessee, EMN has plants in several states in the USA and in several other countries. Eastman makes more than 400 products, including plastics for soft drink bottles, acetate filters for cigarettes, polymer pellets for steering wheels, and other hard molded plastic products.[b] Its single largest product, accounting for about 25 percent of sales, is plastic (PET) for soft drink bottles and other bottles.

The chemical industry is a highly competitive industry with substantial investments in the plant and equipment that produces the chemicals and chemical products in high volume. Many chemical companies run their plant and equipment around the clock because shutting them down would cause problems in many of the processes and clog the equipment.

The complex plant and equipment yield many activities and processes to transform raw materials or generic chemicals into finished chemicals, or products ready for shipment to customers. This makes the flow of material and the processes especially important in a chemical company.

Eastman also recognized that the chemical industry was a globally competitive business. International competitors like Hoechst Celanese, and BASF sold chemical products in the USA, as well as in many other countries. Many countries had their own chemical companies.

Eastman described its "Strategic Intent (Vision) to be the world's preferred chemical company."[c] In such a globally competitive business, how would Eastman realize its strategic intent? How would Eastman grow and prosper in such an industry?

EMN decided to focus on quality by tying process improvement to customer requirements. To implement and communicate this quality emphasis, EMN formulated and widely disseminated its Quality Policy (figure 11.7).[d] Note the emphasis on processes throughout the Quality Policy. Processes are tied into continual improvement through statistical methods to satisfy customers. Eastman's continual process improvement helped to keep its costs in control and provide more value to customers.

Top management leadership and training also play huge parts in Eastman's focus on quality. Earnie Deavenport, President of EMN, remarked: "My senior management team has a quality meeting every week."[e] Each employee spends at least 40 to 60 hours each year learning about TQM methods.[f]

Eastman's long quality journey has paid off handsomely for the firm. EMN felt that its decade-old quality improvement journey helped to generate above-average sales from new products, high customer satisfaction, and a strong safety record.[g]

In October 1993, EMN was notified that it had won a Malcolm Baldrige National Quality Award. Its quality journey was not a short trip. Commenting on the award, Mr Deavenport remarked: "This high honor is the culmination of over a decade of just plain hard work at finding out what our customers wanted and then putting the processes into place that satisfied their needs. Not a simple job for a company with over 7,000 customers worldwide, but we did it – year by year."[h]

Its former parent, Eastman Kodak, under pressure from the financial community to boost its stock price, had decided earlier to divest EMN on January 1, 1994. As it prepared for the future as a standalone company with US$5 billion in sales around the world, EMN was optimistic over winning the Baldrige and preparing for the future. Mr Deavenport commented: "We can't think of any better way to introduce ourselves to the world."[i]

That introduction was successful, as its stock was up about 40 percent in the second year after its divestiture and its profits had doubled.[j] Having used process improvement to stabilize and improve its processes, it was further extending those processes to newly announced plants in Malaysia, Mexico, and Spain. As the firm planned on growing by 10 percent annually, it hoped that much of the growth would be due to increased international operations. By the year 2000, the firm planned on having 30 percent of its manufacturing assets outside the USA, compared to 5 percent in 1995.[k]

Discussion Questions

1 Based on the EMN case, describe the importance of tying process improvement into customer requirements.

2 Why is a reputation for quality so important for a company just starting as an independent company?

3 How will the culture of process improvement or *kaizen* help Eastman in its international expansion?

Sources: a. "Eastman Chemical Company," *Value Line Investment Survey* (March 3, 1995), p. 1889; b. "Eastman Chemical shows it's ready to leave the nest," *USA Today* (October 19, 1993), p. 4B;   c. *Strategic Intent*. Kingsport, TN: Eastman Chemical Company (1993);   d. *Eastman Chemical Company's Quality Journey*. Kingsport, TN: Eastman Chemical Company (1993);   e. "Eastman Chemical shows it's ready to leave the nest," p. 4B;   f. Ibid.;   g. "Kodak Unit, Ames Rubber are given Baldriges amid tougher standards," *Wall Street Journal* (October 19, 1993), p. A22;   h. "Eastman wins '93 Nationwide Quality Award," *The Knoxville News-Sentinel* (October 19, 1993), p. C1;   i. "Eastman Chemical shows it's ready to leave the nest," p. 4B;   j. "Eastman Chemical Company," *Value Line Investment Survey* (March 3, 1995), p. 1889;   k. "Loudon site, growth on Eastman agenda," *The Knoxville News-Sentinel* (May 5, 1995), p. C7.

QUALITY POLICY

Quality Goal

To be the leader in quality and value of products and services

Quality Managment Process

- Focus on customers.
- Establish mission, vision, and indicators of performance.
- Understand, standardize, stabilize, and maintain processes.
- Plan, do, check, act for continual improvement and innovation.

Operational Policy

- Achieve process stability and reliability.
- Control every process to the desired target.
- Improve process capability.

Principles

Customer Satisfaction	Anticipate, understand, and excel at meeting customer needs.
Continual Improvement	Improve the current level of performance of processes, products, and services.
Innovation	Search for and implement creative processes, products, and services.
Process Emphasis	Focus on processes as the means to improve results.
Management Leadership	Create and maintain a shared vision, constancy of purpose, and supportive environment that includes appropriate recognition and reinforcement.
Empowerment	Create a culture where people have the knowledge, skills, authority, and desire to decide, act, and take responsibility for results of their actions and for their contribution to the success of the company.
Statistical Methods	Understand the concept of variation and apply appropriate statistical methods for continual improvement and innovation.
Employee Development	Encourage and support lifelong learning and personal growth.
Partnerships	Build long-term relationships with customers and suppliers.
Assessment	Assess performance and benchmark against world's best.

E. W. Deavenport, Jr.
President

EASTMAN

Figure 11.7 Eastman's quality policy.

"BRITISH AIRWAYS AND CUSTOMER SATISFACTION"

INTERNATIONAL

C A S E

British Airways PLC (BA) needed more than good marketing to change passengers inter-pretation of its acronym from "Bloody Awful" to "Bloody Awesome." In the early 1980s, the company was bloated, inefficient, and losing money at £288,000 (US$432,000) per day – taxpayers' money.[a] Charles Gurassa, regional general manager for the Americas, sums up the prevailing attitude, "we carried *passengers* – the word *customer* was not in our vocabulary." It was clear to many that this could not continue.[b]

Changes began in 1983 with the arrival of Sir Colin Marshall, former COO of Avis Car Rental, who possessed a steely determination to turn BA around.[c] He cut the staff from 60,000 to 36,000, abandoned unprofitable routes, and sold assets to raise cash. Many still recall the overnight termination of a large number of managers as the "night of the long knives."[d] Needless to say, Sir Colin made it clear that transformation was going to happen.

One of the first steps was to throw away the dust-covered, lengthy, almost incomprehensible statement of goals. It was replaced with this new mission statement, "To be the best company in the airline business." Everyone understood, especially the customer service staff, who were shocked to hear some recognition of what they had been saying for a long time.[e]

The change process was driven by three basic goals:

- change our image;
- change our culture;
- achieve profitability.

Changing the corporate image meant developing a completely new identity for the company. BA decided to signal this change to employees and customers through a complete redesign of everything from the interior and exterior of the aircraft to the uniforms, and from the company logo to corporate sales offices around the world. In addition, the quasi-separate identities of two firms that had been merged into British Airways (British Overseas Airways Corporation and British European Airways) were finally eliminated.[f]

Cultural change was a more difficult problem. Extensive market research was conducted for the first time. It showed that there were large gaps between staff and customer expectations of service. The research showed that customers wanted more personal service – spontaneity, warmth, concern, friendliness, and attention to personal needs.[g]

In order to address these needs, BA initiated its first staff training program, called Putting People First. All 36,000 employees attended in groups of 150 – from Concorde pilots to bag-gage handlers, and from flight attendants to marketing managers. They all spent two days discussing three themes: winning and losing attitudes, taking ownership of problems since they *were* BA to customers, listening and responding to customer needs. It was very simple, but very effective in changing attitudes abut the airline. Sir Colin attended practically all the sessions and held open discussion sessions to address any concerns.[h]

Lastly, achieving profitability included the privatization of the company in 1987. By 1988, BA had earned £200 million (US$300 million) of income before taxes. This profit was largely attributable to BA's branding of its service to the business traveler market. It was not an easy thing to actually reduce capacity to offer these customers what they wanted – consistently good service. However, the response was an overwhelming success. For the first time in memory, both customers and staff believed that BA could promise and deliver outstanding quality.[i]

The rest of the 1980s and the early 1990s were spent refining BA's focus on marketing, the employee, and customer service. BA is now in its fourth round of employee training.

Essentially, BA has developed a process that links employee treatment to the treatment of the customer.[j]

BA learned that satisfaction was influenced by a customer's perception of the value received for the price paid. BA is not a low-cost carrier, but passengers are willing to pay a premium if they can consistently be assured of the best service.

BA also discovered that managers need to strive to maintain a corporate culture anchored on service to the staff as well as the customer. Even though the overall goal is profit through customer satisfaction and customer loyalty, weakness in any part of the whole process was recognized as a threat to the overall goal.

Evaluation and control of this process were extremely important, but the traditional methods of setting standards and targets and managing through the bureaucracy had to be completely replaced. Thanks to the revolution in information technology, critical information could be quickly delivered to the decision makers – the employees.

BA's information systems are used to gather, store, and analyze data about employees and customers and their behaviors, but the company has gone beyond traditional market research by investing in technology that captures data about the ongoing interaction between employees and customers. The output is designed to be actionable. BA learns not only that a customer is satisfied, but exactly what interactions gave rise to the higher or lower level of satisfaction. Also, learning *when* something matters has proved as crucial as learning *what* is important.[k]

BA continuously monitors customers' perceptions of their experiences with the airline in order to earn their loyalty. Gathering this information has become easier and less expensive as customers interact with BA via fax, smart cards, Internet connections, and other digital media. Using statistical analyses of data to eliminate variance has also become easier thanks to software that can track the recency, frequency, type, and value of data over time.[l]

The results speak for themselves. According to James Halstead, an official of the Swiss Bank Corporation, "It seems nothing can stop British Airways."[m] The company is expected to achieve a record 1996 pre-tax profit of £570 million (US$872 million), which will again ensure BA's place as the most profitable airline in the world.[n]

Discussion Questions

1 What did Sir Colin Marshall hope to accomplish by attending almost all of the Putting People First sessions?

2 How do the evaluation and control functions fit in with the process of delivering customer satisfaction at BA?

3 Explain why it was important for BA to collect data that went beyond just the determination of customer satisfaction.

Sources: **a.** "British Airways PLC," *Hoover's Handbook of World Business 1995–1996*. Austin, TX: The Reference Press (1995), pp. 146–7; **b.** Gurassa, C., "BA stood for bloody awful," *Across the Board* (January, 1995), p. 55; **c.** "Sir Colin Marshall", *Who's Who 1995*. New York: A&C Black (1995), p. 1279; **d.** Gurassa, C., "BA stood for bloody awful," p. 55; **e.** Ibid.; **f.** Ibid.; **g.** Ibid.; **h.** Ibid.; **i.** Ibid., p. 56; **j.** Blumenthal, B. and Haspeslagh, P., "Toward a definition of corporate transformation," *Sloan Management Review* (Spring 1994), p. 101–2; **k.** Ibid., p. 92; **l.** "Learning from customers," *Information Week* (July 3, 1995), p. 92; **m.** Shifron, C., "Record profits seen for British Airways," *Aviation Week and Space Technology* (February 13, 1995), p. 31; **n.** "British Airways PLC," *Inves Text*, Lehman Brothers Ltd (August 7, 1995).

NOTES

1 Mintzberg, H., "Patterns in strategy formulation," *Management Science*, 24 (1978), p. 945.

2 Lorange, P., Morton, M. and Ghoshal, S., *Strategic Control Systems*. St Paul: West Publishing (1986).

3 "For Mercedes, going global means being less German," *Wall Street Journal* (April 27, 1995), p. B4.

4 Sharfman, M., "Antecedents of organizational slack," *Academy of Management Review*, 13 (1988), pp. 601–14.

5 Sanders, R. S., Leitnaker, M. and Ranney, G., "Managing in the presence of variation," in Stahl, M. J. and Bounds, G. M. (eds), *Competing Globally through Customer Value*. Westport, CT: Quorum Books (1991), pp. 253–74.

6 Deming, W. E., *Out of the Crisis*. Cambridge, MA: MIT Center for Advanced Engineering Study (1986), p. 136.

7 Cole, R., "Introduction," Special Issue on TQM, *California Management Review*, 35 (Spring 1993), p. 7.

8 Sanders, R.S., Leitnaker, M. and Ranney, G., "Managing in the presence of variation," p. 255.

9 Ibid., p. 256.

10 Deming, W. E., *The New Economics for Industry, Government, Education*. Cambridge, MA: Massachusetts Institute of Technology for Advanced Engineering Study (1993), p. 102.

11 *Quality: The ICL Way*. London: ICL (1993), p. 1.

12 "Design to Distribution, an ICL success story," *UK Quality* (March 1995), pp. 21–5.

13 American Quality Foundation and Ernst & Young, *International Quality Study: the Definitive Study of the Best International Quality Management Practices*. Cleveland, OH: Ernst & Young (1991), p. 1.

14 *PACE Program Manual*. Knoxville, TN: Sea Ray Boats (1993), p. 4.

15 Wilkinson, A., Redman, T. and Snape, E., "New patterns of quality management in the United Kingdom," *Quality Management Journal*, 2 (Winter 1995), p. 44.

16 Judge, W., Stahl, M., Scott, R. and Millender, R., "Long-term quality improvement and cost reduction at Capsugel/Warner-Lambert," in Stahl, M. J. and Bounds, G. M. (eds), *Competing Globally through Customer Value*, pp. 703–709.

17 Deming, W. E., Out of the Crisis, p. 136.

18 Cole, R., "Introduction," Special Issue on TQM, *California Management Review*, p. 8.

19 Senge, P., *The Fifth Discipline*. New York: Doubleday (1990); Sitkin, S., Sutcliffe, K. and Schroeder, R., "Distinguishing control from learning in TQM," *Academy of Management Review*, 19 (July 1994), p. 537–64.

Index